Nāgārjuna's *Precious Garland*

Nāgārjuna's *Precious Garland*

Buddhist Advice for Living and Liberation

Analyzed, translated,
and edited by

Jeffrey Hopkins

Snow Lion
Boulder

Snow Lion
An imprint of Shambhala Publications, Inc.
4720 Walnut Street
Boulder, Colorado 80301
www.shambhala.com

This book was originally published under the title *Buddhist Advice for Living and Liberation* (Snow Lion, 1998).

9 8 7 6 5

Printed in the United States of America

♾ This edition is printed on acid-free paper that meets the American National Standards Institute Z39.48 Standard.
♻ Shambhala Publications makes every effort to print on recycled paper.
For more information please visit www.shambhala.com.

Snow Lion is distributed worldwide by Penguin Random House, Inc., and its subsidiaries.

The Library of Congress catalogues the previous edition of this book as follows:

Nāgārjuna, 2nd cent.
[Ratnāvalī, English]
Buddhist advice for living & liberation: Nāgārjuna's precious garland / introduced, translated, and edited by Jeffrey Hopkins.
p. cm.
Includes bibliographical references.
ISBN 978-1-55939-274-7
1. Mādhyamika (Buddhism)—Early works to 1800. I. Hopkins, Jeffrey, 1940– . II. Title.
BQ2872.E5H66 1997
294.3'85—dc21
97-18937
CIP

Contents

Technical Note

- For the names of Indian scholars and systems used in the body of the text, *ch*, *sh*, and *ṣh* are used instead of the more usual *c*, *ś*, and *ṣ* for the sake of easy pronunciation by non-specialists; however, *chchh* is not used for *cch*. In the notes the usual transliteration system for Sanskrit is used.
- The names of Indian Buddhist schools of thought are translated into English in an effort to increase accessibility for non-specialists.
- Transliteration of Tibetan is done in accordance with a system devised by Turrell Wylie, *et al.*; see "A Standard System of Tibetan Transcription," *Harvard Journal of Asiatic Studies*, vol. 22, 1959, 261-67.
- The names of Tibetan authors and religious orders are given in "essay phonetics" for the sake of easy pronunciation; for a discussion of the system used, see the Technical Note at the beginning of my *Meditation on Emptiness* (London: Wisdom Publications, 1983; rev. ed. Boston: Wisdom Publications, 1996), 19-22.
- Endnotes are marked with "1, 2, 3..."; footnotes are marked with "a, b, c..."
- See the Bibliography for editions and translations of Indian and Tibetan texts.

PREFACE

I have sought to make this new translation of Nāgārjuna's *Precious Garland* more accessible by providing an introduction describing Nāgārjuna's life and the themes of his text. I have also cast the translation in a more free-flowing manner in informal poetry so that it reflects meaning units. My original impetus to translate the poem came from attending a series of lectures on Nāgārjuna's Six Collections of Reasoning by His Holiness Tenzin Gyatso, the Fourteenth Dalai Lama, in Dharamsala, India, in May of 1972. After finishing a first draft, I orally re-translated the English into Tibetan for verification and correction by Lati Rinpoche, a senior lama-scholar who himself does not speak English. I also worked with Professor Anne Klein and finally Gerald Yorke to improve the presentation. Again twenty-five years later during this re-translation, I listened to the tapes of the Dalai Lama's earlier lectures.

As a final step in the process of preparing this book for publication, I compared my translation with an excellent rendition by John Dunne and Sara McClintock[a] which they kindly sent me upon learning of my project. Their translation makes thorough use of both Ajitamitra's and Gyel-tsap's commentaries and provided many challenges and corrections for which I am most thankful. Also, many thanks to Paul Hackett for providing bibliographic assistance.

Paul Jeffrey Hopkins
University of Virginia

---

[a] *The Precious Garland: An Epistle to a King* (Boston: Wisdom Publications, 1997). It was printed for distribution to the audience of a lecture series by His Holiness the Dalai Lama in Los Angeles in June, 1997; a commercial edition is forthcoming

PART ONE: *ANALYSIS*

1 NĀGĀRJUNA'S BIOGRAPHY FROM TIBETAN SOURCES: THE IMPORTANCE OF ALTRUISTIC PERSONS IN COSMIC TIME

In Buddhist doctrine and literature individual initiative is considered to be crucially valuable in a world-view of rebirth over eons of time. The biography of Nāgārjuna, the author of the *Precious Garland of Advice*, illustrates an emphasis on the importance of individual enterprise over long periods of history that stands in stark contrast to the unfounded, common notion in Europe, America, and so forth that in Asian religions the cyclical nature of time undermines the importance of individual action.

THE PROPHECIES

Chandrakīrti,[a] at the beginning of the sixth chapter of his *Supplement to (Nāgārjuna's) "Treatise on the Middle,"*[b] mentions two prophecies of Nāgārjuna from two of Buddha's sūtras—the *Superior Sūtra on*

---

[a] My exposition is concerned with the prophecies of Nāgārjuna mentioned by Chandrakīrti, additional citations by D̄zong-ka-b̄a, and Jam-ȳang-shay-b̄a's (*'jam dbyangs bzhad pa ngag dbang brtson grus*, 1648-1721) exploration of D̄zong-ka-b̄a's sources in his *Great Exposition of Tenets* (*grub mtha' chen mo/ grub mtha'i rnam bshad rang gzhan grub mtha' kun dang zab don mchog tu gsal ba kun bzang zhing gi nyi ma lung rigs rgya mtsho skye dgu'i re ba kun skong*) (Musoorie: Dalama, 1962), *ca* 3a.2-6b.7, and *Great Exposition of the Middle* (*dbu ma chen mo/ dbu ma 'jug pa'i mtha' dpyod lung rigs gter mdzod zab don kun gsal skal bzang 'jug ngogs*) (Buxaduor: Gomang, 1967), 193a.4-197a.1. For an excellent bibliography of scholarship on Nāgārjuna's prophecies, see David S. Ruegg's *The Literature of the Madhyamaka School of Philosophy in India* (Wiesbaden: Otto Harrassowitz, 1981), 5 n.11. For a sense of the variety of accounts of Nāgārjuna's life, see especially M. Walleser, *The Life of Nāgārjuna from Tibetan and Chinese Sources*, Asia Major, Introductory Volume (Hirth Anniversary Volume, Leipzig, 1923); rpt. Delhi: Nag Publishers, 1979), 421-55.

[b] *dbu ma la 'jug pa, madhyamakāvatāra*; Peking 5261, 5262, vol. 98. Since Chandrakīrti often refers to Nāgārjuna's *Treatise on the Middle* (*dbu ma'i bstan bcos, madhyamakaśāstra*) merely by the appellation *madhyamaka*, the *madhyamaka* of "*madhyamakāvatāra*" is held to refer to a text propounding the middle, specifically Nāgārjuna's *Treatise on the Middle*. My translation of *avatāra* (*'jug pa*) as "supplement" is controversial; others use "introduction" or "entrance," both of which are attested common translations in such a context. My translation is based on the explanation by D̄zong-ka-b̄a L̄o-sang-drak-b̄a (*tsong ka pa blo bzang grags pa*, 1357-1419) that Chandrakīrti was filling in holes in Nāgārjuna's *Treatise on the Middle;* see Tsong-ka-pa, Kensur Lekden, and Jeffrey Hopkins, *Compassion in Tibetan Buddhism* (London: Rider and Company, 1980; repr. Ithaca: Snow Lion, 1980), 96-99. Among the many meanings of the Tibetan term for *avatāra, 'jug pa* can mean "to affix" or "to add on." According to the late Ken-sur Nga-w̄ang-lek-den (*mkhan zur ngag dbang legs ldan*), *avatāra* means "addition" in the sense that Chandrakīrti's text is a supplement historically necessary so as to clarify the meaning of Nāgārjuna's *Treatise on the Middle*. He wanted to make clear that the *Treatise* should not be interpreted according to the Mind Only system (*sems tsam, cittamātra*) or according to the Middle Way Autonomy School (*dbu ma rang rgyud pa, svatantrikamādhyamika*), the founding of which is attributed to Bhāvaviveka. During Nāgārjuna's lifetime, Bhāvaviveka had not written his commentary on the *Treatise,*

the Descent into Laṅkā[1] and the *Great Cloud Superior Sūtra of Twelve Thousand Stanzas.*[2] He cites these to justify relying on Nāgārjuna for an explication of emptiness, since the initial one prophesies that Nāgārjuna will achieve the first Bodhisattva ground for which direct realization of emptiness is necessary[3] and the second prophesies that he will teach widely. D̄zong-ka-b̄a, in his *Ocean of Reasoning, Explanation of (Nāgārjuna's) "Treatise on the Middle"*[4] makes a longer citation of the first prophecy and gives a short commentary on it. The passage begins with a question by the Bodhisattva Mañjushrī to Buddha. D̄zong-ka-b̄a cites the sūtra and elaborates:[5]

> The *Superior Sūtra on the Descent into Laṅkā* says:
>
> > The vehicle of individual knowledge
> > Is not in the sphere of [false] logicians.
> > Please tell who will uphold it
> > After the Protector has passed away.
>
> [Mañjushrī] asks who, after the Teacher has passed away, will uphold the vehicle pacifying the elaborations of terms and conceptuality, the object of the exalted wisdom of individual knowledge in meditative equipoise. In answer, [Buddha] says:
>
> > Mahāmati, know that after
> > The One Gone to Bliss has passed away
> > There will appear after the passage of time
> > One who will uphold the ways [of emptiness, the essence of the teaching].
> > In the south, in the area of Vidarbha[a]

---

nor had he founded his system; therefore, it was necessary later to supplement Nāgārjuna's text to show why it should not be interpreted in such a way.

Moreover, it is said that Chandrakīrti sought to show that a follower of Nāgārjuna should ascend the ten grounds by practicing the vast paths necessary to do so. This is because some interpret the Middle Way perspective as nihilistic. They see it as a means of refuting the general existence of phenomena rather than just their inherent existence—existence by way of the object's own nature—and conclude that it is not necessary to engage in practices such as the cultivation of compassion. Therefore, in order to show that it is important to engage in three central practices—compassion, non-dual understanding, and the altruistic mind of enlightenment (see pp. 27ff.)—and to ascend the ten Bodhisattva grounds, Chandrakīrti—in reliance on Nāgārjuna's *Precious Garland*—wrote this supplementary text, which, of course, also serves as an introduction, or means of entry, to Nāgārjuna's *Treatise.* (This Tibetanized meaning of *avatāra* as "supplement" perhaps accords with the fifth meaning given in Apte [163], "Any new appearance, growth, rise," though not much of a case can be made from the Sanskrit.)

[a] Louis de la Vallée Poussin (*Madhyamakāvatāra par Candrakīrti*, Bibliotheca Buddhica IX [Osnabrück: Biblio Verlag, 1970], 76.13), the Dharamsala edition (63.14), and D̄zong-ka-b̄a (64.12) read *be ta.* The Sanskrit for X.165-166, as given in P. L. Vaidya, *Saddharmalaṅkāvatārasūtram*, ed. Buddhist Sanskrit Texts No.3. Darbhanga: Mithila Institute, 1963, 118, is:

> *dakṣiṃāpatha**vedalyām** bhikṣuḥ śrīmān mahāyaśāḥ*
> *nāgāḥvayaḥ sa nāmnā tu sadasatpakṣadārakaḥ*
> *prakāśya loke madyānam mahāyānamuttaram*
> *āsādya bhūmiṃ muditāṃ yāsyate 'sau sukhāvatīm*

Nga-w̄ang-b̄el-den (*ngag dbang dpal ldan*, born 1797), *Annotations for (Jam-ȳang-shay-b̄a's) "Great Exposition of Tenets," Freeing the Knots of the Difficult Points, Precious Jewel of Clear Thought* (*grub mtha' chen mo'i mchan 'grel dka' gnad mdud grol blo gsal gces nor*) (Sarnath: Pleasure of Elegant Sayings Press, 1964), *dngos* 58a.3) gives *be da* (misprinted as *pe da*) and identifies the place as Vidarbha (*be dar bha*). He etymologizes the name as a place where a certain type of grass (identified in Sarat Chandra Das, *A Tibetan-English Dictionary* [Calcutta, 1902], as *Andropogon muricatus*) grows (*'jag ma skye ba'i yul*). Poussin (*Muséon*

Will be a monk known widely as Shrīmān
Who will [also] be called Nāga.
Destroying the [extreme] positions of [inherent] existence and [conventional] non-existence,
He will thoroughly teach in the world
The unsurpassed Great Vehicle—my vehicle.
Having done this, he will achieve the Very Joyful[a] ground
And then go to the Blissful[b] [Pure Land upon passing away].

Thus, it says that Nāgārjuna would comment on the definitive vehicle, devoid of the extremes of [inherent] existence and [conventional] non-existence.

Chandrakīrti is appealing to the prophetical authority of Buddha's special cognition of all phenomena—past, present, and future. Though his commentary proceeds by way of reasoning, he does not merely point to the reasonableness of Nāgārjuna's work—though this is clearly the thrust of the remainder of his commentary—but appeals to a higher authority for a justification of his choice of Nāgārjuna's *Treatise* as the source for his own discussion of emptiness. Buddha's authority comes from his special cognition, available for all to develop but for the time being inaccessible.

The second prophecy that Chandrakīrti cites, from the *Great Cloud Superior Sūtra of Twelve Thou-*

11, 274) also identifies the place as Vidarbha. M. Walleser, in his *The Life of Nāgārjuna from Tibetan and Chinese Sources*, further identifies (rpt. 6, n. 2) Vidarbha as now called Berar. E. Obermiller, in his *History of Buddhism by Bu-ston* (Heidelberg: Harrassowitz, 1931), 110, identifies the place as Vedalya, based on the Sanskrit edited by Bunyiu Nanjio (286). The late Tibetan scholar Ye-s̄hay-tup-d̄en (*ye shes thub bstan*) identified the term as meaning a place of *kuśa* grass, which he said is an area near present-day Madras.

Both Poussin (*Muséon* 11, 274) and Obermiller (110) take *dpal ldan* (*śrīmān*) as adjectival to "monk" (*bhikṣuḥ*), the former as "illustrious" (*illustre*) and the latter as "glorious," but Nga-w̄ang-b̄el-den (*Annotations, dngos* 58a.3) takes it as Nāgārjuna's name given at ordination (*dge slong du gyur ba'i ming dpal ldan zhes grags pa*), saying that he was otherwise known in the world as "Nāga" (*de'i ming gzhan 'jig rten na klu zhes 'bod pa ste*). This accords with Jam-ȳang-shay-b̄a's statement (*Great Exposition of Tenets, ca* 5a.4) that the name given at ordination was *dpal ldan blo 'chang*. Bu-d̄ön refers to Nāgārjuna early in his life as *śrīmān* (*dpal ldan*), and Obermiller (123, n. 891) recognizes this but mistakenly does not carry it over to this passage in the *Descent into Laṅkā*.

Nga-w̄ang-b̄el-den (*dngos* 58a.4) incorrectly takes "destroying the positions of existence and non-existence" (*yod dang med pa'i phyogs 'jig pa*) as modifying "my vehicle":

> Having thoroughly—clearly—explained in this world the final path of the Great Vehicle of which there is none higher among my vehicles and which destroys—abandons—the two positions, or extremes, of existence and non-existence which, when apprehended, bring ruination, he, having achieved the first ground, the Very Joyful, will go to the Blissful Land.

Poussin (*Muséon* 11, 274) rightly takes "destroying the positions of existence and non-existence" as referring to Nāgārjuna; this is justified by the Sanskrit *sad-asat-pakṣa-dārakaḥ* (given also in Obermiller, 110 n. 759) which is a nominative whereas the unsurpassed Great Vehicle (*mahāyānamuttaram*) is accusative. Jam-ȳang-shay-b̄a (*Great Exposition of Tenets, ca* 5b.8) gives a different reading of the Tibetan (*yod dang med pa'i phyogs 'jig cing*) which more accurately reflects the Sanskrit in that the particle *cing* prevents taking "destroying the positions of existence and non-existence" as modifying "my vehicle," whereas *yod dang med pa'i phyogs 'jig pa* does not do this.

[a] *rab tu dga' ba, muditā*. This is the first Bodhisattva ground.

[b] *bde ba can, sukhāvatī*.

sand Stanzas, says:

> Ānanda,[a] four hundred years after I [Shākyamuni Buddha] pass away, this Licchavi youth Liked-When-Seen-by-All-the-World will become a monk known as Nāga and will disseminate my teaching. Finally, in the land known as Very Pure Light[b] he will become a One Gone Thus, a Foe Destroyer,[c] a completely perfect Buddha named Light-Which-Is-a-Source-of-All-Wisdom.[a]

---

[a] In his translation, Poussin (*Muséon* 11, 275) incorrectly has Buddha identifying the Licchavi youth as Ānanda ("*Prince Licchavi, cet Ānanda, ainsi nommé parce que toute créature se réjouit en le voyant, quatre siècles après le nirvana, sera le bhikṣu nommé Nāga*"). However, it is clear that Buddha is talking about the Licchavi youth who is a contemporary of Ānanda, and thus Buddha is addressing Ānanda and talking about the Licchavi youth. There is considerable justification for the latter reading because the *Great Drum Sūtra* indicates that Buddha is talking to Ānanda *about* the Licchavi youth who is called Liked-When-Seen-by-All-the-World (*'jig rten thams cad kyis mthong na dga' ba, sarvalokapriyadarśana*), this phrase constituting his name and not describing Ānanda as Poussin has it. For the Sanskrit see *Suvarnaprabhāsottamasūtra, Das Goldglanz-Sūtra*, ed. Johannes Nobel [Leiden: Brill, 1950], Glossary, 65). Poussin was perhaps misled into thinking that *'jig rten thams cad kyis mthong na dga' ba* refers to Ānanda because the literal meaning of the name "Ānanda" is "thoroughly happy."

[b] *rab tu dang ba'i 'od.* Poussin (*Muséon* 11, 275) gives the Sanskrit as "*Suviśuddhaprabhābhūmi,*" whereas Obermiller (*History of Buddhism by Bu-ston*, 129) gives "*Prasannaprabhā.*"

[c] *dgra bcom pa, arhan.* With respect to the translation of *arhan/ arhant* (*dgra bcom pa*) as "Foe Destroyer," I do this to accord with the usual Tibetan translation of the term and to assist in capturing the flavor of oral and written traditions that frequently refer to this etymology. Arhats have overcome the foe which is the afflictive emotions (*nyon mongs, kleśa*), the chief of which is ignorance.

The Indian and Tibetan translators of Sanskrit and other texts into Tibetan were also aware of the etymology of *arhant* as "worthy one," as they translated the name of the "founder" of the Jaina system, Arhat, as *mchod 'od*, "Worthy of Worship" (see Jam-ȳang-shay-b̄a's *Great Exposition of Tenets, ka* 62a.3). Also, they were aware of Chandrakīrti's gloss of the term as "Worthy One" in his *Clear Words*, which reads: *sadevamānuṣāsurāl lokāt pūnārhatvād arhannityuchyate* (*Mūlamadhyamakakārikās de Nāgārjuna avec la Prasannapadā Commentaire de Candrakīrti*, publié par Louis de la Vallée Poussin, Bibliotheca Buddhica IV [Osnabrück: Biblio Verlag, 1970], 486.5), *lha dang mi dang lha ma yin du bcas pa'i 'jig rten gyis mchod par 'os pas dgra bcom pa zhes brjod la* (409.20, Tibetan Cultural Printing Press edition; also, Peking 5260, vol. 98, 75.2.2), "Because of being worthy of worship by the world of gods, humans, and demi-gods, they are called Arhats."

Also, they were aware of Haribhadra's twofold etymology in his *Illumination of the Eight Thousand Stanza Perfection of Wisdom Sūtra.* In the context of the list of epithets qualifying the retinue of Buddha at the beginning of the sūtra (see Unrai Wogihara, ed., *Abhisamayālaṃkārālokā Prajñā-pāramitā-vyākhyā, The Work of Haribhadra* [Tokyo: The Toyo Bunko, 1932-5; rpt. ed., Tokyo: Sankibo Buddhist Book Store, 1973], 8.18), Haribhadra says:

> They are called *arhant* [Worthy One, from the root *arh* "to be worthy"] since they are worthy of worship, religious donations, and being assembled together in a group, etc. (Wogihara, 9.8-9: *sarva evātra pūjā-dakṣiṇā-gaṇa-parikarṣādy-ārhatayarhantaḥ*; Peking 5189, 67.5.7: *'dir thams cad kyang mchod pa dang // yon dang tshogs su 'dub la sogs par 'os pas na dgra bcom pa'o*).

Also:

> They are called *arhant* [Foe Destroyer, *arihan*] because they have destroyed (*hata*) the foe (*ari*).
> (Wogihara, 10.18: *hatāritvād arhantaḥ*; Peking 5189, 69.3.6: *dgra rnams bcom pas na dgra bcom pa'o*).

(My thanks to Gareth Sparham for the references to Haribhadra.) Thus, we are dealing with a considered preference in the face of alternative etymologies—"Foe Destroyer" requiring a not unusual *i* infix to make *ari-han*, with *ari* meaning enemy and *han* meaning to kill, and thus "Foe Destroyer." Unfortunately, one word in English cannot convey both this meaning and "Worthy One"; thus I have gone with what clearly has become the predominant meaning in Tibet, since it is the focus of my study. For an excellent discussion of the two etymologies of *arhat* in Buddhism and Jainism, see L. M. Joshi's "Facets of Jaina Religiousness in Comparative Light," L. D. Series 85 (Ahmedabad: L. D. Institute of Indology, May 1981), 53-58.

This prophecy has a much longer perspective, tracing Nāgārjuna over lifetimes, first as a youth in Shākyamuni Buddha's audience named Liked-When-Seen-by-All-the-World, then as Nāgārjuna, and finally as someone who achieves enlightenment in a certain place and with a certain name in the distant future. The passage gives a sense of the development of a great being over a long period of time.

As Ḏzong-ka-ḇa briefly mentions in his *Illumination of the Thought*[6]—his commentary on Chandrakīrti's *Supplement to (Nāgārjuna's) "Treatise on the Middle"*—the Licchavi youth Liked-When-Seen-by-All-the-World is mentioned in the *Excellent Golden Light Sūtra.*[7] In that sūtra, Liked-When-Seen-by-All-the-World speaks with Kauṇḍinya about whether Buddha would leave relics upon passing away. Kauṇḍinya, inspired by Buddha, answers that because a Buddha's body is not made of blood and bone, there could not be any such relics but that Buddha, out of skillful means, would nevertheless leave relics.[b] Nāgārjuna is a rebirth of this illustrious youth.

Besides the prophecies in the *Sūtra on the Descent into Laṅkā* and the *Great Cloud Sūtra*, Ḏzong-ka-ḇa's commentary refers to two more prophecies but does not quote them; these are from the *Mañjushrī Root Tantra*[8] and the *Great Drum Sūtra.*[9] The *Mañjushrī Root Tantra* says:[c]

> When four hundred years have passed
> After I, the One Gone Thus, have passed away,
> A monk called Nāga will arise.
> Faithful in and helpful to the teaching,
> He will attain the Very Joyful ground.
> Living for six hundred years,
> That great being will also achieve
> The knowledge[-mantra] of *Mahāmayūrī.*[d]
> He will know the meaning of various treatises
> And the meaning of no inherent existence.[e]
> When he leaves that body,
> He will be born in the [Pure Land of] Bliss.
> Finally he will just definitely attain
> Thoroughly the state of Buddhahood.

---

[a] *ye shes 'byung gnas 'od.* Both Poussin (*Muséon* 11, 275) and Obermiller (*History of Buddhism by Bu-ston*, 129) give the Sanskrit as *Jñānākaraprabha.*

[b] An almost identical conversation is reported in the *Great Cloud Sūtra* (Peking 898, vol. 35, 250.1.7-250.4.7).

[c] Peking 162, vol. 6, 259.3.8-259.4.2, Chapter 36. This passage is translated by E. Obermiller in the *History of Buddhism by Bu-ston* (Heidelberg: Harrassowitz, 1932), Part 2, 111. He cites it as Kg. RGYUD. XI. 450a.5-450a.6.

Jam-ẏang-shay-ḇa (*Tenets*, *ca* 4a.3, 5b.8, 6b.5) cites the relevant parts of the passage with a slightly different reading:

> When four hundred years have passed
> After I, the One Gone Thus, have passed away,
> A monk called Nāga will arise...
> Living for six hundred years...
> He will know **many treatises teaching the basic constituent**
> And **the suchness of** the meaning of no inherent existence.

[d] *rma bya chen po.*

[e] *dngos po med pa.*

About this prophecy, the nineteenth-century Mongolian scholar Nga-w̄ang-b̄el-den says in his *Annotations to (Jam-ȳang-shay-b̄a's) "Great Exposition of Tenets"*:[10]

This passage in the *Mañjushrī Root Tantra* prophesies the Superior Nāgārjuna's:

- time of arising
- name
- help to the teaching through proclaiming the first proclamation of doctrine and so forth
- how he gained realization of the first ground through the force of reading the Perfection of Wisdom Sūtras
- his lifespan
- how he effected the welfare of transmigrators through the power of achieving knowledge-mantra
- his composing many treatises—Collections of Advice, Collections of Praises, medical and political treatises, and so forth, and in particular his clarifying the meaning of the profound emptiness by way of the Collections of Reasonings
- his going to the [Pure Land of] Bliss upon passing away from sorrow
- how in the future he will be thoroughly purified [as a Buddha] in the Desire Realm through [the display of] an emanation body.

This prophecy, while adding details, mirrors the series of events mentioned in the *Descent into Laṅkā*.

D̄zong-ka-b̄a reports but does not cite the prophecy in the *Great Drum Sūtra:*

The *Great Drum Sūtra* says that:

- after the Teacher's passing away, when the [average] life-span is eighty years[a] and the teaching [of the Great Vehicle] has degenerated, the Licchavi youth Liked-When-Seen-by-All-the-World, having become a monk bearing the Teacher's name [in the sense of being of the Shākya clan], will extend the teaching
- after one hundred years, he will die and be born in the Blissful [Pure Land].

That this scripture also prophesies the master [Nāgārjuna even though it does not explicitly mention his name] is asserted by Sthavira Bodhibhadra[b] and the Great Elder [Atisha]; they are relying on the explanation that the Licchavi Liked-When-Seen and Nāgārjuna are of one continuum [that is to say, earlier and later births in a single stream of rebirth].

The *Great Drum Sūtra* states that this monk [Nāgārjuna] is a seventh ground [Bodhisattva]. Such an explanation cannot be proven to contradict the former [statement in the *Descent into Laṅkā Sūtra* that Nāgārjuna was a first ground Bodhisattva], for variations among scriptures do occur [due to the fact that some scriptures describe how great beings appeared to ordinary sight and others describe their actual attainment].[c] In some scriptures, for instance, certain Great

---

[a] D̄zong-ka-b̄a's text (Tibetan Cultural Printing Press, 64.22) reads *lo brgyad cu'i dus su* which could mean "when eighty years [old]"; however, Jam-ȳang-shay-b̄a (*Great Exposition of the Middle*, 194b.4) makes it clear that the reference is to lifespan: "...when the [average] lifespan is eighty years" (*tshe lo brgyad cu'i dus su*).

[b] The passage is cited in Jam-ȳang-shay-b̄a's *Great Exposition of Tenets, nga* 3a.2.

[c] The bracketed material is from Ḡön-chok-jik-may-w̄ang-b̄o (*dkon mchog 'jigs med dbang po*), *Analysis of the Great Treatise, (Chandrakīrti's) Supplement to (Nāgārjuna's) "Treatise on the Middle": Lamp of Scripture and Reasoning: Oral Transmission of the Omniscient Lama, Jam-ȳang-shay-b̄ay-dor-jay* (*bstan gcos chen po dbu ma la 'jug pa'i mtha' dpyod lung rigs sgron me zhes bya ba

Kings are said to be Stream Enterers whereas in other scriptures they are said to be Buddhas. Jam-ȳang-shay-b̄a, pursuing D̄zong-ka-b̄a's thought behind these somewhat cryptic statements, gives a detailed account of Nāgārjuna's three proclamations of doctrine. This is done in his *Great Exposition of Tenets*[a] in which he extensively cites the *Great Drum Sūtra.* By arranging his several citations in their order of appearance in the sūtra, a picture of the prophecy and of Nāgārjuna's continuum of lives emerges.

NĀGĀRJUNA'S LIVES ACCORDING TO THE GREAT DRUM SŪTRA

In the initial passage that Jam-ȳang-shay-b̄a cites, Shākyamuni Buddha is reporting a much earlier prophecy by a previous Buddha called Lamp-Maker[b] who was speaking to a prince that in a later birth came to be in the retinue of Shākyamuni Buddha, at which time he was called Liked-When-Seen-by-All-the-World. The Buddha Lamp-Maker is prophesying (1) the prince's appearance at the time of Shākyamuni Buddha in the Licchavi clan as Liked-When-Seen-by-All-the-World, (2) his later birth as Nāgārjuna, (3) Nāgārjuna's assistance to the doctrine, and (4) after his life as Nāgārjuna, rebirth in a Pure Land and subsequent pursuit of the teaching through emitting a magical emanation.[11]

> When the Protector called Shākyamuni emerges in this obdurate[c] world realm, you will become the Licchavi Liked-When-Seen. Then, when the [average] lifespan is eighty years at a time of the diminishment of the teaching after the Protector [Shākyamuni Buddha] has passed away in that worldly realm, you—having become the monk called Mindful,[d] will bring out this sūtra without concern for your own life. Then, dying after a hundred years pass, you will be born in the worldly realm of the Blissful [Pure Land]. At that time you will emit many great magical emanations. Staying on the eighth ground, you will set one body in the Blissful [Pure Land], and upon emanating one body you will set it in the Joyous [Pure Land],[e] questioning the Undaunted Protector [Maitreya] about this sūtra.

About this prophecy, D̄zong-ka-b̄a's *Ocean of Reasoning, Explanation of (Nāgārjuna's) "Treatise on the Middle Way"* cryptically says, "That prophecy in the *Great Drum Sūtra* is said to [refer to Nāgārjuna's] final appearance in the south." It is clear—from Jam-ȳang-shay-b̄a's explanations of Nāgārjuna's life in both his *Great Exposition of Tenets* and *Great Exposition of the Middle*—that from among Nāgārjuna's three appearances in south India and his three proclamations of doctrine, this prophecy is referring to the third and thus is not about his birth in south India or even his becoming a monk (since he did that much earlier) but about his return to south India from the northern continent called Unpleasant

---

kun mkhyen bla ma 'jam dbyangs bzhad pa'i rdo rje'i gsung rgyun), The Collected Works of dkon-mchog-'jigs-med-dbaṅ-po (New Delhi: Ngawang Gelek Demo, 1972), vol. 6, 185.6-186.1. Jam-ȳang-shay-b̄a (*Great Exposition of the Middle*, 195b.6) holds that—according to the sūtra system—in fact Nāgārjuna, in that lifetime, was a seventh grounder who gained the eighth. In addition, from the viewpoint of Highest Yoga Mantra, he is held to have achieved Buddhahood in that lifetime.

[a] His explanation is found at the beginning of the section on the Great Vehicle systems (*ca* 4a.2-6b.7), a synopsis of which is given in Jeffrey Hopkins, *Meditation on Emptiness*, 356-59.

[b] *mar me mdzad, dīpaṃkara.*

[c] *mi mjed.*

[d] *blo 'chang.*

[e] *dga' ldan, tuṣita.*

Sound.[a] When Ḏzong-ka-ḇa says that such is "said," he means, as can be seen from Jam-ȳang-shay-ḇa's annotations to Ḏzong-ka-ḇa's *Great Exposition of the Stages of the Path,*[12] that the *Great Drum Sūtra* itself says this in a verse summation of the prophecy later in the text:[13]

> That is his final emergence
> In the southern direction.

In the next passage that Jam-ȳang-shay-ḇa cites from the *Great Drum Sūtra,* Shākyamuni Buddha himself is speaking—in the presence of a group of Bodhisattvas including Liked-When-Seen-by-All-the-World—to Mahākāshyapa about the future rebirth of Liked-When-Seen-by-All-the-World as Nāgārjuna. He speaks of Nāgārjuna as actually being a seventh ground Bodhisattva but of assuming the aspect of a common being who newly attains the first Bodhisattva ground in that lifetime. He also speaks of Nāgārjuna's three proclamations of doctrine and their content, as well as his death, which, given his high spiritual attainments, is merely a display.[14]

> Having set him on the seventh [Bodhisattva] ground, I will bless him as an ordinary being. Then, when the [average] lifespan is eighty years at a time of the diminishment of the teaching, he—having been born in the family lineage called Kayāgaurī[b] in a village called Base-of-the-Great-Garland[c] in a district called Ayodhyā[d] on the banks of a river in a southern area called *Ru mun de*[e]—will become a monk bearing my name [in that he will be a member of the Shākya clan]. Through skill in sustaining the community he, having emerged from the householder's life among those indolent with regard to my training in virtue, will gather them together through the modes of gathering.[f]
>
> Having found this sūtra, he will hold it to his body, and having purified the spiritual community, initially he will thoroughly eradicate the great bases of unsuitability [at Nālanda], proclaiming the great sound of doctrine. He will proclaim the conch of the doctrine and victory banner of the doctrine spoken in the *Great Drum Sūtra.* As a second [proclamation of doctrine] he will set forth Great Vehicle sūtras discoursing on emptiness. As a third [proclamation of doctrine] he will expound discourse examining the basic constituent[g] [i.e., the Buddha nature] of sentient beings and will discourse on the *Great Drum*....Later, hearing this sūtra at a time of

---

[a] *sgra mi nyan, kuru.*

[b] *ka yo ri.*

[c] *phreng ba chen po rten.*

[d] *dmag gis mi tshugs pa.*

[e] This is the name as it appears in Tibetan; the Sanskrit is unknown.

[f] As Nāgārjuna himself says in the *Precious Garland of Advice* (stanza 133), the four modes of gathering students are by way of giving gifts, giving doctrine, teaching others to fulfill their aims, and oneself acting according to that teaching:

> You should cause the assembling
> Of the religious and the worldly
> Through giving, speaking pleasantly,
> Purposeful behavior, and concordant behavior.

"Speaking pleasantly" is conversation based on high status and definite goodness. "Purposeful behavior" is to cause others to practice what is beneficial. "Concordant behavior" is for one to practice what one teaches others.

[g] *khams, dhātu.*

> great age, he will discourse on this sūtra for a hundred years, making the rain of doctrine fall. After a hundred years pass, he will display a great magical emanation among humans in the south and will display thorough passing beyond sorrow.

By citing this passage, Jam-ȳang-shay-b̄a provides a fuller picture of the three phases of Nāgārjuna's life, which D̄zong-ka-b̄a alludes to only in passing when he mentions the final appearance in south India.

In the final passage from the *Great Drum Sūtra* that Jam-ȳang-shay-b̄a cites, Buddha, still speaking to Mahākāshyapa, prophesies Nāgārjuna's attainment of Buddhahood in the distant future.[15]

> Later he will become a Buddha. After a thousand Buddhas have thoroughly passed away, sixty-two eons will pass. One hundred thousand Solitary Realizers will pass, and then when eight Protectors have also passed, this monk Liked-When-Seen-by-All-the-World, who bears my name [in that he is a member of the Shākya clan] will become a One Gone Thus, a Foe Destroyer, a completely perfect Buddha called Light-Which-Is-A-Source-of-All-Wisdom in a Buddha Land in just this world.

By means of these three passages the continuum of the being who later became Nāgārjuna is shown to have had an illustrious history dating back to an earlier Buddha, then through the time of Shākyamuni Buddha and through the very long lifetime as Nāgārjuna as well as stretching into the distant future when he will become a Buddha. The story conveys the message that spiritual progress is a long-term process, and it emphasizes the importance of extraordinary, compassionately motivated beings over vast stretches of history.

NĀGĀRJUNA'S LIVES ACCORDING TO THE GREAT CLOUD SŪTRA

More information is provided through Jam-ȳang-shay-b̄a's citations of the *Great Cloud Sūtra,* which Chandrakīrti cites only briefly. Again, I will present them in their order of appearance in the sūtra. Shākyamuni Buddha's audience of Bodhisattvas here includes Kauṇḍinya, who later became the great Buddhist king Ashoka, and Liked-When-Seen-by-All-the-World, who later became Nāgārjuna. Also present is the goddess Vimalaprabhā who—long ago during the time of the Buddha Lamp-of-the-Nāga-Lineage[a]—was the wife of King Nāga-of-Great-Effort[b]; that ancient King was an earlier birth of the Licchavi youth Liked-When-Seen-by-All-the-World. The message that lives are interwoven over long periods of rebirth is clear.

In the first passage Buddha is speaking to the "goddess" Vimalaprabhā about Kauṇḍinya, foretelling his rebirth in the future as the great religious king Ashoka:[16]

> Goddess, the prophesied master, the Brahmin Kauṇḍinya also will be born one hundred twenty years after I pass away, in the royal lineage of a half universal emperor[c] called the Maurya lineage.... Goddess, he will become the lay-practitioner[d] King Ashoka. Goddess, that half universal emperor called Ashoka will proclaim the initial great lion's roar of the treatises of doctrine and

---

[a] *klu rigs sgron me, nāgakulapradīpa.*

[b] *brtson 'grus chen po'i klu.*

[c] *'khor los sgyur ba'i rgyal po, cakravartin.* Such a ruler has dominion over from one to four of the continents of our type of world system (there are only four) by means of a wheel made, respectively, from different metals—iron/steel, copper, silver, or gold.

[d] *dge bsnyen, upāsaka.*

will manifestly make worship.

In the next passage, with the same persons among his audience, Buddha addresses the general collection of Bodhisattvas, speaking about the doctrine's remaining for forty years after he passes away and then its decline:[17]

> Children of gods,[a] after I have passed away, those who have created roots of virtue and those who have served many Buddhas will explain sūtras such as this, teaching them also to others extensively. Furthermore, the *Great Cloud Sūtra* will be enjoyed in the Land of Jambu [i.e., this world] for up to forty years and will be disseminated. After that, at a later time, the excellent doctrine will be abandoned, the king[doms] will be disturbed, and the excellent doctrine will vanish….

Having set the scene of the degeneracy of the doctrine, Buddha—speaking through Mahākāshyapa—prophesies the rebirth of Liked-When-Seen-by-All-the-World as Nāgārjuna, who will rescue this doctrine from oblivion in the first of his three proclamations of doctrine. Through Buddha's power, Mahākāshyapa is answering a question about who will uphold the teaching after Buddha's passing away; the question is put by a devaputra king of Scent-Eaters called Liked-When-Seen[b] in the presence of the Licchavi youth Liked-When-Seen-by-All-the-World.[18]

> In the Land of Jambu at a time of the thorough degeneration of the excellent doctrine a monk similar to Mahākāshyapa will be born. Arising in the midst of my hearers, he will, in stages, wipe out famine, will praise the sūtras spoken by the One Gone Thus among unruly ones difficult to tame…he will stay in the monastery, praise the discipline, and defeat the unruly.

In the next passage, Buddha identifies the Licchavi youth Liked-When-Seen-by-All-the-World as a rebirth of a much earlier king, tracing Nāgārjuna back not only to the Licchavi youth Liked-When-Seen-by-All-the-World contemporaneous with Shākyamuni Buddha but also to a distant predecessor of that youth, a Nāga King who lived at the time of an earlier Buddha and whose name was Lamp-of-the-Nāga-Lineage.[19]

> That King, King-Nāga-of-Great-Effort, is presently this Licchavi youth, Liked-When-Seen-by-All-the-World.

According to the *Great Cloud Sūtra of Twelve Thousand Stanzas* as cited by Chandrakīrti but not in the separate translation of the sūtra as it exists in Tibetan, Buddha identifies the illustrious future lifetime of Liked-When-Seen-by-All-the-World by name as Nāgārjuna. (Nāgārjuna's name is not explicitly mentioned in any other passages either in the *Great Cloud Sūtra* or the *Great Drum Sūtra.*) Chandrakīrti cites this particular passage from the *Great Cloud Sūtra* that contains Nāgārjuna's name:

> Ānanda, four hundred years after I [Shākyamuni Buddha] pass away, this Licchavi youth Liked-When-Seen-by-All-the-World will become a monk *known as Nāga* and will extend my teaching widely [in the world]. Finally, in the land known as Very Pure Light he will become a One Gone Thus, a Foe Destroyer, a completely perfect Buddha named Light-Which-Is-A-Source-of-All-Wisdom.

In the sūtra as it is translated into Tibetan, Buddha speaks of Liked-When-Seen-by-All-the-World's three proclamations of doctrine when he takes rebirth as the being that is understood by context to be

---

[a] *lha'i bu, devaputra.*

[b] *lha'i bu mthong na dga' ba dri za'i rgyal po.*

Nāgārjuna:[20]

> Furthermore, look at the greatness of my hearer [Nāgārjuna], a monk concordant in name with the One Gone Thus [in that he will be of the Shākya clan], who will manifestly proclaim three times great proclamations of doctrine and then the time of death will come....

Also, Buddha prophesies the enlightenment of Liked-When-Seen-by-All-the-World, that is, Nāgārjuna, in the very distant future:[21]

> Child of good family, once this good eon has passed, after one thousand Buddhas have thoroughly passed away, for sixty-two eons a Buddha will not arise; one hundred ten million Solitary Realizers will arise. Child of good family, after those sixty-two eons have passed, seven other Buddhas will arise. Then, when the seventh has thoroughly passed away, at that time this worldly realm will be called Manifest Faith.[a] In this worldly realm called Manifest Faith, this [Liked-When-Seen-by-All-the-World, i.e., Nāgārjuna,] will become a One Gone Thus, a Foe Destroyer, a completely perfect Buddha called Light-Which-Is-A-Source-of-All-Wisdom.

Having prophesied Kauṇḍinya to be reborn as King Ashoka and Liked-When-Seen-by-All-the-World to be reborn as Nāgārjuna, Buddha prophesies the future rebirth of the "goddess" Vimalaprabhā as a princess in a family in a city that Nāgārjuna will visit:[22]

> When seven hundred years have passed after I thoroughly pass away through [my skill in] means, this goddess Vimalaprabhā will arise in a lineage of a king of the realm, called Udayana[b] in a city called Definite-As-Endowed-With-Glorious-Qualities[c] on the southern bank of the river Auspicious-Blackness[d] in the district of *Mun can*[e] in a southern area....

SUMMARY

Thus, four hundred years after Shākyamuni Buddha passed away, the prince Liked-When-Seen-by-All-the-World—to fulfill his earlier wish to assist the teaching made when he was King-Nāga-of-Great-Effort in the presence of the Buddha Lamp-of-the-Nāga-Lineage—took birth in South India (the first of three appearances in South India) and became a monk under Saraha. He was given the name Glorious Mindful One[f] and was called Nāgārjuna. In his first proclamation of doctrine Nāgārjuna protected the monks at Nālanda from famine through alchemy, exhorting the indolent, and expelling the wayward. Then, having gained adepthood, somewhere between his fiftieth and hundredth year he went to the land of dragons and, bringing back the *One Hundred Thousand Stanza Perfection of Wisdom Sūtra*, appeared in South India a second time. Having composed the *Treatise on the Middle, the Fundamental Text Called "Wisdom,"* he proclaimed the second proclamation of the doctrine of emptiness for up to a hundred years. Then, he went to the northern continent called Unpleasant Sound, furthering the interests of sentient beings for two hundred years and again appeared in South India for a third time. During this final period, he brought back the *Great Drum Sūtra*, the *Great Cloud Sūtra*, and so forth from

---

[a] *mngon par dad pa.*

[b] *bde spyod.*

[c] *dpal yon can nges pa.*

[d] *nag po bzang.*

[e] This is the Tibetan; the Sanskrit is not known.

[f] *dpal ldan blo 'chang.*

the northern continent and proclaimed the third proclamation of doctrine, discourse examining the basic constituent, the Buddha nature. During this final period of a hundred years he taught about the existence of the Matrix of One Gone Thus[a] in all sentient beings in such works as his *Praise of the Element of Qualities*.[23]

Shākyamuni foretells that after Liked-When-Seen-by-All-the-World's life as Nāgārjuna, he will be reborn in the Blissful Pure Land, from which he will emit a magical emanation to the Joyous Pure Land in order to question the Undaunted Protector Maitreya about the *Great Drum Sūtra*. Shākyamuni goes on to prophecy Nāgārjuna's enlightenment after more than sixty-two eons in the land known as Very Pure Light. About the Buddha whom Nāgārjuna will become Shākyamuni says that:

- his lifespan will be fifteen intermediate eons
- he will be born in lands called Manifestly Liking Doctrine, and so forth
- those places will be without Hearers, Solitary Realizers, and Forders,[b] will be without absence of leisure for the practice of doctrine, will have many Bodhisattvas, and will be adorned always with pleasant sounds
- even after that Buddha passes away, his teaching will remain for one thousand ten million years.

THE FORCE OF ALTRUISM

Through these many sources, what emerges is a personal history of tremendous consequence to this and other worlds over a very long period of time. Nāgārjuna's marvelous history begins, so to speak, with wishes made in the presence of an earlier Buddha. As Jam-ȳang-shay-b̄a says:[24]

> With respect to how this master [Nāgārjuna] raised the doctrine of the Great Vehicle, the *Great Cloud Sūtra* says that in accordance with wishes[c] that he made in the presence of the [earlier] One Gone Thus, Lamp-of-the-Nāga-Lineage, to proclaim three proclamations and so forth of the excellent doctrine during the time of the teaching of Shākyamuni, he proclaimed three proclamations of doctrine here.

The *Great Cloud Sūtra* itself says:[25]

> ...consider the greatness of the monk [Nāgārjuna] similar in name to the One Gone Thus. For, that monk made a promise and planted wishes in the presence of the One Gone Thus, Lamp-of-the-Nāga-Lineage. Having made [the promise and wish], "I will give my life to protect the excellent doctrine also during the teaching of the Supramundane Victor Shākyamuni," he will manifestly proclaim proclamations of the excellent doctrine three times.

However one takes the story, as an actual prophecy or as a religious fiction intended to inculcate a sense of Nāgārjuna's greatness (and many parts do indeed show handicrafting), the fact that the saga begins with a promise and a wish illustrates the power of intentions, the epochal importance of individual initiative. Also, that the narrative takes place over such a long period of time illustrates the doctrine of gradual development over many lifetimes. Thereby, individual lives are put in perspective—showing at once the place of particular lives in a larger history and the importance of individual continuity and initiative.

---

[a] *de bzhin gshegs pa'i snying po, tathāgatagarbha.*

[b] "Forders" (*mu stegs, tīrthika*) are non-Buddhists who propound and follow a path, or ford, to liberation or high status.

[c] *smon lam.*

That Nāgārjuna's lives are enmeshed with others' in different roles illustrates the changeability yet connectedness of situations over the continuum of lives and the relativity of particular relationships of the moment. That the purpose of his activities over so many lives is all for the benefit of others illustrates the boundless extent of altruism advocated in the Great Vehicle. That the teaching of emptiness about to be presented comes from this illustrious being indicates that the source of its presentation is no ordinary being but one whose lives are directed by principle—Nāgārjuna is not just an intelligent scholar but also a special being, this very specialness stemming from altruistic intentions. The religious value of imagining such a special being and thereby mixing one's mind with such compassionate heroism is implicit.

2 Advice for Living

Nāgārjuna's *Precious Garland of Advice* is variously included among his Collections of Advice[a] since it advises how to conduct daily life, etc., or among his Six Collections of Reasonings[b] since it contains a great many reasonings establishing the emptiness of inherent existence (see pp. 51ff.) It is said that he wrote the *Precious Garland* specifically for a Shātavāhana king.[c] He describes the advice as sometimes being unpleasant, comparing it to distasteful but effective medicine: (141-42)

> Rare are helpful speakers,
> Listeners are very rare,
> But rarer still are those who act at once
> On words that though unpleasant are beneficial.
>
> Therefore having realized that though unpleasant
> It is helpful, act on it quickly,
> Just as to cure an illness one drinks
> Dreadful medicine from one who cares.

And: (301-3)

> Monarchs who do what is against the practices
> And senseless are mostly praised
> By their citizens, for it is hard to know
> What will or will not be tolerated.
> Hence it is hard to know
> What is useful or not [to say].
> If useful but unpleasant words
> Are hard to speak to anyone else,
> What could I, a monk, say to you,
> A King who is a lord of the great earth?

---

[a] *gdams tshogs.*

[b] *rigs tshogs.*

[c] Dr. Heramba Chatterjee Sastri identifies the king as "presumably Gautamīputra Śātakarṇī, the lord over the three oceans as recorded in *Nasik Edict* of his mother Bālaśrī, stated to be a friend of Nāgārjuna, as the person to whom two of the friendly epistles were addressed. The date of Gautamīputra as assigned by K. A. N. Sastri is 80-104 A. D." See *The Philosophy of Nāgārjuna as contained in the Ratnāvālī* (Calcutta: Saraswat Library, 1977), 11-12. Robert Thurman identifies the king as Udayi in "Nagarjuna's Guidelines for Buddhist Social Action" in *Engaged Buddhist Reader* edited by Arnold Kotler (Berkeley: Parallax, 1996), 80.

But because of my affection for you
And from compassion for all beings,
I tell you without hesitation
That which is useful but unpleasant.

When Nāgārjuna says that his motivation is not just affection for the King but also "compassion for all beings," he intends others to benefit from reading and contemplating his advice. For, at the end of the poem he announces that these teachings also are for others: (498)

These doctrines were not just taught
Only for monarchs
But were taught with a wish to help
Other sentient beings as befits them.

He extends the attitude of implementing unpleasant but salutary advice to encompass practice in general in that the attainment of a greater end makes temporary difficulties bearable: (374-77)

If even [in ordinary life] pain can bring future benefit,
What need is there to say that [accepting suffering]
Beneficial for one's own and others' happiness will help!
This practice is known as the policy of the ancients.

If through relinquishing small pleasures
There is extensive happiness later,
Seeing the greater happiness
The resolute should relinquish small pleasures.

If such things cannot be borne,
Then doctors giving distasteful medicines
Would disappear. It is not [reasonable]
To forsake [great pleasure for the small].

Sometimes what is thought harmful
Is regarded as helpful by the wise.
General rules and their exceptions
Are commended in all treatises.

At other points, however, the advice is described as being gentle and soothing: (304-6)

The Supramundane Victor said that students are to be told
The truth—gentle, meaningful, and salutary—
At the proper time and from compassion.
That is why you are being told all this.

O Steadfast One, when true words
Are spoken without belligerence,
They should be taken as fit to be heard,
Like water fit for bathing.

Realize that I am telling you
What is useful here and otherwise.

Act on it so as to help
Yourself and also others.

At the end of the poem Nāgārjuna, while presenting the qualifications of spiritual guides, warns against not following helpful advice: (491-93ab)

Those who have qualms that it would be bad for themselves
[If they relied] on one who has purity, love, and intelligence
As well as helpful and appropriate speech,
Cause their own interests to be destroyed.

You should know in brief
The qualifications of spiritual guides.
If you are taught by those knowing contentment
And having compassion and ethics,
As well as wisdom that can drive out your afflictive emotions,
You should realize [what they teach] and respect them.

The purpose of such reliance is to effect personal transformation from a state of being imbued with afflictive emotions and to a state that Nāgārjuna implies would be endowed with the characteristics of a qualified teacher—contentment, love and compassion, the purity of ethics, and intelligence that can help others drive out their afflictive emotions.

REMOVING DEFECTS AND ACQUIRING GOOD QUALITIES

At the beginning of the *Precious Garland of Advice for a King* is an obeisance to Buddha, whom Nāgārjuna describes as having separated from all defects and having acquired all good qualities: (1)

I bow down to the Omniscient,
Freed from all defects,
Adorned with all good qualities,
The sole friend of all beings.

He ends the epistle by calling readers to achieve the same state: (497)

Freed from all defects
And adorned with all good qualities,
Become a sustenance for all sentient beings
And become omniscient.

In both cases, the reason for separating from negative qualities and achieving good qualities is clear—to become a "friend," a "sustenance of all sentient beings." The aim is altruistic.

Near that closing appeal, he advises practitioners three times each day to make wishes to effect the process of shedding negative states and becoming endowed with positive ones: (477)

May I also be adorned completely
With those and all other good qualities,
Be freed from all defects,
And have superior love for all sentient beings.

In the middle of the text, when speaking on the two practices of accumulating stores of merit and wisdom, he exhorts readers not to be lazy about these practices but to identify defects and good qualities:

(227-28)

Hence do not feel inadequate thinking,
"Buddhahood is far away."
Always strive at these [collections]
To remove defects and attain good qualities.

Realizing that desire, hatred, and obscuration
Are defects, forsake them completely.
Realizing that non-desire, non-hatred, and non-obscuration
Are good qualities, inculcate them with vigor.

The framework of removing defects and acquiring good qualities pervades the text. Deprecation of the Great Vehicle, the core of which is altruism,[a] is viewed as an inability to appreciate good qualities: (368-70)

Either through not knowing the good qualities [of altruism] and the defects [of mere self-concern],
Or identifying good qualities as defects,
Or through despising good qualities,
They deride the Great Vehicle.

Those who deride the Great Vehicle—
Knowing that to harm others is defective
And that to help others is a good quality—
Are said to despise good qualities.

Those who despise the Great Vehicle,
Source of all good qualities in that [it teaches] taking delight
Solely in the aims of others due to not looking to one's own,
Consequently burn themselves [in bad transmigrations].

The result of deriding altruism is the ruination of one's own welfare.

In sum, in the beginning, middle, and end of the *Precious Garland of Advice* Nāgārjuna emphasizes personality transformation through adopting beneficent attitudes and actions and through discarding counter-productive attitudes and actions, all within the explicitly stated context of serving others' well-being. This is the overall theme.

LOVE, COMPASSION, HELP, NON-HARMING

Nāgārjuna again and again makes clear the centrality of love, compassion, help, and non-harming. Non-harming and love are two of the six epitomes of religious practice: (10)

Not drinking intoxicants, a good livelihood,
Non-harming, respectful giving,
Honoring the honorable, and love—
Practice in brief is that.

Also, whether or not one is engaged in religious practice depends on whether others are being helped or

[a] The word "altruism" is built from the Latin *alter*, meaning "other"; thus the word basically means "otherism," unselfish concern for the welfare of others.

are still being harmed: (11)

Practice is not done by just
Mortifying the body,
For one has not forsaken injuring others
And is not helping others.

In the section on achieving the thirty-two marks of a great being, love is the cause for having marvelously bright and blue eyes: (195)

Through viewing beings with love
And without desire, hatred, or delusion
Your eyes will be bright and blue
With eyelashes like a bull.

Love figures so prominently in the development of the eighty beauties[a] of a Buddha that it is the only factor mentioned when he summarizes their causation (197). The meritorious power of love is such that an instant of it exceeds offering three hundred pots of food daily to monastics (283).

Though, unlike wisdom, love does not yield liberation, it is promoted as bringing many benefits to oneself—friendliness from gods and humans, protection by spirits, mental and physical pleasures, defense against weapons and poison, effortless achievement, and rebirth in comfort: (284-85)

Though [through love] you are not liberated
You will attain the eight good qualities of love—
Gods and humans will be friendly,
Even [non-humans] will protect you,
You will have mental pleasures and many [physical] pleasures,
Poison and weapons will not harm you,
Without striving you will attain your aims,
And be reborn in the world of Brahmā.

The benefits, however, are not limited to worldly success, for when Nāgārjuna addresses the incompleteness of the Lesser Vehicle[b] with respect to laying out the causes of Buddhahood, he speaks not about wisdom but about the compassionate activities of Bodhisattvas: (390-93)

Bodhisattvas' aspirational wishes, deeds, and dedications [of merit]
Were not described in the Hearers' Vehicle.

---

[a] *dpe byad, anuvyañjana;* this term is often translated as "minor marks," but this does little to reflect the strength of the Sanskrit or the Tibetan.

[b] *theg dman, hīnayāna.* The term "Lesser Vehicle" (*theg dman, hīnayāna*) has its origin in the writings of Great Vehicle (*theg chen, mahāyāna*) authors and was, of course, not used by those to whom it was ascribed. Substitutes such as "non-Mahāyāna," "Nikāya Buddhism," and "Theravādayāna" have been suggested in order to avoid the pejorative sense of "Lesser." However, "Lesser Vehicle" is a convenient term in this particular context for a type of tenet system and/or practice that is seen in Great Vehicle scholarship to be surpassed but not negated by a "higher" system. It needs to be realized that the "Lesser Vehicle" is not despised, most of it being incorporated into the "Great Vehicle." The monks' and nuns' vows are Lesser Vehicle as is much of the course of study in monastic universities in Tibetan Buddhism—years of study are put into the topics of Epistemology (*tshad ma, pramāṇa*), Manifest Knowledge (*chos mngon pa, abhidharma*), and Discipline (*'dul ba, vinaya*), all of which are mostly Lesser Vehicle in perspective.

Therefore how could one become
A Bodhisattva through it?
[In the Hearers' Vehicle] Buddha did not explain
The foundations for a Bodhisattva's enlightenment.
What greater authority for this subject
Is there other than the Victor?

How could the fruit of Buddhahood be superior
[If achieved] through the path common to Hearers
Which has the foundations [of the Hearer enlightenment],
The meanings of the four noble truths, and the harmonies with enlightenment?

The subjects concerned with the Bodhisattva deeds
Were not mentioned in the [Hearers' Vehicle] sūtras
But were explained in the Great Vehicle.
Hence the wise should accept it [as Buddha's word].[a]

Identifying the uniquely Great Vehicle practice of the six perfections as well as compassion and their effects, he says that compassion fulfills all aims: (435-38)

Briefly the good qualities
Observed by Bodhisattvas are
Giving, ethics, patience, effort,
Concentration, wisdom, compassion, and so forth.

Giving is to give away one's wealth.
Ethics is to help others.
Patience is to have forsaken anger.
Effort is enthusiasm for virtues.

Concentration is unafflicted one-pointedness.
Wisdom is ascertainment of the meaning of the truths.
Compassion is a mind having the one savor
Of mercy for all sentient beings.

From giving there arises wealth, from ethics happiness,
From patience a good appearance, from [effort in] virtue brilliance,
From concentration peace, from wisdom liberation,
From compassion all aims are achieved.

With respect to how to attain Buddhahood, he speaks of three causes, two of which are compassion and the altruistic intention to become enlightened whereas the other is wisdom: (174c-75)

If you and the world wish to attain
Unparalleled enlightenment,
Its roots are the altruistic aspiration to enlightenment
Firm like the monarch of mountains,

---

[a] For Ďzong-ka-ƃa's discussion of 390 and 393, see Tsong-ka-pa, Kensur Lekden, and Jeffrey Hopkins, *Compassion in Tibetan Buddhism*, 173.

Compassion reaching to all quarters,
And wisdom not relying on duality.[a]

The seventh-century Indian scholar Chandrakīrti, who became renowned especially in the Tibetan cultural region for his commentaries on four commentaries on Middle Way texts,[b] etc., draws on Nāgārjuna's specifying these three causes of enlightenment in the *Precious Garland of Advice.* Paying homage to compassion at the beginning of his *Supplement to the Middle,* he reiterates the same three:

Hearers and middling realizers of suchness [i.e., Solitary Realizers][c] are born from the Kings of Subduers [i.e., Buddhas].
Buddhas are born from Bodhisattvas.
The mind of compassion, non-dual understanding, and the altruistic mind of enlightenment
Are the causes of Children of Conquerors [i.e., Bodhisattvas].

Mercy alone is seen as the seed of a Conqueror's rich harvest,
As water for development,
And as a ripened state of long enjoyment,
Therefore at the start I praise compassion.

Chandrakīrti pays homage to compassion because it is the chief distinguishing feature of a Bodhisattva. Also, since Bodhisattvas are the causes of Buddhas, by paying homage to their main practice, he implicitly honors Buddhas who arise from this practice. He pays respect to the causes of Buddhahood because if one wants to become a Buddha, one must generate compassion and enter the Bodhisattva path. Also, compassion is crucial not just in the beginning but also in the middle and after the end of the path in the state of Buddhahood.

Nāgārjuna says that love and compassion have to be completely unbiased: (437cd)

Compassion is a mind having the one savor
Of mercy for all sentient beings.

He also emphasizes the concordant relationship in terms of the limitless beings who are objects of compassion, the consequent limitless merit accumulated through such an attitude, and the limitless good qualities that are attained at Buddhahood through such merit: (216-20)

Through their compassion
Bodhisattvas are determined to lead

---

[a] For Dzong-ka-ba's discussion of 174c-175 see Tsong-ka-pa, Kensur Lekden, and Jeffrey Hopkins, *Compassion in Tibetan Buddhism,* 111-113.

[b] These are:

Clear Words, Commentary on (Nāgārjuna's) "Treatise on the Middle" (dbu ma rtsa ba'i 'grel pa tshig gsal ba, mūlamadhyamakavṛttiprasannapadā; P5260, vol. 98)

Commentary on (Nāgārjuna's) "Sixty Stanzas of Reasoning" (rigs pa drug cu pa'i 'grel pa, yuktiṣaṣṭikāvṛtti; P5265, vol. 98)

Commentary on (Nāgārjuna's) "Seventy Stanzas on Emptiness" (stong pa nyid bdun cu pa'i 'grel pa, śūnyatāsaptativṛtti; P5268, vol. 99)

Commentary on (Āryadeva's) "Four Hundred Stanzas on the Yogic Deeds of Bodhisattvas" (byang chub sems dpa'i rnal 'byor spyod pa gzhi brgya pa'i rgya cher 'grel pa, bodhisattvayogacaryācatuḥśatakaṭīkā; P5266, vol. 98)

[c] *rang rgyal, pratyekabuddha.*

These limitless sentient beings out of suffering
And establish them in Buddhahood.

[Hence] whether sleeping or not sleeping,
After thoroughly assuming [such compassion]
Those who remain steadfast—
Even though they might not be meticulous—

Always accumulate merit as limitless as all sentient beings
Since sentient beings are limitless.
Know then that since [the causes] are limitless,
Limitless Buddhahood is not hard to attain.

[Bodhisattvas] stay for a limitless time [in the world];
For limitless embodied beings they seek
The limitless [qualities of] enlightenment
And perform limitless virtuous actions.

Hence though enlightenment is limitless,
How could they not attain it
With these four limitless collections
Without being delayed for long?

Here Nāgārjuna first suggests that enlightenment is far away after a limitless period of practice and then shows in the last stanza why it is not far away. However, below this, he says that since Bodhisattvas have little or no suffering, their extremely long period of practice is not difficult: (224-26)

Since thus they are not greatly harmed
By physical and mental suffering,
Why should they be discouraged
Though they lead beings in all worlds?

It is hard to bear suffering even for a little,
What need is there to speak of doing so for long!
What could bring harm even over limitless time
To happy beings who have no suffering?

They have no physical suffering;
How could they have mental suffering?
Through their compassion they feel pain
For the world and so stay in it long.[a]

Later he describes how a compassionate motivation ameliorates what pain there is: (373)

It is renowned [in Great Vehicle scriptures] that motivation determines practices
And that the mind is most important.
Hence how could even suffering not be helpful
For one who gives help with an altruistic motivation?

---

[a] Ḏzong-ka-ƃa explains that the statement that Bodhisattvas do not suffer pain refers to those who have at least the first of the ten Bodhisattva grounds; see Tsong-ka-pa, Kensur Lekden, and Jeffrey Hopkins, *Compassion in Tibetan Buddhism,* 187.

Chapter Three concludes with an argument that compassion helps both others and oneself, due to a concordance between the practices as causes and the effects gained in Buddhahood: (298-300)

Through meditatively cultivating the wisdom of reality
Which is the same [for all phenomena] and is moistened with compassion
For the sake of liberating all sentient beings,
You will become a Conqueror endowed with all supreme aspects.

Through multitudes of pure wishes
Your Buddha Land will be purified.
Through offering gems to the Kings of Subduers[a]
You will emit infinite light.

Therefore knowing the concordance
Of actions and their effects,
Always help beings in fact.
Just that will help yourself.

Here an appeal for practice is made from the viewpoint of both other-concern and self-concern and reflects a statement made in Chapter One: (7)

Having analyzed well
All deeds of body, speech, and mind,
Those who realize what benefit self and others
And always perform these are wise.

This appeal also to self-help is echoed later when he compares practicing to taking care of one's own body and then declares that it will indeed do just that: (489)

Those who feel a dearness for the practices
Have in fact a dearness for their body.
If dearness [for the body] helps it,
The practices will do just that.

Nevertheless, earlier he exhorted the king to provide help without looking for reward: (272ab)

Without hope of reward
Provide help to others.

Also, he listed altruism motivated by desire among the fifty-seven defects: (427)

Conceptuality concerned with attachment to others
Is an intention to help or not help others
Due to being affected by desire
Or an intent to harm.

Thus he appeals not to self-desire but to intelligent self-concern, although one might more starkly characterize his maneuvers as calling for altruism within appealing to selfish concerns. In a similar way, the current Dalai Lama recommends "wise selfishness" for those who cannot be altruistic without hope for return—that is to say, selfishness realizing that other-concern yields far better effects for oneself.

---

[a] That is, Buddhas.

In the final stanza of the *Precious Garland of Advice* the appeal solely is to other-concern without hope for reward: (500)

> For the sake of enlightenment aspirants should always apply themselves
> To ethics, supreme respect for teachers, patience, non-jealousy, non-miserliness,
> Endowment with the wealth of altruism without hope for reward, helping the destitute,
> Remaining with supreme people, leaving the non-supreme, and thoroughly maintaining the doctrine.

In this final chapter Nāgārjuna, after recommending a recitation that is to be performed three times daily (466-87), presents the logic behind the limitlessness of the causes of enlightenment. The prayer is comprised of wishes for fulfillment for all sentient beings through favorable situations that range from worldly advantages such as leisure, freedom of action, good livelihood, wealth, the necessities of life, a good complexion, health, strength, and long life to religious values such as the four immeasurables—love, compassion, joy, and even-mindedness devoid of the afflictive emotions—as well the six perfections—giving, ethics, patience, effort, concentration, and wisdom—as well as liberation, completion of the two collections of merit and wisdom, completion of the ten Bodhisattva grounds, and attainment of the marks and beautiful features of a Buddha. Wishes also are made always to relieve others' pain, to be such a person that beings distressed from fear could become entirely fearless through merely hearing one's name, to bring help and happiness always in all ways to all sentient beings, to stop all beings in all worlds who wish to commit ill deeds, to be an object of enjoyment for all, to be as dear to them as their own life, to take on oneself the fructification of all their non-virtues, to give the fructification of all one's virtues to them, and to remain in the world as long as any sentient being anywhere has not been liberated for their sake even though one has attained highest enlightenment. Nāgārjuna declares that the merit of such wishes is limitless and then gives both a scriptural source and reasoning: (486-87)

> If the merit of saying this
> Had form, it would never fit
> Into realms of worlds as numerous
> As the sand grains of the Ganges.
>
> The Supramundane Victor said so,
> And the reasoning is this:
> [The limitlessness of the merit of] wishing to help limitless realms
> Of sentient beings is like [the limitlessness of those beings].

In this way he presents the wishes and dedications of Bodhisattvas and the means for the highest enlightenment to which he earlier alluded (390-93) as lacking in the Lesser Vehicle. He demonstrates the concordance between the practices for enlightenment and enlightenment itself. Still, it is clear that the fruits of practice are not limited to the spiritual. As he says: (398)

> Through faith in the Great Vehicle
> And through practicing what is explained in it
> The highest enlightenment is attained
> And, along the way, even all [wordly] pleasures.

HIGH STATUS

Nāgārjuna identifies the practices of eliminating defects and gaining good qualities to be those performed by persons seeking high status within the realms of gods and humans. He identifies the practices of wisdom as for those seeking definite goodness: (230)

Eliminating defects and acquiring good qualities
Are the practices of those seeking high status.
Thoroughly extinguishing conceptions through consciousness [of reality]
Is the practice of those seeking definite goodness.

Despite the overall structure, described above, in which the framework of the removal of defects and acquisition of good qualities is especially related to Buddhahood, here he seems to limit the elimination of defects and the gaining of good qualities to seeking advancement in cyclic existence—the round of birth, suffering, sickness, and death. This delimitation is reinforced by the two preceding stanzas where he defines defects and good qualities. There he identifies the effects of defects as low rebirths as a hell-being, animal, or hungry-ghost and identifies the results of good qualities as rebirths as a god or a human: (228-29)

Realizing that desire, hatred, and obscuration
Are defects, forsake them completely.
Realizing that non-desire, non-hatred, and non-obscuration
Are good qualities, inculcate them with vigor.

Through desire one goes into a hungry ghost transmigration,
Through hatred one is impelled into a hell,
Through obscuration one mostly goes into an animal transmigration.
Through stopping these one becomes a god or a human.

His descriptions of the meaning of "high status" (*abhyudaya, mngon mtho*) suggest that it refers only to elevated (Sans. *ud*) states, i.e., the happinesses, of humans and gods relative to animals, hungry ghosts, and hell-beings within the five types of lives in cyclic existence: (3-4)

In one who first practices high status
Definite goodness arises later,
For having attained high status,
One comes gradually to definite goodness.

High status is considered to be happiness,[a]
Definite goodness is liberation.
The quintessence of their means
Is briefly faith and wisdom.

In commentary on the first line of the third stanza, the sole Indian commentator on the *Precious Garland*, Ajitamitra,[b] says:[c]

---

[a] *bde ba, sukha.*

[b] *mi 'pham bshes gnyen.* Little is known about Ajitamitra; his composition (*rin po che'i phreng ba'i rgya cher bshad pa, ratnāvaliṭīkā;* P5659, vol. 129; Golden Reprint, vol. 183, *nge*) is placed no "later than the beginning of the ninth century"; see Michael Hahn, *Nāgārjuna's Ratnāvalī*, vol.1, The Basic Texts (Sanskrit, Tibetan, and Chinese) (Bonn: Indica et Tibetica Verlag, 1982), xv.

[c] *mngon par mtho ba'i rgyu yin pa'i phyir mngon par mtho ba ste/ rgyu la 'bras bu btags pa'i phyir// dper na tshe ni mar yin no zhes*

> Because they are the causes of high status, they are [called] high status, since this is a case of designating [the name of] the effect to the causes, as, for example, in saying, "Life is ghee."

Commenting on the fourth stanza, Ajitamitra says:[a]

> Those which are the practices[b] of high status are called "happiness" because they are concordant with attaining all the excellent happinesses of the world.

The fifteenth century Tibetan commentator Gyel-tsap Dar-ma-rin-chen[c] more succinctly says:[d]

> [High status/states] are any happinesses or neutral [feelings] included within the continuums of gods of humans.

Thus, roughly speaking, *abhyudaya* is glossed as (worldly) happiness. Since *abhyudaya* is derived from *abhi* + *ud* and Vaman Shivaram Apte's *Sanskrit-English Dictionary*[26] gives as translations "rise (of heavenly bodies), sunrise; rise, prosperity, good fortune, elevation, success" etc., *abhyudaya*—both from the viewpoint of meaning and of etymology—means *elevated* or *high status* within the realms of cyclic existence.[e]

However, I suggest that this is not Nāgārjuna's only meaning in the *Precious Garland of Advice*, for, as we have seen, he uses the vocabulary of removing defects and achieving good qualities also in the context of full enlightenment. In fact, after the two main expositions of high status and definite goodness in the first two chapters, it is in Chapter Three on the two collections *that are the causes of Buddhahood* that he defines respective practices of high status and definite goodness: (230)

> Eliminating defects and acquiring good qualities
> Are the practices of those seeking high status.
> Thoroughly extinguishing conceptions through consciousness [of reality]
> Is the practice of those seeking definite goodness.

The context of his identification suggests that there are two levels of high status—within cyclic existence and above cyclic existence. Possible confirmation is found in the section on fifty-seven defects that he specifies are abandoned by Bodhisattvas. The topic occurs at the beginning of Chapter Five entitled "Bodhisattva Deeds" which is tied to achieving not just liberation from cyclic existence but the full enlightenment of a Buddha: (402)

> Then, you should forsake
> These which are called assorted faults.

---

pa lta bu'o: Golden Reprint, vol. 183, 373.3.

[a] *mngon par mtho ba'i chos gang yin pa de ni 'jig rten pa'i phun sum tshogs pa'i bde ba mtha' dag 'thob pa dang mthun pa'i phyir bde ba zhes bya'o:* Golden Reprint, vol. 183, 374.3.

[b] *chos, dharma.*

[c] *rgyal tshab dar ma rin chen,* 1364-1432. He is one of the two main students of Ḏzong-ka-ḇa Ḻo-sang-drak-ḇa, founder of what has come to be known as the Ge-luk (*dge lugs*) order of Tibetan Buddhism.

[d] *dbu ma rin chen 'phreng ba'i snying po'i don gsal bar byed pa,* Collected Works, (lha sa: zhol par khang, 15th rab 'byung in the fire rooster year, i.e., 1897), *ka* 6a.4: *lha dang mi'i rgyud kyis bsdus pa'i bde ba dang / btang snyoms ci rigs pa yin la.*

[e] Tibetan and Indian scholars brought the term into Tibetan not as the gloss *bde ba* (happiness) but as *mngon mtho,* literally "manifestly high." I hold that the same should be done in English through using a term such as "high states" or "high status."

With vigor you should definitely realize
Those renowned as the fifty-seven.

He describes the fifty-seven defects in stanzas 403-33, concluding: (434)

[Householder] Bodhisattvas abandon those.
Those diligent in [monastic] vows abandon more.
Freed from these defects
Good qualities are easily observed.

When looked at this way, the practices of high status are seen to be concordant with those of definite goodness, which otherwise might seem to be totally foreign, or even contradictory—a passage into a realm obviating the need for acquisition of good qualities.

Nevertheless, Nāgārjuna seems to suggest such categorical separation when he says: (125)

Therefore, as long as the doctrine removing
The conception of I is not known,
Take heed of the practices
Of giving, ethics, and patience.

Also, Gyel-tsap describes this stanza as "Advice to strive for high status as long as emptiness is not realized." However, it is clear that the power of meritorious actions is the means for achieving the marvelous good qualities of Buddhahood which is the final goal: (208)

Through multiplying a hundred thousand-fold
The merit for the hair-treasure
A Protector's crown-protrusion
Is produced, imperceptible as it actually is.

And: (219)

[Bodhisattvas] stay for a limitless time [in the world];
For limitless embodied beings they seek
The limitless [good qualities of] enlightenment
And perform limitless virtuous actions.

Bodhisattvas' aims are not the pleasures of lives of cyclic existence nor removal from involvement through meditative withdrawal into emptiness but the limitless advantageous qualities of full enlightenment that is concordant with realization of emptiness. Hence I would suggest that performance of the practices of high status such as charity is not limited in scope to worldly aims.

Nāgārjuna uses the vocabulary of good qualities also for the wisdom that Bodhisattvas seek: (435)

Briefly the good qualities
Observed by Bodhisattvas are
Giving, ethics, patience, effort,
Concentration, wisdom, compassion, and so forth.

Moreover, near the conclusion of the set of wishes for others' welfare that he advises practitioners repeat three times daily, he adds: (476-77)

Completing the two collections [of merit and wisdom],
May they have the brilliant marks and beautiful features [even while on the path],

And may they cross without interruption
The ten inconceivable grounds.
May I also be adorned completely
With those and all other good qualities,
Be freed from all defects,
And have superior love for all sentient beings.

The description recalls his initial homage to Buddha: (1)

I bow down to the Omniscient,
Freed from all defects,
Adorned with all good qualities,
The sole friend of all beings.

Hence it is clear that the removal of defects and achievement of good qualities—the practices of high status—extend right to Buddhahood.

THE PRACTICES OF HIGH STATUS

Nāgārjuna first treats the practices for high status in Chapter One (8-24) and Chapter Two (124-74b).[a] In both sections he speaks of practices for both advancement within cyclic existence and attaining the good qualities of Buddhahood. In Chapter One he presents what Gyel-tsap describes as sixteen practices for high status. Thirteen activities are to be stopped:

- the ten non-virtues—three physical, four verbal, and three mental negative activities—that are to be restrained: (8-9)

  Not killing, not stealing,
  Forsaking the mates of others,
  Refraining completely from false,
  Divisive, harsh, and senseless speech,
  Thoroughly forsaking covetousness, harmful intent,
  And the views of Nihilists—
  These are the ten gleaming paths of action;
  Their opposites are dark.

- three additional activities to be restrained: (10ab)

  Not drinking intoxicants, a good livelihood,
  Non-harming,

He then gives three positive activities to be adopted: (10bcd)

respectful giving,
Honoring the honorable, and love—
Practice in brief is that.

He immediately criticizes self-mortification for a double reason—it still involves harming other beings in one's own body and does not help others: (11)

---

[a] It seems that the advice in Chapter Five (402-34b) to abandon the fifty-seven defects also could be included in the topic of high status.

Practice is not done by just
Mortifying the body,
For one has not forsaken injuring others
And is not helping others.

To explain what helping others means, he speaks of the first three among the six perfections renowned in the Great Vehicle—giving, ethics, and patience: (12)

Those not esteeming the great path of excellent doctrine
Bright with giving, ethics, and patience,
Afflict their bodies, taking
An aberrant path like a cow path [deceiving oneself and those following].

The triad of giving, ethics, and patience epitomize the practice of high status, and later he adds that the essence of these three is compassion: (399)

At that time [when you are a ruler] you should internalize
Firmly the practices of giving, ethics, and patience,
Which were especially taught for householders
And which have an essence of compassion.[a]

Still, the mere fact that he lists giving, ethics, and patience in their order in the list of the six perfections that are the central practice for the achievement of Buddhahood in the Great Vehicle does not rule out aiming at advantageous situations within cyclic existence in order to continue practice over a series of lifetimes. Chandrakīrti makes this point in his *Supplement to (Nāgārjuna's) "Treatise on the Middle"*:[b]

Therefore the Conqueror, having discoursed on giving,
Spoke upon its accompaniment by ethics.
When virtues are nurtured on the field of ethics,
The enjoyment of effects is unceasing.

D̄zong-ka-b̄a's *Illumination of the Thought* makes the point clearly:[27]

Defective ethics is a source of many faults, such as being led to a bad transmigration; therefore, immediately after discoursing on giving, the Conqueror who had overcome all ill-deeds spoke on the achievement of accompanying giving with ethics so that the benefits thereof would not be wasted. The reason for this is that ethics is the base of all auspicious qualities and, therefore, is alone the field. If the virtues of giving and so forth are nurtured on the field of ethics, the con-

---

[a] In his *Illumination of the Thought* D̄zong-ka-b̄a quotes this stanza, identifies the three practices, and explains that Nāgārjuna does not mean either that householder Bodhisattvas do not have the other three perfections—effort, concentration, and wisdom—or that monastic Bodhisattvas do not have the first three:

> Among the three practices that are easy for householder Bodhisattvas, giving covers the donation of articles and bestowal of non-fright [taking bugs out of water, etc.] Ethics is that of householders, and patience is mainly a mind determined about the doctrine. Effort, concentration, and wisdom are easier for monastic Bodhisattvas, but this does not mean that householders and monastics do not have the other three perfections.

See Tsong-ka-pa, Kensur Lekden, and Jeffrey Hopkins, *Compassion in Tibetan Buddhism*, 221-22.

[b] II.6.

tinuation of engaging in causes, such as giving, and of using effects, such as a good body and good resources, will increase more and more. The collections of effects grow, and one is able to enjoy them for a long time. Otherwise, this is not possible.

This indicates that givers of gifts should not just consider the marvelous resources that are effects of giving but should think about the physical support with which they will enjoy them. They should consider the continuation of resources in many lives. Thus, you should know that keeping proper ethics—the means of achieving these—is very important.

Novice Bodhisattvas should, as was explained above, make effort at giving gifts, and they should do this in order to attain Buddhahood for the sake of all sentient beings, who are their field of intent. Temporarily, however, they need a ripening of the fruits of giving on the base of happy transmigrations over many lifetimes. This too depends on ethics because without ethics the favorable circumstances for training in the Bodhisattva deeds are not complete.

Chandrakīrti makes a similar case for patience:[a]

If you get angry with those who have done you harm,
Is that harm stopped because of your resentment of them?
Resentment thus is certainly senseless here
And unfavorable for future lives.

In the same way, dependence upon a suitable situation for continuation of practice most likely is the meaning of Nāgārjuna's saying: (3-6)

In one who first practices high status
Definite goodness arises later,
For having attained high status,
One comes gradually to definite goodness.
High status is considered to be happiness,
Definite goodness is liberation,
The quintessence of their means
Is briefly faith and wisdom.
Due to having faith one relies on the practices,
Due to having wisdom one truly knows.
Of these two wisdom is the chief,
Faith is its prerequisite.

One who does not neglect the practices
Through desire, hatred, fear, or bewilderment
Is known as one of faith,
A superior vessel for definite goodness.

High status serves as a foundation for definite goodness in the sense that through gaining a favorable lifetime endowed with the prerequisites for continued practice, wisdom becomes possible.

Nāgārjuna singles out faith as the quintessential means for achieving high status, but his student Āryadeva in his *Four Hundred Stanzas on the Yogic Deeds of Bodhisattvas* shows how faith can depend on

[a] III.4.

wisdom:[a]

Whoever has generated doubt
Toward what is not obvious in Buddha's word
Will believe that only Buddha [is omniscient]
Based on [his profound teaching of] emptiness.

Āryadeva's point is that if Buddha is correct with respect to such a profound topic as emptiness, he must also be correct with respect to less profound but more hidden topics such as the minute details of the cause and effects of actions. Consequently, through confirming Buddha's teaching of emptiness, a person with doubt about Buddha's teachings concerning the means of achieving specific effects such as high status can gain belief.

Tibetan scholars have used this type of reasoning as justification for accepting cosmological explanations, and so forth, that are not contradicted by direct perception, logical inference, and internal contradictions. Over centuries Tibetan traditions have developed a sense of what, within Buddha's teachings on very hidden topics, can be accepted literally. Among these is the teaching of a flat earth, now obviously contradicted by direct perception from satellites, and this has brought into question the whole scope of teachings on very obscure topics, not only cosmological but also ethical, hitherto considered safely verified. Nowadays, the issue is being bridged to some extent by reconsidering the general process of causation of high status through holding that, for instance, the teaching that resources in a future lifetime are generated by generosity in this lifetime[b] is accessible to usual logical inference based on the correspondence of cause and effect but the exact particulars of a certain type of charity leading to a specific effect at a specific time, etc., is not accessible to usual logical inference.

If we combine Nāgārjuna's and Āryadeva's statements, it appears that though the faith that is the prime means of high status makes one a receptacle for definite goodness, the wisdom involved in definite goodness can, for some persons, be a prerequisite for faith in the practices that yield high status.

When Nāgārjuna describes the jungle-like situation of cyclic existence that comes from not engaging in the practices of high status, he does not use reasoned argument based on a concordance between cause and effect but also he does not explicitly appeal to Buddha's special cognition as the source for detailing the dreadful effects of counter-productive actions, though such an appeal may be implicit. Here the list of negative deeds includes the ten non-virtues, intoxicants, lack of generosity, wrong livelihood, arrogance, jealousy, anger, and stupidity: (13-18)

Their bodies embraced by the vicious snakes
Of the afflictive emotions, they enter for a long time
The dreadful jungle of cyclic existence
Among the trees of endless beings.[c]

---

[a] *bstan bcos bzhi brgya pa zhes bya ba'i tshig le'ur byas pa, catuḥśatakaśāstrakārikā;* P5246, vol. 95; stanza 280 which occurs in Chapter 12; parenthetical additions are from Gyel-tsap's commentary, 90b.3-91a.2; see *Yogic Deeds of Bodhisattvas: Gyel-tsap on Āryadeva's Four Hundred,* commentary by Geshe Sonam Rinchen, translated and edited by Ruth Sonam (Ithaca: Snow Lion Publications: 1994), 241-42.

[b] See stanza 438.

[c] It is interesting to note that the jungle is not viewed as an ecological heaven but as an entangling nightmare.

A short life comes through killing.
Much suffering comes through harming.
Poor resources, through stealing.
Enemies, through adultery.

From lying arises slander.
From divisiveness, a parting of friends.
From harshness, hearing the unpleasant.
From senselessness, one's speech is not respected.

Covetousness destroys one's wishes,
Harmful intent yields fright,
Wrong views lead to bad views,
And drink to confusion of the mind.

Through not giving comes poverty,
Through wrong livelihood, deception,
Through arrogance, a bad lineage,
Through jealousy, little beauty.

A bad color comes through anger,
Stupidity, from not questioning the wise.
These are effects for humans,
But prior to all is a bad transmigration.

The last line means that rebirth as an animal, hungry ghost, or hell-being will occur prior to these results as a human.

The practices of high status are presented in direct opposition to such unfavorable results: (19-24)

Opposite to the well-known
Fruits of these non-virtues
Is the arising of effects
Caused by all the virtues.

Desire, hatred, ignorance, and
The actions they generate are non-virtues.
Non-desire, non-hatred, non-ignorance,
And the actions they generate are virtues.

From non-virtues come all sufferings
And likewise all bad transmigrations,
From virtues, all happy transmigrations
And the pleasures of all lives.

Desisting from all non-virtues
And always engaging in virtues
With body, speech, and mind—
These are called the three forms of practice.

Through these practices one is freed from becoming
A hell-being, hungry ghost, or animal.
Reborn as a human or god one gains
Extensive happiness, fortune, and dominion.

Through the concentrations, immeasurables, and formlessnesses
One experiences the bliss of Brahmā and so forth.
Thus in brief are the practices
For high status and their fruits.

Nāgārjuna here describes the fruits of the practice of high status solely within the scope of lifetimes in cyclic existence, ranging from human births to those in Form Realm and Formless Realm that are attained through engaging in special meditations during this lifetime.

In Chapter Two he calls for practice of the first three perfections—giving, ethics, and patience—in order to thwart the process of bad rebirths: (124-25)

If this doctrine is not understood thoroughly,
The conception of an I prevails,
Hence come virtuous and non-virtuous actions
Which give rise to good and bad rebirths.

Therefore, as long as the doctrine removing
The conception of I is not known,
Take heed of the practices
Of giving, ethics, and patience.

Seemingly, he calls for such practice *only* until the wisdom of selflessness is gained, but this cannot be his meaning since later (440-61b) when discussing the Bodhisattva grounds, he still speaks of the perfections of giving, ethics, etc., as well as other practices. Rather, since the practices of high status can serve as temporary antidotes to lower rebirth, they are necessary if the underpinning of the process of rebirth itself—the conception of inherent existence—has not been demolished.

Still, the appeal is often to gaining favorable states within cyclic existence as when he appeals to the King to perform the practices of high status for five personal benefits: (126-27)

A Lord of the Earth who performs actions
With their prior, intermediary,
And final practices
Is not harmed here or in the future.

Through the practices there are fame and happiness here,
There is no fear now or at the point of death,
In the next life happiness flourishes,
Therefore always observe the practices.

He also associates the practice of the four means of drawing people together as well as truth, generosity, peace, and wisdom (128-42; for discussion of these see pp. 74ff.) with good qualities that are useful for the King politically.

Turning to consideration of the process of downward movement in cyclic existence, Nāgārjuna calls ...inual realization of impermanence and death and thus the imminence of the ineluctable effects of bad karma: (143-45)

Always considering the impermanence
Of life, health, and dominion,
You thereby will make intense effort
Solely at the practices.

Seeing that death is certain
And that, having died, you suffer from ill deeds,
You should not commit ill deeds
Though there might be temporary pleasure.

Sometimes no horror is seen
And sometimes it is.
If there is comfort in one,
Why do you have no fear for the other?

Sometimes the horrible effects of a bad deed are not seen until the next life, and sometimes they are seen in this life. If comfort is taken because the effects are not seen, why is fear of those actions not generated when the effects are seen! Correspondingly, engagement in religious practice, impelled by realizing impermanence, yields happiness for both oneself and others: (278-79)

The causes of death are many,
Those of staying alive are few,
These too can become causes of death,
Therefore always perform the practices.

If you always perform thus the practices,
The mental happiness which arises
In the world and in yourself
Is most favorable.

Nāgārjuna identifies specific problems that draw beings into bad transmigrations—intoxicants, gambling, and sexual lust. Intoxicants have four faults ruining one's own life: (146)

Intoxicants lead to worldly scorn,
Your affairs are ruined, wealth is wasted,
The unsuitable is done from delusion,
Therefore always avoid intoxicants.

Gambling has nine faults that involve strongly stirring up harsh afflictive emotions: (147)

Gambling causes avarice,
Unpleasantness, hatred, deception, cheating,
Wildness, lying, senseless talk, and harsh speech,
Therefore always avoid gambling.

Indicating an appreciation for the strength of sexual attachment, Nāgārjuna produces a multi-staged argument over twenty-three stanzas (148-70) to diminish lust. Since he is speaking to a heterosexual man, the argument centers around the unsuitability of lust for a woman's body, but as he says later, this same message is to be applied to the male body (165).

The exposition is constructed in a confrontational way, mainly to overcome perception of what is actually unclean as clean—to remove adherence to a delusionary appearance of purity: (148)

Lust for a woman mostly comes
From thinking that her body is clean,
But there is nothing clean
In a woman's body in fact.

A realistic list of substances found in the body are given (149-51):

- in the mouth—saliva and dental scum
- in the nose— snot, slime, and mucus
- in the eyes—tears and other excretions
- in the abdomen and chest—feces, urine, lungs, and liver.

Due to refusing to see realistically what is there, lust is generated, just as a fool might drool over a decorated pot filled with feces.

He taunts those who claim to want wisdom in order to achieve freedom from desire but who desire this body which, if seen clearly, would itself lead to less attachment (152). Even worse, given the constituents of the body, those who lust after it are like pigs rushing to filth (153). In addition to its constitution, the body has holes from which what is inside drips out, moistening the skin (154-55, 157). Also, the substances from which the body grows are nothing pure, but are blood (considered in ancient times to be the woman's contribution) and semen (156). He mockingly asks what possible attribute could give rise to such lust (158). If it is color and shape, then is it alright to lust after nicely colored and shaped feces (159)?

Taking another tack, he compares the body to a putrid corpse covered on the outside by skin, which since it is over a mass of impurity should not itself be considered clean, just as a pot, though beautiful on the outside, is reviled if filled with filth (160-62). After all, the body befouls perfumes, garlands, good, and drink; thus if one's own and others' impurities are to be reviled, why not the body in which they are contained and from which they ooze (163-64)?

In a stunning provocation, he ridicules whose who want religious instruction but who cannot realize that their own bodies are unclean despite the fact that they themselves have to keep washing this which drips from nine orifices—eyes, ears, nostrils, mouth, genitalia, and anus (166). Earlier he chided his listeners in a similar way: (116-17)

When the body, which is unclean,
Coarse, and an object of the senses,
Does not stay in the mind [as having a nature of uncleanliness and pain]
Although it is continually in view,

Then how could this doctrine
Which is most subtle, profound,
Baseless, and not manifest,
Easily appear to the mind?

Those who write poetry glorifying the body are worthy of derision: (167)

Whoever composes poetry
With metaphors elevating this body—

O how shameless! O how stupid!
How embarrassing before [wise] beings!

In addition, lust leads to fights just as dogs quarrel over some dirty thing (168).

Concluding, Nāgārjuna calls for realization that there is greater pleasure in liberation than in the minor happy events of cyclic existence (169). He says that, at minimum, the type of analysis that has been presented will cause desire to diminish and physical lust to disappear for the time being (170). Long-term goals are to be emphasized over short-term pleasures; this principle is repeated in a milder format later in the poem: (375)

If through relinquishing small pleasures
There is extensive happiness later,
Seeing the greater happiness
The resolute should relinquish small pleasures.

Hunting. In Chapter Two, the section on high status ends with the faults of hunting, which indeed stands in direct contradiction to the over-all theme of compassion. Hunters are described as persons who, having stained themselves with malevolence, create fright in others, as if spewing out venom (172). By their actions they are themselves drawn into fear, short life, and rebirth in a hell (171). He calls his readers to become the opposite—persons who generate pleasure in others much as a gathering rain-cloud delights farmers (173).

This altruistic perspective is described and fortified in the final chapter within the thrice-daily wishes that he commends: (479-84)

May those beings in all worlds
Who are distressed through fear
Become entirely fearless
Even through merely hearing my name.

Through seeing or thinking of me or only hearing my name
May beings attain great joy,
Naturalness free from error,
Definiteness toward complete enlightenment,

And the five clairvoyances
Throughout their continuum of lives.
May I always in all ways bring
Help and happiness to all sentient beings.

May I always without harm
Simultaneously stop
All beings in all worlds
Who wish to commit ill deeds.

May I always be an object of enjoyment
For all sentient beings according to their wish
And without interference, as are the earth,
Water, fire, wind, herbs, and wild forests.

May I be as dear to sentient beings as their own life,
And may they be even more dear to me.
May their ill deeds fructify for me,
And all my virtues fructify for them.

RESULTS OF MERITORIOUS PRACTICE

Nāgārjuna describes in detail the positive effects of religious practice (281-99), which Gyel-tsap organizes into five common good qualities and twenty-five particular good qualities:

common good qualities

happiness
fame
respect from officials
sleeping and awakening happily
happy dreams.

particular good qualities and their causes

1 becoming a monarch of gods due to serving one's parents, respecting elders in one's greater family, using resources well, being patient, generous, and having kindly speech, being without divisiveness, and being truthful
2 the eight good qualities of love—friendliness from gods and humans, protection by spirits, mental and physical pleasures, defense against weapons and poison, effortless achievement, and rebirth in comfort—due to being loving
3 firm altruistic intention to attain enlightenment due to causing others to generate the same aspiration
4 leisure due to faith
5 goods rebirths due to ethics
6 detachment due to accustoming to emptiness
7 mindfulness due to not wavering
8 intelligence due to thinking
9 realization of meaning due to respect
10 wisdom due to protecting the doctrine
11 being in the company of Buddhas and attaining quick success due to making the doctrine unobstructedly available
12 achievement of the meaning of doctrines due to non-attachment
13 increase of resources due to non-miserliness
14 becoming the center among respected persons due to not being proud
15 retention of the doctrine through enduring difficulties in its acquisition
16 being free from demons and endowed with mightiness due to giving others sugar/molasses, ghee, honey, sesame oil, and salt as well as non-fright to the frightened
17 visual clairvoyance due to offering lamps at monuments and in dark places
18 auditory clairvoyance due to offering musical instruments for worship at monuments
19 clairvoyance knowing others' minds due to refraining from speaking of their mistakes or their defective limbs but protecting their feelings

20 clairvoyance of magical display—the ability to reduce many emanations to one and vice versa, and so forth—due to giving shoes and conveyances, serving the feeble, and providing teachers with transport
21 clairvoyance remembering past lives due to activities supporting the doctrine—such as building temples and enduring difficulties for the sake of the doctrine—memorizing doctrines, retaining the meaning, and providing the doctrine for others
22 clairvoyance knowing the extinction of all contamination due to correct knowledge that all phenomena lack inherent existence
23 Buddhahood due to cultivating the wisdom of the emptiness of all phenomena equally which is moistened with compassion for all beings
24 a pure Buddha Land due to making multitudes of pure wishes for the welfare of other beings
25 emitting infinite light due to offering gems to Buddhas.

He concludes with a reminder that, due to the concordance of cause and effect, helping others is the way to help oneself: (300)

Therefore knowing the concordance
Of actions and their effects,
Always help beings in fact.
Just that will help yourself.

Two types of high status. The line between the practices of high status directed at improvement within cyclic existence and those exhibiting the profound altruism of the Great Vehicle that leads to Buddhahood is hard to draw—and probably should not be drawn since it would not reflect how fluidly Nāgārjuna moves between the two topics. Similarly, it is difficult to draw a completely distinct line between the examination of sexual lust that is included within the section on high status and the examination of pleasure in Chapter Four (346-63, to be discussed below, pp. 65ff.) and included within the topic of liberation and thus of definite goodness.

3 ADVICE FOR LIBERATION

DEFINITE GOODNESS

Let us first consider the Sanskrit and Tibetan terms that I translate as "definite goodness"—*naiḥśreyasa* and *nges par legs pa.* For *naiḥśreyasa,*[a] Apte[b] gives "final beatitude, absolution; happiness; faith, belief; apprehension, conception." I find his etymology of the term as *niścitaṃ śreyasaḥ* more to the point; for *niścita* he gives "ascertained, determined, decided, settled, concluded," and, as an indeclinable, "decidedly, positively, certainly." For *śreyas,* Apte[28] gives "virtue, righteous deeds, moral or religious merit; bliss, good fortune, blessing, good, welfare, felicity, a good or auspicious result; any good or auspicious occasion; final beatitude, absolution." Thus for *naiḥśreyasa* I prefer the literal translation "definite goodness" in order to convey the sense that the state of liberation from cyclic existence (as well as the great liberation of Buddhahood) are stable and thus unlike high status within cyclic existence which can deteriorate. Also, there is evidence that Ajitamitra reads the compound as "definitely good," or "decidedly good," for in commentary on verse 25a he says:[c]

> From these [practices] one achieves the definitely good and virtuous liberation; therefore, these are [the practices of] definite goodness; just it is definitely good.

His emphasis on *just* liberation as definitely good is echoed in Gyel-tsap's commentary on stanza 4:[d]

> Definite goodness is asserted as liberation, [a state of] separation that is an abandonment of sufferings and their origins through the wisdom realizing selflessness. Since it is a [state of] separation [from obstructions] that has the attribute of irreversibility, it is definitely good.

I do not agree with a translation such as "final beatitude" since "beatitude" means bliss or happiness and thus has more the meaning of high status and it strays too far from the literal meaning, goodness. Also, "final" which is stronger and less literal than "definite" does not leave room for identifying the referents of *naiḥśreyasa* as twofold, the liberation from cyclic existence not being final and the latter the great liberation[e] of Buddhahood being final. "Final beatitude" could give the mistaken impression that liberation from cyclic existence is the *final* accomplishment—an implication inappropriate in the con-

---

[a] Also: *niḥśreyasa;* see *Quadralingual Mahāvyutpatti,* reproduced by Lokesh Chandra (New Delhi: International Academy of Indian Culture, 1981), 1729, and Lokesh Chandra, *Tibetan-Sanskrit Dictionary* (New Delhi: International Academy of Indian Culture, 1959), 610.

[b] *Sanskrit-English Dictionary,* 892.

[c] *'di las nges par legs shing dge ba thar pa 'grub pas na nges par legs pas te/ de nyid nges par legs pa yin no:* Golden Reprint, vol. 183, 392.3.

[d] *nges par legs pa ni bdag med rtogs pa'i shes rab kyis sdug kun spangs pa'i bral ba thar par 'dod do// slar mi ldog pa'i chos can gyi bral ba yin pas/ negs par legs pa zhes bya'o:* 6a.4.

[e] *thar pa chen po.*

text of a Great Vehicle system in which Buddhahood is the only final achievement.

Nāgārjuna presents the process of definite goodness in ninety-nine continuous stanzas (25-123) and again discusses the topic of the path of liberation in Chapter Four (346-65).[a] In the latter, he returns to the topic of pleasure, analyzing it from many viewpoints in order to establish that pleasure, and by extension all phenomena, are empty of inherent existence. In the course of presenting the topic of definite goodness, he interweaves many issues—the frightening nature of selflessness, the process of bondage, the nature of liberation, reasonings establishing emptiness, and the faults of misunderstanding the view of emptiness. Let us consider these.

FRIGHTENING NATURE OF SELFLESSNESS

Nāgārjuna describes the doctrines of definite goodness as deep, subtle, and frightening to childish beings. Immature persons, out of ignorantly clinging to I and mine, fear the very selflessness that for the wise extinguishes fear; due to being frightened, the childish fail to examine it (25-26, 39). He chides proponents of Lesser Vehicle tenets for being like the childish in that they:

- hold that in the nirvana without remainder—that is to say, the nirvana after the death of a liberated being—the person and the mental and physical aggregates do not exist
- yet are frightened by the non-existence of these now (40-41).

(The meaning of "non-existence" is discussed below, 69ff.) The scolding clearly indicates that he sees his system as different from the *systems* of the proponents of the Lesser Vehicle even though in his *Fundamental Treatise on the Middle, Called "Wisdom"* he uses *scriptures* of the Lesser Vehicle to establish emptiness.

The wise do not regard the world as really existent or really non-existent (38) and thus the doctrine of definite goodness is profound, unapprehendable, and baseless whereas the ignorant delight in a base, are frightened by the baseless, and ruin themselves by being caught in existence and non-existence, thereupon ruining others (75-77). The doctrine of definite goodness is beyond virtue and non-virtue yet has the function of liberation—a doctrine unshared with non-Buddhists and other Buddhists as well (79).

PROCESS OF BONDAGE

All ills arise from the conception of I and mine, which do not exist as ultimates but are so conceived (27-28).[b] The misconception of I as an ultimate depends upon conceiving the mental and physical aggregates as ultimates, and thus without the latter misconception the former does not exist (31-33). Nāgārjuna says that when Ānanda (a Lesser Vehicle practitioner but not a proponent of a Lesser Vehicle system) found insight into the meaning of this, he attained the eye of doctrine, that is to say, reached the path of seeing and "repeatedly spoke of it to monastics" (34).[c] Since Nāgārjuna thereby says

---

[a] He does not use the term "definite goodness" during the latter discussion, and Gyel-tsap does not identify that section with this term, but Nāgārjuna identifies definite goodness as liberation (4b) and uses the term "liberation" (*grol, mukti*) in stanza 363.

[b] When Nāgārjuna says that I and mine are "wrong as ultimates" (28), he suggests that the negation of I and mine that he will present does not include non-ultimate, or conventional, I and mine. This indeed is how Ge-luk scholars interpret the statement.

[c] This is one of two etymologies of "Hearer" (*nyan thos, śrāvaka*) that Chandrakīrti offers in his *Commentary on the Supplement.*

that a Lesser Vehicle practitioner, a Hearer, realized emptiness and he does not describe another emptiness deeper than this one, a distinction must be made between Lesser Vehicle systems of tenets[a] and Lesser Vehicle practitioners, such as Hearers and Solitary Realizers, who could follow the tenets of any Buddhist school including those of the Great Vehicle.[b] Those Hearers who understood the type of emptiness that he is portraying still would not have the strong altruism that Bodhisattvas have, as per his discussion about their lacking "the aspirational wishes, deeds, and dedications of Bodhisattvas" (390a), etc.

The conception that the mental and physical aggregates exist as ultimates serves as the foundation of the misconception that the I exists as an ultimate. The latter leads to contaminated virtuous and non-virtuous actions, which themselves induce birth (35, 124). Still, the conception of I can be said to produce the mental and physical aggregates (29) in the sense that it leads to contaminated actions that produce rebirth; this does not contradict the main point that the misconception of the aggregates is the foundation of the misconception of I. In sum, the afflictive emotions (ignorance, desire, and hatred—the chief being ignorance), contaminated action, and rebirth mutually feed on each other beginninglessly (36).

NATURE OF LIBERATION

Since the process of suffering stems from misconceiving the mental and physical aggregates to exist the way they appear, that is to say, as ultimates, then by understanding that the aggregates do not exist this way, the misconception of I is overcome, contaminated actions are not performed, and thereby new mental and physical aggregates caught in cyclic existence are not produced (30). Just as, with respect to sexual desire, Nāgārjuna emphasized the discrepancy between an appearance of purity and fact of impurity, so with respect to the mental and physical aggregates he draws a comparison between perceiving the water of a mirage and then going close and not seeing it at all: (52-53)

> A form seen from a distance
> Is seen clearly by those nearby.
> If a mirage were water,
> Why is water not seen by those nearby?
>
> The way this world is seen
> As real by those afar
> Is not so seen by those nearby
> For whom it is signless like a mirage.

In his *Illumination of the Thought* Ḏzong-ka-ḇa (Tsong-ka-pa, Kensur Lekden, and Jeffrey Hopkins, *Compassion in Tibetan Buddhism,* 102) gives the first etymology as:

> Hearers are so called because they listen to correct instructions from others and after attaining the fruit of their meditation—the enlightenment of a Hearer—they cause others to hear about that fact. They say, "I have done what was to be done; I will not know another birth," and so forth. Many such instances appear in the scriptures.

For more discussion of the two etymologies, see Jeffrey Hopkins, *Meditation on Emptiness,* n. 495, 840-45.

[a] These are widely known as the Great Exposition School and the Sūtra School; however, these terms never appear in Nāgārjuna's extant works.

[b] These are usually identified as the Mind Only School and the Middle Way School; however, the Mind Only School was yet to be formed during Nāgārjuna's six-hundred year lifetime.

In a similar way, the aggregates appear to be inherently existent but, when analyzed, are seen not to be so (54-55). Rather, for that consciousness they are "signless" in the sense that to a consciousness that has analyzed whether they exist the way they appear, they no longer appear at all: (94-97)

Earth, water, fire, and wind
Do not have a chance
In the face of that undemonstrable consciousness
Complete lord over the limitless.

Here[a] long and short, subtle and coarse,
Virtue and non-virtue,
And here names and forms
All are ceased.

All those that earlier appeared to consciousness
Because of not knowing that [reality]
Will later cease for consciousness in that way
Because of knowing that [reality].

All these phenomena of beings
Are seen as fuel for the fire of consciousness.
They are pacified through being burned
By the light of true discrimination.

Upon having discovered that the water of a mirage is not water, one would be just silly to think that previously existent water now does not exist (55). The absence of the appearance of phenomena to such a mind does not mean that what formerly was actually existent now has been destroyed: (98)

The reality is later ascertained
Of what was formerly imputed by ignorance.
When a thing is not found,
How can there be a non-thing?

This is why Buddha remained silent when asked whether the world has an end: (73-74)

Hence, in fact there is no disappearance
Of the world through nirvana.
Asked whether the world has an end
The Conqueror remained silent.

Because he did not teach this profound doctrine
To worldly beings who were not receptacles,
The All-Knowing is therefore known
By the wise to be omniscient.

In this sense, it is only ignorant to conceive that the mirage-like world either exists or does not exist: (56)

---

[a] "Here" means "in the face of a Superior's meditative equipoise.

One who conceives of the mirage-like world
That it does or does not exist
Is consequently ignorant.
When there is ignorance, one is not liberated.

Liberation is found when one ceases to conceive of things and non-things, existence and non-existence: (42-45)

If nirvana is not a non-thing,
Just how could it have thingness?
The extinction of the misconception
Of things and non-things is called nirvana.

In brief the view of nihilism
Is that effects of actions do not exist.
Without merit and leading to a bad state,
It is regarded as a "wrong view."

In brief the view of existence
Is that effects of actions exist.
Meritorious and conducive to happy transmigrations
It is regarded as a "right view."

Because existence and non-existence are extinguished by wisdom,
There is a passage beyond meritorious and ill deeds.
This, say the excellent, is liberation from
Bad transmigrations and happy transmigrations.

And: (57)

A follower of non-existence goes to bad transmigrations,
And a follower of existence goes to happy transmigrations.
Through correct and true knowledge
One does not rely on dualism and becomes liberated.

However, non-reliance on dualism with regard to the ultimate does not leave mere non-assertion, for Nāgārjuna accepts the conventions of the world, which he specifies as meaning cause and effect: (50)

Having thus seen that effects arise
From causes, one asserts what appears
In the conventions of the world
And does not accept nihilism.

And: (46ab)

Seeing production as caused
One passes beyond non-existence.

His long exposition of the causes for achieving the effects of high status exemplifies the assertion of cause and effect as does his detailing the causes for attaining the thirty-two marks of a Buddha (176-96) and the progression of the ten grounds of Bodhisattvas (440-61b). However, he holds that this does not force him into the view of existence since he asserts a state of cessation beyond conventions: (51)

One who asserts, just as it is, cessation
That does not arise from conventions
Does not pass into [a view of] existence.
Thereby one not relying on duality is liberated.

And: (46cd)

Seeing cessation as caused
One also does not assert existence.

(For more discussion of what "existence" and "non-existence" may mean, see 69ff.)

REASONINGS ESTABLISHING EMPTINESS

Two stanzas at the end of the long analysis of pleasure clearly indicate the relationship between reasoning and release from suffering: (363, 365)

Thus attachment to meeting with pleasure
And attachment to separating from pain
Are to be abandoned because they do not inherently exist.
Thereby those who see thus are liberated.
Knowing thus correctly, just as it is,
That transmigrating beings do not exist in fact,
One passes [from suffering] not subject [to rebirth and hence][29] without appropriating [rebirth],
Like a fire without its cause.

Reasoning leads to seeing that phenomena do not inherently exist whereupon liberation is gained. Notice that in stanza 363 Nāgārjuna speaks of realizing the absence of *inherent* existence[a] of pleasure and pain; Ge-luk scholars hold that this qualification of the existence that is being refuted as being inherent existence applies to all instances when he speaks of the extreme of existence.

REASONING REFUTING PRODUCTION

Nāgārjuna presents many and various reasonings—most with a mere mention and a few with more explanation. The first is the reasoning refuting production which is also the reasoning given in the very first stanza of Chapter One in his *Treatise on the Middle:*

There is never production
Anywhere, of any thing
From itself, from others,
From both, or causelessly.

Given the extensive treatment that he gives to other reasonings in the twenty-seven chapters of the *Treatise on the Middle*, it is amazing that even in the *Treatise* he says no more than this one stanza to establish these four negative propositions; rather, he immediately passes on to an examination of conditions. Similarly, in the *Precious Garland* this reasoning is mentioned in the context of the three factors that appear to be the wheel of cyclic existence—the conception of I, action, and rebirth—but is not elaborated: (37)

---

[a] *ngo bo nyid med phyir, naiḥsvabhāvyāt.*

Because this wheel is not obtained from self, other,
Or from both, in the past, the present, or the future,
The conception of I is overcome
And thereby action and rebirth.

However, in their commentaries on the *Treatise on the Middle*, Buddhapālita and Chandrakīrti elaborate on the four reasons:

- If things were produced from themselves (or from something the same entity as themselves) their production would be senseless, since they would already exist, and if it were claimed that such production is sensible, then it would be endless, for if there were a purpose to the re-duplication of something once, the same would hold true forever.
- If things were produced from what is other, then darkness could be produced from a flame, etc.
- If things were produced from both self and other, then all the fallacies of production from self and production from other would be entailed.
- If things were produced causelessly, it would be senseless to work at their causes.[a]

Production from self is propounded by the Sāṃkhyas, production from other is propounded by other Buddhist schools, production from both is propounded by the Jainas, and causeless production is propounded by the Nihilists. However, the intention of the reasoning is not just to dispose of philosophical arguments on production. The aim is to be shaken to the point where the conclusion is drawn that the phenomena of cyclic existence and nirvana are not inherently produced and hence do not inherently exist, whereupon after extensive meditation liberation from cyclic existence can be gained.

ANOTHER REASONING REFUTING PRODUCTION

Next Nāgārjuna considers whether causes are produced before their effects or simultaneously with their effects. He says no more than that such production is not established either imputedly, that is to say, conventionally, or ultimately: (47)

Previously produced and simultaneously produced [causes]
Are non-causes; [thus] there are no causes in fact,
Because [such] production is not confirmed at all
As [existing] conventionally or in reality.

In commentary, Ajitamitra[30] adds that since a cause is the basis producing the effect, if it exists before its effect, it cannot be its basis. Also, if a cause exists at the same time as its effect, there is no way of delimiting that certain things are needed to produce other things. He glosses "in fact" in the second line with "ultimately."[31]

In the *Treatise on the Middle* Nāgārjuna says:[32]

If the entity of the effect exists,
What will a cause produce?
If the entity of the effect does not exist,
What will a cause produce?

---

[a] For more discussion, see my *Emptiness Yoga*, 156-203, 383-390; and *Meditation on Emptiness*, 57-60, 131-150, 639-650.

If it is not producing,
A cause is not possible.
If causes are not existent,
Of what would there be an effect?

Similarly, in his *Seventy Stanzas on Emptiness* he says:[33]

Because the existent exists, it is not produced.
Because the non-existent does not exist, it is not [produced].
Because the qualities are incompatible,
The existent and non-existent is not [produced].
Because there is no production,
There is no abiding and no ceasing.

In his own commentary on this he says:[34]

> Because a thing[a] exists, it could not be produced from causes. For the existent is explained as "the presently existent." Because the non-existent does not exist, it could not be produced from causes. Because the existent and non-existent are not concordant, such is not produced, for they are mutually exclusive. The existent and the non-existent possess mutually exclusive qualities; hence, due to their incompatibility how could that which is both existent and non-existent be produced? Because there is no production, there also is no abiding and no ceasing.

Chandrakīrti applies this reasoning solely to production from other; his *Supplement to (Nāgārjuna's) "Treatise on the Middle"* says:[35]

> If producers are causes producing products that are other [than themselves], it is to be considered whether they produce an existent, non-existent, that which is both, or that which lacks both. If it exists, of what use are producers? What could these producers do for the non-existent? What could they do for that which is both? What could they do for that which lacks both?[b]

Therefore, it is concluded that production from previously existent causes and simultaneously existent causes does not occur in the conventions of the world nor does it exist in the face of an ultimate reasoning consciousness.

REASONING OF DEPENDENT-ARISING

However, this does not mean that conditionality[c] is refuted, for in the *Precious Garland* Nāgārjuna immediately affirms dependent-arising and uses it as a reasoning showing that things do not exist by way of their own nature: (48-49)

When this is, that arises,
Like short when there is long.
Due to the production of this, that is produced,
Like light from the production of a flame.

---

[a] *dngos po, bhāva.*

[b] For more discussion, see my *Meditation on Emptiness*, 151-154, and *Emptiness Yoga*, 390.

[c] *rkyen nyid 'di pa tsam, idaṃ pratyayatāmātra.* See Ajitamitra, Golden Reprint, vol. 183, 403.6.

When there is long, there is short.
They do not exist through their own nature,
Just as due to the non-production
Of a flame, light also does not arise.

As can be seen from these stanzas, although Nāgārjuna refutes the extreme of existence, he is not averse to using the word "is" or "exists"[a] in the context of such conditionality. The second line of stanza 49 states a certain type of existence as what is being refuted, "They do not exist *through their own nature.*"[b] Thus, as Ajitamitra[c] says, conditionality is conventional. (For more discussion of what it means to exist conventionally, see p. 72.)

REASONING REFUTING MOTION AND REST

Nāgārjuna briefly mentions the refutation of going, coming, and staying (or resting): (63)

How could the world exist in fact,[d]
With a nature passed beyond the three times,[e]
Not going when disintegrating, not coming,
And not staying even for an instant?

The reasoning refuting motion is found in multiple forms in the twenty-five stanzas of Chapter Two in the *Treatise on the Middle.* In that text, Nāgārjuna first considers in six stanzas where present going takes place—the part of the path already gone over, that yet to be gone over, and that presently being gone over. Since the last of these is the most likely possibility, it is refuted through indicating that two goings would be required—that which makes the area the being-gone-over and that which is the going on it.

Then, in five stanzas he analyzes whether a non-goer goes or a goer goes, the former being ridiculous and the latter requiring two goings. Next, in two stanzas he analyzes the beginning of going—where it is begun and who begins it; let us cite this analysis as an example of the reasoning. In his commentary on the *Treatise on the Middle,* Chandrakīrti frames Nāgārjuna's stanzas as responses to objections:[36]

Qualm: Going exists because its beginning exists. Devadatta begins to go through abandoning standing still, and a cloak of non-existent turtle hairs and so forth are not begun.

Answer: Going would exist if its beginning existed [but it does not.] For, Nāgārjuna says:

Going is not begun on the gone-over,
Going is not begun on the not-yet-gone-over,
Going is not begun on the being-gone-over,
Where is going begun?

If a beginning of going existed, going would be begun on the path already gone over, or on the not-yet-gone-over, or on the being-gone-over. With respect to these [alternatives], going is not

---

[a] *'di yod pas na 'di 'byung, asmin satīdaṃ bhavati:* Hahn, 20.

[b] *rang gi ngo bo las ma yin/ na bhavaty asvabhāvataḥ:* Hahn, 20.

[c] Golden Reprint, vol. 183, 404.5: *tha snyad pa.*

[d] I.e., ultimately.

[e] Past, present, and future.

begun on the gone-over because its action of going has ceased. If going were begun there, it would not be "the gone-over" because the past and the present are mutually exclusive.

Going is also not begun on the not-yet-gone-over because the future and the present are mutually exclusive. Going is also not begun on the being-gone-over because the being-gone-over does not exist and because [if going did exist on the being-gone-over] two actions would be entailed and two agents would be entailed. Thus, not seeing a beginning of going in any of these ways, Nāgārjuna said, "Where is going begun?"

Also, showing how going does not occur, Nāgārjuna says:

Before going is begun there is no
Being-gone-over and no gone-over
Where going would be begun. How could
Going be on the not-yet-gone-over?

When Devadatta is standing still, he does not begin going; for, prior to his beginning going, there is no form of the path being gone over or already gone over where going would be begun. Thus, because the gone-over and the being-gone-over do not then exist, going is not begun on either of them.

Qualm: Even if the gone-over and the being-gone-over do not exist prior to a beginning of going, the not-yet-gone-over nevertheless exists, and the beginning of going occurs there.

Answer: "How could going be on the not-yet-gone-over?" The not-yet-gone-over is that [part of the path] on which an action of going has not been produced or has not been begun. The position that the beginning of going occurs on the not-yet-gone-over is senseless. Therefore, Nāgārjuna says, "How could going be on the not-yet-gone-over?"

In the remaining twelve stanzas, Nāgārjuna also considers the opposite of going—staying, or resting—as well as stopping going, whether the goer and going are one or different, etc., finally drawing the conclusion:[37]

Therefore going, goer, and
Place of going do not exist.

Chandrakīrti qualifies the refutation by saying, "Thus, goer, place of going, and going, are not found *when analyzed this way.*" The qualification leaves room for conventionally existent goer, going, and place of going. Ajitamitra[38] explicitly says that Nāgārjuna's thought is that these exist conventionally.

Nāgārjuna draws the conclusion that ultimately cyclic existence and nirvana do not differ: (64)

Because the coming, going, and staying
Of the world and nirvana do not exist
As [their own] reality, what difference
Is there in fact[a] between the two?

REASONING REFUTING THE THREE CHARACTERISTICS OF PRODUCTS

Instead of giving a separate analysis of the three characteristics of products—production, staying, and disintegration (or ceasing)—as he does in Chapter Seven of the *Treatise*, Nāgārjuna extrapolates from

---

[a] I.e., ultimately.

the refutation of motion and rest that since there is no staying, there also could not be any production or cessation of an object: (65)

If, due to the non-existence of staying,
Production and cessation do not exist as [their own] reality,
How could production, staying,
And ceasing exist in fact?

REASONING REFUTING STASIS AND CHANGE

Nāgārjuna refutes the Vaisheṣhikas' notion that minute particles themselves are permanent and their states change, but the refutation also applies to the general question of change. If the states of particles change, then they are not permanent; however, if the states do not change, a thing could not change from one state to another, such as from a child to a youth. Partial disintegration of a phenomenon is not observed, whereas complete disintegration would involve dropping the assertion of permanence: (66-67)

If always changing,
How are things non-momentary?
If not changing,
How can they be altered in fact?

Do they become momentary
Through partial or complete disintegration?
Because an inequality is not apprehended,
This momentariness cannot be admitted either way.

Vaiṣhṇavas might respond that they avoid all these problems by asserting a permanent, beginningless and endless, "old" person. Nāgārjuna takes them literally, questioning whether this old person is momentary, in which case each moment becomes entirely non-existent as it passes and thus the person could not become old. On the other hand, if the person is constant, then it also could never become old: (68)

If momentary, then it becomes entirely non-existent;
Hence how could it be old?
Also if non-momentary, it is constant;
Hence how could it be old?

The same reasoning would seem to apply to Buddhist notions of the complete momentariness of compounded things. How could anything age? As the Dalai Lama said when lecturing on this text in 1972, everything is always new.

REASONING REFUTING MOMENTS

A moment, however small, must end, so it must have a beginning and a middle. When subjected to the analysis of whether a moment is its beginning, its middle, or end, it is not found. Likewise, the beginning of a moment also has a beginning, middle, and end, and thus it cannot be found under such analysis: (69-70)

Just as a moment has an end, so a beginning
And a middle must be considered.

Thus due to this triple nature of a moment,
There is no momentary abiding of the world.
Also the beginning, middle, and end
Are to be analyzed like a moment.
Therefore beginning, middle, and end
Are also not [produced] from self or other.

REASONING REFUTING WHAT HAVE PARTS

Since everything has parts, Nāgārjuna extends the above reasoning to all phenomena: (71ab)

Due to having many parts there is no unity,
There is not anything without parts.

REASONING OF THE LACK OF BEING ONE OR MANY

Moreover, without one, the plural cannot exist, and there is nothing that is not either singular or plural: (71c)

Further, without one, there is not many.[a]

REASONING REFUTING EMPTINESS, DISINTEGRATION, AND ANTIDOTE

Given these refutations, one might think that emptiness itself is findable under analysis; however, if the substratum of an emptiness does not exist, how could the emptiness that depends on that substratum exist?[39] (71d)

Also, without existence there is no non-existence.

The same applies to disintegration or an antidote in that without an analytically findable existent, its analytically findable disintegration or overcoming by a counter-agent is also not analytically findable: (72)

If it is thought that through disintegration or an antidote
An existent becomes non-existent,
Then how without an existent
Could there be disintegration or an antidote?

REASONING REFUTING PERSONS AND OTHER PHENOMENA

The refutation of persons is twofold—first through considering the six constituents and then through considering the five aggregates, these being two ways of considering the phenomena in dependence upon which a person is designated. Immediately after the first reasoning, the six constituents themselves are refuted, and immediately after the second the five aggregates are refuted. As Ajitamitra[40] says, this is done in order to oppose notions that although the person or the self are refuted, the constituents or aggregates exist.

The six constituents related with a person are earth (the hard factors of the body that provide obstructiveness), water (fluids that afford cohesiveness), fire (heat that matures), wind (motility), space (open places), and consciousness. A person is not any of these individually, nor a composite of them,

---

[a] For an extensive discussion of this reasoning, see Donald S. Lopez, *A Study of Svātantrika* (Ithaca: Snow Lion Publications, 1987), 356-79.

nor something other than them: (80-81)

> A person is not earth, not water,
> Not fire, not wind, not space,
> Not consciousness, and not all of them.
> What person is there other than these?
>
> Just as a person is not real
> Due to being a composite of six constituents,
> So each of the constituents also
> Is not real due to being a composite.

In the second reasoning, Nāgārjuna refutes the self through a fivefold analysis of its relation with the aggregates—forms, feelings, discriminations, compositional factors, and consciousnesses: (82)

> The aggregates are not the self, they are not in it,
> It is not in them, without them it is not,
> It is not mixed with the aggregates like fire and fuel.
> Therefore how could the self exist?

This reasoning mirrors that presented in the first stanza of Chapter Twenty-two in the *Treatise on the Middle* where the One Gone Thus, i.e., the Buddha, is used as an example of a self, a person:

> The One Gone Thus is not the aggregates; the One Gone Thus is not other than the aggregates;
> The aggregates are not in the One Gone Thus; the One Gone Thus is not in the aggregates;
> The One Gone Thus does not possess the aggregates.
> What One Gone Thus is there?

Let us consider the reasoning in more detail.

The first position: that the self is the aggregates. Chandrakīrti says in commentary on the first stanza of Chapter Eighteen of the *Treatise*:[41]

> With respect to this, if the self were thought to be the aggregates, then the self would have production and disintegration because of depending on the production and disintegration of the aggregates. Also, the self is not asserted thus because of the consequence of many faults.[a] As [Nāgārjuna] will explain:[42]
>
> > Also it does not arise [newly]
> > Not having existed [in a former life]
> > For fallacy follows there,
> > The self would be a product
> > And its arising would be causeless.
>
> And similarly:[43]
>
> > The appropriated [aggregates] are not the self,
> > [For] the aggregates arise and disintegrate.

---

[a] The Buddhist Sanskrit Texts edition of the Sanskrit (145.22) emends the text to read, "due to the consequence of the fault of manyness." However, the Tibetan accords with Poussin's Bibliotheca Buddhica edition (341) and allows for fallacies other than manyness.

How indeed could the appropriated
Be the appropriator?

Furthermore, this position is to be understood from the extensive analysis in the *Supplement:*[44]

If the aggregates were the self,
Then because those aggregates are many, the selves would also just be many.
Also the self would be a substantiality and viewing it as such
Would not be erroneous if it is acting on a substantiality.
In nirvana annihilation of the self would definitely occur.
There would be destruction and production of the self in the moments prior to nirvana.
Due to the destruction of the agent, effects of those [actions] would be non-existent.
Also another would experience [the effects of actions] accumulated by another....

Here I will not extensively elaborate on it. Thus, respectively the aggregates are not the self.

The Fifth Dalai Lama's expansion on these reasonings in his *Sacred Word of Mañjushrī*[a] clarifies how the impermanence, etc., of the self could be a fallacy:

It is not sufficient just to doubt whether [the I and the aggregates] are the same or different; a decision must be reached. Therefore, you should analyze [first] whether the I which is conceived by an innate [consciousness] conceiving true existence is one with body and mind. In that case, the I could not be anything but either one with the body or one with the mind. If the I were one with the body, it would not be sensible to say, "My body," from the viewpoint of associating an attribute, body, with a base, I. Also, you would [absurdly] have to say, "My I," or "The body's body." Generate ascertainment that it is the same also if the I were one with the mind.

If, having thought thus, [your attempt at understanding] is merely verbal and you do not gain strong conviction, contemplate the following. Nāgārjuna's *Treatise on the Middle*[45] says:

When it is taken that there is no self
Except the appropriated [aggregates],
The appropriated [aggregates] themselves are the self.
If so, your self is non-existent.

Because the I and the aggregates would be inherently one, they would be one in all respects with utterly no division. Hence, they would be none other than partless. Then you could not present—in the context of that partless one—the two different things: the "I" that is the appropriator of the five aggregates and the "five aggregates" that are appropriated by it. In that case, an assertion of "my body" or "my aggregates" would be senseless.

If this also does not get to the heart of the matter, think that because the I and the body are one, after death when the body is burned, the I also would be burned. Or, just as the I transmigrates to the next life, so the body also would have to transmigrate. Or, just as the body does not transmigrate, so the I also would not transmigrate. Consider the application of such fallacies.

---

[a] *ngag dbang blo bzang rgya mtsho* (Dalai Lama V; 1617-1682), *Instruction on the Stages of the Path to Enlightenment, Sacred Word of Mañjushrī* (*byang chub lam gyi rim pa'i khrid yig 'jam pa'i dbyangs kyi zhal lung*), (Thimphu: kun-bzang-stobs-rgyal, 1976), 182.5-210.6. For an English translation, see Jeffrey Hopkins, "Practice of Emptiness" (Dharamsala: Library of Tibetan Works and Archives, 1974).

Through having meditated thus, you come to think, "[The I] is probably not the same as the body." Then, if you think, "The I is probably one with the mind," consider this fallacy:

> The suffering of cold arises when the I is without clothes, and the sufferings of hunger and thirst arise when the I lacks food and drink. Therefore, if after death the mind were born in a Formless Realm, then because the mind would be one with the I, it would still have to make use of gross forms such as food and clothing.

The above modes of reasoning are suitable and easy for beginners to develop. However, if you have been disciplined through discriminating wisdom, a little more elaboration will decide the matter. Therefore, consider the fallacy of the selves becoming many. Chandrakīrti's *Supplement to (Nāgārjuna's) "Treatise on the Middle"* says:[46]

> If the aggregates were the self,
> Then because those aggregates are many, the selves would also just be many.

Just as the aggregates are five, so the I would also become five, or just as the I is no more than one, so the aggregates could not be five. Similarly, Nāgārjuna's *Treatise on the Middle*[47] says, "If the self were the aggregates, it would have production and disintegration." Because the five aggregates would be inherently produced and would inherently disintegrate, you would have to assert that the I also is produced and disintegrates in that way.

The I of the former birth and the I of this life can be only either one or different. If one, through the force of their being inherently one, the sufferings of the I in the former life as an animal—such as stupidity and enslavement for others' use—would also be experienced on the occasion of the I's being a human in this birth. Also the human pleasures of this life would have been experienced as an animal in the former life. Contemplate such absurd consequences.

Similarly, Chandrakīrti's *Supplement* (VI.61cd) says:

> Whatever are inherently separate are not
> Suitable to be included in one continuum.

If the I of the former life and the I of the next life were inherently different, they would be totally, unrelatedly different. Thereby it would be impossible to remember, "I was born in such and such a former birth," just as Devadatta does not remember that he was born in a former birth as [his contemporary] Yajñadatta.

Furthermore, your accumulating actions for birth in a happy transmigration would be wasted because another would enjoy the fruition of the effects in a life of high status, and you yourself would not experience it. Why? The agent of the actions and the experiencer of the effects would not be included into the one base of a mere-I [a nominally existent I] and would be unrelated.

Therefore, if an action accumulated in a former life brought help or harm in this life, you would be meeting with [the effects of] actions not done [by yourself]. If help and harm did not arise [from deeds done], there would be no sense in abandoning ill-deeds and adopting virtues in this life because their effects would not ripen for the future I.

Through contemplating such, you will gain ascertainment with respect to the third essential: ascertaining a lack of true oneness [of the I and the aggregates].

Oneness of the I and its bases of designation—the mental and physical aggregates—is impossible.

The second position: that the self is other than the aggregates. That the self and the aggregates are different is equally inadmissible; Nāgārjuna's *Treatise on the Middle* says:[48]

> If [the self] were other than the aggregates,
> It would not have the character of the aggregates.

Chandrakīrti's *Clear Words* comments:[49]

> If the self were separate from the aggregates, it would have the character of non-aggregates. The five aggregates have the character of suitability as form,[a] experiencing, apprehending signs, composition, and realizing objects individually. Also, just as consciousness [is different] from form, so the self which is being asserted to be different from the aggregates would be established as having a character different [from the aggregates]. Also, its different character would be apprehended just as [the character of] mind [is apprehended separate] from form, but it is not apprehended so. Therefore, the self also is not separate from the aggregates.

The Fifth Dalai Lama expands:

> Now, you might think that the I and the five aggregates cannot be anything but different. Chandrakīrti's *Supplement* (VI.120ab) says:
>
> > There is no self other than the aggregates because
> > Apart from the aggregates, its conception does not exist.
>
> The inherently different must be unrelated. Therefore, just as within the aggregates you can identify each individually—"This is the aggregate of form," and so forth—so, after clearing away the five aggregates, you would have to be able to identify the I, "This is the I." However, no matter how finely you analyze, such an I is not at all to be found.
>
> It is not sufficient that the mode of non-finding be just a repetition of the impoverished phrase, "Not found." For example, when an ox is lost, one does not take as true the mere phrase, "It is not in such and such an area." Rather, it is through searching for it in the highland, midland, and lowland of the area that one firmly decides it cannot be found. Here also, through meditating until a decision is reached, you gain conviction.

---

[a] "Suitability as form" (*rūpana, gzugs su rung ba*) is cogently rendered by J. W. De Jong in his *Cinq Chapitres De La Prasannapadā* (Paris: Libraire Orientaliste Paul Geuthner, 1949, 4) as "le pouvoir d'être brisé," "capable of being broken." The latter is how Ajitamitra interprets the term in his commentary on the *Precious Garland* (notation lost). Therefore, it appears that the translators into Tibetan were aware of both meanings and chose "suitability as form" here. However, according to Lati Rin-bo-chay (oral explanation) "capable of being broken" is not appropriate as a definition of form at least in those schools that assert partless particles as these cannot be broken down either physically or mentally. Perhaps this is the reason why the translation as "that which is suitable as form," meaning whatever one points to when asked what form is, was preferred. Still, according to Geshe Gedün Lodrö (oral explanation) partless particles could not be further reduced without disappearing; thus, if we take their physical disappearance as their susceptibility to being broken, this interpretation of *rūpaṇa* as that which is susceptible to being broken would be an appropriate definition of form.

"That which is suitable as form" (*gzugs su rung ba*) appears to be uninformative since it repeats the very term being defined, form; however, it does illustrate the notion that reasoning meets back to common experience in that with form we are at a level of common experience with little else to come up with as a definition other than saying that it is what we point to when we identify a form.

The third and fourth positions: that the self is in the aggregates and that the aggregates are in the self. That the self is in, or dependent upon, the aggregates is also inadmissible, as is the proposition that the aggregates are in, or dependent upon, the self. Buddhapālita's *Commentary on (Nāgārjuna's) Treatise* says:[50]

> Aggregates do not exist in a One Gone Thus like a forest of trees in snow. Why? Those which are supported [i.e., the aggregates] and their base [i.e., a One Gone Thus] would be other; therefore, it would follow that a One Gone Thus was permanent. Also, a One Gone Thus does not exist in aggregates like a lion in a forest of trees. Why? There would be the fallacy just indicated.

Chandrakīrti's own *Commentary on the "Supplement"* says:[51]

> If [the self and the aggregates] were other, they would be fit to be the entities of that which is supported and its support like yogurt in a metal bowl, for example. Since the two, yogurt and bowl, are just other in worldly conventions, they are seen to be the entities of that which is supported and its support. However, the aggregates are not thus different from the self, and the self also is not different from the aggregates. Therefore, these two are not entities of support and supported.

The fifth position: that the self possesses the aggregates. Buddhapālita's *Commentary on (Nāgārjuna's) Treatise* says:[52]

> A One Gone Thus does not possess aggregates in the way that a tree possesses a core. Why? A One Gone Thus would not be other than the aggregates; therefore, there would be the fallacy of his being impermanent.

Chandrakīrti's *Supplement* says:[a]

> It is not accepted that the self possesses the body. For the self [has already been refuted as inherently one with or different from the aggregates and thus] is not [inherently existent]. Therefore, the relationship of the self's possessing the aggregates does not exist [inherently]. If it is said that they are other [entities, like Devadatta's] possessing a cow or that they are not other [entities like Devadatta's] possessing his body, [the answer is that] the self is not one with or other than the body.

Chandrakīrti's own *Commentary on the "Supplement"* says:[53]

> Also, the suffix indicating possession [*mat-* or *vat-pratyaya*] is employed for the non-different in *rūpavān devadattaḥ*, "Devadatta is a possessor of a form [a body]." It is employed for the different in *gomān*, "Devadatta is a possessor of a cow." Since form and the self do not have sameness or otherness, there is no saying that the self possesses form.

When sought in these five ways the self, or person, or I is not found.

---

[a] Peking 5262, vol. 98 104.3.7ff, VI.143; Poussin's translation is *Muséon*, n.s. v. 12, 310-11. In accordance with Ďzong-ka-ɓa's *Illumination* (Peking 6143, vol. 154 89.1.7ff) the passage should be qualified so as to read:

> It is not accepted that the self [inherently] possesses the body. For the self [has already been refuted as inherently one with or different from the aggregates and thus] is not [inherently existent]. Therefore, the relationship of the self's possessing the aggregates does not exist [inherently]. If it is said that they are other [entities, like Devadatta's] possessing a cow or that they are not other [entities like Devadatta's] possessing his body, [the answer is that] the self is not one with or other than the body. [Therefore, the self's possessing form does not inherently exist.]

EXTENDING THE REASONING REFUTING COMPOSITES TO THE FOUR ELEMENTS

In the *Precious Garland* Nāgārjuna extends the fivefold reasoning, minus the position of possession, to the four elements—earth, water, fire, and wind. The four elements always work together, within the context of one being predominate, much like four forces that manifest in various ways due to a preponderance of one or the other: (83-85)

> The three elements[a] are not earth, they are not in it,
> It is not in them, without them it is not;
> Since this also applies to each,
> The elements, like the self, are false.
>
> Earth, water, fire, and wind
> Individually also do not inherently exist.
> When any three are absent, an individual one does not exist.
> When one is absent, the three also do not exist.
>
> If when three are absent, an individual one does not exist
> And if when one is absent, the three also do not exist,
> Then each itself does not exist.
> How could a composite be produced?

If the elements existed in and of themselves, there absurdly would be water without motility, obstructiveness, or maturation; there absurdly would be wind without obstructiveness, maturation, or cohesion; there absurdly would be earth without motility, maturation, and cohesion: (86)

> Otherwise, if each itself exists,
> Why without fuel is there no fire?
> Likewise why is there no water, wind, or earth
> Without motility, obstructiveness, or cohesion?

AGAIN, THE REASONING OF DEPENDENT-ARISING

To a hypothetical objection that it is well known that fire cannot exist without fuel, but earth, water, and wind can exist without the others, Nāgārjuna relies on the dictum that everything is a dependent-arising: (87)

> If [it is answered that] fire is well known [not to exist without fuel but the other three elements exist by way of their own entities],
> How could your three exist in themselves
> Without the others? It is impossible for the three
> Not to accord with dependent-arising.

He may be speaking to the questioner's own assertion that all phenomena are dependent-arisings, since in his next move he undermines a solidly existent notion of dependent-arising.

REASONING REFUTING DEPENDENT-ARISING

If the elements, or anything else, exist individually, how could they depend on each other? Yet, if they do not exist in themselves, how can they depend on each other?: (88)

---

[a] Water, fire, and wind; or cohesion, heat, and motility.

How could those—that themselves
Exist individually—be mutually dependent?
How could those—that do not themselves
Exist individually—be mutually dependent?

It is clear that "existence" here means existence in and of itself.

Furthermore, do these mutually dependent elements occupy the same place or separate places? If they are not intermingled, they could not be in one place, but if they are intermingled, they do not exist separately: (89)

If it is the case that they do not themselves exist individually,
But where there is one, the other three exist,
Then if unmixed, they are not in one place,
And if mixed, they do not themselves exist individually.

Once the elements cannot stand alone, they do not have their own character, and if they do not have their own character, the one cannot predominate over the others. This train of reasoning undermines the very notion that forms are produced through a predominance of one element over the others within a combination of all four: (90)

The elements do not themselves exist individually,
So how could their own individual characters exist?
What do not themselves individually exist cannot predominate.
Their characters are regarded as conventionalities.

Despite the refutation of such entities, Nāgārjuna declares that the characters of the elements are "conventionalities," the implication being that therefore the elements also exist in this way and hence forms composed of the elements exist as conventionalities. (For discussion of the issue of ultimate and conventional existence, see 69ff.)

EXTENDING THE REFUTATION TO ALL PHENOMENA

Nāgārjuna proceeds to list various types of objects as illustrations of the fact that all phenomena are subject to this type of analysis and concludes by saying that all these are ceased in the face of such an analytical consciousness (91-93, 100). He undercuts adherence to the inherent existence of the mere nominal or conventional existence of phenomena by declaring that even nominality does not exist: (99)

Because the phenomena of forms
Are only names, space too is only a name.
Without the elements how could forms exist?
Therefore even name-only does not exist.

Everything is like a banana (or plantain) tree which appears to have a solid trunk but is merely composed of layers (like an onion), without any core: (101-2)

Just as when a banana tree
With all its parts is torn apart, there is nothing,
So when a person having the [six] constituents
Is divided, it is the same.

Therefore the Conquerors said,
"All phenomena are selfless."
Since this is so, all six constituents
Have been delineated as selfless for you.

REASONINGS REFUTING PLEASURE AND PAIN

In Chapter Four Nāgārjuna gives an extensive refutation of pleasure and pain over eighteen stanzas (346-63), after which he extends the impact of the analysis to all phenomena. The movement from the earlier analysis of lust in Chapter Two (148-70) for the sake of suppressing a specific behavior to a deeper analysis in Chapter Four that yields liberation mirrors his description of the progression of Buddha's teaching: (394-96)

Just as a grammarian [first] has students
Read a model of the alphabet,
So Buddha taught trainees
The doctrines that they could bear.

To some he taught doctrines
To turn them away from ill-deeds;
To some, for the sake of achieving merit;
To some, doctrines based on duality;

To some, doctrines based on non-duality;
To some what is profound and frightening to the fearful—
Having an essence of emptiness and compassion—
The means of achieving [unsurpassed] enlightenment.

It is noteworthy that the first three lines of the middle stanza refer to the doctrines of high status—the essence of which he has said is compassion (399)—and the third line of the last stanza, which concerns the highest level of practice, speaks also of compassion. The practice of compassion is clearly not limited to lower levels of the path as if it were surpassed by wisdom.

Unlike his earlier brief style, here in the analysis of pleasure and pain topics are laid out more gradually through expansion and repetition. The first sixteen stanzas treat the topic of pleasure through:

- employing five new reasonings that are outflows of the reasoning of dependent-arising
- recalling the earlier reasoning refuting the elements
- extending this reasoning to consciousness.

The first approach is to undermine the seemingly solid nature of pleasure 1) by pointing out that physical pleasure is only a lessening of pain that is misconceived to be real pleasure and 2) by pointing out that mental pleasure is only a creation of conceptual thought. Uncharacteristic of his earlier brevity, he makes these points twice: (346-48)

Although Universal Monarchs rule
Over the four continents, their pleasures
Are regarded as only two—
The physical and the mental.

Physical feelings of pleasure
Are only a lessening of pain.
Mental pleasures are made of thought,
Created only by conceptuality.

All the wealth of worldly pleasures
Are just a lessening of suffering,
Or are only [creations of] thought,
Hence they are in fact not meaningful.

The second tack is to point out that since objects are pleasurable only one by one, all other objects are at that time not causes of pleasure and hence not real. In this sequence he names thirteen types of objects and repeats the punch-line three times with slight variation: (349-52)

Just one by one there is enjoyment
Of continents, countries, towns, homes,
Conveyances, seats, clothing, beds,
Food, drink, elephants, horses, and women.

When the mind has any [one of these as its object],
Due to it there is said to be pleasure,
But since at that time no attention is paid to the others,
The others are not then in fact meaningful [causes of pleasure].

When [all] five senses, eye and so forth,[a]
[Simultaneously] apprehend their objects,[b]
A thought [of pleasure] does not refer [to all of them],
Therefore at that time they do not [all] give pleasure.

Whenever any of the [five] objects is known
[As pleasurable] by one of the [five] senses,
Then the remaining [objects] are not so known by the remaining [senses]
Since they then are not meaningful [causes of pleasure].

He explains that actually the mental consciousness pays attention to an object already apprehended by the senses and imputes it to be pleasurable, the point being that the mental consciousness can do this with only one object at a time: (353)

The mind apprehends an image of a past object
Which has been apprehended by the senses
And imagines and fancies
It to be pleasurable.

Having explained that multiple objects cannot be pleasurable simultaneously, in the third through fifth parts of the argument he refutes sense faculties, sense consciousnesses, and objects and thus indirectly refutes that there is pleasure. First he attacks the notion that one sense faculty knows one object. This is done by showing that the sense faculty and the object depend upon each other. The suggestion

---

[a] Eye, ear, nose, tongue, and body sense consciousnesses.

[b] Visual forms (i.e., colors and shapes), sounds, odors, tastes, and tangible objects.

is that we view sense faculties and their objects as existing in their own right whereas they do not, and hence there is no real physical pleasure: (354)

Also the one sense which here [in the world
Is said to] know one object
Is meaningless without an object,
And the object also is meaningless without it.

In the fourth reasoning, he uses the example of a visual consciousness to make the point that it arises in dependence upon a visual sense organ and a form and hence there is no real pleasure: (355)

Just as a child is said to be born
In dependence on a father and a mother,
So a [visual] consciousness is said to arise
In dependence on an eye sense and on a form.

In the fifth and final phase of the new reasonings, objects of the past, future, and present are declared to be unreal due to their interdependence. The present must depend on the past and the future in order to be present, but if the present does not exist in the past and the future, then it cannot truly depend on them. However, if the present does exist in the past and the future, then it is not different from them: (356-57)

Past and future objects
And the senses are meaningless,
So too are present objects
Since they are not distinct from these two.

Just as due to error the eye perceives
A whirling firebrand as a wheel,
So the senses apprehend
Present objects [as if real].

To cap the presentation of the unreality of pleasure, he cites the fact that the sense organs and their respective objects—colors and shapes, sounds, odors, tastes, and tangible objects—are composed of the four elements and thus are subject to the faults adduced in Chapter One:[a] (358-60)

The senses and their objects are regarded
As being composed of the elements.
Since the elements are meaningless individually,
These also are meaningless in fact.

If the elements are each different,
It follows that there could be fire without fuel.
If mixed, they would be characterless.
Such is also to be ascertained about the other elements.

Because the elements are thus meaningless in both these ways,
So too is a composite.

---

[a] See pp. 63ff.

Because a composite is meaningless
So too are forms meaningless in fact.

He extends this type of analysis to feeling, which, according to Buddhist psychology, must operate in conjunction with consciousness, discrimination, and other mental factors which are included within the fourth aggregate, compositional factors. Thus feeling is subject to the same analysis as the elements: either feeling, consciousness, discrimination, and other mental factors would exist individually in which case they would not depend on each other, or if they did not exist individually, they could not depend on each other: (361)

Also because consciousnesses, feelings,
Discriminations, and compositional factors
Altogether and individually are without essential factuality,
[Pleasures] are not ultimately meaningful.

The brunt of this multi-staged argument is extended to feelings of pain through merely mentioning the initial corresponding reasoning: (362)

Just as lessening of pain
Is fancied to be pleasure in fact,
So destruction of pleasure
Is also fancied to be pain.

The conclusion is that both types of attachment—to meeting with pleasure and to separating from pain—are overcome through knowledge that they do not inherently exist. Through such knowledge, gained through reflecting on reasoning, liberation is attained: (363)

Thus attachment to meeting with pleasure
And attachment to separating from pain
Are to be abandoned because they do not inherently exist.
Thereby those who see thus are liberated.

Liberation is found through seeing the absence of inherent existence; it is clear from the flow of the text that such perception is born from these types of reasoning.

REASONING REFUTING PERCEPTION OF REALITY

Again, if it is thought that the mind perceiving reality is an inherently existent entity, this is refuted through considering that a mind only works together with mental factors. Thus, the same reasoning used for the elements and for pleasure and pain applies to a mind seeing emptiness. Consequently, only conventionally is it said that the mind sees reality: (364)

What sees [reality]?
Conventionally it is said to be the mind
[For] without mental factors there is no mind
[And hence minds and mental factors] are meaningless, due to which it is not asserted that they are simultaneous.[a]

---

[a] I see this stanza as extending the type of reasoning Nāgārjuna used with regard to the elements, but Gyel-tsap (58a.5) intriguingly sees the issue as revolving around whether the mind that sees the ultimate truth is itself an ultimate truth:

Question: Then what sees?

FAULTS OF MISUNDERSTANDING THE VIEW OF EMPTINESS

Nāgārjuna berates those who misunderstand the doctrine of emptiness in either of two ways—(1) accepting it but taking it to mean nothingness and thereby not practicing the adoption of virtues and the overcoming of non-virtues or (2) taking emptiness to mean a denial of cause and effect and therefore rejecting it: (119-20)

> This doctrine wrongly understood
> Causes the unwise to be ruined
> Because they sink into the uncleanliness
> Of nihilistic views.
> Further, the stupid who fancy
> Themselves wise, having a nature
> Ruined by rejecting [emptiness], go headfirst
> To a terrible hell due to their wrong understanding.

> Answer: The mind seeing the ultimate truth does not become an ultimate truth, and conventionally it is said that an awareness of meditative equipoise on the ultimate truth in the manner of the disappearance of dualistic appearance—the awareness being produced and ceasing moment by moment—sees the ultimate truth [which is not a momentary phenomenon]. Moreover, this is only posited relatively and is not inherently established, for without mental factors mind does not occur and also without mind mental factors do not occur and hence [that the mind sees the ultimate truth] does not have the meaning of being inherently established. Also, the mind does not see the mind because the tip of a finger itself does not touch itself, and moreover it is not asserted that two minds occur simultaneously.

According to this interpretation, the stanza would be translated:

> What sees [reality]?
> Conventionally it is said to be the mind,
> Without mental factors there is no mind
> [And hence] there is no meaning [of inherent existence. Also the mind itself does not know the mind because] it is not asserted that [two minds] are simultaneous.

(For Ḏzong-ka-ḇa's discussion of 363d-364b see Tsong-ka-pa, Kensur Lekden, and Jeffrey Hopkins, *Compassion in Tibetan Buddhism*, 132-33.) Gyel-tsap's interpretation reflects a concern found in Ḏzong-ka-ḇa's *The Essence of Eloquence* in which even with respect to the Mind Only School he handles apparent evidence in Āryadeva's *Compilation of the Essence of Wisdom* (*ye shes snying po kun las btus pa, jñānasārasamuccaya*; Peking 5251, *tsha* vol. 95, 144.2.8) that seems to declare the wisdom knowing reality is an ultimate. Āryadeva seems to say:

> That a consciousness which is released
> From apprehended-object and apprehending-subject exists **as the ultimate** (***dam pa'i don du***)
> Is renowned in the texts of the Yogic Practitioners
> Who have passed to the other shore of the ocean of awareness.

However, Ḏzong-ka-ḇa holds that the passage actually means:

> That a consciousness which is released
> From apprehended-object and apprehending-subject exists **ultimately** [i.e., exists by way of its own character]
> Is renowned in the texts of the Yogic Practitioners
> Who have passed to the other shore of the ocean of awareness.

For this and other similar points see Jeffrey Hopkins, *Emptiness in "Mind-Only" Buddhism*, Translation: Chapter 7 and Synopsis: Chapter 7 (Berkeley: University of California Press, 1999).

And: (371)

> One type with faith [in emptiness forsakes it] through misconception [of it as denying cause and effect].
> Others who are angry [forsake emptiness] through despising it.
> If even the faithful type is said [in sūtra] to be burned,
> What can be said about those who turn their backs on it through despising it!

Gyel-tsap[54] draws the conclusion that even if one does not have interest in emptiness, one should not deprecate it.

Correspondingly, Nāgārjuna extols the merits of properly digesting the doctrine: (121-23)

> Just as one comes to ruin
> Through wrong eating but obtains
> Long life, freedom from disease,
> Strength, and pleasures through right eating,
>
> So one comes to ruin
> Through wrong understanding
> But obtains bliss and highest enlightenment
> Through right understanding.
> Therefore having forsaken with respect to this [doctrine of emptiness]
> Nihilistic views and rejection,
> Be supremely intent on correct understanding
> For the sake of achieving all aims.

The enormity of the task of gaining a proper perspective on the doctrine of emptiness can be seen from his taunts to those who call it nihilism. Although in other places—as we have seen—he stresses the importance of conventional assertions and specifies that the existence being refuted is inherent existence, he lays claim to this doctrine's being beyond existence and non-existence: (58-62)

> If through correct and true knowledge
> [Such wise persons] do not assert existence and non-existence
> And thereby [you think] that they follow non-existence,
> Why should they not be followers of existence?
>
> If from refuting existence
> Non-existence would accrue to them,
> Why from refuting non-existence
> Would existence not accrue to them?
>
> They implicitly have no nihilistic thesis
> And also have no nihilistic behavior
> And due to relying on [the path to] enlightenment have no nihilistic thought.
> Hence how can they be regarded as nihilists?
>
> Ask the Sāṃkhyas, the followers of Kaṇaḍa, Nirgranthas,
> And the worldly proponents of a person and aggregates,

Whether they propound
What passes beyond "is" and "is not."
Thereby know that the ambrosia
Of the Buddhas' teaching is called profound,
An exclusive doctrine passing
Far beyond "is" and "is not."

Nevertheless, qualifications of the type of existence being refuted are particularly clear in the section on Buddha's initial silence: (103-18)

Thus neither self nor non-self
Are to be apprehended **as real**.
Therefore the Great Subduer rejected
Views of self and non-self.

Sights, sounds, and so forth were said by the Subduer
Not to be true and not to be false.
If from one position its opposite arises,
Both do not exist **in fact**.

Thus **ultimately** this world
Is beyond truth and falsity.
Therefore the Subduer does not assert
That it **really** exists or does not.

...

That which is secret for a common being
Is the profound doctrine,
The world as like an illusion,
The ambrosia of the Buddhas' teaching.

Just as the production and disintegration
Of an illusory elephant are seen,
But the production and disintegration
Do not **really** exist,

So the production and disintegration
Of the illusion-like world are seen,
But the production and disintegration
Do not **ultimately** exist.

Just as an illusory elephant,
Being only a bewildering of consciousness,
Does not come from anywhere,
Nor go anywhere, nor **really** stay,

So the illusion-like world,
Being only a bewildering of consciousness,

Does not come from anywhere,
Nor go anywhere, nor **really** stay.
Thus it has a nature beyond the three times.
Other than as the imputation of a convention
What world is there **in fact**
Which would exist or not?

...

Realizing that because of its profundity
This doctrine is difficult for beings to understand,
The Subduer, having become enlightened
[At first] turned away from teaching doctrine.

Also, in other places, Nāgārjuna says that phenomena exist conventionally: (90)

The elements do not themselves exist individually,
So how could their own individual characters exist?
What do not themselves individually exist cannot predominate.
Their characters are regarded as **conventionalities**.

Just what it means to be a conventionality remains a topic of much debate among Nāgārjuna's followers. In this text Nāgārjuna indicates that:

- conventionally existing and really existing are two exhaustive possibilities (47)
- asserting what appears in worldly conventions prevents nihilism (50)
- asserting cessation that is outside worldly conventions prevents falling into exaggerated notions of existence (51)
- the world is just an imputation of conventions (114)
- only conventionally is it said that the mind sees reality (364).

Existing conventionally is opposed to existing inherently,[a] existing in fact,[b] existing as real (or really existing, or existing as reality, or existing as its own reality),[c] and existing ultimately.[d] Thus, at times it appears that Nāgārjuna denies inherent existence (and its equivalents) and affirms conventional existence, whereas at other times he speaks of a reality beyond assertions of either existence or non-existence without any qualification. It may be that the latter type of statement refers to the psychologi-

---

[a] 84: *ngo bo nyid du med;* 297: *ngo bo nyid med par;* 363: *ngo bo nyid med phyir, naiḥsvābhāvyāt.*

[b] 29, 47, 54d, 63, 64, 65, 66, 73, 104, 114, 348, 358, 360, 362: *don du, arthataḥ.* Also, a related word is "meaningless"—354, 356, 358d, 360, 364, 365: *don med, vyartham;* 358c, 361: *don med, vaiyarthyaṃ.* "In fact" is used more loosely in 54b, 148, 300, 350, 386, and 489 where it does not seem to stand in contradistinction to existing conventionally but indicates that something, such as the purity of the body, does not exist even conventionally. The term *don med, anartha* also appears in 327 where it means "contrary to one's aims."

[c] 32: *yang dag nyid du, tattvena;* 38: *yang dag nyid du, tattvataḥ;* 47: *yang dag nyid du na, tattvataḥ;* 53: *yang dag, yathābhuto;* 64: *yang dag tu, tattvataḥ;* 65: *yang dag nyid, tattvataḥ;* 81: *yang dag;* 103: *yang dag ji bzhin, yathābhutyena;* 105: *yang dag tu, tattvena;* 110: *don kyi yang dug tu, tattvena;* 113: *yang dag nyid du, bhāvatvena.* There are loose usages in reference to the image of a face in 31 (*yang dag nyid du, tattvataḥ*) and an illusory elephant in 112 (*yang dag nyid du, bhāvatvena*).

[d] 28, 105, 361: *dam pa'i don du, parmārthaḥ;* 111: *dam pa'i don du, parmārthena.*

cal state of perceiving reality directly, in the face of which there are no assertions. For instance, he says: (93-97)

Earth, water, fire, and wind,
Long and short, subtle and coarse,
As well as virtue and so forth are said by the Subduer
To be ceased in the consciousness [of reality].

Earth, water, fire, and wind
Do not have a chance
In the face of that undemonstrable consciousness
Complete lord over the limitless.

Here[a] long and short, subtle and coarse,
Virtue and non-virtue,
And here names and forms
All are ceased.

All those that earlier appeared to consciousness
Because of not knowing that [reality]
Will later cease for consciousness in that way
Because of knowing that [reality].

All these phenomena of beings
Are seen as fuel for the fire of consciousness.
They are pacified through being burned
By the light of true discrimination.

Still, it is clear that a combination of wisdom and compassion is needed for the achievement of Buddhahood, which itself is not a blank withdrawal but is endowed with all supreme qualities: (298)

Through meditatively cultivating the wisdom of reality
Which is the same [for all phenomena] and is moistened with compassion
For the sake of liberating all sentient beings,
You will become a Conqueror endowed with all supreme aspects.

Thus it appears that when Nāgārjuna speaks about all phenomena being burned by the fire of wisdom, he is referring to a particular state of meditation on the path to complete enlightenment in which analysis undermines an over-concretized appearance of phenomena. Since he wants to draw his readers into the experience of this wisdom-consciousness that does not find these phenomena, he does not over-load the text with the qualification "inherent existence" or the like. Rather, the literature itself draws the reader into a state beyond phenomena.[b]

---

[a] "Here" means "in the face of a Superior's meditative equipoise."

[b] This is the reason why I have not loaded the translation with such qualifications in brackets. In previous translations I have wanted to show how many qualifications must be made in the process of a typical Ge-luk-ba exegesis—that being my topic—but here I have not done so since the literature of Nāgārjuna's text demands otherwise. Although I mostly follow Gyel-tsap's interpretation of the syntax of Nāgārjuna's stanzas, I am not following his constant interpolation of such qualifications.

4 Compassion and Wisdom in Public Policy

At the end of Chapter Four, Nāgārjuna summarizes his advice to the Shātavāhana king on how to conduct political rule.[a] He refers to the triad of charity, morality, and tolerance,[b] all of which have a core of compassion: (399)

> At that time [when you are a ruler] you should internalize
> Firmly the practices of giving, ethics, and patience,
> Which were especially taught for householders
> And which have an essence of compassion.

Similarly, in Chapter Two, he praises this triad of practices as the best politics and then derides those politicians intent on deception as paving the way for their own demise in this and future lifetimes: (128-31)

> The practices are the best policy,
> It is through them that the world is pleased;
> Neither here nor in the future is one cheated
> By a world that has been pleased.
>
> The world is displeased
> By the policies of non-practice.
> Due to the displeasure of the world
> One is not pleased here or in the future.
>
> How could those with senseless deviant minds
> On a path to bad transmigrations,
> Wretched, intent on deceiving others,
> Have understood what is meaningful?
>
> How could those intent on deceiving others
> Be persons of policy?
> Through it they themselves will be cheated
> In many thousands of births.

CHARACTER OF A LEADER

As qualities of leadership Nāgārjuna extols truth, generosity, peace, and wisdom (134-39). Later he singles out patience, respect, and generosity within employing a splendid metaphor: (340)

---

[a] Nāgārjuna's political advice is not limited to Chapter Four but is found in Chapters Two and Three also, as indicated below.

[b] This triad figures also in stanzas 12 and 125.

The birds of the populace will alight upon
The royal tree providing the shade of patience,
Flourishing flowers of respect,
And large fruits of resplendent giving.

Also, he speaks of four means of bringing people together: (133)

You should cause the assembling
Of the religious and the worldly
Through giving, speaking pleasantly,
Purposeful behavior, and concordant behavior.

Here, "giving" means to give material things; "speaking pleasantly" is to converse on the topics of high status and definite goodness; "purposeful behavior" is to cause others to practice what is beneficial; "concordant behavior" is for one to practice what one teaches others. Giving, or generosity, appears in all three of these lists.

GENEROSITY

The quintessence of Nāgārjuna's advice on charity is to be as focused on helping others as one is on helping oneself. From that perspective, one should make oneself available for others' use just as air, for instance, is: (256-57)

Just as you are intent on thinking
Of what could be done to help yourself,
So you should be intent on thinking
Of what could be done to help others.

If only for a moment make yourself
Available for the use of others
Just as earth, water, fire, wind, medicine,[a]
And forests [are available to all].

Generosity draws political allegiance as long as one is not witlessly soft: (341)

Monarchs whose nature is generosity
Are liked if they are strong,
Like a sweet hardened outside
With cardamom and pepper.

Charity calls for analysis of what will help, contingent upon circumstances: (263-64)

Even give poison
To those whom it will help,
But do not give even the best food
To those whom it will not help.
Just as it is said that it will help
To cut off a finger bitten by a snake,

---

[a] *sman:* whether the reference is to medicine itself or herbs is unclear.

So the Subduer says that if it helps others,
One should even bring [temporary] discomfort.

Nāgārjuna's advice about generosity is presented in the context of reasoned arguments that it helps both one's country and oneself. At the beginning he makes an appeal to self-interest since charity during this life will bring wealth to oneself in future lives multiplied exponentially: (307-8)

If you do not make contributions of the wealth
Obtained from former giving to the needy,
Through your ingratitude and attachment
You will not obtain wealth in the future.

Here in the world workers do not carry
Provisions for a journey unpaid,
But lowly beggars, without being bribed, carry to your future life
[What you give them] multiplied a hundred times.

Impermanence means that all wealth must be left behind, whereas if one's resources are used for beneficial purposes the resultant good karma is carried to the next lifetime: (313-17)

Having let go of all possessions,
[At death] powerless you must go elsewhere,
But all that has been used for the doctrine
Precedes you [as good karma].

When all the possessions of a previous monarch
Come under the control of the successor,
Of what use are they then to the former monarch
For practice, happiness, or fame?

Through using wealth there is happiness here in this life,
Through giving there is happiness in the future,
From wasting it without using or giving it away,
There is only misery. How could there be happiness?

Because of lack of power while dying,
You will be unable to make donations by way of your ministers
Who will shamelessly lose affection for you
And will seek to please the new monarch.

Hence while in good health create foundations of doctrine
Immediately with all your wealth,
For you are living amidst the causes of death
Like a lamp standing in a breeze.

At the end of the section on charity, the appeal is to the welfare of the country within recognition that the ruler is merely a temporary occupant of the seat of power due to former virtuous actions: (343)

You did not bring your dominion with you from your former life
Nor will you take it to the next.

Since it was gained through religious practice,
You would be wrong to act against the practices.

On the negative side, to do otherwise would result in the ruination of the country: (344-45)

O King, exert yourself
To avert a sequence
Of miserable supplies for the realm
Through [misuse of] royal resources.
O King, exert yourself
To increase the succession
Of the dominion's resources
Through [proper use of] royal resources.

Also, generosity is implicitly recommended as a means to hide one's own faults: (136)

Just as a single splendid charity
Conceals the faults of kings,
So avarice destroys
All their wealth.

TYPES OF CHARITABLE ASSISTANCE

Care for the disadvantaged. Those afflicted by disease, lack of family, pain, low class, poverty, and the conquered are to be objects of compassion: (243, 251, 320)

Always care compassionately
For the sick, the unprotected, those stricken
With suffering, the lowly, and the poor
And take special care to nourish them.
Provide extensive care
For the persecuted, the victims of crop failure,
The stricken, those suffering contagion,
And for beings in conquered areas.
Cause the blind, the sick, the lowly,
The protectorless, the destitute,
And the crippled equally to obtain
Food and drink without interruption.

Also, the government should provide medical care for the old, the young, and the ill: (240)

In order to alleviate the suffering
Of sentient beings—the old, young, and infirm—
You should establish through the estates [that you control]
Doctors and barbers throughout your country.

Beggars are to be treated with food and even special adornments: (244, 261)

Until you have given to monastics and beggars
Seasonally-appropriate food and drink,

As well as produce, grain, and fruit,
You should not partake of them.
Lovingly give to beggars
Various and glittering
Clothes, adornments, perfumes,
Garlands, and enjoyments.

Care for prisoners. Criminals are to be treated like one's own children with a compassionate wish to reform them: (336)

Just as deficient children are punished
Out of a wish to make them competent,
So punishment should be carried out with compassion,
Not through hatred nor desire for wealth.

Even when ministers have jailed criminals, the ruler should be concerned for them (330). Those who have committed particularly awful crimes are to be treated with special compassion (331-32). Weaker prisoners are to be freed after brief incarceration and all others eventually (333-34), and while incarcerated, they should be kept in good condition (335). If, upon analysis, some prisoners are determined to be particularly dangerous, they should be exiled (337). It is clear that for Nāgārjuna there are no limits to the compassion required of a religious government.

Creating and supporting religious institutions. He advises that leaders engage in expansive, high-minded deeds (309), creating religious institutions and monuments (231-34) beyond the ken of lowly rulers (310), generating the respect of wealthy rulers (311), and causing admiration in all (312). Also, the religious institutions founded by previous rulers are to be maintained as before (318). The government is to provide for the upkeep of religious centers by capable caretakers (232ab, 235abc, 319, 322) and for upkeep for religious practitioners both within and without the kingdom (262, 321). Pages and books of Buddha's word and treatises about it, as well as pens and ink, are to be provided (238). The implicit message is that for the values of Buddhist doctrine to be inculcated on a popular level, impressive, well-endowed institutions are required.

Public education. The government is to support public education through providing for the livelihood of teachers: (239)

As ways to increase wisdom,
Wherever there is a school in the land
Provide for the livelihood of teachers
And give lands to them [for their provision].

Public parks and facilities for travelers. Nāgārjuna calls for the government to pay particular attention to travelers through providing extensive facilities: (241-42)

O One of Good Wisdom, please provide
Hostels, parks, dikes,
Ponds, rest-houses, water-vessels,
Beds, food, hay, and wood.

Please establish rest-houses
In all towns, at temples, and in all cities

And provide water-vessels
On all arid roadways.

And: (245-48)

At the sites of the water-vessels
Place shoes, umbrellas, water-filters,
Tweezers for removing thorns,
Needles, thread, and fans.

Within vessels place the three medicinal fruits,
The three fever medicines, butter,
Honey, eye medicines, and antidotes to poison,
And write out mantras and prescriptions.

At the sites of the vessels place
Salves for the body, feet, and head,
As well as wool, stools, gruel,
Jars [for getting water], cooking pots, axes, and so forth.

Please have small containers
In the shade filled with sesame,
Rice, grains, foods, molasses,
And suitable water.

Care for animals and hungry ghosts. He makes a moving call for the King to provide for ants: (249)

At the openings of ant-hills
Please have trustworthy persons
Always put food, water,
Sugar, and piles of grain.

The next stanza suggests that ants are an illustration for other animals and hungry ghosts: (250)

Before and after taking food
Always appropriately offer fare
To hungry ghosts, dogs,
Ants, birds, and so forth.

Commercial regulation. Farmers are to be protected at times of poor harvest and at all times from high taxes: (252)

Provide stricken farmers
With seeds and sustenance.
Eliminate high taxes [levied by the previous monarch].
Reduce the tax rate [on harvests].

Other techniques to achieve an active economy are to distribute resources to the poor, reduce tolls, remove red-tape, establish law and order, and implement price controls at times of scarcity: (253-54)

Protect [the poor] from the pain of wanting [your wealth].
Set up no [new] tolls and reduce those [that are heavy].

Also free [traders from other areas] from the afflictions
That come from waiting at your door.
Eliminate robbers and thieves
In your own and others' countries.
Please set prices fairly
And keep profits level [even during scarcity].

Providing sex. In seeming contradiction with the two extended analyzes—first of sexual lust (148-70) and then of pleasure (346-63)—Nāgārjuna advises the king to provide prostitutes to those seeking sexual pleasure, perhaps when it suits governmental needs for entertainment. He backs up the advice with the account that in a former life Shākyamuni Buddha provided eighty thousand prostitutes. It strikes me as unfathomable that the concordant result of such charity is the ability to retain the words and meanings of doctrine: (259-60)

If you give to those so seeking
Girls of beauty well adorned,
You will thereby attain
Thorough retention of the excellent doctrine.

Formerly the Subduer provided
Along with every need and so forth
Eighty thousand girls
With all adornments.

TRUTH

As a desirable characteristic of a leader, truthfulness brings trust: (134-35)

Just as by themselves the true words
Of kings generate firm trust,
So their false words are the best means
To create distrust.

What is not deceitful is the truth;
It is not an intentional fabrication.
What is solely helpful to others is the truth.
The opposite is falsehood since it does not help.

It is not clear whether this means that the truth is constituted by what is helpful or that the helpful is constituted by the truth; however, he also says that the King should always speak the truth even if it costs his life or dominion: (274)

For your sake always speak the truth.
Even should it cause your death
Or ruin your governance,
Do not speak in any other way.

Still, he calls for clever usage of self-development to undermine the influence of enemies; rather than repeating their faults one should remove one's own defects and acquire good qualities and thereby bring disfavor to the enemy: (132)

Even if you seek to harm an enemy,
You should remove your own defects and cultivate good qualities.
Through that you will help yourself,
And the enemy will be displeased.

PEACE

Peace is extolled as bestowing power: (137)

In peace there is profundity.
From profundity the highest respect arises,
From respect come influence and command,
Therefore observe peace.

WISDOM

Wisdom allows for independent judgment: (138)

From wisdom one has a mind unshakable,
Non-reliance on others, firmness,
And is not deceived. Therefore,
O King, be intent on wisdom.

Wisdom depends upon the company one keeps, who, for rulers, are their counselors: (140)

Wisdom and practice always grow
For one who keeps company
With those who speak with advice,
Who are pure, and who have unstained wisdom and compassion.

Gyel-tsap marks off twelve stanzas in Chapter Three (265-76) as branches of the collection of wisdom. These practices promote the development of intelligence:

- respecting the doctrine and its proponents and offering presents to teachers
- reverently listening to the doctrine and imparting it to others, causing the growth of good qualities in others just as you wish for them in yourself
- not being satisfied with merely hearing doctrine but retaining and differentiating the meaning
- keeping away from nihilists' ideas
- not paying attention to worldly talk but being focused on the supramundane
- refraining from talking about others with evil intent
- not debating out of pride and, when debating, not attacking to the quick
- not praising your own good qualities but speaking of those even of enemies
- analyzing your own mistakes, rooting out your own faults, and causing others to do so
- looking on the harm that others do to you as created by your former deeds, thereby preventing anger at others which itself would cause more suffering in the future; instead of that, bearing suffering alone
- helping others without hope of reward
- sharing pleasures with beggars
- avoiding arrogance when prosperous and depression when poor
- always speaking truthfully even if it costs your life or power.

Nāgārjuna concludes that if the King follows this prescription for the development of wisdom he will become a supreme leader: (275)

> Always observe the discipline
> Of actions just as it has been explained.
> In that way, O glorious one, you will become
> The best of authoritative beings upon the earth.

The faculty of judgement is needed for each and every action, yielding independence: (276)

> You should always analyze well
> Everything before you act,
> And through seeing things correctly as they are
> Do not put full reliance on others.

RESPECT

Honoring those worthy of honor is one of the six epitomes of religious practice: (10)

> Not drinking intoxicants, a good livelihood,
> Non-harming, respectful giving,
> Honoring the honorable, and love—
> Practice in brief is that.

Paying respect involves serving parents and the principals of one's larger family (281) as well as revering religious teachers through offering goods and services and accomplishing what they teach (235). He chillingly adds that the King should not respect, revere, or pay homage to non-Buddhists since the ignorant "would become enamored of the faulty" (237). Although he never calls for persecution of non-Buddhists, it is clear that he seeks for the King to support only Buddhism within the context that its values promote social well-being. How such advice could be adapted to multi-cultural societies in the present day is an enigma yet to be worked out. In the last two centuries, experiments have been tried (1) in communist systems through putting the State above all else as an entity separate even from the people and (2) in capitalist systems through putting greed as the prime motivating factor. Both have failed due to not being based in humane values, but how socially beneficial attitudes can be taught separate from particular religions in public education remains a puzzle. Perhaps many of the principles that Nāgārjuna advocates, such as the six epitmoes just mentioned but stripped of any embeddedness in Buddhism, could contribute to public education and a more caring, multi-cultural society.

CHARACTER OF APPOINTEES

Nāgārjuna details the character traits of ministers, generals, and administrators: (328-29, 323-26)

> O Lord of Humans, since in this world nowadays
> Most are prone to wreak havoc on each other,
> Listen to how your governance
> And your practice should be.
>
> Let there always be around you many persons
> Old in experience, of good lineage,
> Knowing good policy, who shrink from ill deeds,
> Are agreeable, and know what should be done.

Appoint ministers who know good policy,
Who practice the doctrine, are civil,
Pure, harmonious, undaunted, of good lineage,
Of excellent ethics, and grateful.

Appoint generals who are generous,
Without attachments, brave, kindly,
Who use [the treasury] properly, are steadfast,
Always conscientious, and practice the doctrine.

As administrators appoint elders
Of religious disposition, pure, and able,
Who know what should be done, are skilled in the [royal] treatises,
Understand good policy, are unbiased, and are kindly.

Every month you should hear from them
About all the income and expenses,
And having heard, you yourself should tell them
All that should be done for the centers of doctrine and so forth.

Their counsel is to be followed only if it offers nourishment for the people: (255)

You should know full well [the counsel]
That your ministers offer,
And should always enact it
If it nurses the world.

Secret agents are to be used to report on conditions in the country so that the government may act in accordance with religious principles: (338)

In order to maintain control, oversee all the country
Through the eyes of agents.
Always conscientious and mindful,
Do what accords with the practices.

RESULTS OF PRINCIPLED RULE

Nāgārjuna warns that if the King's rule does not accord with religious practice—which by context is understood to be constituted by giving, ethics, patience, and compassion or the six perfections plus compassion—the result will be ruination: (327)

If your realm exists for the doctrine
And not for fame or desire,
Then it will be extremely fruitful.
If not, its fruit will be misfortune.

5 *The Vehicles*

HEARERS AND BODHISATTVAS BOTH REALIZE THE SUBTLEST EMPTINESS

Immediately after the analysis of pleasure and pain (346-66), Nāgārjuna declares that it is through realization built on such analysis that beings are liberated from the round of suffering. He thereby indicates that not only Great Vehicle practitioners but also Hearers (Lower Vehicle practitioners, namely, persons without special great compassion) must realize this type of emptiness to achieve liberation: (365)

> Knowing thus correctly, just as it is,
> That transmigrating beings do not exist in fact,
> One passes [from suffering] not subject [to rebirth and hence][55] without appropriating [rebirth],
> Like a fire without its cause.[a]

Further confirmation that both Hearers and Bodhisattvas perceive the same emptiness is found in the next two lines when he says that Bodhisattvas *also*[b] perceive such a reality: (366ab)

> Bodhisattvas also who have seen it thus,
> Seek perfect enlightenment with certainty.

Furthermore, in Chapter One he makes the point that as long as the mental and physical aggregates are misconceived to inherently exist, the I also is misconceived to have the same status, as a result of which there is karma due to which birth occurs: (35)

> As long as the aggregates are conceived,
> So long thereby does the conception of I exist.
> Further, when the conception of I exists,
> There is action, and from it there also is birth.

Thus it is necessary for both Hearers and Bodhisattvas to realize that all phenomena, not just persons, do not inherently exist.

Later he makes the same point by indicating that the extinction taught in the scriptures of Lower Vehicle tenet systems is the same as the absence of production taught in the Great Vehicle:[c] (386)

---

[a] For Ɗzong-ka-ɓa's extensive discussion of this topic, including stanzas 35-37, 365-366, and 386 of the *Precious Garland,* see Tsong-ka-pa, Kensur Lekden, and Jeffrey Hopkins, *Compassion in Tibetan Buddhism,* 150-171.

[b] *kyang, api.* The *zhol* reads *'ang.*

[c] It needs to be kept in mind that Nāgārjuna is not speaking about Lower Vehicle systems of tenets but about Lower Vehicle scriptures. He is calling the Lower Vehicle systems of tenets to recognize the subtle emptiness that is taught in their own scriptures.

> The absence of production taught in the Great Vehicle
> And the extinction of the others are in fact the same emptiness
> [Since they indicate] the non-existence of [inherently existent] production and the extinction [of inherent existence].
> Therefore let [the Great Vehicle] be allowed [as Buddha's word].

The meaning of this cryptic stanza is not readily apparent; therefore let us consult Ďzong-ka-ƃa's and Gyel-tsap's commentaries on it. Ďzong-ka-ƃa's explanation is multi-staged; first he gives a brief commentary that repeats the vocabulary of Nāgārjuna's stanza in an easy-to-understand format:[56]

> Just this meaning of the absence of inherent existence of phenomena is taught in the scriptural divisions of the Lower Vehicle. Nāgārjuna's *Precious Garland* (386) says:
>
> > The absence of production taught in the Great Vehicle
> > And the extinction of the others are in fact the same emptiness
> > [Since they indicate] the non-existence of [inherently existent] production and the extinction [of inherent existence].
> > Therefore let [the Great Vehicle] be allowed [as Buddha's word].
>
> Great Vehicle sūtras teach as emptiness the non-existence of inherently existent production, and when emptiness is taught in others, that is to say, in the sūtras of the Lower Vehicle, an extinction of compounded phenomena is taught. Hence the two teachings of emptiness are equivalent. Therefore, do not be impatient with the teaching of emptiness in the Great Vehicle.[a]

He proceeds to refute what for him is a crude explanation of Nāgārjuna's meaning. In that interpretation it is held that Nāgārjuna's point is merely that an absence of inherent existence is a basic requirement for something to become extinct. Ďzong-ka-ƃa draws the absurd conclusion that then any phenomenon, such as a sprout, and an emptiness of inherent existence would be equivalent. He does not explain why this is not acceptable but the reason is that a sprout is a compounded, positive phenomenon whereas an emptiness is an uncompounded, negative phenomenon.[b] He says:

> In what way do these two teachings have the same meaning? Some say, "Hearers assert an extinction of things, but if things inherently existed, then extinction would not be feasible. Consequently, when an extinction of things is asserted, it is necessary to assert an absence of inherent existence from the beginning. Therefore, these two have the same meaning."
>
> This is very incorrect. For, if such were so, then phenomena such as sprouts which the Proponents of the Middle assert to exist would have that reason [i.e., they are things that become extinguished]; and, therefore, it would absurdly follow that the two—everything such as sprouts

---

[a] As per Ďzong-ka-ƃa's explanation of this stanza, it should be translated:

> The teaching of emptiness in the Great Vehicle as the absence of production
> And others' [teaching of emptiness as] extinction are equivalent
> [Since they indicate] the non-existence of [inherently existent] production and the extinction [of inherent existence].
> Therefore let [the Great Vehicle] be allowed [as Buddha's word].

[b] It might seem odd that Ďzong-ka-ƃa is unwilling to hold that a sprout and its emptiness are equivalent since the *Heart Sūtra* says that emptiness is form and form is emptiness and since Chandrakīrti says that emptiness and dependent-arising are synonymous. However, Ďzong-ka-ƃa takes the first to mean that the *entity* of a form and its emptiness are the same and takes the latter to mean that an understanding of dependent-arising aids in understanding emptiness, and vice versa.

and so forth—and emptiness are equivalent.

Then he brushes off Ajitamitra's statement that the absence of production—that is to say, the emptiness of inherently existent production—and impermanence have the same meaning. Again he does not give his reason, but it likely is that if the emptiness of inherent existence meant impermanence, then even those following Lower Vehicle tenet systems would realize the subtlest emptiness since realization of impermanence would constitute realization of emptiness. From Ḏzong-ka-ƀa's point of view, Ajitamitra's interpretation is way off the mark; his reaction may suggest why his student, Gyel-tsap, wrote his own commentary on Nāgārjuna's text. He says:

> Also, Ajitamitra's *Commentary on the Precious Garland*[a] says that there is no difference in meaning at all between the absence of production and momentariness. However, this is the explanation of one who has not understood the meaning of [Nāgārjuna's] text.

Having refuted two misinterpretations, Ḏzong-ka-ƀa now gives his own reading, first utilizing Chandrakīrti's identification of a Lower Vehicle sūtra that teaches the type of extinction to which Nāgārjuna is referring. Although there are many Lower Vehicle scriptures that speak about a practitioner's achieving a state of release such that there will be no future suffering, what is required here is a passage that speaks about the extinction of the mental and physical aggregates *at present* while the practitioner is still alive, if "extinction" is somehow to have the same meaning as the absence of (inherently existent) production. Chandrakīrti cites such a sūtra passage in his *Commentary on (Nāgārjuna's) "Sixty Stanzas of Reasoning,"* but it takes some maneuvering to make it say what he wants. He has to split the passage into two parts—one referring to the extinction of present suffering or the present mental and physical aggregates and the other referring to the extinction of future suffering. The point is that since the first one refers to the extinction of present suffering or the present mental and physical aggregates, it does not refer to a cessation brought about by the path but to the natural extinction that these phenomena have always had and is seen when perceiving emptiness. Chandrakīrti justifies distinguishing between the two parts through pointing to the presence of the proximate term "these" in the first part but its absence in the second. Ḏzong-ka-ƀa continues:

> A Lower Vehicle sūtra quoted in Chandrakırti's *Commentary on (Nāgārjuna's) "Sixty Stanzas of Reasoning"* says:[b]
>
> > This which is complete abandonment of *these* sufferings, definite abandonment, purification, extinction, separation from desire, cessation, thorough pacification, disappearance, non-connection to other suffering, non-arising, and non-production is peace, this is auspiciousness. It is like this: the definite abandonment of all the aggregates, the extinction of cyclic existence, freedom from desire, cessation, nirvana.

Commenting on this, Chandrakīrti says that because the phrase "these sufferings" uses the proximate term "these," the passage "complete abandonment of these sufferings, definite abandonment, purification, extinction, separation from desire, cessation, thorough pacification, disappearance" refers only to the sufferings or aggregates that exist presently in one's own continuum. The passage "non-connection to other suffering, non-arising, and non-production is peace,

---

[a] Golden Reprint, vol. 183, 471.3.

[b] *rigs pa drug cu pa'i 'grel pa, yuktiṣaṣṭikāvṛtti;* Golden Reprint, vol. 113, 25.2.

this is auspiciousness. It is like this: the definite abandonment of all the aggregates, the extinction of cyclic existence, freedom from desire, cessation, nirvana" refers to future suffering.

Ḏzong-ka-ḇa next raises a hypothetical objection that no part of this sūtra passage is about primordial extinction but in its entirety is concerned with a nirvana attained by the path since "sufferings" and "aggregates" can be understood as referring to afflictive emotions. He responds that if the more general meaning is applicable, it should be utilized without resorting to a more exceptional meaning.

Objection: "Sufferings" and "aggregates" are general terms used here for their instances, the afflictive emotions [and thus the passage refers to the abandonment of the afflictive emotions by the path and does not refer to a primordial extinction of the aggregates].

Answer: This also is not feasible. Even though if general terms are not amenable to explanation with a general meaning, they must be explained as referring to their instances, here ["sufferings" and "aggregates"] are explicable in the context of [their] general [meaning].

Ḏzong-ka-ḇa concludes his presentation by identifying that "extinction" in this context refers to primordial extinction, which means that sufferings and the aggregates have from the start been without inherently existent production. Otherwise, extinction of the mental and physical aggregates would have to mean that through cultivation of the path the aggregates are totally abandoned, resulting in the absurdity that there would not be anyone left to actualize nirvana, or if there were someone, there could not be any nirvana.

Otherwise, in accordance with the Proponents of True Existence, it would not be fitting to explain [this sūtra passage] as primordial extinction in the sense that the aggregates have been primordially without inherently existent production as [the line] in Maitreya's *Sublime Continuum,*[a] "The afflictions are primordially extinguished," is explained. Rather, it must [incorrectly] be explained as a total abandonment [of the aggregates] by means of the path. If it is [explained this way, then there are the following faults]: When the nirvana that is to be actualized exists, the actualizer would not exist. Also, when the actualizer exists, the nirvana to be actualized would not exist because the aggregates would not have been extinguished. Thereby, they are unable to explain this sūtra.

According to us, it is permissible to explain extinction here in accordance with the statement:

> Extinction [in this case] is not [caused] by means of an antidote.
> It is so called because of primordial extinction.

Hence we are able to explain well the meaning of the sūtra [as referring to a natural or primordial absence of inherent existence in phenomena].

Therefore, the two:

---

[a] *Great Vehicle Treatise on the Sublime Continuum/ Treatise on the Later Scriptures of the Great Vehicle*, Chapter 1.15 (*theg pa chen po rgyud bla ma'i bstan bcos, mahāyānottaratantraśāstra;* P5525, vol. 108):

> Due to realizing the quiescent nature of transmigrating beings, [that is, all persons and phenomena]*
> They [perceive] the very mode [of being of phenomena],
> This being because of the natural thorough purity
> And because the afflictive emotions are extinguished from the start.

*From Asaṅga's commentary, P5526, vol. 108, 35.3.7.

- the teaching in sūtra of a nirvana that is a cessation of suffering upon having taught such a [primordial] extinction
- and the teaching of cessation in the sense of an absence of inherently existent production

are said by the Superior Nāgārjuna to be equivalent. Because his statement appears not to have been understood, I have explained it in detail.

Gyel-tsap summarizes Ḏzong-ka-ḇa's points but strangely refers to the sūtra passage as being a Great Vehicle scripture:[57]

A Great Vehicle scripture[a] cited in Chandrakīrti's *Commentary on (Nāgārjuna's) "Sixty Stanzas of Reasoning"* says:

> This which is complete abandonment of these sufferings, definite abandonment, purification, extinction, separation from desire, cessation, thorough pacification, disappearance, non-connection to other suffering, non-arising, and non-production is peace, this is auspiciousness. It is like this: the definite abandonment of all the aggregates, the extinction of cyclic existence, freedom from desire, cessation, nirvana.

And also a [Lower Vehicle] sūtra says:

> Births are extinct; pure behavior has been observed; what was to be done has been done; other than this, another worldly existence will not be known.

When Nāgārjuna condenses the meaning of these, he says in the *Sixty Stanzas of Reasoning*, "Just as a state of destructedness is known...." [In commentary, Chandrakīrti[b]] says that when [the state of] a Lower Vehicle Foe Destroyer is attained, the knowledge, "My births are extinct," definitely must be explained as meaning knowledge of the absence of inherently existent production because otherwise it would contradict the former sūtra.[c] [Chandrakīrti[58] says that] it would not be suitable to explain [the former sūtra passage] as just the extinction of births in the sense of making a connection to a later rebirth because, in reference to the absence of production even during the nirvana with remainder [that is to say, while still alive], the proximate term "these" is used and in terms of not being born in future lives it says, "non-connection to other suffering...nirvana."

Objection: The general term "these sufferings" is used here for their instances, whereby the thought is that all afflictive emotions are extinct and non-produced.

Answer: Even though if general terms are not amenable to explanation with a general meaning, they must be explained as referring to their instances, here there is not the slightest contradiction

---

[a] Notice that Ḏzong-ka-ḇa refers to the first sūtra passage as "a Lower Vehicle sūtra" whereas Gyel-tsap (62a.4; Guru Deva edition, *ka*, 469.3: *theg chen gyi sde snod*) calls it "a Great Vehicle scripture." Whether Gyel-tsap was correcting Ḏzong-ka-ḇa or whether he slipped up is yet to be determined; Jam-ȳang-shay-ḇa (*Great Exposition of Tenets, cha* 40a.2) refers to it as a "Hearer sūtra."

[b] Golden Reprint, vol. 113, 25.5. After quoting the former passage Chandrakīrti says:

> Therefore, here also the phrase [in the second passage], "Births are extinct," indicates the absence of production just like that [in the former passage]. It is definite that the phrase, "Other than this, another worldly existence will not be known," is in reference to future suffering.

[c] It is difficult to fathom the relevance of contradicting the former sūtra if that sūtra were indeed a "Great Vehicle scripture" as Gyel-tsap says.

in explaining ["these sufferings"] in a general context.

Therefore, the two:

- the teaching in the scriptures of the Great Vehicle of cessation in the sense of the absence of inherently existent production
- and the teaching in the scriptures of others—that is to say, in the scriptures that the Proponents of Hearer Vehicle tenets assert as the word [of Buddha]—of extinction, emptiness,

are the same as meaning the absence of production and extinction, that is to say, the absence of inherently existent production and the extinction of inherent existence, and knowing this [emptiness of inherent existence] is the same as knowing the absence of production and knowing extinction. Consequently, let [the fact] that the scriptures of the Great Vehicle are the word [of Buddha] be an object of your awareness. Therefore let [the Great Vehicle] be allowed [as Buddha's word].[a]

Nāgārjuna makes the appeal that those who are skeptical about Great Vehicle scriptures should consider them to be the word of Buddha since both the Hearer scriptures (although not as interpreted by the Hearer schools of tenets) and the Great Vehicle teach the same emptiness.

VALIDATING THE GREAT VEHICLE

Nāgārjuna shows that despite the similarity between the Lesser Vehicle and the Great Vehicle in their teaching of emptiness, they do differ in that Bodhisattvas remain in the world out of compassion: (366)

Bodhisattvas also who have seen it thus,
Seek perfect enlightenment with certainty.
They make the connection between lives
Until enlightenment only through their compassion.

Over the next thirty-two stanzas (367-98) he defends the Great Vehicle scriptures as the word of Buddha through an argument that mainly shows why the Great Vehicle is derided (367-79, 383) and the nature of the Great Vehicle itself (380-87, 390-93).

Why the Great Vehicle is derided. It is despised out of:

- a sense of inadequacy and antagonism born of bewilderment about the full extent of the paths and fruits taught in the Great Vehicle (367, 379, 383)
- not identifying the value of altruism and the harm from mere self-concern (368a)
- misidentifying altruism as harmful (368b)
- knowing that altruism is beneficial and harming others is bad but still despising altruism (368c, 369).

The results of deriding the doctrines of compassion as well as of emptiness are rebirths in bad transmigrations (370-71).

Nāgārjuna exhorts those who might be concerned about the hardships required in Great Vehicle practice to consider that undergoing difficulties now can avoid great pain later and relinquishing small

[a] Following Gyel-tsap's interpretation, it seems that the stanza should be translated this way:

The teaching in the Great Vehicle of the absence of production
And others' [teaching of] extinction, emptiness,
Are the same as meaning the absence of [inherently existent] production and the extinction [of inherent existence].
Therefore let [the Great Vehicle] be allowed [as Buddha's word].

pleasures now can bring great pleasure later (372-77). The implication is that some who deride the Great Vehicle cannot bear to contemplate its demands for long practice over eons of lives.

The nature of the Great Vehicle. What is described in Great Vehicle scriptures? Compassion and wisdom (378).[a] The six perfections and compassion are the epitome of the Great Vehicle; giving and ethics bring about other beings' welfare; one's own welfare is achieved through patience and effort; concentration and wisdom bring about liberation (379-80). The Great Vehicle also addresses the inconceivable good qualities of a Buddha (384-85), Nāgārjuna's suggestion being that some who deride it merely cannot accept the inconceivable great nature of a Buddha.

Thus when it is seen that the emptiness explained in the Great Vehicle is the same as the extinction described in Hearer scriptures and that the Great Vehicle has the special task of addressing the great nature of a Buddha and how to achieve it through the special practices of Bodhisattvas (390-93), it should be accepted that the Hearer Vehicle and Solitary Realizer Vehicle on the one hand and the Great Vehicle on the other are all the word of Buddha (387-88). Nāgārjuna makes the point that Buddha made certain teachings "with a special intention," such as sometimes teaching three final vehicles (thereby indicating that some beings never achieve Buddhahood) and sometimes teaching one final vehicle (thereby indicating that all beings eventually attain Buddhahood); since the purpose for this is difficult to understand, at minimum it would be best to remain neutral about the Great Vehicle scriptures (388-89).

Nāgārjuna's argument—built on an appeal to altruism, fear of the consequences of selfishness, chidings about willingness to accept hardship, similarity of teachings in the Lower Vehicle and the Great Vehicle, the special teachings of the Great Vehicle, and the mystery of Buddhahood—ends with a description of the series of teachings that a Buddha dispenses: (394-96)

> Just as a grammarian [first] has students
> Read a model of the alphabet,
> So Buddha taught trainees
> The doctrines that they could bear.
>
> To some he taught doctrines
> To turn them away from ill-deeds;
> To some, for the sake of achieving merit;
> To some, doctrines based on duality;
>
> To some, doctrines based on non-duality;
> To some what is profound and frightening to the fearful—
> Having an essence of emptiness and compassion—
> The means of achieving [unsurpassed] enlightenment.

As Gyel-tsap says:[59]

> Just as a grammarian first has students read a model of the alphabet, the Buddhas do not teach trainees from the very beginning doctrines that are difficult to realize. Rather, they teach the doctrines that they can bear as objects of their minds. The stages are as follows:

---

[a] For Ḏzong-ka-ƃa's brief discussion of 378 see Tsong-ka-pa, Kensur Lekden, and Jeffrey Hopkins, ***Compassion in Tibetan Buddhism,*** 114-115.

- to some they teach doctrines to turn them away from ill-deeds such as killing; this is so that these trainees who have the thought-patterns of beings of small capacity may achieve the ranks of gods or humans as fruits of their merit
- to some trainees who have the thought-patterns of beings of middle capacity they teach doctrines based on the duality of apprehended object and apprehending subject and that cyclic existence one-pointedly is to be abandoned and nirvana is one-pointedly to be adopted
- to some trainees they teach ultimately established consciousness empty of a difference in substantial entity between apprehended object and apprehending subject, thereby teaching to them [doctrine that is] not based on duality
- to some trainees of highest faculties, who will achieve the unsurpassed enlightenment, they teach [doctrine] that has an essence of emptiness—the profound mode of subsistence [of phenomena] frightening to the fearful who adhere to the true existence of things—and compassion.[a]

The suggestion is that it is out of a Buddha's omniscience that different modes of practice are taught.

From the beginning of the *Precious Garland* when Nāgārjuna pays homage to the Buddha as a being who has become freed from all defects and adorned with all good qualities to the end (497) when he calls on his listeners to free themselves from all defects and become adorned with all good qualities and thereby transform themselves into a sustenance for all beings, he interweaves advice for the development of compassion and the wisdom realizing emptiness. It is clear that far from being incompatible, the two are viewed as parts of a harmonious path to a state of supreme service for others.

[a] Gyel-tsap's interpretation of this highest level of the teaching (64a.6) finds little support in the Sanskrit syntax but conveys much of the intent.

Part Two: *Precious Garland of Advice for a King*

Sanskrit: *rājaparikathā-ratnamālā / ratnāvalī*

Tibetan: *rgyal po la gtam bya ba rin po che'i phreng ba / rin chen phreng ba*

By Nāgārjuna

As interpreted for the most part by Gyel-tsap Dar-ma-rin-chen

Translator's Remarks

Although I have consulted both the surviving Sanskrit portions of Nāgārjuna's text[a] and the sole Indian commentary, the *Extensive Explanation of (Nāgārjuna's) "Precious Garland"*[b] by Ajitamitra,[c] the translation mainly follows the lengthy commentary in Tibetan by Gyel-tsap Dar-ma-rin-chen, entitled *Illumination of the Essential Meanings of (Nāgārjuna's) "Precious Garland of Madhyamaka."*[d] In addition to a running interpretation of all five chapters,[e] Gyel-tsap breaks Nāgārjuna's text into a complicated series of sections and sub-sections in order to clarify shifts of topic and inter-relations of points. I have extracted this guide and placed it both beside the stanzas themselves and separately at the end as a table of contents. Most often, the guide provides crucial help in orienting comprehension but occasionally can seem tediously over-done due to fitting every stanza (and every line) into a patterned whole. However, the tedium is mitigated by appreciating the creative task of fabricating such a detailed outline.

---

[a] The Sanskrit survives for stanzas 1-77, 101-146c, 301-400, 401-455b, and 478d-500ab; for an excellent critical edition of the Sanskrit and the Tibetan translated by Jñānagarbha and Lu-gyel-tsen (*klu'i rgyal mtshan*) in the first half of the eighth century and revised by Kanakavarman and Ba-tsap Nyi-ma-drak (*pa tshab nyi ma grags*) in the eleventh century, as well as a copy of Paramārtha's Chinese translation, discussion of translations, and works in progress, see Michael Hahn, *Nāgārjuna's Ratnāvalī*, vol.1, The Basic Texts (Sanskrit, Tibetan, and Chinese), (Bonn: Indica et Tibetica Verlag, 1982). I used an edition of the Tibetan not found in a printed canon, published at the *zhol* Printing Press below the Potala in Hla-sa, as my basis, compared it to the Peking edition and Gyel-tsap's commentary, and constructed an improved *zhol* edition, given below, that also incorporates some of Gyel-tsap's preferences. As Hahn (20-22) says, the *zhol* edition is often preferable to these four canonical editions with respect to reflecting the Sanskrit, but a thorough-going analysis is yet to be done. In addition, the Sanskrit frequently differs from the Tibetan texts, and it would be most interesting once another edition of the Sanskrit is made available (rumored now to be stolen from Tibet and kept in Beijing) for analysis to be conducted as to whether the fact that the Tibetan revisers compared three Sanskrit editions could make the Tibetan more reliable in places than the present Sanskrit edition.

[b] *rin po che phreng ba'i rgya cher bshad pa, ratnāvaliṭīkā;* translated into Tibetan by Vidyākaraprabha and Bel-dzek (*zhu chen gyi lo tstsha ba dpal brtsegs*); Peking 5659, vol. 129, 183.2.4-201.4.6; Golden Reprint, vol. 183 (*nge*), 363-482. Of the 118 folios of Ajitamitra's commentary, Chapter 1 takes 67 folios (Golden Reprint, vol. 183, 364.3-431.6); Chapter 2, 25 folios (431.6-456.1); Chapter 3, 7 folios (456.1-463.2); Chapter 4, 10 folios (463.2-473.5); Chapter 5, 9 folios (473.5-482.5). From this, it is clear that Ajitamitra's focus was on the first Chapter with much less for the last four. See also Hahn, 18.

[c] *mi pham bshes gnyen.*

[d] *dbu ma rin chen 'phreng ba'i snying po'i don gsal bar byed pa,* Collected Works, *ka,* (lha sa: zhol par khang, 15th rab 'byung in the fire rooster year, i.e., 1897), 78 folios; also, Collected Works, *ka,* (New Delhi: Guru Deva, 1980), 349-504. In the translation, all references are to the 1897 edition except as noted. Leonard W. J. van der Kuijp ("Notes on the Transmission of Nagarjuna's Ratnavali in Tibet," *The Tibet Journal,* Summer 1985, vol. X, No. 2, 8) reports that the only other Tibetan commentary "listed in the indigenous bibliographies is the one written by Zhang Thang-sag-pa Ye-shes byung-gnas," and identifies it as MHTL no. 11345.

[e] Chapter 1 takes 21 folios (4a.3-25b.3); Chapter 2, 13 folios (25b.3-38a.5); Chapter 3, 11 folios (38a.5-49b.2); Chapter 4, 15 folios (49b.2-64b.5); Chapter 5, 12 folios (64b.5-76b.6). Gyel-tsap liberally borrows from Ajitamitra without attribution as is the frequent custom, somewhat like revising a textbook.

1 High Status and Definite Goodness

Homage to all Buddhas and Bodhisattvas.[a]

I. Introduction 1-2

A. Obeisance to and praise of Buddha 1

1 I bow down to the Omniscient,
Freed from all defects,
Adorned with all good qualities,
The sole friend of all beings.

B. Promise to compose the book 2

2 O King, I will explain practices solely virtuous
To generate in you the doctrine,
For the practices will be established
In a vessel of the excellent doctrine.

II. Actual book 3-487

A. Chapter One: Cause and effect of high status and definite goodness 3-100

1. Setting the scene 3-7

a. Order of the two doctrines 3

3 In one who first practices high status
Definite goodness arises later,
For having attained high status,
One comes gradually to definite goodness.

b. Identification of their causes and of them as effects 4

4 High status is considered to be happiness,
Definite goodness is liberation.
The quintessence of their means
Is briefly faith and wisdom.

c. Difference of main and secondary of the two causes 5

5 Due to having faith one relies on the practices,
Due to having wisdom one truly knows.
Of these two wisdom is the chief,
Faith is its prerequisite.

d. Characteristics of a trainee who is a vessel 6-7

6 One who does not neglect the practices
Through desire, hatred, fear, or bewilderment
Is known as one of faith,
A superior vessel for definite goodness.

7 Having analyzed well
All deeds of body, speech, and mind,
Those who realize what benefit self and others
And always perform these are wise.

[a] This is an obeisance by the translators from Sanskrit into Tibetan, whose names are listed in the colophon (p. 164).

2. Actual explanation of the causes and effects of high status and definite goodness 8-100

a. Cause and effect of high status 8-24

(1) Extensive exposition 8-24b

(a) Practices for high status 8-21

1' Sixteen practices for high status 8-10

a' Thirteen activities to be ceased 8-10b

1" Ceasing the ten non-virtues 8-9

8 Not killing, not stealing,
Forsaking the mates of others,
Refraining completely from false,
Divisive, harsh, and senseless speech,

9 Thoroughly forsaking covetousness, harmful intent,
And the views of Nihilists—
These are the ten gleaming paths of action;
Their opposites are dark.

2" Ceasing other improprieties 10ab

b' Three practices to engage in 10bc

c' Summation 10d

10 Not drinking intoxicants, a good livelihood,
Non-harming, respectful giving,
Honoring the honorable, and love—
Practice in brief is that.

2' Non-existence of those in other systems 11-13

a' Harming self and others through entering a bad path 11

11 Practice is not done by just
Mortifying the body,
For one has not forsaken injuring others
And is not helping others.

b' Persons who go on bad paths 12

12 Those not esteeming the great path of excellent doctrine
Bright with giving, ethics, and patience,
Afflict their bodies, taking
An aberrant path like a cow path [deceiving oneself and those following].[60]

c' Faults of entering a bad path 13

13 Their bodies embraced by the vicious snakes
Of the afflictive emotions, they enter for a long time
The dreadful jungle of cyclic existence
Among the trees of endless beings.

3' Fruits of wrongly engaging in those practices 14-19

a' Fruits concordant with non-virtuous causes, a short life, etc. 14-18b

14 A short life comes through killing.
Much suffering comes through harming.
Poor resources, through stealing.
Enemies, through adultery.

15 From lying arises slander.
From divisiveness, a parting of friends.
From harshness, hearing the unpleasant.
From senselessness, one's speech is not respected.

16 Covetousness destroys one's wishes,
Harmful intent yields fright,
Wrong views lead to bad views,
And drink to confusion of the mind.

17 Through not giving comes poverty,
Through wrong livelihood, deception,
Through arrogance, a bad lineage,
Through jealousy, little beauty.

18 A bad color comes through anger,
Stupidity, from not questioning the wise.
These are effects for humans,
But prior to all is a bad transmigration.[a]

b' Fructifications into a whole lifetime in a bad transmigration 18cd

c' Arising of fruits of virtue opposite from those 19

19 Opposite to the well-known
Fruits of these non-virtues
Is the arising of effects
Caused by all the virtues.

4' Virtuous and non-virtuous causes and effects 20-21

20 Desire, hatred, ignorance, and
The actions they generate are non-virtues.
Non-desire, non-hatred, non-ignorance,
And the actions they generate are virtues.

21 From non-virtues come all sufferings
And likewise all bad transmigrations,
From virtues, all happy transmigrations
And the pleasures of all lives.

(b) Modes of practice 22

22 Desisting from all non-virtues
And always engaging in virtues
With body, speech, and mind—
These are called the three[b] forms of practice.

(c) Fruits of practice 23-24b

23 Through these practices one is freed from becoming
A hell-being, hungry ghost, or animal.
Reborn as a human or god one gains
Extensive happiness, fortune, and dominion.

---

[a] The fruits previously described are effects within a human life that accord with the causes, but rebirth as an animal, hungry ghost, or hell-being will occur prior to these results as a human; Ajitamitra, Golden Reprint, vol. 183, 388.3.

[b] The *zhol* edition reads "three" (*gsum*), as does Gyel-tsap's commentary (367.2) which says:

> These are described as the **three** forms of practice of the three approaches [of body, speech, and mind] ('di ni sgo gsum gyis chos rnam pa **gsum** du bshad do).

The *sde dge* edition (214.6) has "two" (*gnyis*), as does the Peking (5658, vol. 129, 174.2.5) and Ajitamitra (Peking 5659, vol. 129, 187.2.8; *sde dge* 269.4). Since it is clear that Gyel-tsap used Ajitamitra's commentary, he must have been aware of the alternate reading.

24 Through the concentrations, immeasurables, and formlessnesses[a]
One experiences the bliss of Brahmā and so forth.
Thus in brief are the practices
For high status and their fruits.

(2) Summation 24cd

b. Cause and effect of definite goodness 25-100

(1) How definite goodness is described in sūtra 25-77

(a) Brief explanation of the Conqueror's description of definite goodness 25-27

1' How definite goodness is described 25

25 The doctrines of definite goodness
Are said by the Conquerors
To be deep, subtle, and frightening
To the childish, who are not learned.

2' Generation and non-generation of fear for the profound meaning by the ignorant and the wise 26

26 "I am not, I will not be.
I have not, I will not have,"
That frightens all the childish
And extinguishes fear in the wise.

3' The Teacher's saying that fear arises from conception of self 27

27 By him who speaks only to help beings,
It was said that all beings
Have arisen from the conception of I
And are enveloped with the conception of mine.

(b) Extensive explanation of definite goodness 28-74

1' Proving the conceptions of I and mine to be false 28-34

a' Actual proof 28-29

28 "The I exists, the mine exists."
These are wrong as ultimates,
For the two are not [established]
By a thorough consciousness of reality just as it is.

29 The mental and physical aggregates arise
From the conception of I which is false in fact.[b]
How could what is grown
From a false seed be true?

b' Attainment of liberation through abandoning these conceptions 30

30 Having seen thus the aggregates as untrue,
The conception of I is abandoned,
And due to abandoning the conception of I
The aggregates arise no more.

c' Teaching reality through the example of a reflection 31-33

1" Example for ceasing sufferings and their sources through realizing the person and aggregates as not truly existing 31-32

31 Just as it is said
That an image of one's face is seen

[a] These are the four concentrations (called the first, second, third, and fourth concentrations), the four immeasurables (love, compassion, joy, and equanimity), and the four formless absorptions (infinite space, infinite consciousness, nothingness, and peak of cyclic existence).

[b] "In fact" means "ultimately" or "as existing able to bear analysis." See stanza 35 for a description of how misconception of I leads to rebirth, that is to say, the arising of new mental and physical aggregates.

Depending on a mirror
But does not really exist [as a face],

32 So the conception of I exists
Dependent on the aggregates,
But like the image of one's face
The I does not at all really exist.[a]

2" The opposite example 33

33 Just as without depending on a mirror
The image of one's face is not seen,
So too the conception of I does not exist
Without depending on the aggregates.

d' Realization of emptiness as the cause of liberation 34

34 When the Superior Ānanda
Heard what this means,
He attained the eye of doctrine
And repeatedly spoke of it to monastics.

2' Refutation of inherently existent bondage and liberation 35-45

a' Order of entry into cyclic existence 35-36

1" Identifying the root of cyclic existence 35

35 As long as the aggregates are conceived,
So long thereby does the conception of I exist.
Further, when the conception of I exists,
There is action, and from it there also is birth.

2" Example for cyclic existence 36

36 With these three pathways[b] mutually causing each other
Without a beginning, a middle, or an end,
This wheel of cyclic existence
Turns like the wheel of a firebrand.[c]

b' Order of ceasing cyclic existence 37-38

37 Because this wheel is not obtained from self, other,
Or from both, in the past, the present, or the future,
The conception of I is overcome
And thereby action and rebirth.

38 One who sees how cause and effect
Are produced and destroyed
Does not regard the world
As really existent or really non-existent.

---

[a] "Really exist" is often taken in Ge-luk-ba scholarship to mean "as its own reality," that is to say, "to be established as its own mode of abiding" (*khyod khyod kyi gnas lugs su grub pa*).

[b] The three are afflictive emotions, actions, and production. From among the twelve links of dependent-arising, the first of these three—afflictive emotions—is identified as ignorance, attachment, and grasping. The second—actions—is identified as compositional action and "existence." The third—production—is identified as the other seven of the twelve links: consciousness, name and form, six sense fields, contact, feeling, birth, and aging and death.

[c] When a firebrand is twirled, it looks like a complete circle, or wheel, of fire.

c' Benefits of realizing emptiness 39

39 One who has heard thus the doctrine extinguishing
All suffering, but does not examine it
And fears the fearless state
Trembles due to ignorance.

d' Nature of liberation 40-45

1" Unsuitability of fearing the extinction of the conception of a self at the time of the nirvana without remainder 40

40 That all these will not exist in nirvana
Does not frighten you.[a]
Why does their non-existence
Explained here cause you fright?

2" Liberation as the extinction of all conceptions of true existence 41-42

a" Impossibility of an inherently existent non-thing as liberation 41

41 "In liberation there is no self and are no aggregates."
If liberation is asserted thus,
Why is the removal here of the self
And of the aggregates not liked by you?

b" Impossibility of a thing as liberation 42ab

42 If nirvana is not a non-thing,
Just how could it have thingness?

c" Meaning of liberation 42cd

The extinction of the misconception
Of things and non-things is called nirvana.

3" Difference between wrong and right views 43-44

43 In brief the view of nihilism
Is that effects of actions do not exist.
Without merit and leading to a bad state,
It is regarded as a "wrong view."

44 In brief the view of existence
Is that effects of actions exist.
Meritorious and conducive to happy transmigrations
It is regarded as a "right view."

4" Liberation as the extinction of the conception of true existence even during the nirvana with remainder 45

45 Because existence and non-existence are extinguished by wisdom,
There is a passage beyond meritorious and ill deeds.
This, say the excellent, is liberation from
Bad transmigrations and happy transmigrations.

[a] The referent of "you" is a practitioner of the Lesser Vehicle.

3' All phenomena as free of the extremes of permanence and annihilation 46-74

a' Extensive exposition 46-56

1" Refuting inherently existent cause and effect 46-47

a" Cause and effect as free of the extremes of existence and non-existence 46

46 Seeing production[a] as caused
One passes beyond non-existence.
Seeing cessation as caused
One also does not assert existence.

b" Refuting inherently existent cause and effect 47

47 Previously produced and simultaneously produced[b] [causes]
Are non-causes; [thus] there are no causes in fact,
Because [such] production is not confirmed at all
As [existing] conventionally or in reality.[c]

2" Avoiding contradiction with what is renowned in the world 48-49

48 When this is, that arises,
Like short when there is long.
Due to the production of this, that is produced,
Like light from the production of a flame.

49 When there is long, there is short.
They do not exist through their own nature,
Just as due to the non-production
Of a flame, light also does not arise.

3" Liberation through realizing the meaning of non-duality 50-51

50 Having thus seen that effects arise
From causes, one asserts what appears
In the conventions of the world
And does not accept nihilism.

51 One who asserts, just as it is, cessation
That does not arise from conventions
Does not pass into [a view of] existence.
Thereby one not relying on duality is liberated.[d]

---

[a] The production of suffering is caused by the conception of inherent existence; its cessation is caused by the path.

[b] Previous to and simultaneously with their effects.

[c] Production from previously existent causes and simultaneously existent causes does not occur in the conventions of the world nor does it exist in the face of an ultimate reasoning consciousness; see Ajitamitra, Golden Reprint, vol. 183, 403.4-403.6.

[d] According to Gyel-tsap's interpretation of this stanza (lha sa: zhol par khang, 15th rab 'byung in the fire rooster year, i.e., 1897, *ka* 16a.1-16a.4) it would read:

> One who asserts refutation [of inherently existent cause and effect]
> Does not pass into [a view of exaggerated] existence
> [As one would do by asserting] as real what does not arise from conventions;
> Thereby one not relying on duality is liberated.

It seems that Gyel-tsap resorts to this interpretation in order to avoid having to present the opinion that the ultimate does not conventionally exist.

4" Illustrative example 52-56

a" Example for realizing and not realizing the reality of things 52-53

52 A form seen from a distance
Is seen clearly by those nearby.
If a mirage were water,
Why is water not seen by those nearby?

53 The way this world is seen
As real by those afar
Is not so seen by those nearby
For whom it is signless like a mirage.

b" Refuting inherently existent aggregates 54

54 Just as a mirage is seemingly water
But not water and does not in fact exist [as water],
So the aggregates are seemingly a self
But not a self and do not exist in fact.[a]

c" No liberation from cyclic existence if views of existence and non-existence are not abandoned 55-56

55 Having thought a mirage to be water
And then having gone there,
Someone would just be stupid to surmise,
"That water does not exist."

56 One who conceives of the mirage-like world
That it does or does not exist
Is consequently ignorant.
When there is ignorance, one is not liberated.

b' Absence of the fallacy of thereby falling to the view of annihilation 57-60

1" Necessity of realizing non-duality to attain liberation 57

57 A follower of non-existence goes to bad transmigrations,
And a follower of existence goes to happy transmigrations.
Through correct and true knowledge
One does not rely on dualism and becomes liberated.

2" Flinging the absurd consequence that a realization of what is free of the extremes views existence and non-existence 58-59

58 If through correct and true knowledge
[Such wise persons] do not assert existence and non-existence
And thereby [you think] that they follow non-existence,
Why should they not be followers of existence?

59 If from refuting existence
Non-existence would accrue to them,

---

[a] Gyel-tsap (16b.2) comments:

> Just as the image of water in a mirage is in fact, that is to say, when analyzed, not water, so these aggregates are in fact not inherently existent because although they appear as if an inherently established self, they are not a self.

Why from refuting non-existence
Would existence not accrue to them?

3" Absence of the fault of annihilation in realizing the non-conceptual 60

60 They implicitly have no nihilistic thesis
And also have no nihilistic behavior
And due to relying on [the path to][a] enlightenment have no nihilistic thought.
Hence how can they be regarded as nihilists?

c' Freedom from extremes as an uncommon feature of Buddhism 61-62

61 Ask the Sāṃkhyas, the followers of Kaṇāda,[b] Nirgranthas,[c]
And the worldly proponents of a person and aggregates,[d]
Whether they propound
What passes beyond "is" and "is not."

62 Thereby know that the ambrosia
Of the Buddhas'[e] teaching is called profound,
An exclusive doctrine passing
Far beyond "is" and "is not."

d' Refuting inherently existent things 63-74

1" Refuting inherently existent going and coming 63-64

63 How could the world exist in fact,[f]
With a nature passed beyond the three times,[g]
Not going when disintegrating, not coming,
And not staying even for an instant?

64 Because the coming, going, and staying
Of the world and nirvana do not exist
As [their own] reality, what difference
Is there in fact[h] between the two?

2" Refuting inherently existent production, staying, and disintegration as characteristics of products 65

65 If, due to the non-existence of staying,
Production and cessation do not exist as [their own] reality,
How could production, staying,
And ceasing exist in fact?

[a] Gyel-tsap, 17a.6.

[b] The Vaisheṣhikas.

[c] The Jainas.

[d] Gyel-tsap (17b.3) identifies these as some Buddhist sects and non-Buddhist sects that assert a substantially existent person and/or substantially existent aggregates.

[e] Since it is a Sanskritic convention to use the plural as an honorific, this could refer only to Shākyamuni Buddha.

[f] I.e., ultimately.

[g] Past, present, and future.

[h] Ajitamitra (Golden Reprint, vol. 183, 411.6) glosses this as "ultimately" (*don dam par na*).

66 If always changing,
How are things non-momentary?
If not changing,
How can they be altered in fact?

3" Tangentially refuting the assertions of non-Buddhists 66-68

a" Refuting the Vaisheṣhikas' assertion of permanent atoms 66-67

67 Do they become momentary
Through partial or complete disintegration?
Because an inequality[a] is not apprehended,
This momentariness cannot be admitted either way.

68 If momentary, then it becomes entirely non-existent;
Hence how could it be old?
Also if non-momentary, it is constant;
Hence how could it be old?

b" Refuting the Vaiṣhṇavas' assertion of a permanent person 68

69 Just as a moment has an end, so a beginning
And a middle must be considered.
Thus due to this triple nature of a moment,
There is no momentary abiding of the world.

4" Refuting inherently existent moments 69-74

a" All moments as having parts 69

70 Also the beginning, middle, and end
Are to be analyzed like a moment.
Therefore beginning, middle, and end
Are also not [produced][61] from self or other.

b" Refuting inherent existence of what has parts 70

71 Due to having many parts there is no unity,
There is not anything without parts.
Further, without one, there is not many.
Also, without existence there is no non-existence.

c" Refuting inherently existent things through the reason of their not being one or many 71-73b

72 If it is thought that through disintegration or an antidote
An existent becomes non-existent,
Then how without an existent
Could there be disintegration or an antidote?

73 Hence, in fact there is no disappearance
Of the world through nirvana.
Asked whether the world has an end
The Conqueror remained silent.

d" Reason for not holding the world as having an end 73c-74

[a] It is not seen that only part of a thing changes. Also, if a particle changed completely, it could not be said, as the Vaisheṣhikas do, that it is permanent but its states are impermanent.

74 Because he did not teach this profound doctrine
To worldly beings who were not receptacles,
The All-Knowing is therefore known
By the wise to be omniscient.

(c) Summation 75-77

1' Conquerors' descriptions of the profound 75

75 Thus the doctrine of definite goodness
Was taught by the perfect Buddhas,
The seers of reality, as profound,
Unapprehendable, and baseless.[a]

2' Faults of fearing the profound 76-77b

76 Frightened by this baseless doctrine,
Delighting in a base, not passing
Beyond existence and non-existence,
Unintelligent beings ruin themselves.

77 Afraid of the fearless abode,
Ruined, they ruin others.

3' Exhorting the king to realize the profound 77cd

O King, act in such a way
That the ruined do not ruin you.

(2) Exhorting the king to train in the profound 78-100

(a) Setting the scene 78-79

78 O King, lest you be ruined
I will explain through the scriptures
The mode of the supramundane, just as it is,
The reality not partaking of dualism.

79 This profundity endowed with meanings drawn [from scriptures][b]
And beyond ill-deeds and meritorious deeds
Has not been tasted by those who fear the baseless—
The others—the Forders[c]—and even by our own.[d]

(b) Two selflessnesses 80-100

1' Selflessness of persons 80-82

a' Unsuitability of the six constituents as the person 80-81

80 A person is not earth, not water,
Not fire, not wind, not space,
Not consciousness, and not all of them.
What person is there other than these?

---

[a] "Baseless" means not providing a base for the conception that things inherently exist.

[b] Following Gyel-tsap, 21a.4: *'khor ba'i rgyu gyur pa'i sdig dang bsod nams bya ba las 'das pa'i zab mo gsung rab las* ***bkrol*** *ba'i don dang ldan pa.* For an extensive discussion of whether 79b should read *bkrol* or *bkol* see van der Kuijp, "Notes on the Transmission of Nagarjuna's Ratnavali in Tibet," *The Tibet Journal,* Summer 1985, vol. X, No. 2, 76; van der Kuijp settles on *bkrol.* My translation was prompted by Dunne and McClintock's "derived (from the scriptures)."

[c] "Forders" (*mu stegs, tīrthika*) are non-Buddhists who propound and follow a path, or ford, to liberation or high status.

[d] "Our own" refers to those following lower systems of Buddhist tenets.

81 Just as a person is not real
Due to being a composite of six constituents,
So each of the constituents also
Is not real due to being a composite.

b' Refuting an inherently existent person through a fivefold analysis 82

82 The aggregates are not the self, they are not in it,
It is not in them, without them it is not,
It is not mixed with the aggregates like fire and fuel.[a]
Therefore how could the self exist?

2' Selflessness of other phenomena 83-100
a' Refuting an inherently existent form aggregate 83-99
1" Refuting inherently existent dependent-arisings 83-90
a" Their not being established as one or many 83

83 The three elements[b] are not earth, they are not in it,
It is not in them, without them it is not;
Since this also applies to each,
The elements, like the self, are false.

b" Therefore the elements are not inherently existent 84

84 Earth, water, fire, and wind
Individually also do not inherently exist.
When any three are absent, an individual one does not exist.
When one is absent, the three also do not exist.

c" Absence of inherent existence of composites 85-87
1: Contradiction of inherent existence and dependence of composites 85

85 If when three are absent, an individual one does not exist
And if when one is absent, the three also do not exist,
Then each itself does not exist.
How could a composite be produced?

2: Refuting an answer to that 86

86 Otherwise, if each itself exists,
Why without fuel is there no fire?
Likewise why is there no water, wind, or earth
Without motility, obstructiveness, or cohesion?[c]

[a] According to Ajitamitra (Golden Reprint, vol. 183, 423.2) this means that if the aggregates and the self were mingled like fire and fuel, then they could not be distinguished, as is the case with a mixture of water and milk. According to Gyel-tsap (22b.2), this means that the aggregates and the self are not inexpressible as either one or different because all phenomena are either one or different.

[b] Water, fire, and wind; or cohesion, maturing, and motility.

[c] There absurdly would be water without motility, obstructiveness, or maturation. There absurdly would be wind without obstructiveness, maturation, or cohesion. There absurdly would be earth without motility, maturation, and cohesion.

3: Dispelling further debate 87

87 If [it is answered that] fire is well known [not to exist without fuel but the other three elements exist by way of their own entities],
How could your three exist in themselves
Without the others? It is impossible for the three
Not to accord with dependent-arising.

d" Refuting proofs for inherent existence 88-90

88 How could those—that themselves
Exist individually—be mutually dependent?
How could those—that do not themselves
Exist individually—be mutually dependent?

89 If it is the case that they do not themselves exist individually,
But where there is one, the other three exist,
Then if unmixed, they are not in one place,
And if mixed, they do not themselves exist individually.

90 The elements do not themselves exist individually,
So how could their own individual characters[a] exist?
What do not themselves individually exist cannot predominate.[b]
Their characters are regarded as conventionalities.

2" Refuting inherent existence of evolutes of the elements 91ab

91 This mode [of refutation] is also to be applied
To colors, odors, tastes, and objects of touch;

3" Applying the refutation to other phenomena 91c-98

a" Actual application 91c-92

Eye, consciousness, and form;[c]
Ignorance, action, and birth;

92 Agent, object, and action,
Number, possession, cause and effect,

---

[a] In Tibetan scholastic literature the characters of the four elements are:
earth—that which is hard and obstructive
water—that which is wet and moistening
fire—that which is hot and burning
wind—that which is light and moving.

[b] The potencies of the four elements are said to be present in everything; the predominance of one element over the others determines what is manifested, but if they do individually exist, how could one predominate?

[c] These three are the visual sense organ, the visual consciousness, and the form (color and shape) seen by the visual consciousness.

Time, short and long, and so forth,
Name and name-bearer as well.

b" Sources for the emptiness of inherent existence 93-98
1: All phenomena as empty of inherent existence 93

93 Earth, water, fire, and wind,
Long and short, subtle and coarse,
As well as virtue and so forth are said by the Subduer
To be ceased in the consciousness [of reality].

2: Explanation 94-95

94 Earth, water, fire, and wind
Do not have a chance[a]
In the face of that undemonstrable consciousness
Complete lord over the limitless.

95 Here[b] long and short, subtle and coarse,
Virtue and non-virtue,
And here names and forms
All are ceased.

3: Stating proofs 96-97

96 All those that earlier appeared to consciousness
Because of not knowing that [reality][c]
Will later cease for consciousness[d] in that way
Because of knowing that [reality].

97 All these phenomena of beings
Are seen as fuel for the fire of consciousness.
They are pacified through being burned
By the light of true discrimination.

4: No fault of falling to a view of annihilation 98

98 The reality is later ascertained
Of what was formerly imputed by ignorance.[e]

---

[a] Gyel-tsap (24b.1) takes this as meaning to that consciousness "earth, water, fire, and wind do not find a location in the face of its perception" (*sa dang chu dang me dang ni rlung gis khyod kyi gzigs ngor gnas thob par 'gyur ba min*). The *zhol* edition reads *rlung gi gnas **mthong** 'gyur ma yin;* Hahn (37) reads *rlung **gis** gnas **thod** 'gyur ma yin* which is confirmed by Ajitamitra (Golden Reprint, vol. 183, 430.1) who then glosses it with *gnas skabs rnyed par mi 'gyur ro*.

[b] "Here" means "in the face of meditative equipoise directly realizing emptiness."

[c] Gyel-tsap (24b.3) identifies what is not known as "the primordially existent absence of inherently existent production" (*gdod nas grub pa'i rang bzhin gyis skye ba med pa'i don*).

[d] Gyel-tsap (24b.5) glosses "for consciousness" with "in the face of perception by a Superior's meditative equipoise" (*'phags pa'i mnyam gzhag gi gzigs ngor*).

[e] The translation of these lines follows the Tibetan as well as Gyel-tsap's commentary (25a.2):

Objection: Since in that case you have asserted that everything does not exist, you become a Nihilist.

Answer: Not so. Afflictive ignorance previously imputed inherent existence where there is no inherent existence, and later upon having delineated the emptiness of inherent existence, one ascertains suchness and realizes the mode of abiding of things, but there is no fallacy of deprecating things even in the slightest.

When a thing is not found,
How can there be a non-thing?

4" Refuting inherently existent space 99

99 Because the phenomena of forms
Are only names,[a] space too is only a name.
Without the elements how could forms exist?
Therefore even name-only does not exist.

b' Applying the refutation to the remaining aggregates 100

100 Feelings, discriminations, compositional
factors,
And consciousnesses are to be considered
Like the elements and the self.
Thereby the six constituents[b] are selfless.

The first chapter of the *Precious Garland*, An Indication of High Status and Definite Goodness, is finished.

---

[a] *gzugs kyi dngos po ming tsam phyir.* Chandrakīrti's citation of this in his *Prasannapadā* has a different reading, "because of being just the non-existence of form" (*rūpasyābhāvamātratvād*). This reading is not reflected in any of the Tibetan texts, either of the *Ratnāvalī* or of the *Prasannapadā* (Tibetan Cultural Printing Press, 346.6) or in their commentaries. Though both readings make sense, I am following the Tibetan because it was checked against three Sanskrit editions and here I am seeking to present a translation of the *Precious Garland* in the light of Gyel-tsap's commentary (25.5).

"Only name" means "merely nominally existent," the word "merely" eliminating that phenomena are established by way of their own character. In Ge-luk-ɓa scholastic literature it is said that "only name" does not mean "merely sounds" even though names are sounds, since otherwise the only phenomena that would exist would be sounds.

[b] The constituents are earth, water, fire, wind, space, and consciousness, which are the basis in dependence upon which a self is imputed.

2 THE INTERWOVEN

101 Just as when a banana tree
With all its parts is torn apart, there is nothing,
So when a person having the [six] constituents
Is divided, it is the same.

102 Therefore the Conquerors said,
"All phenomena are selfless."
Since this is so, all six constituents
Have been delineated as selfless for you.

103 Thus neither self nor non-self
Are to be apprehended as real.
Therefore the Great Subduer rejected
Views of self and of non-self.

104 Sights, sounds, and so forth were said by the Subduer
Not to be true and not to be false.
If from one position its opposite arises,
Both do not exist in fact.[a]

105 Thus ultimately this world
Is beyond truth and falsity.
Therefore the Subduer does not assert
That it really exists or does not.

106 [Knowing that] these in all ways do not exist,
How could the All-Knower say
They have limits or no limits,
Or have both or neither?

107 "Innumerable Buddhas have come,
And likewise will come and are here at present.
There are zillions of sentient beings,
And in addition the Buddhas intend to abide in the three times.

B. Chapter Two: Interwoven explanation of the cause and effect of definite goodness and high status

1. Cause and effect of definite goodness 101-23

a. Refuting extreme views 101-15

(1) Recalling the former explanation through another example 101

(2) Actual refutation of extreme views 102-14

(a) Absence of inherent existence of self and selflessness 102-3

(b) Absence of inherent existence of existents and non-existents 104-6

1' Actual explanation 104-5

2' Reason for not answering in any of the four extremes 106

(c) Dispelling an objection that not teaching an end to cyclic existence is wrong 107-14

1' Objection 107-8

[a] It has already been established that there are no inherently existent things and no inherently existent trueness; thus, there are no inherently existent non-things and no inherently existent falseness, because the latter exist only in relation to the former.

108 "The extinguishing of the world in the three
Times does not cause it to increase,
Then why was the All-Knower silent
About the limits of the world?"[a]

2' Answer 109-14

a' Example for the absence of inherent existence of the world's production and cessation 109-11

1" The profound as what is secret for non-receptacles 109

109 That which is secret for a common being
Is the profound doctrine,
The world as like an illusion,
The ambrosia of the Buddhas' teaching.

2" Actual example 110-11

110 Just as the production and disintegration
Of an illusory elephant are seen,
But the production and disintegration
Do not really exist,

111 So the production and disintegration
Of the illusion-like world are seen,
But the production and disintegration
Do not ultimately exist.

b' Example for the absence of inherent existence of going and coming 112-13

112 Just as an illusory elephant,
Being only a bewildering of consciousness,
Does not come from anywhere,
Nor go anywhere, nor really stay,

113 So the illusion-like world,
Being only a bewildering of consciousness,
Does not come from anywhere,
Nor go anywhere, nor really stay.

c' Things are only nominally imputed 114

114 Thus it has a nature beyond the three times.
Other than as the imputation of a convention
What world is there in fact
Which would exist or not?

(3) Therefore the four extremes were not taught 115

115 For this reason the Buddha,
Except for keeping silent, said nothing
About the fourfold format: having or
Not having a limit, both, or neither.[b]

---

[a] An objector wonders, "Innumerable Buddhas are effecting the liberation of even more sentient beings; there are no new sentient beings; thus in time all would be liberated. Since, of course, such extinguishing, or liberating, of worldly beings does not increase the number of beings, the world must eventually have an end. Thus, why did Buddha remain silent about an end to the world?"

[b] The first extreme of the world's having limits is propounded by the Dialectician Nihilists who say that the self is finished at the end of this life and does not go on to a future life. The second extreme of the world's not having limits is propounded by the Sāṃkhyas who say that the very self of this life goes to the next life. The third extreme of the world's both having and not having limits is propounded by the Jainas who say that the states of the self have limits but the nature of the self has no limits. The fourth extreme of the world's neither having nor not having limits is propounded by the Buddhist Proponents of a Self

b. Difficulty of realizing the profound 116-23

(1) Reason for the difficulty of realizing the profound 116-17

116 When the body, which is unclean,
Coarse, and an object of the senses,
Does not stay in the mind [as having a nature of uncleanliness and pain]
Although it is continually in view,

117 Then how could this doctrine
Which is most subtle, profound,
Baseless, and not manifest,
Easily appear to the mind?

(2) Reason why Buddha did not explain the profound to non-receptacles 118

118 Realizing that because of its profundity
This doctrine is difficult for beings to understand,
The Subduer, having become enlightened
[At first] turned away from teaching doctrine.[a]

(3) Explaining the reason 119-23

(a) Faults of misconceiving the profound 119-20

119 This doctrine wrongly understood
Causes the unwise[b] to be ruined
Because they sink into the uncleanliness
Of nihilistic views.

120 Further, the stupid who fancy
Themselves wise,[c] having a nature
Ruined by rejecting [emptiness], go headfirst
To a terrible hell due to their wrong understanding.

(b) Example for the defects of misconception and the good qualities of correct conception 121-22

121 Just as one comes to ruin
Through wrong eating but obtains
Long life, freedom from disease,
Strength, and pleasures through right eating,

122 So one comes to ruin
Through wrong understanding
But obtains bliss and highest enlightenment
Through right understanding.

(c) Advice to be conscientious about realizing the profound 123

123 Therefore having forsaken with respect to this [doctrine of emptiness]
Nihilistic views and rejection,

(*gang zag yod par smra ba, pudgalavādin*) who say that there is a real self that is utterly unpredicable as being either permanent or impermanent.

[a] His initial display of reluctance to teach is considered to be his first teaching—pointing to the profundity of what he realized and its difficulty of realization.

[b] Those who accept emptiness but take it to mean nothingness thereby turn away from the practice of virtue and the overcoming of non-virtuous activities.

[c] These are those who take emptiness to mean a denial of cause and effect and therefore reject emptiness.

Be supremely intent on correct understanding
For the sake of achieving all aims.

2. Cause and effect of high status 124-74b

a. Setting the scene 124-25

(1) Travelling in cyclic existence due to not realizing emptiness 124

124 If this doctrine is not understood thoroughly,
The conception of an I prevails,
Hence come virtuous and non-virtuous actions
Which give rise to good and bad rebirths.

(2) Advice to strive for high status as long as emptiness is not realized 125

125 Therefore, as long as the doctrine removing
The conception of I is not known,
Take heed of the practices
Of giving, ethics, and patience.

b. Actual explanation of the cause and effect of high status 126-74b

(1) Achieving the causes for high status 126-43

(a) General exhortation to practice the causes for high status 126-32

1' Practicing causes having five benefits 126-27

126 A Lord of the Earth who performs actions
With their prior, intermediary,
And final practices
Is not harmed here or in the future.

127 Through the practices there are fame and happiness here,
There is no fear now or at the point of death,
In the next life happiness flourishes,
Therefore always observe the practices.

2' Practice is the best policy 128

128 The practices are the best policy,
It is through them that the world is pleased;
Neither here nor in the future is one cheated
By a world that has been pleased.

3' Forsaking bad policies 129-32

a' Unsuitability of relying on bad treatises 129

129 The world is displeased
By the policies of non-practice.
Due to the displeasure of the world
One is not pleased here or in the future.

b' Scorning reliance on bad treatises 130-31

130 How could those with senseless deviant minds
On a path to bad transmigrations,
Wretched, intent on deceiving others,
Have understood what is meaningful?

131 How could those intent on deceiving others
Be persons of policy?
Through it they themselves will be cheated
In many thousands of births.

c' Special policy for practice 132

132 Even if you seek to harm an enemy,
You should remove your own defects and cultivate good qualities.
Through that you will help yourself,
And the enemy will be displeased.

133 You should cause the assembling
Of the religious and the worldly
Through giving, speaking pleasantly,
Purposeful behavior, and concordant behavior.[a]

(b) Training in the special causes of high status 133-43

1' Training in the four ways of assembling students 133

134 Just as by themselves the true words
Of kings generate firm trust,
So their false words are the best means
To create distrust.

2' Training in the four: speaking truth, generosity, peace, and wisdom 134-39

a' The four individually 134-38

1" Training in truth 134-35

135 What is not deceitful is the truth;
It is not an intentional fabrication.
What is solely helpful to others is the truth.[b]
The opposite is falsehood since it does not help.

136 Just as a single splendid charity
Conceals the faults of kings,
So avarice destroys
All their wealth.

2" Training in giving 136

137 In peace there is profundity.
From profundity the highest respect arises,
From respect come influence and command,
Therefore observe peace.

3" Training in peace 137

138 From wisdom one has a mind unshakable,
Non-reliance on others, firmness,
And is not deceived. Therefore,
O King, be intent on wisdom.

4" Training in wisdom 138

139 A lord of humanity having the four goodnesses—
Truth, generosity, peace, and wisdom—
Is praised by gods and humans
As are the four good practices themselves.

b' Summation 139

140 Wisdom and practice always grow
For one who keeps company
With those who speak advisedly,
Who are pure,[c] and who have unstained wisdom and compassion.

3' Relying on special associates who cause increase of virtue 140-43

a' Characteristics of special associates 140

---

[a] "Giving" means to give material things; "speaking pleasantly" is to converse on the topics of high status and definite goodness; "purposeful behavior" is to cause others to practice what is beneficial; "concordant behavior" is for one to practice what one teaches others.

[b] For discussion of this stanza, see p. 80.

[c] Gyel-tsap (31b.3) describes purity as having few desires and knowing satisfaction and (thus) pure intention.

b' Suitability of following special associates 141-42

141 Rare are helpful speakers,
Listeners are very rare,
But rarer still are those who act at once
On words that though unpleasant are
beneficial.

142 Therefore having realized that though
unpleasant
It is helpful, act on it quickly,
Just as to cure an illness one drinks
Dreadful medicine from one who cares.[62]

c' Continuously meditating on the imminence of death 143

143 Always considering the impermanence
Of life, health, and dominion,
You thereby will make intense effort
Solely at the practices.

(2) Forsaking the causes of bad transmigrations 144-73

(a) Brief explanation 144-45

144 Seeing that death is certain
And that, having died, you suffer from ill
deeds,
You should not commit ill deeds
Though there might be temporary pleasure.

145 Sometimes no horror is seen
And sometimes it is.
If there is comfort in one,
Why do you have no fear for the other?[a]

(b) Extensive explanation 146-73

1' Stopping attachment to intoxicants 146

146 Intoxicants lead to worldly scorn,
Your affairs are ruined, wealth is wasted,
The unsuitable is done from delusion,
Therefore always avoid intoxicants.

2' Stopping attachment to gambling 147

147 Gambling causes avarice,
Unpleasantness,[b] hatred, deception, cheating,
Wildness, lying, senseless talk, and harsh
speech,
Therefore always avoid gambling.

3' Stopping attachment to women 148-70

a' General refutation of the cleanliness of a woman's body 148

148 Lust for a woman[c] mostly comes
From thinking that her body is clean,

[a] Sometimes the horrible effects of a bad deed are not seen until the next life, and sometimes they are seen in this life. If comfort is taken because the effects are not seen, why is fear of those actions not generated when the effects are seen?

[b] Gyel-tsap (32b.2) identifies this as due to the discomfort of wondering whether one will win or not.

[c] Since Nāgārjuna is speaking to a heterosexual man, he speaks about a woman's body; but as he says later, this same message is to be applied to the male body.

But there is nothing clean
In a woman's body in fact.

149 The mouth is a vessel of foul saliva
And scum between the teeth,
The nose a vessel of snot, slime, and mucus,
The eyes are vessels of tears and other
excretions.

b' Specific refutation of the cleanliness of a woman's body 149-69

1" Refuting that a woman's parts are beautiful 149-54

a" Unsuitability of attachment to a woman's body because of its only having a nature of the unclean 149-50

150 The abdomen and chest is a vessel
Of feces, urine, lungs, liver, and so forth.
Those who through obscuration do not see
A woman this way, lust for her body.

b" Example 151

151 Just as some fools desire
An ornamented pot filled with what is unclean,
So ignorant, obscured
Worldly beings desire women.[a]

c" Absence of the state of desirelessness if attached to women 152

152 If the world is greatly attached
Even to this ever-so-smelly body
Which should cause loss of attachment,
How can it be led to freedom from desire?

d" Though a woman's body is unclean, the stupid call it a cause of pleasure 153-54

153 Just as pigs are greatly attached
To a site of excrement, urine, and vomit,
So some lustful ones desire
A site of excrement, urine, and vomit.

154 This city of a body with protruding holes
From which impurities emerge
Is called an object of pleasure
By beings who are stupid.

2" Refuting that the whole body is beautiful 155-68

a" Stopping attachment to a woman's body in general 155-57

155 Once you yourself have seen the impurities
Of excrement, urine, and so forth,
How could you be attracted
To a body composed of those?

156 Why should you lust desirously for this
While recognizing it as an unclean form
Produced by a seed whose essence is impure,
A mixture of blood and semen?

157 One who lies on this impure mass
Covered by skin moistened

[a] Hahn (61) identifies this stanza as a spurious addition in the Tibetan; indeed, if it is, it would explain why the chapter has an extra stanza.

With those fluids, merely lies
On top of a woman's bladder.

b" Stopping attachment to its color and shape 158-65b
1: Stopping attachment to the color and shape of a woman's body in general 158

158 If whether beautiful or ugly,
Whether old or young,
All female bodies are unclean,
From what attribute does your lust arise?

2: Stopping attachment to a beautiful body 159-63
a: Unsuitability of attachment 159-61

159 Just as it is not fit to desire
Filth although it has a good color,
Is very fresh, and has a nice shape,
So is it with a woman's body.

160 How could the nature of this putrid corpse,
A rotten mass covered outside by skin,
Not be seen when it looks
So very horrible?

161 "The skin is not foul,
It is like a garment."
Like a hide over a mass of impurities
How could it be clean?

b: Suitability of disgust 162-63

162 A pot though beautiful outside,
Is reviled when filled with impurities.
Why is the body, filled with impurities
And foul by nature, not reviled?

163 If you revile against impurities,
Why not against this body
Which befouls clean scents,
Garlands, food, and drink?

3: Thinking that one's own body, like a woman's, is unclean 164-65b

164 Just as one's own or others'
Impurities are reviled,
Why not revile against one's own
And others' unclean bodies?

165 Since your own body is
As unclean as a woman's,
Is it not suitable to part
From desire for self and other?

c" Consequent unsuitability of attachment to a woman's body 165c-66

166 If you yourself wash this body
Dripping from the nine wounds[a]
And still do not think it unclean,
What use is [religious] instruction for you?

[a] The nine orifices are eyes, ears, nostrils, mouth, genitalia, and anus.

d" Chiding persons who praise women 167-68

167 Whoever composes poetry
With metaphors elevating this body—
O how shameless! O how stupid!
How embarrassing before [wise][63] beings!

168 Moreover, these sentient beings—
Obscured by the darkness of ignorance—
Quarrel most over what they desire,
Like dogs for the sake of some dirty thing.

3" Refuting that attachment to a woman is a cause of happiness 169

169 There is pleasure when a sore is scratched,
But to be without sores is more pleasurable
still.
Just so, there are pleasures in worldly desires,
But to be without desires is more pleasurable
still.

c' Effect of meditating on uncleanliness 170

170 If you analyze thus, even though
You do not achieve freedom from desire,
Because your desire has lessened
You will not lust for women.

4' Stopping hunting 171-73

a' Forsaking killing 171

171 To hunt game is a horrible
Cause of short life,
Fear, suffering, and hell,
Therefore always steadfastly keep from killing.

b' Forsaking generating fear in others 172

172 Those who frighten embodied beings
When they encounter them are malevolent
Like a snake spitting poison,
Its body completely stained with impurity.

c' Generating pleasure in others 173

173 Just as farmers are gladdened
When a great rain-cloud gathers,
So those who gladden embodied beings
When encountering them are beneficent.

(3) Summary: Abandoning non-practices and achieving the practices 174ab

174 Thus observe the practices incessantly
And abandon those counter to them.

3. Cause and effect of definite goodness 174c-200

a. Condensing the principal causes of highest enlightenment into three and training in them 174c-75

If you and the world wish to attain
Unparalleled enlightenment,

175 Its roots are the altruistic aspiration to
enlightenment
Firm like the monarch of mountains,
Compassion reaching to all quarters,
And wisdom not relying on duality.

b. Training in the causes for achieving the thirty-two signs of a Buddha 176-96

(1) Exhortation to listen 176

176 O great King, listen to how
Your body will be adorned
With the thirty-two signs
Of a great being.

(2) Actual explanation of the thirty-two marks of a Buddha 177-96

177 Through proper honoring of stūpas,[a]
Honorable beings, Superiors, and the elderly
You will become a Universal Monarch,
Your glorious hands and feet marked with [a design of] wheels.

178 O King, always maintain firmly
What you have vowed about the practices,
You will then become a Bodhisattva
With feet that are very level.

179 Through giving, speaking pleasantly,
Purposeful behavior, and concordant behavior[b]
You will have hands with glorious
Fingers joined by webs [of light].

180 Through abundant giving
Of the best food and drink
Your glorious hands and feet will be soft;
Your hands, feet, shoulder blades,
And the nape of your neck will broaden,
So your body will be large and those seven areas broad.

181 Through never doing harm and freeing the condemned
Your body will be beautiful, straight, and large,
Very tall with long fingers
And broad backs of the heels.

182 Through spreading the vowed practices
You will have glory, a good color,
Your ankles will not be prominent,
Your body hairs will stand upwards.

183 Through your zest for knowledge, the arts,
And so forth, and through imparting them

---

[a] Stūpas, which often are monuments commemorating Buddha's marvelous activities, here can be considered actual Buddhas because they contain relics or because Buddha blesses them, "Whatever I am, this is," (*nga gang yin pa de nyid 'di nyid yin no;* Ajitamitra, Golden Reprint, vol. 183, 453.5).

[b] These are the four means of gathering students as mentioned in stanza 133.

You will have the calves of an antelope,
A sharp mind, and great wisdom.

184 If others seek your wealth and possessions,
Through the discipline of immediate giving
You will have broad arms and a pleasant appearance[a]
And will become a leader of the world.

185 Through reconciling well
Friends who have become divided
You will become the best of those
Whose glorious secret organ retracts inside.[b]

186 Through giving good houses
And nice comfortable carpets
Your color will be very soft
Like refined stainless gold.

187 Through giving the highest powers[c]
And following a teacher properly
You will be adorned by each and every hair
And by a spiraling hair between the eyebrows.

188 Through speech that is pleasant and pleasing
And by acting upon the good speech [of others]
You will have curving shoulders
And a lion-like upper body.

189 Through nursing and curing the sick,
The area between your shoulders will be broad,
You will live in a natural state,
And all tastes will be the best.

190 Through initiating activities concordant
With the practices, your crown protrusion[d]
Will stand out well, and [your body] will be
Symmetrical like a banana tree.

191 Through speaking true and soft words
Over a long time, O lord of humanity,
Your tongue will be long
And your voice that of Brahmā.

---

[a] Gyel-tsap, 36b.5: *sku'i zo mdog bde ba.*

[b] Like an elephant or a horse (Gyel-tsap, 185.5).

[c] That is to say, kingdoms.

[d] This is a round, fleshy swelling on the crown or top of a Buddha's head; it is perceptible but its size is not.

192 Through speaking true words
Always and continuously
You will have cheeks like a lion,
Be glorious, and hard to overcome.

193 Through showing great respect,
Serving others, and doing what is fitting,
Your teeth will be very white,
Shining, and even.

194 Through using true and non-divisive
Speech over a long time
You will have forty glorious teeth
That are set evenly and are wondrous.

195 Through viewing beings with love
And without desire, hatred, or delusion
Your eyes will be bright and blue
With eyelashes like a bull.

196 Thus in brief know well
These thirty-two signs
Of a great lion of beings
Together with their causes.

c. Reason for not elaborating here on the causes and effects of the beautiful features 197

197 The eighty beautiful features arise
From a concordant cause of love.
Fearing this text would be too long,
I will not, O King, explain them.

d. Difference between the marks of a Buddha and of a Universal Emperor 198-200

(1) Difference in effects 198

198 All Universal Emperors
Are regarded as having these,
But their purity, beauty, and luster
Cannot match even a little those of a Buddha.

(2) Difference in causes 199-200d

199 The auspicious signs and beautiful features
Of a Universal Emperor
Are said to arise [even][64] from the single cause
Of faith in the King of Subduers.

200 But such virtue accumulated one-pointedly
For a hundred times ten million eons
Cannot produce even one
Of the hair-pores of a Buddha.

(3) Example 200efgh

Just as the brilliance of suns
Is slightly like that of fireflies,
So the signs of a Buddha are slightly like
Those of a Universal Emperor.

The second chapter of the *Precious Garland*, The Interwoven, is finished.

3 Collections for Enlightenment

C. Chapter Three: Advice to train in the two collections of merit and wisdom—the causes of highest enlightenment

1. Modes of the collections 201-11

a. Exhorting the king to listen 201

201 Great king, hear from the great scriptures
Of the Great Vehicle
How the marks of a Buddha
Arise from inconceivable merit.

b. Limitlessness of the collection of merit 202-9

(1) Actual explanation 202-8

(a) Achieving one hair-pore of a Buddha through ten times the merit of Solitary Realizers, etc. 202-3

202 The merit giving rise to all
Solitary Realizers, to Learners, and Non-
Learners,
And all the merit of the transient world
Is measureless like the universe itself.

203 Through such merit ten times extended
One hair-pore of a Buddha is achieved.
All the hair-pores of a Buddha
Arise in just the same way.

(b) Achieving one beautiful feature of a Buddha through a hundred times the merit for achieving a hair-pore 204-5

204 Through multiplying by a hundred
The merit which produces
All the hair-pores of a Buddha
One auspicious beauty is acquired.

205 O King, as much merit as is required
For one auspicious beautiful feature,
So much also is required
For each up to the eightieth.

(c) Achieving one mark of a Buddha through a hundred times the merit for producing all the beautiful features 206

206 Through multiplying a hundred-fold
The collection of merit which achieves
The eighty auspicious beautiful features
One mark of a great being arises.

(d) Achieving the hair-spiral on a Buddha's brow through a thousand times the merit for producing all the marks 207

207 Through multiplying a thousand-fold
The extensive merit that is the cause
Of achieving the thirty signs
The hair-treasure like a full moon arises.[a]

(e) Achieving the crown protrusion through a thousand times the above merit 208

208 Through multiplying a hundred thousand-fold
The merit for the hair-treasure

[a] This is a single hair, spiraling to the right, between the brows.

A Protector's crown-protrusion
Is produced, imperceptible as it actually is.
Through increasing ten million times
A hundred thousand the merit
For the crown-protrusion there comes
The excellence producing the euphony
Of a Buddha's speech and its sixty qualities.[a]

(2) The collections are infinite but are taught to trainees as measurable 209

209 Though such merit is measureless,
It is said for brevity to have a measure,
Just as [the merit of][65] the world is said
For brevity to be included in the ten directions.

c. Limitlessness of the collection of wisdom 210

210 When the causes of even the Form Body
Of a Buddha are as immeasurable
As the world, how then could the causes
Of the Truth Body be measured?

d. Limitlessness of effects of the two collections 211

211 If the causes of all things are small
But they produce extensive effects,
The thought that the measureless causes of
Buddhahood
Have measurable effects should be eliminated.

2. Effects of each collection 212-13

212 The Form Body of a Buddha
Arises from the collections of merit.
The Truth Body in brief, O King,
Arises from the collections of wisdom.

213 Thus these two collections
Are the causes of attaining Buddhahood,
So in sum always rely
Upon merit and wisdom.

3. Advice not to feel inadequate about accumulating the two collections 214-27

a. Brief indication 214

214 Do not feel inadequate about this
[accumulation]
Of merit to achieve enlightenment,
Since reasoning and scripture
Can restore one's spirits.

b. Extensive explanation 215-26

(1) Advice not to be lazy about the collection of merit 215-20

(a) Limitlessness of the merit of generating the aspiration to enlightenment 215-16

215 Just as in all directions
Space, earth, water, fire, and wind
Are without limit,
So suffering sentient beings are limitless.

216 Through their compassion
Bodhisattvas are determined to lead

[a] The chapter has an extra stanza, and Gyel-tsap does not comment on this stanza which also has an extra line.

These limitless sentient beings out of suffering
And establish them in Buddhahood.

(b) Ease of attaining Buddhahood through that cause 217-18

217 [Hence] whether sleeping or not sleeping,
After thoroughly assuming [such compassion]
Those who remain steadfast—
Even though they might not be meticulous—

218 Always accumulate merit as limitless as all sentient beings
Since sentient beings are limitless.
Know then that since [the causes] are limitless,
Limitless Buddhahood is not hard to attain.

(c) Ease of attaining Buddhahood by reason of having the four limitlessnesses 219-20

219 [Bodhisattvas] stay for a limitless time [in the world];
For limitless embodied beings they seek
The limitless [good qualities of] enlightenment
And perform limitless virtuous actions.

220 Hence though enlightenment is limitless,
How could they not attain it
With these four limitless collections
Without being delayed for long?

(2) Advice not to be lazy about accumulating the two collections 221-26

(a) General teaching that through the two collections physical and mental suffering is removed 221

221 The limitless collection of merit
And the limitless collection of wisdom
Eradicate just quickly
Physical and mental sufferings.

(b) Removal of physical suffering by the collection of merit 222

222 The physical sufferings of bad transmigrations
Such as hunger and thirst arise from ill deeds;
Bodhisattvas do not commit ill deeds,
And due to meritorious deeds do not have physical suffering in other lives.

(c) Removal of mental suffering by the collection of wisdom 223

223 The mental sufferings of desire, hatred, fear,
Lust, and so forth arise from obscuration.
Through knowing them to be baseless
They just quickly forsake mental suffering.

(d) No cause for laziness about accumulating the two collections 224-25

224 Since thus they are not greatly harmed
By physical and mental suffering,
Why should they be discouraged
Though they lead beings in all worlds?

225 It is hard to bear suffering even for a little,
What need is there to speak of doing so for long!

What could bring harm even over limitless time
To happy beings who have no suffering?

(e) The power of great compassion 226

226 They have no physical suffering;
How could they have mental suffering?
Through their compassion they feel pain
For the world and so stay in it long.[a]

c. Summation 227

227 Hence do not feel inadequate thinking,
"Buddhahood is far away."
Always strive at these [collections]
To remove defects and attain good qualities.

4. The entities of the two collections 228-30

a. Advice to forsake the opposites of merit and to rely on the meritorious 228

228 Realizing that desire, hatred, and obscuration
Are defects, forsake them completely.
Realizing that non-desire, non-hatred, and non-obscuration
Are good qualities, inculcate them with vigor.

b. Effects of three poisons and of their opposites 229

229 Through desire one goes into a hungry ghost transmigration,
Through hatred one is impelled into a hell,
Through obscuration one mostly goes into an animal transmigration.
Through stopping these one becomes a god or a human.

c. Actual two collections 230

230 Eliminating defects and acquiring good qualities
Are the practices of those seeking high status.
Thoroughly extinguishing conceptions through consciousness [of reality]
Is the practice of those seeking definite goodness.

5. Branches of the two collections 231-76

a. Brief indication 231-39

(1) Branches of the collection of merit 231-37

(a) Establishing objects of worship 231-33

1' Newly establishing objects of worship 231-32

231 You should respectfully and extensively construct
Images of Buddha, monuments,[b] and temples
And provide residences,
Abundant riches, and so forth.

232 Please construct from all precious substances
Images of Buddha with fine proportions,

[a] This pain is a special form of virtue, and the word does not imply that it is unwanted.

[b] *mchod rten, stūpa.*

Well designed and sitting on lotuses,
Adorned with all precious substances.

2' Worshipping them once established 233

233 You should sustain with all endeavor
The excellent doctrine and the communities
Of monastics, and decorate monuments
With gold and jeweled friezes.

(b) Worship 234-36

234 Revere the monuments
With gold and silver flowers,
Diamonds, corals, pearls,
Emeralds, cat's eye gems, and sapphires.

235 To revere propounders of doctrine
Is to do what pleases them—
[Offering] goods and services
And relying firmly on the doctrine.[a]

236 Listen to teachers with homage
And respect, serve, and pray to them.
Always respectfully revere
The [other] Bodhisattvas.

(c) Ceasing to worship unworthy objects 237

237 You should not respect, revere,
Or do homage to others, the Forders,[b]
Because through that the ignorant
Would become enamored of the faulty.

(2) Branches of the collection of wisdom 238-39

238 You should make donations of pages and books
Of the word of the King of Subduers
And of the treatises they gave rise to,[c]
Along with their prerequisites, pens and ink.

239 As ways to increase wisdom,
Wherever there is a school in the land
Provide for the livelihood of teachers
And give lands to them [for their provision].

b. Extensive exposition 240-76

(1) Branches of the collection of merit 240-64

(a) Giving one's own property 240-51

240 In order to alleviate the suffering
Of sentient beings—the old, young, and infirm—

[a] The last line follows an alternative reading given by Gyel-tsap (43a.5); otherwise, it is, "And respectfully rely on them with the six practices," the six most likely being those given in stanza 10—not drinking intoxicants, a good livelihood, non-harming, respectful giving, honoring the honorable, and love.

[b] These are non-Buddhist Tīrthikas.

[c] These are the treatises written by scholar-adepts to explain Buddha's word.

You should establish through the estates [that you control][66]
Doctors and barbers throughout your country.

241 O One of Good Wisdom, please provide
Hostels, parks, dikes,
Ponds, rest-houses, water-vessels,
Beds, food, hay, and wood.

242 Please establish rest-houses
In all towns, at temples, and in all cities
And provide water-vessels
On all arid roadways.

243 Always care compassionately
For the sick, the unprotected, those stricken
With suffering, the lowly, and the poor
And take special care to nourish them.

244 Until you have given to monastics and beggars
Seasonally-appropriate food and drink,
As well as produce, grain, and fruit,
You should not partake of them.

245 At the sites of the water-vessels
Place shoes, umbrellas, water-filters,
Tweezers for removing thorns,
Needles, thread, and fans.

246 Within vessels place the three medicinal fruits,
The three fever medicines,[a] butter,
Honey, eye medicines, and antidotes to poison,
And write out mantras and prescriptions.[b]

247 At the sites of the vessels place
Salves for the body, feet, and head,
As well as wool, stools,[c] gruel,
Jars [for getting water],[67] cooking pots, axes, and so forth.

248 Please have small containers
In the shade filled with sesame,
Rice, grains, foods, molasses,
And suitable water.

---

[a] *tsha ba gsum:* see also Gyel-tsap, 44a.1.

[b] Spells for relieving illness as well as the names and purposes of medicines are to be posted.

[c] These are for children (Gyel-tsap, 44a.2).

249 At the openings of ant-hills
Please have trustworthy persons
Always put food, water,
Sugar, and piles of grain.

250 Before and after taking food
Always appropriately offer fare
To hungry ghosts, dogs,
Ants, birds, and so forth.

251 Provide extensive care
For the persecuted, the victims of crop failure,
The stricken, those suffering contagion,
And for beings in conquered areas.

252 Provide stricken farmers
With seeds and sustenance.

(b) Other giving 252c-56

Eliminate high taxes [levied by the previous monarch].[68]
Reduce the tax rate [on harvests].[69]

253 Protect [the poor] from the pain of wanting [your wealth].
Set up no [new] tolls and reduce those [that are heavy].
Also free [traders from other areas] from the afflictions
That come from waiting at your door.

254 Eliminate robbers and thieves
In your own and others' countries.
Please set prices fairly
And keep profits level [even during scarcity].

255 You should know full well [the counsel]
That your ministers offer,
And should always enact it
If it nurses the world.

256 Just as you are intent on thinking
Of what could be done to help yourself,
So you should be intent on thinking
Of what could be done to help others.

(c) Giving away all wealth 257-58

257 If only for a moment make yourself
Available for the use of others

Just as earth, water, fire, wind, medicine,[a]
And forests [are available to all].

258 Even during their seventh step
Merit measureless as the sky
Is generated in Bodhisattvas
Whose attitude is to give all wealth away.

(d) Giving based on different needs 259-64

1' Giving to humans with certain needs 259-60

259 If you give to those so seeking
Girls of beauty well adorned,
You will thereby attain
Thorough retention[b] of the excellent doctrine.

260 Formerly the Subduer provided
Along with every need and so forth
Eighty thousand girls
With all adornments.

2' Giving to the needy 261

261 Lovingly give to beggars
Various and glittering
Clothes, adornments, perfumes,
Garlands, and enjoyments.

3' Giving that accords with doctrine 262-64

262 If you provide [facilities]
For those most deprived who lack
The means [to study] the doctrine,
There is no greater gift than that.

263 Even give poison
To those whom it will help,
But do not give even the best food
To those whom it will not help.

264 Just as it is said that it will help
To cut off a finger bitten by a snake,
So the Subduer says that if it helps others,
One should even bring [temporary][70]
discomfort.

(2) Branches of the collection of wisdom 265-76

265 You should respect most highly
The excellent doctrine and its proponents.
You should listen reverently to the doctrine
And also impart it to others.

266 Take no pleasure in worldly talk;
Take delight in what passes beyond the world.

---

[a] *sman:* whether the reference is to medicine itself or herbs is unclear.

[b] *gzungs, dhāraṇī:* special capacities to retain the words and meanings of doctrine.

Cause good qualities to grow in others
In the same way [you wish them] for yourself.

267 Please do not be satisfied with doctrine heard,
But retain and discriminate meanings.
Please always be intent
On offering presents to teachers.

268 Do not recite [the books of] worldly Nihilists, and so forth.
Forsake debating in the interest of pride.
Do not praise your own good qualities.
Speak of the good qualities even of your foes.

269 [When debating][71] do not attack to the quick.
Do not talk about others
With bad intent. Individually
Analyze your own mistakes yourself.

270 You should root out completely from yourself
The faults the wise decry in others,
And through your influence
Also cause others to do the same.

271 Considering the harm others do to you
As created by your former deeds, do not anger.
Act such that further suffering will not be created
And your own faults will disappear.

272 Without hope of reward
Provide help to others.
Bear suffering alone,
And share your pleasures with beggars.

273 Do not be inflated
Even by the prosperity of gods.
Do not be depressed
Even by the poverty of hungry ghosts.

274 For your sake always speak the truth.
Even should it cause your death
Or ruin your governance,
Do not speak in any other way.

275 Always observe the discipline
Of actions just as it has been explained.
In that way, O glorious one, you will become
The best of authoritative beings upon the earth.

276 You should always analyze well
Everything before you act,
And through seeing things correctly as they are
Do not put full reliance on others.

6. Benefits arising to one who amasses merit 277-300

a. Arising of five common good qualities 277-80 [1: 277a; 2: 277bc; 3: 277d-279; 4: 280ab; 5: 280cd]

277 (1) Through these practices your realm will be happy,
(2) A broad canopy of fame
Will rise in all directions,
And (3) your officials will respect you fully.

278 The causes of death are many,
Those of staying alive are few,
These too can become causes of death,
Therefore always perform the practices.

279 If you always perform thus the practices,
The mental happiness which arises
In the world and in yourself
Is most favorable.

280 (4) Through the practices you will sleep happily
And will awaken happily.
(5) Because your inner nature will be without defect,
Even your dreams will be happy.

b. Arising of twenty-five particular good qualities 281-300 [1: 281-82; 2: 283-85; 3: 286; 4: 287a; 5: 287b; 6: 287cd; 7: 288a; 8: 288b; 9: 288c; 10: 288d; 11: 289; 12: 290a; 13: 290b; 14: 290c; 15: 290d; 16: 291; 17: 292; 18: 293; 19: 294; 20: 295; 21: 296; 22: 297; 23: 298; 24: 299ab; 25: 299cd; summation 300]

281 (1) Intent on serving your parents,
Respectful to the principals of your lineage,
Using your resources well, patient, generous,
With kindly speech, without divisiveness, and truthful,

282 Through performing such discipline for one lifetime
You will become a monarch of gods
Whereupon even more so you will be a monarch of gods.
Therefore observe such practices.

283 (2) Even three times a day to offer
Three hundred cooking pots of food
Does not match a portion of the merit
In one instant of love.

284 Though [through love] you are not liberated
You will attain the eight good qualities of love—

Gods and humans will be friendly,
Even [non-humans][a] will protect you,

285 You will have mental pleasures and many [physical][72] pleasures,
Poison and weapons will not harm you,
Without striving you will attain your aims,
And be reborn in the world of Brahmā.

286 (3) If you cause sentient beings to generate
The altruistic aspiration to enlightenment and make it firm,
You will always attain an altruistic aspiration to enlightenment
Firm like the monarch of mountains.

287 (4) Through faith you will not be without leisure,[b]
(5) Through good ethics you will move in good transmigrations,
(6) Through becoming familiar with emptiness
You will attain detachment from all phenomena.

---

[a] *mi ma yin pa de dag:* Gyel-tsap, 48a.2.

[b] *mi khom, akṣaṇa.* Apte (8) renders *akṣaṇa* as "inopportune, unseasonable," and for the second meaning of *kṣaṇa* gives "leisure," the first being "instant" which is obviously inappropriate here. Sir Monier Monier-Williams' *A Sanskrit-English Dictionary* (3) similarly gives *akṣaṇa* as "inopportune," and, again, the second meaning of *kṣaṇa* (324) is "a leisure moment, vacant time, leisure." In Franklin Edgerton's *Buddhist Hybrid Sanskrit Grammar and Dictionary* (2), *akṣaṇa* is translated as "inopportune birth, birth under such circumstances that one cannot learn from a Buddha." Even Edgerton's rendering, which is far from the literal reading, offers nothing to oppose the more literal rendering as "leisure." Though the implication of "non-leisure" is that one lacks the leisure or opportunity for religious practice, the explanation of a term need not become the translation itself; what is implicit in the Sanskrit can be left implicit in the English as well. Similarly, with respect to the Tibetan, Sarat Chandra Das' *A Tibetan-English Dictionary* (956) renders *mi khom pa* as "uninterrupted uneasiness, want of leisure"; Das also refers to "the eight states of perpetual uneasiness or the states where there are no opportunities for doing religious works." Das renders *dal ba* as "languor, ease, quietude, leisure; also the state of *dalwa,* and so the being at ease or in the state of leisurely comfort or repose." The eight conditions of non-leisure are:

1 birth as a hell-being
2 birth as a hungry ghost
3 birth as an animal
4 birth in an uncultured area
5 possessing defective sense faculties
6 having wrong views
7 birth as a god of long life
8 birth in a world system where a Buddha did not come.

288 (7) Through not wavering you will attain
mindfulness,
(8) Through thinking you will attain
intelligence,
(9) Through respect you will be endowed with
realization of meaning,
(10) Through guarding the doctrine you will
become wise.

289 (11) Through making the hearing and the giving
Of the doctrine be unobstructed
You will company with Buddhas
And will quickly attain your wishes.

290 (12) Through non-attachment you will achieve
the meaning [of doctrines],[a]
(13) Through not being miserly your resources
will increase,
(14) Through not being proud you will become
chief [of those respected],
(15) Through enduring the doctrine you will
attain retention.

291 (16) Through giving the five essentials[b]
As well as non-fright to the frightened
You will not be harmed by any demons
And will become the best of the mighty.

292 (17) Through offering series of lamps at
monuments
And through offering lamps in dark places
As well as the oil for them
You will attain the divine eye.

293 (18) Through offering musical instruments and
bells
For the worship of monuments
And through offering drums and trumpets
You will attain the divine ear.

294 (19) Through not mentioning others' mistakes
And not talking of others' defective limbs
But protecting their minds
You will attain knowledge of others' minds.

---

[a] *chos kyi don:* Gyel-tsap, 48b.2.

[b] Sugar/molasses, ghee, honey, sesame oil, and salt (Ajitamitra, Golden Reprint, vol. 183, 462.1).

295 (20) Through giving shoes and conveyances,
Through serving the feeble,
And through providing teachers with transport
You will attain the skill to create magical emanations.[a]

296 (21) Through acting for the doctrine,[b]
Remembering books of doctrine and their meaning,
And through stainless giving of the doctrine
You will attain memory of your continuum of lives.

297 (22) Through knowing thoroughly, correctly, and truly
That all phenomena lack inherent existence,
You will attain the sixth clairvoyance—
The excellent extinction of all contamination.

298 (23) Through meditatively cultivating the wisdom of reality
Which is the same [for all phenomena] and is moistened with compassion
For the sake of liberating all sentient beings,
You will become a Conqueror endowed with all supreme aspects.

299 (24) Through multitudes of pure wishes
Your Buddha Land will be purified.
(25) Through offering gems to the Kings of Subduers
You will emit infinite light.

300 Therefore knowing the concordance
Of actions and their effects,
Always help beings in fact.[c]
Just that will help yourself.

The third chapter of the *Precious Garland*, A Compendium of the Collections for Enlightenment, is finished.

---

[a] The skill of reducing many emanations to one and vice versa, etc.

[b] Such as building temples and enduring difficulties for the sake of the doctrine.

[c] Gyel-tsap (49a.1) takes *don du* (translated here as "in fact") as meaning "for the purpose of helping yourself" (*rang la phan pa'i dgos pa'i don du*), which would repeat what is said in the final line of the stanza. Ajitamitra (Golden Reprint, vol. 183, 463.1) more cogently interprets it as "the causes should be achieved by way of fact" (*don gyi sgo nas rgyu bsgrub par bya'o*). I assume that emphasis is being put on actually carrying out the practices.

4 Royal Policy

D. Chapter Four: Advice to train in flawless policy

1. Transition 301-6a

a. Because most do not dare to chide a monarch but give praise, it is fitting to listen to a good explanation 301-3

301 Monarchs who do what is against the practices
And senseless are mostly praised
By their citizens, for it is hard to know
What will or will not be tolerated.
Hence it is hard to know
What is useful or not [to say].[a]

302 If useful but unpleasant words
Are hard to speak to anyone else,
What could I, a monk, say to you,
A King who is a lord of the great earth?

303 But because of my affection for you
And from compassion for all beings,
I tell you without hesitation
That which is useful but unpleasant.

b. Instruction to listen to helpful words in accordance with Buddha's advice 304

304 The Supramundane Victor said that students
are to be told
The truth—gentle, meaningful, and salutary—
At the proper time and from compassion.
That is why you are being told all this.

c. Actual exhortation to listen to words helpful to oneself and others 305-6

305 O Steadfast One,[b] when true words
Are spoken without belligerence,
They should be taken as fit to be heard,
Like water fit for bathing.

306 Realize that I am telling you
What is useful here and otherwise.[c]
Act on it so as to help
Yourself and also others.

---

[a] In the Tibetan this stanza has six lines to accommodate a variant rendering, or perhaps a double meaning, of the Sanskrit (*krcchrād vetti ksamāksamam*): "for it is hard to know/ What they will or will not tolerate./ Hence it is hard to know/ What is useful or not." The first uses *gang phyir* (*yasmāt*), and the second *de yi phyir* (*tasmāt*) which appears in the Sanskrit (Hahn, 92).

[b] Following Gyel-tsap's reading as vocative, 50a.2.

[c] Gyel-tsap (50a.4) takes "here and otherwise" as referring either to this life and future lives or to politics and religion.

2. Extensive exposition of flawless policy 307-98

a. Royal policies 307-27

(1) Increasing giving 307-8

307 If you do not make contributions of the wealth
Obtained from former giving to the needy,
Through your ingratitude and attachment
You will not obtain wealth in the future.

308 Here in the world workers do not carry
Provisions for a journey unpaid,
But lowly beggars, without payment, carry to your future life
[What you give them] multiplied a hundred times.

(2) Founding temples 309-17

(a) Training in exalted thoughts and deeds 309

309 Always be of exalted mind
And take delight in exalted deeds.
From exalted actions arise
All effects that are exalted.

(b) Achieving the four good qualities 310

310 Create foundations of doctrine, abodes
Of the Three Jewels—fraught with glory and fame—
That lowly kings have not even
Conceived in their minds.

(c) Special achievement 311-317

311 O King, it is preferable not to create
Foundations of doctrine that do not stir
The hairs of wealthy kings
Because [those centers] will not become famous even after your death.

312 Through your great exaltation,[a] use even all your wealth
Such that the exalted become free from pride,
[The equal][73] become delighted,
And the inclinations of the lowly are reversed.

313 Having let go of all possessions,
[At death] powerless you must go elsewhere,
But all that has been used for the doctrine
Precedes you [as good karma].

314 When all the possessions of a previous monarch
Come under the control of the successor,
Of what use are they then to the former monarch
For practice, happiness, or fame?

[a] "Great exaltation" refers to the wide scope of temple building and so forth (Gyel-tsap, 51a.1).

315 Through using wealth there is happiness here in this life,
Through giving there is happiness in the future,
From wasting it without using or giving it away,
There is only misery. How could there be happiness?

316 Because of lack of power while dying,
You will be unable to make donations by way of your ministers
Who will shamelessly lose affection for you
And will seek to please the new monarch.

317 Hence while in good health create foundations of doctrine
Immediately with all your wealth,
For you are living amidst the causes of death
Like a lamp standing in a breeze.

(3) Maintaining what was established earlier 318-20
(a) General teaching 318

318 Also you should maintain other centers of doctrine
Established by the previous kings—
All the temples and so forth—
As they were before.

(b) Way of appointing caretakers 319

319 Please have them attended by those
Who are not harmful, are virtuous,
Keep their vows, are kind to visitors, truthful,
Patient, non-combative, and always diligent.

(c) Equal maintenance 320

320 Cause the blind, the sick, the lowly,
The protectorless, the destitute,
And the crippled equally to obtain
Food and drink without interruption.

(4) Providing even for those who do not seek it 321

321 Provide all types of support
For practitioners who do not seek it
And even for those living
In the countries of other monarchs.

(5) Way of appointing ministers 322-27
(a) Appointing religious leaders 322

322 At all centers of the doctrine
Appoint attendants who are
Not negligent, not greedy, skillful,
Religious, and not harmful to anyone.

(b) Appointing ministers 323

323 Appoint ministers who know good policy,
Who practice the doctrine, are civil,[a]
Pure, harmonious, undaunted, of good lineage,
Of excellent ethics, and grateful.

(c) Appointing generals 324

324 Appoint generals who are generous,
Without attachments, brave, kindly,
Who use [the treasury] properly, are steadfast,
Always conscientious, and practice the doctrine.

(d) Appointing treasurers, etc. 325-27

325 As administrators appoint elders
Of religious disposition, pure, and able,
Who know what should be done, are skilled in the [royal][74] treatises,
Understand good policy, are unbiased, and are kindly.

326 Every month you should hear from them
About all the income and expenses,
And having heard, you yourself should tell them
All that should be done for the centers of doctrine and so forth.

327 If your realm exists for the doctrine
And not for fame or desire,
Then it will be extremely fruitful.
If not, its fruit will be misfortune.

b. Instruction in non-degeneration and development 328-35

(1) Instruction in non-degeneration of previously existent practices 328-37

(a) Transition 328

328 O Lord of Humans, since in this world nowadays
Most are prone to wreak havoc on each other,
Listen to how your governance
And your practice should be.

(b) Actual instruction in non-degeneration 329-37

1' Gathering those of special powers 329

329 Let there always be around you many persons
Old in experience, of good lineage,
Knowing good policy, who shrink from ill deeds,
Are agreeable, and know what should be done.

2' Making oneself compassionate 330-32

a' Providing out of compassion 330

330 Even to those whom they have rightfully fined,
Bound, punished, and so forth,

---

[a] Ajitamitra (vol. 183, 466.1) glosses *'jar ba* as a "non-harsh mind/attitude" (*sems mi rtsub pa*). Hahn (101) reads "soft/kindly" (*'jam*).

You, being moistened with compassion,
Should always be caring.

b' Being compassionate especially to the wicked 331

331 O King, through compassion you should
Always generate just an attitude of altruism
Even for all those embodied beings
Who have committed awful ill deeds.

c' The correctness of the above 332

332 Especially generate compassion
For those whose ill deeds are horrible, the murderers.
Those of fallen nature are receptacles
Of compassion from those whose nature is magnanimous.

3' Freeing prisoners and making prisons comfortable 333-36

333 Free the weaker prisoners
After a day or five days.
Do not think the others
Are not to be freed under any conditions.

334 For each one whom you do not think to free
You will lose the [layperson's] vow.
Due to having lost the vow,
Faults will constantly be amassed.

335 As long as prisoners are not freed,
They should be made comfortable
With barbers, baths, food, drink,
Medicine, and clothing.[a]

336 Just as deficient children are punished
Out of a wish to make them competent,
So punishment should be carried out with compassion,
Not through hatred nor desire for wealth.

4' If not reformable, banishing them from the country 337

337 Once you have analyzed and thoroughly recognized
The angry murderers,
Have them banished
Without killing or tormenting them.

[a] Tibetan omits "clothing."

(2) Developing previously non-existent practices 338-45

(a) Achieving practices 338-42

1' Sending out representatives 338-39

338 In order to maintain control,[a] oversee all the country
Through the eyes of agents.
Always conscientious and mindful,
Do what accords with the practices.

339 Continually honor in an exalted way
Those who are foundations of good qualities
With gifts, respect, and service,
And likewise honor all the rest.

2' Examples 340-42

340 The birds of the populace will alight upon
The royal tree providing the shade of patience,
Flourishing flowers of respect,
And large fruits of resplendent giving.

341 Monarchs whose nature is generosity
Are liked if they are strong,
Like a sweet hardened outside
With cardamom and pepper.

342 If you analyze with reason thus,
Your governance will not degenerate.
It will not be without principle
Nor become unreligious but be religious.

(b) Ceasing non-virtues 343-45

343 You did not bring your dominion with you from your former life
Nor will you take it to the next.
Since it was gained through religious practice,
You would be wrong to act against the practices.

344 O King, exert yourself
To avert a sequence
Of miserable supplies for the realm
Through [misuse of] royal resources.

345 O King, exert yourself
To increase the succession
Of the dominion's resources
Through [proper use of] royal resources.

---

[a] Gyel-tsap (54a.3): *rang dbang yod par bya ba'i ched du.*

c. Achieving liberation and not forsaking the scriptures of the Great Vehicle 346-98

(1) Training in the path of liberation 346-66

(a) Refuting inherently existent objects of attachment, pleasant and painful feelings 346-64

1' Refuting real feelings of pleasure 346-61

a' Transition 346-47

346 Although Universal Monarchs rule
Over the four continents, their pleasures
Are regarded as only two—
The physical and the mental.

347 Physical feelings of pleasure
Are only a lessening of pain.
Mental pleasures are made of thought,
Created only by conceptuality.

b' Brief indication 348

348 All the wealth of worldly pleasures
Are just a lessening of suffering,
Or are only [creations of] thought,
Hence they are in fact not meaningful.

c' Extensive explanation 349-61

1" Refuting proofs of real pleasure 349-60

a" Refuting proofs for real mental pleasure 349-50

349 Just one by one there is enjoyment
Of continents, countries, towns, homes,
Conveyances,[a] seats, clothing, beds,
Food, drink, elephants, horses, and women.

350 When the mind has any [one of these as its object],
Due to it there is said to be pleasure,
But since at that time no attention is paid to the others,
The others are not then in fact meaningful [causes of pleasure].

b" Refuting proofs for real physical pleasure 351-60

1: Refuting an aggregation of the five objects as a proof for real physical pleasure 351-53

351 When [all] five senses, eye and so forth,[b]
[Simultaneously] apprehend their objects,[c]
A thought [of pleasure] does not refer [to all of them],
Therefore at that time they do not [all] give pleasure.

352 Whenever any of the [five] objects is known
[As pleasurable] by one of the [five] senses,
Then the remaining [objects] are not so known by the remaining [senses][d]
Since they then are not meaningful [causes of pleasure].

[a] *khyogs:* palanquin, swing. The Sanskrit *pradeśa* is inexplicable.

[b] Eye, ear, nose, tongue, and body sense consciousnesses.

[c] Visual forms (i.e., colors and shapes), sounds, odors, tastes, and tangible objects.

[d] The objects apprehended by the other senses cannot be known to be pleasurable because the thought of pleasure can pay attention only to one object at a time (Gyel-tsap, 56a.6).

353 The mind apprehends an image of a past object
Which has been apprehended by the senses
And imagines and fancies
It to be pleasurable.

2: Refuting individual objects as proofs of real physical pleasure 354-60

a: Actual refutation 354

354 Also the one sense which here [in the world
Is said to] know one object
Is meaningless without an object,
And the object also is meaningless without it.

b: Refuting proofs of real physical pleasure 355-60

1 Refuting inherently existing consciousnesses 355*

355 Just as a child is said to be born
In dependence on a father and a mother,
So a [visual] consciousness is said to arise
In dependence on an eye sense and on a form.

2 Refuting inherently existing objects 356-57*

356 Past and future objects
And the senses are meaningless,
So too are present objects
Since they are not distinct from these two.[a]

357 Just as due to error the eye perceives
A whirling firebrand as a wheel,
So the senses apprehend
Present objects [as if real].

3 Refuting inherently existent senses 358-60*

a Refuting inherently existent senses and objects through refuting inherently existent elements 358*

358 The senses and their objects are regarded
As being composed of the elements.
Since the elements are meaningless individually,
These also are meaningless in fact.

b Refuting inherently existent elements 359*

359 If the elements are each different,
It follows that there could be fire without fuel.
If mixed, they would be characterless.[b]
Such is also to be ascertained about the other elements.

c Therefore forms are not inherently existent 360*

360 Because the elements are thus meaningless in both these ways,
So too is a composite.
Because a composite is meaningless
So too are forms meaningless in fact.

---

[a] The present must depend on the past and the future in order to be present, but if the present does not exist in the past and the future, then it cannot truly depend on them. If the present does exist in the past and the future, then it is not different from them (Gyel-tsap, 56b.6).

[b] If the four elements were completely intermingled, they would lose their individual characters.

2" Refuting the entity of real pleasure 361

361 Also because consciousnesses, feelings,
Discriminations, and compositional factors
Altogether and individually are without essential factuality,
[Pleasures] are not ultimately meaningful.

2' Refuting inherently existing pain 362

362 Just as lessening of pain
Is fancied to be pleasure in fact,
So destruction of pleasure
Is also fancied to be pain.

3' Result of the refutation 363-64

a' Liberation through realizing emptiness 363

363 Thus attachment to meeting with pleasure
And attachment to separating from pain
Are to be abandoned because they do not inherently exist.
Thereby those who see thus are liberated.

b' Identifying the mind realizing emptiness 364

364 What sees [reality]?
Conventionally it is said to be the mind
[For] without mental factors there is no mind
[And hence minds and mental factors] are meaningless, due to which it is not asserted that they are simultaneous.[a]

(b) Both Lesser Vehicle practitioners and Great Vehicle practitioners equally realize the subtle emptiness 365-66

1' Necessity of realizing subtle emptiness even to attain liberation 365

365 Knowing thus correctly, just as it is,
That transmigrating beings do not exist in fact,
One passes [from suffering] not subject [to rebirth and hence][75] without appropriating [rebirth],
Like a fire without its cause.

2' Difference between Lesser Vehicle and Great Vehicle 366

366 Bodhisattvas also who have seen it thus,
Seek perfect enlightenment with certainty.
They make the connection between lives
Until enlightenment only through their compassion.

(2) Stopping forsaking the scriptures of the Great Vehicle 367-98

(a) Extensive exposition 367-96

1' Reason for unsuitability of forsaking the Great Vehicle scriptures 367-79

a' Faults of deriding the Great Vehicle 367-71

1" How the Great Vehicle is derided 367

367 Since the collections [of merit and wisdom] of Bodhisattvas
Were taught by the One Gone Thus in the Great Vehicle,
Those who are bewildered [about the full extent of the paths and fruits of the Great Vehicle][76]
Deride them out of antagonism.

[a] For Gyel-tsap's interpretation of this stanza, see p. 68.

2" Reasons for the derision 368-69

368 Either through not knowing the good qualities [of altruism][77] and the defects [of mere self-concern],
Or identifying good qualities as defects,
Or through despising good qualities,
They deride the Great Vehicle.

369 Those who deride the Great Vehicle—
Knowing that to harm others is defective
And that to help others is a good quality—
Are said to despise good qualities.

3" Faults of deriding the Great Vehicle 370-71

370 Those who despise the Great Vehicle,
Source of all good qualities in that [it teaches] taking delight
Solely in the aims of others due to not looking to one's own,
Consequently burn themselves [in bad transmigrations].[78]

371 One type with faith [in emptiness forsakes it][79] through misconception [of it as denying cause and effect].
Others who are angry [forsake emptiness] through despising it.
If even the faithful type is said [in sūtra] to be burned,
What can be said about those who turn their backs on it through despising it![a]

b' Therefore, the unsuitability of despising the Great Vehicle 372-79

1" Elimination of great suffering through a little suffering 372

372 Just[b] as it is explained in medicine
That poison can removed by poison,
What contradiction is there in saying
That what is injurious [in the future][80] can be removed by suffering?

2" Though there is a little suffering in the deeds of the Great Vehicle, it is unsuitable to despise what completely eliminates suffering 373-74

373 It is renowned [in Great Vehicle scriptures][81] that motivation determines practices
And that the mind is most important.

[a] Gyel-tsap (59b.5) draws the conclusion that even if one does not have interest in emptiness, one should not deprecate it.

[b] Gyel-tsap (60a.1) explains that Nāgārjuna has moved to a new issue, responding to a concern that the Great Vehicle calls for much hardship. An objector has said: It *is* suitable to despise the Great Vehicle because asceticism such as giving away one's head is unbearable and because the profound is difficult to realize.

Hence how could even suffering not be helpful
For one who gives help with an altruistic motivation?

374 If even [in ordinary life] pain can bring future benefit,
What need is there to say that [accepting suffering][82]
Beneficial for one's own and others' happiness will help!
This practice is known as the policy of the ancients.[a]

3" Rightness of making effort for the sake of great bliss; wrongness of being attached to small pleasures 375-77

375 If through relinquishing small pleasures
There is extensive happiness later,
Seeing the greater happiness
The resolute should relinquish small pleasures.

376 If such things cannot be borne,
Then doctors giving distasteful medicines
Would disappear. It is not [reasonable]
To forsake [great pleasure for the small].

377 Sometimes what is thought harmful
Is regarded as helpful by the wise.
General rules and their exceptions
Are commended in all treatises.

4" Suitability of liking the Great Vehicle 378

378 Who with intelligence would deride
The explanation in the Great Vehicle
Of deeds motivated by compassion
And of stainless wisdom!

5" Summation 379

379 Feeling inadequate about its great extent and profound depth
Untrained beings—foes of themselves and others—
Nowadays deride the Great Vehicle
Because of bewilderment.

2' Proving that the Great Vehicle scriptures are the word of Buddha 380-89

a' Deeds of the six perfections 380-82

1" Not the slightest bad explanation in the scriptures of the Great Vehicle 380

380 The Great Vehicle has a nature
Of giving, ethics, patience, effort,
Concentration, wisdom, and compassion.
Hence how could there be any bad explanations in it?

[a] Gyel-tsap (60a.6) takes this as the way of the Buddhas of the three times, or as the way of the good.

2" The aims of the Great Vehicle are taught in the Great Vehicle scriptures 381

381 Others' aims are [achieved][83] through giving
and ethics.
One's own are [achieved] through patience and
effort.
Concentration and wisdom are causes of
liberation.
These epitomize the sense of the Great Vehicle.

3" Therefore, those scriptures are proved to be the word of Buddha 382

382 The aims of benefiting oneself and others and
the meaning of liberation
As briefly taught by the Buddha [in the
Hearers' Vehicle][a]
Are contained in the six perfections.
Therefore these [scriptures of the Great
Vehicle][84] are the word of Buddha.

b' Necessity of knowing the complete path of great enlightenment from the Great Vehicle scriptures 383

383 Those blind with ignorance cannot stand
This Great Vehicle where Buddhas taught
The great path of enlightenment
Consisting of merit and wisdom.

c' Necessity of knowing the great nature of a Buddha from the Great Vehicle which therefore is the word of Buddha 384-89

1" Limitless causes of the Form Body are explained in the Great Vehicle 384-85

384 Conquerors are said to have inconceivable
good qualities
Because the [causal][85] good qualities are
inconceivable like the sky.
Therefore let this great nature of a Buddha
Explained in the Great Vehicle be allowed.

385 Even [Buddha's] ethics were beyond
The scope of Shāriputra.
So why is the inconceivable great nature
Of a Buddha not accepted?

2" Knowledge of extinction described in the Lesser Vehicle and extinction and no production described in the Great Vehicle have the same meaning of the realization of emptiness 386-87

386 The absence of production taught in the Great
Vehicle
And the extinction of the others[b] are in fact the
same emptiness

[a] Gyel-tsap, 61b.2. I use "Hearers' Vehicle" rather than "Lesser Vehicle" in that this is the way Nāgārjuna explicitly refers to this vehicle (390, 440), whereas Gyel-tsap uses "Lesser Vehicle." Nāgārjuna uses the term "Great Vehicle" eighteen times; thus the implication that the Hearers Vehicle is lesser is clear.

[b] That is to say, as taught in the scriptures that the Proponents of Hearer Vehicle tenets assert (Gyel-tsap, 62b.5).

[Since they indicate] the non-existence of
[inherently existent] production and the
extinction [of inherent existence].
Therefore let [the Great Vehicle] be allowed [as
Buddha's word].

387 If emptiness and the great nature of a Buddha
Are viewed in this way with reason,
How could what is taught in the Great Vehicle
and the other
Be unequal for the wise?[a]

3" If the meaning of the Great Vehicle is not understood, it is right to be indifferent toward it but not to despise it 388-89

388 What the One Gone Thus taught with a
special intention
Is not easy to understand.
Therefore since he taught one as well as three
vehicles,
You should protect yourself through
neutrality.[b]

389 There is no fault with neutrality, but there is
fault
From despising it. How could there be virtue?
Therefore those who seek good for themselves
Should not despise the Great Vehicle.

3' Incompleteness of the paths and fruits of the Great Vehicle as explained in the Lesser Vehicle scriptures 390-93

a' The deeds of Bodhisattvas are not completely explained in the Lesser Vehicle scriptures 390-91

390 Bodhisattvas' aspirational wishes, deeds, and
dedications [of merit]
Were not described in the Hearers' Vehicle.
Therefore how could one become
A Bodhisattva through it?

391 [In the Hearers' Vehicle] Buddha[c] did not
explain
The foundations[d] for a Bodhisattva's
enlightenment.

---

[a] The inequality would be to consider one as the word of Buddha and one as not (Gyel-tsap, 63a.1).

[b] If due to the complexity of Buddha's teaching one cannot understand it, neutrality is better since despising it is sinful (Gyel-tsap, 388.3).

[c] The Sanskrit *buddhair* is plural but can be interpreted as an honorific.

[d] Gyel-tsap (63b.3) comments:

> Buddha did not set forth the complete path of the Great Vehicle in the scriptural divisions of the Lower Vehicle because he did not, for the time being, teach [such] to Hearers. Because moreover [such] is blessed for the sake of the unsurpassed enlightenment of Bodhisattvas.

It may be that Gyel-tsap was aware of the reading as "foundations" (*rten rnams*) and thus spoke of "the complete path of the Great Vehicle" as well as of the reading as "blessings" (*byin rlabs;* Hahn 129) which he uses in the final "because" clause.

What greater authority for this subject
Is there other than the Victor?

392 How could the fruit of Buddhahood be superior
[If achieved] through the path common to Hearers
Which has the foundations [of the Hearer enlightenment],
The meanings of the four noble truths, and the harmonies with enlightenment?

b' Buddhahood cannot be achieved through practicing just the four noble truths and the auxiliaries to enlightenment 392

393 The subjects concerned with the Bodhisattva deeds
Were not mentioned in the [Hearers' Vehicle] sūtras
But were explained in the Great Vehicle.
Hence the wise should accept it [as Buddha's word].

c' The Great Vehicle scriptures are suitable to be considered by the wise as the word of Buddha 393

394 Just as a grammarian [first] has students
Read a model of the alphabet,
So Buddha taught trainees
The doctrines that they could bear.

4' Purpose of teaching three vehicles 394-96

395 To some he taught doctrines
To turn them away from ill-deeds;
To some, for the sake of achieving merit;
To some, doctrines based on duality;

396 To some, doctrines based on non-duality;
To some what is profound and frightening to the fearful—
Having an essence of emptiness and compassion—
The means of achieving [unsurpassed][86] enlightenment.[a]

397 Therefore the wise should extinguish
Any belligerence toward the Great Vehicle
And generate special faith
For the sake of achieving perfect enlightenment.

(b) Summation 397-98

398 Through faith in the Great Vehicle
And through practicing what is explained in it

---

[a] For Gyel-tsap's interpretation of these two stanzas see p. 90.

The highest enlightenment is attained
And, along the way, even all [worldly][87] pleasures.

399 At that time [when you are a ruler][88] you should internalize
Firmly the practices of giving, ethics, and patience,
Which were especially taught for householders
And which have an essence of compassion.

3. Summation 399

400 However, if from the unrighteousness of the world
It is difficult to rule religiously,
Then it is right for you to become a monastic
For the sake of practice and grandeur.

4. Advice to become a monastic if unable to learn the special royal ways 400

The fourth chapter of the *Precious Garland*, An Indication of Royal Policy, is finished.

5 Bodhisattva Deeds

E. Chapter 5: Advice for even Bodhisattvas wishing quickly to attain liberation to become monastics 401-87

1. Brief teachings of what is to be adopted and discarded by Bodhisattva householders and monastics 401-2

401 Then having become a monastic
You should first be intent on the training [in ethics].[89]
You should endeavor at the discipline of individual liberation,
At hearing frequently,[a] and delineating their meaning.

402 Then, you should forsake
These which are called assorted faults.[b]
With vigor you should definitely realize
Those renowned as the fifty-seven.[c]

2. Extensive exposition 403-87

a. Forsaking defects 403-34b

(1) Extensive explanation of fifty-seven defects to be forsaken 403-33

(a) The first fifteen, anger, etc. 403-12

1' One through fourteen, anger, etc. 403-6b

403 (1) Belligerence is a disturbance of mind.
(2) Enmity is a [tight][90] hanging onto that.
(3) Concealment is a hiding of ill-deeds[d] [when confronted].[91]
(4) Malevolence is to cling to ill-deeds.

404 (5) Dissimulation is deceptiveness.
(6) Deceit is crookedness of mind.
(7) Jealousy is to be bothered by others' good qualities.
(8) Miserliness is a fear of giving.

---

[a] This means to become learned in the three scriptural collections—discipline, discourses, and manifest knowledge.

[b] Dunne and McClintock (p. 124, n. 100) offer an ingenious alternative translation for these two lines: "Then you should eliminate those faults which are cited in the *Kṣudravastuka.*"

[c] For a most interesting article on the fifty-seven, see Michael Hahn, "On a Numerical Problem in Nāgārjuna's Ratnāvalī," in *Indological and Buddhist Studies: Volume in Honour of Professor J. W. de Jong on his Sixtieth Birthday* (Canberra: Faculty of Asian Studies, 1982), 161-185. Hahn's study is aimed as explaining the problem that Nāgārjuna says that there are fifty-seven faults but there appear to be either fifty-three (when the seven prides are counted as one) or 59 (when they are counted as seven). Hahn rejects Gyel-tsap's creative presentation of fifty-seven (which is based on counting the seven prides as one and finding two faults each in stanzas 416, 418, 427, and 428ab) but has no solution himself. See also Christian Lindtner's ingenious construction of a quite different list of fifty-seven in *Nagarjuniana,* Indiske Studier 4 (Copenhagen: Akademisk Forlag, 1982), 167-69. My translation follows Gyel-tsap's rendering.

[d] *sdigs pa, pāpa.* The term could be translated as "sins" and refers to mental, physical, and verbal actions that contravene either natural laws or formulated codes that one has vowed to uphold.

405 (9) Non-shame and (10) non-embarrassment
Are insensibility concerning oneself and others [respectively].[a]
(11) Inflatedness is not to pay respect.
(12) Faulty exertion is to be polluted by belligerence.

406 (13) Arrogance is haughtiness [due to wealth, and so forth].[92]
(14) Non-conscientiousness is non-application at virtues.
(15) Pride has seven forms
Each of which I will explain.

2' Pride 406c-12

407 Fancying that one is lower than the lowly,
Or equal with the equal,
Or greater than or equal to the lowly—
All are called the pride of selfhood.

408 Boasting that one is equal to those
Who by some good quality are superior to oneself
Is called exceeding pride.
Fancying that one is superior to the superior,

409 Thinking that one is higher than the very high,
Is pride beyond pride;
Like sores on an abscess
It is very vicious.

410 Conceiving an I through obscuration
In the five empty [aggregates][b]
Which are called the appropriation
Is said to be the pride of thinking I.

411 Thinking one has won fruits [of the spiritual path]
Not yet attained is the pride of conceit.
Praising oneself for faulty deeds
Is known by the wise as erroneous pride.

412 Deriding oneself, thinking
"I am useless," is called

---

[a] The first is not to refrain from ill-deeds out of concern for one's own self-image, whereas the second is not to refrain from ill-deeds out of concern for others' opinions of oneself (Gyel-tsap, 65b.1).

[b] Sanskrit reads "aggregates" instead of "empty."

The pride of inferiority.
Such is a brief description of the seven prides.

(b) From hypocrisy to the forty-first, not thinking of death 413-25

413 (16) Hypocrisy is to control the senses
For the sake of goods and respect.
(17) Flattery is to speak pleasant phrases
For the sake of goods and respect.

414 (18) Indirect acquisition is to praise
Another's wealth in order to acquire it.
(19) Pressured acquisition is manifest derision[a]
Of others in order to acquire goods.

415 (20) Desiring profit from profit
Is to praise previous acquisitions.
(21) Repeating faults is to recite again and again
The mistakes made by others.

416 (22) Non-collectedness is inconsiderate irritation
Arisen from illness.[b]

---

[a] To make derision as by saying that the person is very miserly, etc. (Gyel-tsap, 65a.5).

[b] The translation follows Gyel-tsap, 66a.6. The central term of the first two lines, *spungs med* ("Non-collectedness") is inexplicably different from the Sanskrit, *staimityam* which Dunne and McClintock (75) translate as "stupefaction" and thus render these two lines as: "Stupefaction is the state of being overwhelmed/ that comes from not thinking clearly or from illness." I have no solution for the disparity.

The Tibetan of the *zhol* edition:

spungs med so sor ma brtags par//
nad las gyur pa'i blong ba'o//
kun chags bdag gi yo byad ngan//
chags pa le lo can gyi yin//

differs significantly from the four printed canonical editions mentioned above (Hahn, 139):

spungs med so sor ma brtags par//
nad las gyur pa'i blong ba 'am//
bdag gi yo byad ngan pa la//
chags ngan le lo can gyi yin//

The *zhol* reading clearly presents two of the fifty-seven faults, *spungs med* and *kun chags*. Also, even the other reading which offers an "or" between the first two and last two lines can be seen as listing two types of *spungs med* and thus two faults. It would then be translated as:

(23) Non-collectedness is inconsiderate irritation
Arisen from illness,
(23) Or bad attachment to bad possessions
Is that [i.e., another non-collectedness] of the lazy.

This reading also applies to the Sanskrit as long as one takes account of *staimityam*. Thus both the *zhol* reading and an available alternative interpretation of the four canonical editions (and the Sanskrit) undermine Hahn's claim ("Numerical," 174) that the Tibetan clearly does not allow an interpretation of this stanza as presenting two of the fifty-seven faults.

(23) Clinging is the attachment
Of the lazy to their bad possessions.

417 (24) Discrimination of differences is
discrimination
Impeded by desire, hatred, or obscuration.
(25) Not looking into the mind is explained
As not applying it to anything.[a]

418 (26) Degeneration of respect and reverence for
deeds
Concordant with the practices occurs through
laziness.
(27) A bad person is regarded as being a spiritual
guide
[Pretending] to have the ways of the
Supramundane Victor.[b]

419 (28) Yearning is a small entanglement
Arising from lustful desire.
(29) Obsession, a great entanglement
Arising from desire.

420 (30) Avarice is an attitude
Of clinging to one's own property,
(31) Inopportune avarice is attachment
To the property of others.

421 (32) Irreligious lust is desirous praise
Of women who ought to be avoided.
(32) Hypocrisy is to pretend that one possesses
Good qualities that one lacks, while desiring ill
deeds.

422 (34) Great desire is extreme greed
Gone beyond the fortune of knowing
satisfaction.
(35) Desire for advantage is to want to be known
By whatever way as having superior good
qualities.

423 (36) Non-endurance is an inability
To bear injury and suffering.

---

[a] Gyel-tsap (66b.1) describes this as not taking to mind either desire, hatred, or bewilderment or as not taking to mind either virtues or non-virtues.

[b] With considerable ingenuity, Gyel-tsap (66b.2) breaks this stanza into two parts to make it yield two faults.

(37) Impropriety is not to respect the activities
Of a teacher or spiritual guide.

424 (38) Not heeding advice is to not respect
Counsel concordant with practice.
(39) Intention to meet with relatives
Is sentimental attachment to one's kin.

425 (40) Attachment to objects[a] is to relate
Their good qualities in order to acquire them.
(41) Fancying immortality is to be
Unaffected by concern over death.

(c) The forty-second, proclaiming one's own good qualities, etc. 426-33

426 (42) Conceptuality concerned with approbation
Is the thought that—no matter what—
Others will take one as a spiritual guide
Due to possessing good qualities.

427 (43, 44) Conceptuality concerned with attachment to others
Is an intention to help or not help others
Due to being affected by desire
Or an intent to harm.[b]

428 (45) Dislike is a mind that is unsteady.
(46) Desiring union is a dirtied mind.[c]
(47) Indifference is a laziness with a sense of inadequacy
Coming from a listless body.

429 (48) Distortion is for the afflictive emotions
To influence body and color.
(49) Not wishing for food is explained
As physical sluggishness due to over-eating.

430 (50) A very dejected mind is taught
To be fearful faintheartedness.
(51) Longing for desires is to desire
And seek after the five attributes.[d]

431 (52) Harmful intent arises from nine causes
Of intending to injure others—

---

[a] Following Gyel-tsap (67a.2). The Sanskrit, however, means "country" or "area," as in being over-attached to one's own locale.

[b] Gyel-tsap (67a.4.) splits this item into two.

[c] Gyel-tsap (67a.5) views the first two lines of this stanza as indicating two items—a reading that clearly accords with the *zhol* edition (see text).

[d] Pleasant forms, sounds, odors, tastes, and tangible objects.

Having senseless qualms concerning oneself,
friends, and foes[a]
In the past, present, and future.

432 (53) Sluggishness is non-activity
Due to heaviness of mind and body.
(54) Drowsiness is sleepiness.
(55) Excitement is strong disquiet of body and
mind.

433 (56) Contrition is regret for bad deeds
Which arises afterwards from grief about them.
(57) Doubt is to be of two minds
About the [four] truths,[b] the Three Jewels,[c] and
so forth.

(2) Summation 434ab

434 [Householder] Bodhisattvas abandon those.
Those diligent in [monastic] vows abandon
more.

b. Adopting good qualities 434c-87b

(1) Temporary good qualities 434c-61b

(a) General teaching 434c-9

1' Brief description of the entities of good qualities 434c-35

Freed from these defects
Good qualities are easily observed.

435 Briefly the good qualities
Observed by Bodhisattvas are
Giving, ethics, patience, effort,
Concentration, wisdom, compassion, and so
forth.

2' Identifying the individual entities of good qualities 436-37

436 Giving is to give away one's wealth.
Ethics is to help others.
Patience is to have forsaken anger.
Effort is enthusiasm for virtues.

437 Concentration is unafflicted one-pointedness.
Wisdom is ascertainment of the meaning of the
truths.
Compassion is a mind having the one savor
Of mercy for all sentient beings.

3' Individual effects 438

438 From giving there arises wealth, from ethics
happiness,
From patience a good appearance, from [effort
in] virtue brilliance,

[a] The qualms are that oneself and/or one's friends will be harmed and that one's enemies will be helped (Gyel-tsap, 67b.2).

[b] Suffering, origin of suffering, cessation of suffering, and path.

[c] Buddha, doctrine (realizational and scriptural), and spiritual community.

From concentration peace, from wisdom liberation,
From compassion all aims are achieved.

439 From the simultaneous perfection
Of all those seven is attained
The sphere of inconceivable wisdom,
The protectorship of the world.[a]

4' General effect 439

440 Just as eight grounds of Hearers
Are described in the Hearers' Vehicle,
So ten grounds of Bodhisattvas
Are described in the Great Vehicle.[b]

(b) Good qualities of the ten grounds 440-61b

1' Just as there are eight grounds of Hearers, so there are ten Bodhisattva grounds 440

2' Entities and good qualities of the ten grounds 441-60

441 The first of these is the Very Joyful
Because those Bodhisattvas are rejoicing
From having forsaken the three entwinements[c]
And being born into the lineage of Ones Gone Thus.

442 Through the maturation of those [good qualities][d]
The perfection of giving becomes supreme.

---

[a] That is to say, Buddhahood (Gyel-tsap, 68b.2.

[b] As Ḏzong-ka-ɓa says about Chandrakīrti's *Supplement:*

> Chandrakīrti's explanation here of eleven grounds—the Very Joyful and so forth—is based on Nāgārjuna's rough presentation of the ten grounds of the eleventh [Buddhahood]....Chandrakīrti also bases his explanation on the *Sūtra on the Ten Grounds* (*mdo sde sa bcu pa, daśabhūmikasūtra*).

See Tsong-ka-pa, Kensur Lekden, and Jeffrey Hopkins, *Compassion in Tibetan Buddhism,* 131.

[c] Viewing the mental and physical aggregates which are a transitory collection as a real self, afflicted doubt, and considering bad ethics and disciplines to be superior (Gyel-tsap, 69b.3). Based on five stanzas in the *Precious Garland,* Ḏzong-ka-ɓa presents the argument that the afflictive emotions abandoned on the first Bodhisattva ground are artificial, or acquired, defilements and not innate defilements:

> In commenting, Chandrakīrti does not clearly state either that the artificial afflictive emotions are abandoned on the first ground or that the innate afflictive emotions are abandoned from the second ground. However, Nāgārjuna's *Precious Garland* explains that until the eighth ground is attained, the seeds of all afflictive emotions are not removed [stanzas 455-56], that the conception of true existence is assigned as an afflictive emotion [stanza 35], that until that conception is removed the view of the transitory is not removed [stanza 35], and that the three links [view of the transitory collection as real "I" and "mine," afflicted doubt, and viewing bad ethics and codes of discipline as superior] are abandoned on the first ground [stanza 441]. Therefore, it is extremely clear that afflictive emotions in general are divided into two [artificial and innate] and that the view of the transitory in particular must be divided in the same way.

See Tsong-ka-pa, Kensur Lekden, and Jeffrey Hopkins, *Compassion in Tibetan Buddhism,* 220.

[d] "Qualities" in each of these ten is added from Gyel-tsap, 70a.1.

They vibrate a hundred worlds
And become Great Lords of Jambudvīpa.[a]

443 The second is called the Stainless
Because all ten [virtuous] actions
Of body, speech, and mind are stainless
And they naturally abide in those [deeds of ethics].

444 Through the maturation of those [good qualities]
The perfection of ethics becomes supreme.
They become Universal Monarchs helping beings,
Masters of the glorious [four continents][93] and of the seven precious objects.[b]

445 The third ground is called the Luminous
Because the pacifying light of wisdom arises.
The concentrations and clairvoyances are generated,
And desire and hatred are completely extinguished.

446 Through the maturation of those [good qualities]
They practice supremely the deeds of patience
And become a great wise monarch of the gods.
They put an end to desire.

447 The fourth is called the Radiant
Because the light of true wisdom arises.
They cultivate supremely
All the harmonies with enlightenment.[c]

---

[a] This is the southern continent of a four continent world-system.

[b] Precious—that is to say, valuable—chariots, jewels, consorts, ministers, elephants, horses, and generals.

[c] The thirty-seven harmonies with enlightenment are divided into seven sections:

I. four establishments through mindfulness: 1 mindful establishment on body; 2 mindful establishment on feeling; 3 mindful establishment on mind; 4 mindful establishment on phenomena. **II. four thorough abandonings:** 5 generating virtuous qualities not yet generated; 6 increasing virtuous qualities already generated; 7 not generating non-virtuous qualities not yet generated; 8 thoroughly abandoning non-virtuous qualities already generated. **III. four legs of manifestation:** 9 aspiration; 10 effort; 11 contemplation; 12 analytical meditative stabilization. **IV. five faculties:** 13 faith; 14 effort; 15 mindfulness; 16 meditative stabilization; 17 wisdom. **V. five powers:** 18 faith; 19 effort; 20 mindfulness; 21 meditative stabilization; 22 wisdom. **VI. seven branches of enlightenment:** 23 correct mindfulness; 24 correct discrimination of phenomena; 25 correct effort; 26 correct joy; 27 correct pliancy; 28 correct meditative stabilization; 29 correct equanimity. **VII. eightfold path:** 30 correct view; 31 correct realization; 32 correct speech; 33

448 Through the maturation of those [good qualities]
They become monarchs of the gods in [the heaven] Without Combat.
They are skilled in quelling the arising of the view
That the transitory collection [is inherently existent I and mine].

449 The fifth is called the Extremely Difficult to Overcome
Because all evil ones find it extremely hard to conquer them.
They become skilled in knowing
The subtle meanings of the noble truths and so forth.

450 Through the maturation of those [good qualities]
They become monarchs of the gods abiding in the Joyous Land,
They overcome the foundations of all Forders
Afflictive emotions and views.

451 The sixth is called the Approaching
Because they are approaching the good qualities of a Buddha.
Through familiarity with calm abiding and special insight
They attain cessation and hence are advanced [in wisdom].

452 Through the maturation of those [good qualities]
They become monarchs of the gods [in the land] of Liking Emanation.
Hearers cannot surpass them.
They pacify those with the pride of superiority.

453 The seventh is the Gone Afar
Because the number [of good qualities] has increased.
Moment by moment they [can][94] enter
The equipoise of cessation.

correct aims of actions; 34 correct livelihood; 35 correct exertion; 36 correct mindfulness; 37 correct meditative stabilization.

454 Through the maturation of those [good qualities]
They become masters of the gods [in the land] of Control over Others' Emanations.
They become great leaders of teachers
Who know direct realization of the [four] noble truths.

455 The eighth is the Immovable, the youthful ground.
Through non-conceptuality they are immovable,
And the spheres of activity
Of their body, speech, and mind are inconceivable.

456 Through the maturation of those [good qualities]
They become a Brahmā, master of a thousand worlds.
Foe Destroyers, Solitary Realizers, and so forth
Cannot surpass them in positing the meaning [of doctrines].[95]

457 The ninth ground is called Excellent Intelligence.
Like a regent they have attained
Correct individual realization
And therefore have good intelligence.

458 Through the maturation of those [good qualities]
They become a Brahmā, master of a million worlds.
Foe Destroyers and so forth cannot surpass them
In [responding to] questions in the thoughts of sentient beings.

459 The tenth is the Cloud of Doctrine
Because the rain of holy doctrine falls.
The Bodhisattva is bestowed empowerment
With light rays by the Buddhas.

460 Through the maturation of those [good qualities]
They become master of the gods of Pure Abode.
They are supreme great lords,
Master of the sphere of infinite wisdom.

3' Summation 461ab

461 Thus those ten grounds are renowned
As the ten Bodhisattva grounds.

(2) Final good qualities 461c-87

(a) Each of a Buddha's good qualities is limitless 461c-63

1' The Buddhas' limitless good qualities depend on the ten powers 461c-62b

The ground of Buddhahood is different.
Being in all ways inconceivable,

462 Its great extent is merely said
To be endowed with the ten powers.

2' Examples of the limitlessness of Buddhas' good qualities 462c-63

Each power is immeasurable too
Like [the limitless number of] all transmigrators.

463 The limitlessness of a Buddha's [good qualities]
Is said to be like the limitlessness
Of space, earth, water, fire,
And wind in all directions.

(b) Causes for generating belief and faith in the limitless good qualities of Buddhas 464-87

1' The reason why Buddhas' good qualities are limitless is that the causal merits are limitless 464-68

a' Source for the limitlessness of Buddhas' good qualities 464

464 If the causes are [reduced][96] to a mere [measure]
And not seen to be limitless,
One will not believe the limitlessness
[Of the good qualities][97] of the Buddhas.

b' Way to amass limitless merit 465

465 Therefore in the presence of an image
Or monument or something else
Say these twenty stanzas
Three times every day:

c' Brief presentation of the seven branches 466-68

466 Going for refuge with all forms of respect
To the Buddhas, excellent Doctrine,
Supreme Community, and Bodhisattvas,
I bow down to all that are worthy of honor.

467 I will turn away from all ill deeds
And thoroughly take up all meritorious actions.
I will admire all the merits
Of all embodied beings.

468 With bowed head and joined palms
I petition the perfect Buddhas
To turn the wheel of doctrine and remain
As long as transmigrating beings remain.

2' Limitlessness of the causes because of aspiring to help limitless beings 469-85

469 Through the merit of having done thus
And through the merit that I did earlier and will do
May all sentient beings aspire
To the highest enlightenment.

470 May all sentient beings have all the stainless faculties,
Release from all conditions of non-leisure,
Freedom of action,
And endowment with good livelihood.

471 Also may all embodied beings
Have jewels in their hands,
And may all the limitless necessities of life remain
Unconsumed as long as there is cyclic existence.

472 May all women at all times
Become supreme persons.[a]
May all embodied beings have
The intelligence [of wisdom][98] and the legs [of ethics].

473 May embodied beings have a pleasant complexion,
Good physique, great splendor,
A pleasing appearance, freedom from disease,
Strength, and long life.

474 May all be skilled in the means [to extinguish suffering][99]
And have liberation from all suffering,
Inclination to the Three Jewels,
And the great wealth of Buddha's doctrine.

[a] Here I am following Ajitamitra (Golden Reprint, vol. 183, 479.4) who reads *skyes mchog* as *skyes pu'i mchog* "supreme person" and thus takes Nāgārjuna as referring to Buddhas "since Buddhas are the supreme over all sentient beings." As an alternate reading, he says the reference could be to other supreme persons not included among Buddhas. Gyel-tsap (73a.6), however, takes the line in a sexist way as, "May all women at all times/ Become supreme men," (reading *skyes mchog* as *skyes pa mchog*). The Sanskrit of this stanza is not extant but would be clear as to its referent, and thus Ajitamitra is the accurate source. Still, the line has a sexist bent, and thus contemporary practitioners could adapt these line to read, "May all beings at all times/ Be born as supreme beings." It is said that in Nāgārjuna's exposition of Highest Yoga Mantra (*sngags bla med, anuttarayogamantra*) male and female are considered to be equal.

475 May they be adorned with love, compassion, joy,
Even-mindedness [devoid of][100] the afflictive emotions,
Giving, ethics, patience, effort,
Concentration, and wisdom.

476 Completing the two collections [of merit and wisdom],
May they have the brilliant marks and beautiful features [even while on the path],[101]
And may they cross without interruption
The ten inconceivable grounds.

477 May I also be adorned completely
With those and all other good qualities,
Be freed from all defects,
And have superior love for all sentient beings.

478 May I perfect all the virtues
For which all sentient beings hope,
And may I always relieve
The sufferings of all embodied beings.

479 May those beings in all worlds
Who are distressed through fear
Become entirely fearless
Even through merely hearing my name.

480 Through seeing or thinking of me or only hearing my name
May beings attain great joy,
Naturalness free from error,
Definiteness toward complete enlightenment,

481 And the five clairvoyances[a]
Throughout their continuum of lives.
May I always in all ways bring
Help and happiness to all sentient beings.

482 May I always without harm
Simultaneously stop
All beings in all worlds
Who wish to commit ill deeds.

---

[a] These are visual clairvoyance, auditory clairvoyance, clairvoyance knowing others' minds, clairvoyance knowing magical emanation, and clairvoyance knowing former lives.

483 May I always be an object of enjoyment
For all sentient beings according to their wish
And without interference, as are the earth,
Water, fire, wind, herbs, and wild forests.

484 May I be as dear to sentient beings as their own life,
And may they be even more dear to me.
May their ill deeds fructify for me,
And all my virtues fructify for them.

485 As long as any sentient being
Anywhere has not been liberated,
May I remain [in the world][102] for the sake of that being
Though I have attained highest enlightenment.

3' Immeasurability of the merit of those virtues 486

486 If the merit of saying this
Had form, it would never fit
Into realms of worlds as numerous
As the sand grains of the Ganges.

4' Sources 487

487 The Supramundane Victor said so,
And the reasoning is this:
[The limitlessness of the merit of][103] wishing to help limitless realms
Of sentient beings is like [the limitlessness of those beings].

III. Conclusion 488-500

A. Advice to generate inspiration for the practices and to observe the four practices 488-90

488 These practices that I have explained
Briefly to you in this way
Should be as dear to you
As your body always is.

489 Those who feel a dearness for the practices
Have in fact a dearness for their body.
If dearness [for the body][104] helps it,
The practices will do just that.

490 Therefore pay heed to the practices as you do to yourself.
Pay heed to achievement as you do to the practices.
Pay heed to wisdom as you do to achievement.
Pay heed to the wise as you do to wisdom.

B. Faults of not relying on a teacher and qualifications of a teacher 491-93ab

491 Those who have qualms that it would be bad
for themselves
[If they relied] on one who has purity, love,
and intelligence
As well as helpful and appropriate speech,
Cause their own interests to be destroyed.

492 You should know in brief
The qualifications of spiritual guides.
If you are taught by those knowing
contentment
And having compassion and ethics,

493 As well as wisdom that can drive out your
afflictive emotions,
You should realize [what they teach] and
respect them.

C. The supreme fruit is achieved through excellent behavior 493c-97

1. Achieving the supreme fruit 493cd

You will attain the supreme achievement
By following this excellent system:

2. Advice to perform the special deeds 494-97

a. Extensive mode of behavior 494-97

494 Speak the truth, speak gently to sentient
beings.
Be of pleasant nature, compelling.
Be politic, do not wish to defame,
Be independent, and speak well.

495 Be well-disciplined, contained, generous,
Magnificent, of peaceful mind,
Not excitable, not procrastinating,
Not deceitful, but amiable.[a]

b. Condensed mode of behavior 496

496 Be gentle[b] like a full moon.
Be lustrous like the sun in autumn.
Be deep like the ocean.
Be firm like Mount Meru.

c. Very condensed mode of behavior 497

497 Freed from all defects
And adorned with all good qualities,

---

[a] Although *nges par* (certain) appears in both the *zhol* and the *sde dge* (250.6) editions and in Gyel-tsap (76a.3, who refers to two readings *nges par* and *nges pa*), the Sanskrit is *dakṣiṇaḥ* (able, clever, upright, amiable) which would be *des par* in Tibetan—orthographically easily mistaken to be *nges par*. The Peking (183.1.6), Golden Reprint (vol. 183, 360.6), and Hahn (167) read *des par*.

[b] Although *nges pa* (certain) appears in both the *zhol* and the *sde dge* (250.6) editions and in Gyel-tsap (76.3) who says, "Be disciplined, brave, and certain like the full moon" (*zla ba nya ba bzhin dul zhing mdzangs la nges pa*), the Sanskrit is *saumyas* (gentle, agreeable, pleasant, mild) which would be *des pa* in Tibetan—orthographically easily mistaken to be *nges pa*. The Peking (183.1.6), Golden Reprint (vol. 183, 360.6), and Hahn (167) read *des pa*.

Become a sustenance for all sentient beings
And become omniscient.

D. These doctrines are not just for monarchs but also for all others 498

498 These doctrines were not just taught
Only for monarchs
But were taught with a wish to help
Other sentient beings as befits them.

E. Exhorting the king to heed the advice 499-500

1. Suitability of continuously thinking of the welfare of others 499

499 O King, it would be right for you
Each day to think about this advice
So that you and others may achieve
Complete and perfect enlightenment.

2. Suitability of adopting virtues 500

500 For the sake of enlightenment aspirants should always apply themselves
To ethics, supreme respect for teachers, patience, non-jealousy, non-miserliness,
Endowment with the wealth of altruism without hope for reward, helping the destitute,
Remaining with supreme people, leaving the non-supreme, and thoroughly maintaining the doctrine.

The fifth chapter of the *Precious Garland*, An Indication of the Bodhisattva Deeds, is finished.

Here ends the *Precious Garland of Advice for a King* by the great master, the Superior Nāgārjuna. It was translated by the Indian professor Vidyākaraprabha[a] and the Tibetan translator and monastic Ḃel-ḋzek.[b] Consulting three Sanskrit editions, the Indian professor Kanakavarman and the Tibetan monastic Ḃa-tsap Nyi-ma-drak[c] corrected translations and other points that did not accord with the unique thought of the Superior [Nāgārjuna] and his spiritual son [Āryadeva]. It was printed at the great publishing house below [the Potala in Hla-ṡa].

[a] King Tri-ṡong-day-ḋzen (*khri srong lde btsan*) invited him to Tibet in the latter half of the eighth century CE (Hahn, 16).

[b] *dpal brtsegs;* see George N. Roerich, *The Blue Annals,* 102, 331, 344.

[c] *pa tshab nyi ma grags,* born 1055. For discussion of his contribution to Tibetan understanding of Mādhyamika, see Karen Lang, "sPa tshab Nyi ma grags and the Introduction of Prāsaṅgika Madhyamaka into Tibet," in *Reflections on Tibetan Culture: Essays in Memory of Turrell V. Wylie,* edited by Lawrence Epstein and Richard Sherburne (Lewiston, NY: Edwin Mellen Press, 1990). For discussion of his birth year, see van der Kuijp, "Notes on the Transmission of Nagarjuna's Ratnavali in Tibet," *The Tibet Journal,* Summer 1985, vol. X, No. 2, 4.

PART 3:
TIBETAN TEXT

In 1972 when I originally translated the *Precious Garland*, I primarily used the edition printed by the press at the base of the Potala in Hla-ša (*zhol* edition)[a] and in the possession of the Ñam-gyel[b] College in Dharamsala. Since it was error-laden, I compared it with the Peking edition as found in the *Tibetan Tripiṭaka* (Tokyo-Kyoto: Tibetan Tripiṭaka Research Foundation, 1956)[c] and with the readings found in Gyel-tsap's commentary, *Illumination of the Essential Meanings of (Nāgārjuna's) "Precious Garland of Madhyamaka"*; it is clear Gyel-tsap consulted at least two editions of the text[d] as well as Ajitamitra's commentary. The intended result is an improved edition of the *zhol*, accessible here in the same volume as the translation. A critical edition of the surviving Sanskrit and four editions in written canons—*snar thang*, Peking, *sde dge*, and *co ne*—but not the *zhol* edition has been published by Michael Hahn,[e] and a critical edition of the same four editions as well as the *zhol* together with Ajitamitra's commentary on the same page has been published by Ācārya Ngawang Samten[f]; hence here I have kept listings of variants to a bare minimum.

The edited text was written out by Palden in Dharamsala in December, 1972. Gyel-tsap's outline of the stanzas is given in Tibetan script following the text, after which is a list of emendations.

---

[a] Translated by the Indian Vidyākaraprabha (*rigs byed 'od zer*) and the Tibetan Translator from Shu-chen Ɓel-ḋzek (*zhu chen kyi lo tstsha ba dpal brtsegs*) and emended by the Indian Kanakavarman and the Tibetan Ɓa-tsap Nyi-ma-drak (*pa tshab nyi ma grags*).

[b] *rnam rgyal*.

[c] Translated by the Indian Jñānagarbha and the Tibetan Ḻu-gyel-tsen (*klu'i rgyal mtshan*) and emended by the Indian Kanakavarman and the Tibetan Ɓa-tsap Nyi-ma-drak (*pa tshab nyi ma grags*). My notes were taken in the margins of a photo-offset publication of a hand-written copy of the *zhol* edition in Prof. Mr. L. P. Lhalungpa, *Dbuma Rigs Tshogs Drug: The Six Yuktishastra of Madhyamika* (Delhi: 1970); however, I am not including here an indication of the few further errors in that edition since the purpose is to present a critical edition of the *zhol*.

[d] For instance, with respect to verse 235d Gyel-tsap (43a.5) gives two readings—first *chos drug gus par bsten par mdzod* and then a variant from another edition *chos ni nge par bsten pa mdzod*:

> sngar bshad pa'i chos drug gis gus par bsten par
> mdzod ces gdams so// dpe kha cig las/ chos ni nge
> par bsten pa mdzod ces 'byung ngo

As Ācārya Ngawang Samten (*Ratnāvalī of Ācārya Nāgārjuna with the Commentary by Ajitamitra*, Bibliotheca Indo-Tibetica Series-XXI [Sarnath: Central Institute of Higher Tibetan Studies, 1990], 19.15) says, this reading is not found either in the *zhol* or the other four currently available editions, thus indicating that Gyel-tsap had an edition that is not currently available.

Also, in his commentary on stanza 356 Gyel-tsap (56b.6) incorporates two readings without saying he is doing so: *'das ma 'ongs* ***de gnyis las ni ma 'das pa*** (56b.6) as in the *zhol* reading and *'das ma 'ongs* ***de gnyis las tha dad du grub pa med*** (57a.1) as in the four editions found in the written canons; in addition he uses both *da lta'i* (57a.2) as in *zhol* and *da ltar* (57a.1) as in the four. Such instances indicate that van der Kuijp's speculation ("Notes on the Transmission of Nagarjuna's Ratnavali in Tibet," *The Tibet Journal*, Summer 1985, vol. X, No. 2, 5) that Gyel-tsap had only one edition available to him is unfounded.

[e] *Nāgārjuna's Ratnāvalī*, vol.1, The Basic Texts (Sanskrit, Tibetan, and Chinese) (Bonn: Indica et Tibetica Verlag, 1982).

[f] For bibliographic information see the previous footnote. For Ācārya Ngawang Samten's well-reasoned presentation on the different editions, see the same, 15.14-21.2.

༄། །མགོན་པོ་ཀླུ་སྒྲུབ་ཀྱིས་མཛད་པའི།

རྒྱལ་པོ་ལ་གཏམ་བྱ་བ་རིན་པོ་ཆེའི་ཕྲེང་བ

བཞུགས་སོ། །

༄། །རྒྱ་གར་སྐད་དུ། རཱ་ཛ་པ་རི་ཀ་ཐཱ་ར་ཏྣ་མཱ་ལཱི།
བོད་སྐད་དུ། རྒྱལ་པོ་ལ་གཏམ་བྱ་བ་རིན་པོ་ཆེའི་ཕྲེང་བ།

སངས་རྒྱས་དང་བྱང་ཆུབ་སེམས་དཔའ་ཐམས་ཅད་ལ་ཕྱག་འཚལ་ལོ། །

༡ ཉེས་པ་ཀུན་ལས་རྣམ་གྲོལ་ཞིང་། །
ཡོན་ཏན་ཀུན་གྱིས་བརྒྱན་པ་པོ། །
སེམས་ཅན་ཀུན་གྱི་གཉེན་གཅིག་པུ། །
ཐམས་ཅད་མཁྱེན་ལ་ཕྱག་འཚལ་ལོ། །

༢ རྒྱལ་པོ་ཁྱོད་ལ་ཆོས་བསྒྲུབ་ཕྱིར། །
གཅིག་ཏུ་དགེ་བའི་ཆོས་བཤད་དེ། །
དམ་པའི་ཆོས་ཀྱི་སྣོད་ལ་ནི། །
ཆོས་འགྲུབ་འགྱུར་ཏེ་གང་ཞིག་ལ། །

༣ དང་པོར་མངོན་པར་མཐོ་བའི་ཆོས། །
ཕྱིས་ནི་ངེས་པར་ལེགས་འབྱུང་བའོ། །
གང་ཕྱིར་མངོན་པར་མཐོ་ཐོབ་ནས། །
རིམ་གྱིས་ངེས་པར་ལེགས་པ་འོང་། །

༤ དེ་ལ་མངོན་མཐོ་བདེ་བ་སྟེ། །
ངེས་པར་ལེགས་པ་ཐར་པར་འདོད། །
དེ་ཡི་སྒྲུབ་པ་མདོར་བསྡུ་ན། །
མདོར་ན་དད་དང་ཤེས་རབ་བོ། །

༥ དད་ཅན་ཉིད་ཕྱིར་ཆོས་ལ་བརྟེན། །
ཤེས་རབ་ལྡན་ཕྱིར་ཡང་དག་རིག །
འདི་གཉིས་གཙོ་བོ་ཤེས་རབ་སྟེ། །
དེ་ཡི་སྔོན་འགྲོ་དད་པ་ཡིན། །

༦ འདུན་དང་ཞེ་སྡང་འཇིགས་པ་དང་། །
རྨོངས་པས་གང་ཞིག་ཆོས་མི་འདའ། །
དེ་ནི་དད་པ་ཅན་ཞེས་བྱ། །
ངེས་པར་ལེགས་པའི་སྣོད་མཆོག་ཡིན། །

༧ གང་ཞིག་ལུས་ངག་ཡིད་ཀྱི་ལས། །
ཐམས་ཅད་ལེགས་པར་ཡོངས་བརྟགས་ཏེ། །
བདག་དང་གཞན་ལ་ཕན་ཤེས་ནས། །
རྟག་ཏུ་བྱེད་པ་དེ་མཁས་པ། །

༨ མི་གསོད་པ་དང་རྐུ་སྤོང་དང་། །
གཞན་གྱི་ཆུང་མ་སྤོང་བ་དང་། །
ལོག་དང་ཕྲ་མ་རྩུབ་ཉིད་དང་། །
མ་འབྲེལ་སྨྲ་བ་ཡང་དག་སྡོམ། །

༩ ཆགས་དང་གནོད་སེམས་མེད་པ་པ། །
ཉིད་ཀྱི་ལྟ་བ་ཡོངས་སྤོང་བ། །
འདི་དག་ལས་ལམ་དཀར་བཅུ་སྟེ། །
བཟློག་པ་དག་ནི་ནག་པོ་ཡིན། །

༡༠ ཆང་མི་འཐུང་དང་འཚོ་བ་བཟང་། །
རྣམ་མི་འཚེ་དང་གུས་སྦྱིན་དང་། །
མཆོད་འོས་མཆོད་དང་བྱམས་པ་སྟེ། །
མདོར་ན་ཆོས་ནི་དེ་ཡིན་ནོ། །

༡༡ ལུས་གདུང་བྱེད་པ་འབའ་ཞིག་ལས། །
ཆོས་མེད་འདི་ལྟར་དེ་ཡིས་ནི། །
གཞན་ལ་གནོད་པ་སྤོང་མེད་ཅིང་། །
གཞན་ལ་ཕན་འདོགས་ཡོད་མ་ཡིན། །

༡༢ སྦྱིན་དང་ཚུལ་ཁྲིམས་བཟོད་གསལ་ལ་བ། །
དམ་ཆོས་ལམ་པོ་ཆེ་ལ་གང་། །
མ་གུས་ལུས་གདུང་གནག་ལམ་ལྟ་རི། །
ལམ་གོལ་དགནས་འགྲོ་བ་དེ། །

༡༣ འཁོར་བའི་འབྲོག་ནི་མི་བཟད་པ། །
མཐའ་ཡས་སྐྱེ་བོའི་ཤིང་ཅན་དུ། །
ཉོན་མོངས་གདུག་པས་འཁྱུད་པའི་ལུས། །
ཤིན་ཏུ་ཡུན་རིང་འཇུག་པར་འགྱུར། །

༡༤ གསོད་པ་ཡིས་ནི་ཚེ་ཐུང་འགྱུར། །
རྣམ་པར་འཚེ་བས་གནོད་པ་མང་། །
རྐུ་བ་ཡིས་ནི་ལོངས་སྤྱོད་ཕོངས། །
ཀྱི་པོ་བྱེད་པས་དགྲ་དང་བཅས། །

༢༥ བརྫུན་དུ་སྨྲ་བས་སྐུར་པ་སྟེ། །
ཕྲ་མ་ཡིས་ནི་བཤེས་དང་འབྱེད། །
རྩུབ་མོ་ཉིད་ཀྱིས་མི་སྙན་ཐོས། །
མི་འབྲེལ་བ་ཡིས་ཚིག་མི་བཙུན། །

༢༦ བརྣབ་སེམས་ཡིད་ལ་རེ་བ་འཇོམས།།
གནོད་སེམས་འཇིགས་པ་སྦྱིན་པར་བྱེད།།
ལོག་པར་ལྟ་བས་ལྟ་ངན་ཉིད། །
ཆང་འཐུང་བ་ཡིས་བློ་འཁྲུལ་ཏེ། །

༢༧ མ་བྱིན་ལེན་པས་དབུལ་བ་ཉིད།།
ལོག་པར་འཚོ་བས་བསླུས་པ་སྟེ།།
ཁེངས་པ་ཡིས་ནི་རིགས་ངན་ཉིད།།
ཕྲག་དོག་གིས་ནི་གཟི་ཆུང་ཉིད།།

༢༨ ཁྲོ་བས་ཁ་དོག་ངན་པ་ཉིད། །
མཁས་ལ་མི་འདྲི་བླུན་པ་ཉིད།།
མི་ཉིད་ལ་ནི་འབྲས་བུ་འདི།།
ཀུན་གྱིས་དང་པོར་ངན་འགྲོ་འོ།།

༢༩ མི་དགེ་ཞེས་བྱ་དེ་དག་གི །
རྣམ་སྨིན་བསྔགས་པ་གང་ཡིན་པ།།
དགེ་བ་དག་ནི་ཐམས་ཅད་ལ།།
འབྲས་བུ་དེ་ནི་བཟློག་སྟེ་འབྱུང་།།

༣༠ ཆགས་དང་ཞེ་སྡང་གཏི་མུག་དང་།
དེས་བསྐྱེད་ལས་ནི་མི་དགེ་བ།།
མ་ཆགས་ཞེ་སྡང་གཏི་མུག་མེད།།
དེས་བསྐྱེད་ལས་ནི་དགེ་བ་ཡིན།།

༣༡ མི་དགེ་བ་ལས་སྡུག་བསྔལ་ཀུན། །
དེ་བཞིན་ངན་འགྲོ་ཐམས་ཅད་དོ། །
དགེ་ལས་བདེ་འགྲོ་ཐམས་ཅད་དང་། །
སྐྱེ་བ་ཀུན་ཏུ་བདེ་བ་དག །

༣༣ ཡིད་དང་ལུས་དང་ངག་གིས་ནི། །
མི་དགེ་ཀུན་ལས་ལྡོག་བྱ་ཞིང་། །
དགེ་ལ་རྟག་ཏུ་འཇུག་བྱ་བ། །
འདི་ནི་ཆོས་རྣམ་གསུམ་དུ་བཤད།།

༢༣ ཆོས་འདི་དམྱལ་བ་ཡི་དྭགས་དང་།།
དུད་འགྲོ་དག་ལས་ནམ་གྲོལ་ཞིང་།།
ལྷ་དང་མི་ཡི་ནང་དག་ཏུ། །
བདེ་དཔལ་ལ་རྒྱལ་སྲིད་རྒྱས་པ་འཐོབ།།

༢༤ བསམ་གཏན་ཚད་མེད་གཟུགས་མེད་ནི། །
ཚངས་སོགས་བདེ་བ་སྤྱོད་པར་བྱེད། །
དེ་ལྟར་མངོན་མཐོའི་ཆོས་འདི་དང་།།
དེ་ཡི་འབྲས་བུ་མདོར་བསྡུས་པའོ། །

༢༥ ༄ ངེས་པར་ལེགས་པའི་ཆོས་དག་ཀྱང་། །
ཕྲ་ཞིང་ཟབ་པར་སྣང་བ་དང་། །
བྱིས་པ་ཐོས་དང་མི་ལྡན་པ། །
སྐྲག་པར་བྱེད་པར་རྒྱལ་བས་གསུངས། །

༢༦ བདག་ཡོད་མ་ཡིན་ཡོད་མི་འགྱུར།།
བདག་གི་ཡོད་མིན་མི་འགྱུར་ཞེས།།
བྱིས་པ་དག་ནི་དེ་ལྟར་སྐྲག །
མཁས་པ་ལ་ནི་སྐྲག་པ་ཟད། །

༢༧ སྐྱེ་དགུ་འདི་ནི་མ་ལུས་པ། །
ངར་འཛིན་པ་ལས་བྱུང་བ་དང་།།
ང་ཡིར་འཛིན་ལྡན་སྐྱེ་དགུ་ལ། །
ཕན་པ་གཅིག་ཏུ་གསུང་བས་གསུངས།།

༢༨ བདག་ཡོད་བདག་གི་ཡོད་ཅེས་པ།།
འདི་ནི་དམ་པའི་དོན་དུ་ལོག །
གང་ཕྱིར་ཡང་དག་ཇི་ལྟ་བ། །
ཡོངས་སུ་ཤེས་པས་གཉིས་མི་འབྱུང་། །

༢༩ ངར་འཛིན་ལས་བྱུང་ཕུང་པོ་རྣམས།།
ངར་འཛིན་དེ་ནི་དོན་དུ་བརྫུན། །
གང་གི་ས་བོན་བརྫུན་པ་དེའི། །
སྐྱེ་བ་བདེན་པ་ག་ལ་ཞིག །

༣༠ ཕུང་པོ་དེ་ལྟར་མི་བདེན་པར། །
མཐོང་ནས་ངར་འཛིན་སྤོང་བར་འགྱུར།།
ངར་འཛིན་པ་དག་སྤངས་ནས་ནི། །
ཕྱིས་ནི་ཕུང་པོ་འབྱུང་མི་འགྱུར། །

༣༡ ཇི་ལྟར་མེ་ལོང་བརྟེན་ནས་སུ། །
རང་བཞིན་གཟུགས་བརྙན་སྣང་མོད་ཀྱི།།
དེ་ནི་ཡང་དག་ཉིད་དུ་ན།།
ཅུང་ཟད་ཀྱང་ནི་ཡོད་མིན་པ། །

༣༢ དེ་བཞིན་ཕུང་པོ་རྣམས་བརྟེན་ནས། །
ངར་འཛིན་པ་ནི་དམིགས་པར་འགྱུར།།
རང་གི་བཞིན་གྱི་གཟུགས་བརྙན་བཞིན།།
ཡང་དག་ཉིད་དུ་དེ་འགའ་འང་མེད། །

༣༣ ཇི་ལྟར་མེ་ལོང་མ་བརྟེན་པར། །
རང་བཞིན་གཟུགས་བརྙན་མི་སྣང་ལྟར།།
ཕུང་པོ་རྣམས་ལམ་བརྟེན་པར། །
ངར་འཛིན་པ་ཡང་དེ་དང་འདྲ། །

༣༤ འཕགས་པ་ཀུན་དགའ་བོ་ཡིས་ནི།།
དེ་ལྟ་བུ་ཡི་དོན་ཐོས་ནས། །
ཆོས་ལ་མིག་ཐོབ་བདག་ཉིད་ཀྱིས། །
དགེ་སློང་རྣམས་ལ་བཟླས་ཏེ་སྨྲས། །

༣༥ ཇི་སྲིད་ཕུང་པོར་འཛིན་ཡོད་པ། །
དེ་སྲིད་དེ་ལས་ངར་འཛིན་ཡོད། །
ངར་འཛིན་ཡོད་ན་ཡང་ལས་ཏེ། །
དེ་ལས་ཡང་ནི་སྐྱེ་བ་ཡིན། །

༣༦ ལམ་གསུམ་ཐོག་མཐའ་དབུས་མེད་པ། །
འཁོར་བའི་དཀྱིལ་འཁོར་མགལ་མེ་ཡི། །
དཀྱིལ་འཁོར་ལྟ་བུ་ཕན་ཚུན་གྱི། །
རྒྱུ་ཅན་འདི་ནི་འཁོར་བར་འགྱུར། །

༣༧ དེ་ནི་རང་གཞན་གཉི་ག་དང་། །
དུས་གསུམ་ཉིད་དུའང་མ་ཐོབ་ཕྱིར། །
ངར་འཛིན་པ་ནི་ཟད་པར་འགྱུར། །
དེ་ནས་ལས་དང་སྐྱེ་བ་ཡང་། །

༣༨ དེ་ལྟར་རྒྱུ་འབྲས་སྐྱེ་བ་དང་། །
དེ་དག་ཟད་པ་ཉིད་མཐོང་ནས། །
ཡང་དག་ཉིད་དུ་འཇིག་རྟེན་ལ།།
ཡོད་མེད་ཉིད་དུ་མི་སེམས་སོ།།

༣༩ སྡུག་བསྔལ་ཐམས་ཅད་ཟད་པ་ཡི། །
ཆོས་འདི་ཐོས་ནས་རྟོག་མེད་པ། །
མི་འཇིགས་གནས་ལ་སྦྱར་བ་དག །
ཡོངས་སུ་མི་ཤེས་ཕྱིར་སྐྲག་གོ། །

༤༠ མྱ་ངན་འདས་ལ་འདི་དག་ཀུན། །
མེད་པར་འགྱུར་ན་ཁྱོད་མི་འཇིགས། །
འདིར་ནི་མེད་པར་བཤད་པ་ལ། །
ཁྱོད་ནི་ཅི་སྟེ་འཇིགས་པར་བྱེད། །

༤༡ ཐར་ལ་བདག་མེད་ཕུང་པོ་མེད། །
གལ་ཏེ་ཐར་པ་དེ་འདྲ་འདོད། །
བདག་དང་ཕུང་པོ་གསལ་བ་ལ། །
འདིར་ནི་ཁྱོད་ཀོ་ཅིས་མི་དགའ། །

༤༢ མྱ་ངན་འདས་པ་དངོས་མེད་པའང་། །
མིན་ན་དེ་དངོས་ག་ལ་ཡིན། །
དངོས་དང་དངོས་པོ་མེད་འཛིན་པ། །
ཟད་པ་མྱ་ངན་འདས་ཞེས་བྱ། །

༤༣ མདོར་ན་མེད་པར་ལྟ་བ་ཉིད། །
ལས་ཀྱི་འབྲས་བུ་མེད་ཅེས་པ། །
བསོད་ནམས་མ་ཡིན་ངན་སོང་བ།།
དེ་ནི་ལོག་པར་ལྟ་ཞེས་བཤད། །

༤༤ མདོར་ན་ཡོད་པར་ལྟ་བ་ཉིད། །
ལས་ཀྱི་འབྲས་བུ་ཡོད་ཅེས་པ། །
བསོད་ནམས་བདེ་འགྲོ་རྒྱུ་མཐུན་པ།།
ཡང་དག་ལྟ་བ་ཞེས་བཤད་དོ། །

༤༥ ཤེས་པས་མེད་དང་ཡོད་ཞི་ཕྱིར། །
སྡིག་དང་བསོད་ནམས་ལས་འདས་པ། །
དེ་ཡིས་ངན་འགྲོ་བདེ་འགྲོ་ལས།
དེ་ནི་ཐར་པར་དམ་པས་བཤད།།

༤༦ སྐྱེ་བ་རྒྱུ་དང་བཅས་མཐོང་བས།།
མེད་པ་ཉིད་ལས་འདས་པ་ཡིན།
འགོག་པ་རྒྱུ་དང་བཅས་མཐོང་བས།།
ཡོད་པ་ཉིད་དུའང་ཁས་མི་ལེན། །

༤༧ སྒྱུར་སྐྱེས་པ་དང་ལྷན་ཅིག་སྐྱེས། །
རྒྱུ་མིན་དོན་དུ་རྒྱུ་མེད་དོ། །
བརྟགས་དང་ཡང་དག་ཉིད་དུ་ན།།
སྐྱེ་བ་འདང་རབ་ཏུ་མ་གྲགས་ཕྱིར།།

༤༨ འདི་ཡོད་པས་ན་འདི་འབྱུང་དཔེར།།
རིང་པོ་ཡོད་ན་ཐུང་ངུ་བཞིན། །
འདི་སྐྱེས་པས་ན་འདི་སྐྱེས་དཔེར། །
མར་མེ་བྱུང་བས་འོད་བཞིན་ནོ། །

༤༩ རིང་པོ་ཡོད་ན་ཐུང་བ་ཉིད། །
རང་གི་ངོ་བོ་ལས་མ་ཡིན། །
མར་མེ་འབྱུང་བ་མེད་པའི་ཕྱིར།།
འོད་ཀྱང་འབྱུང་བ་མེད་པ་བཞིན།།

༥༠ དེ་ལྟར་རྒྱུ་འབྲས་སྐྱེ་མཐོང་ཞིང་།།
འཇིག་རྟེན་འདིན་ཇི་བཞིན་དུ།།
སྒྲོས་ལས་བྱུང་བར་ཁས་བླངས་པས།།
མེད་པ་ཉིད་དུ་ཁས་མི་ལེན།།

༥༡ འགོག་པ་སྒོམས་ལས་མཐུང་བ།།
ཡང་དག་ཇི་བཞིན་ཉིད་ཕྱུར་པ། །
ཁམས་ལེན་ཡོད་པ་ཉིད་མི་འབྱུར།།
དེས་ན་གཉིས་མི་བརྟེན་པ་གྲོལ།།

༥༢ ཐག་རིང་ནས་ནི་མཐོང་བའི་གཟུགས། །
ཉེ་བ་རྣམས་ཀྱིས་གསལ་བར་མཐོང་།།
སྨིག་རྒྱུ་ག་ལ་ཏེ་ཆུ་ཡིན་ན། །
ཉེ་བ་རྣམས་ཀྱིས་ཅིས་མི་མཐོང་། །

༥༣ ཇི་ལྟར་རིང་བ་རྣམས་ཀྱིས་ནི། །
འཇིག་རྟེན་འདི་ནི་ཡང་དག་མཐོང་། །
དེ་ལྟར་དེ་དང་ཉེ་རྣམས་ཀྱིས། །
མི་མཐོང་མཚན་མེད་སྨིག་རྒྱུ་བཞིན།།

༥༤ ཇི་ལྟར་སྨིག་རྒྱུ་ཆུ་འདྲ་བ།།
ཆུ་མིན་དོན་དུ་མ་ཡིན་པ།།
དེ་བཞིན་ཕུང་པོ་བདག་འདྲ་བ།།
དེ་དག་བདག་མིན་དོན་དུ་མིན།།

༥༥ སྨིག་རྒྱུ་ལ་ནི་འདི་རྒྱུ་ཞེས། །
བསམས་ཏེ་དེར་ནི་སོང་བ་ལས། །
གལ་ཏེ་ཆུ་དེ་མེད་དོ་ཞེས། །
འཛིན་པ་དེ་ནི་བླུན་པ་ཉིད། །

༥༦ དེ་བཞིན་སྨིག་རྒྱུ་ལྟ་བུ་ཡི། །
འཇིག་རྟེན་ཡོད་ཅེའམ་མེད་པ་ཞེས། །
འཛིན་པ་དེ་ནི་རྨོངས་པ་སྟེ། །
རྨོངས་པ་ཡོད་ན་མི་གྲོལ་ལོ། །

༥༧ མེད་པ་པ་ནི་ངན་འགྲོར་འགྲོ། །
ཡོད་པ་པ་ནི་བདེ་འགྲོར་འགྲོ། །
ཡང་དག་ཇི་བཞིན་ཡོངས་ཤེས་ཕྱིར། །
གཉིས་ལ་མི་བརྟེན་ཐར་པར་འགྱུར། །

༥༨ ཡང་དག་ཇི་བཞིན་ཡོངས་ཤེས་པས། །
མེད་དང་ཡོད་པ་མི་འདོད་པས། །
དེ་ཕྱིར་མེད་པ་པར་འགྱུར་ན། །
ཅི་ཕྱིར་ཡོད་པ་པར་མི་འགྱུར། །

༥༩ གལ་ཏེ་ཡོད་པ་བསྙུན་ཕྱུང་བས། །
དོན་གྱིས་དེ་ནི་མེད་པར་བསྟན། །
དེ་བཞིན་མེད་པ་སྙུན་ཕྱུང་བས། །
ཡོད་པར་ཅི་ཡི་ཕྱིར་མི་བསྟན། །

༦༠ གང་དག་དོན་གྱིས་མེད་དུ། །
དམ་མི་འཆའ་ཞིང་མི་སྤྱོད་ལ། །
བྱང་ཆུབ་བརྟེན་ཕྱིར་སེམས་མེད་ལ། །
དེ་དག་ཇི་ལྟར་མེད་པར་བཤད། །

༦༡ གང་ཟག་ཕུང་པོར་སྨྲ་བ་ཡི། །
འཇིག་རྟེན་གྲངས་ཅན་འུག་ཕྲུག་དང་། །
གོས་མེད་བཅས་ལ་གལ་ཏེ་ཞིག །
ཡོད་མེད་འདས་པ་སྨྲས་ན་དྲིས། །

༦༢ དེ་ཕྱིར་སངས་རྒྱས་རྣམས་ཀྱིས་ནི། །
བསྟན་པ་འཆི་མེད་ཡོད་མེད་ལས། །
འདས་པ་ཟབ་མོ་ཞེས་བཤད་པ། །
ཆོས་ཀྱི་ཁྱད་པ་ཡིན་ཤེས་བྱིས། །

༦༣ ཞིག་ནས་འགྲོ་མེད་འོང་མེད་ཅིང་། །
སྐད་ཅིག་ཀྱང་ནི་མི་གནས་པ། །
དུས་གསུམ་འདས་བདག་འཇིག་རྟེན་ནི།།
དེ་འདྲ་དོན་དུ་ཅི་ཡོད་དམ། །

༦༤ གང་ཕྱིར་གཉིས་ཡང་དག་ཏུ། །
འགྲོ་དང་འོང་དང་གནས་མེད་པ། །
དེ་ཕྱིར་འཇིག་རྟེན་མྱ་ངན་འདས། །
དོན་དུ་ཁྱད་པར་ཇི་ལྟ་བུ། །

༦༥ གནས་པ་མེད་ཕྱིར་སྐྱེ་བ་དང་། །
འགག་པ་ཡང་དག་ཉིད་མིན་ན།།
སྐྱེ་བ་དང་ནི་གནས་པ་དང་། །
འགག་པ་དོན་དུ་ག་ལ་ཞིག །

༦༦ གལ་ཏེ་རྟག་ཏུ་འགྱུར་ན་ནི། །
ཇི་ལྟར་སྐད་ཅིག་མ་ཡིན་དངོས། །
གལ་ཏེ་འགྱུར་བ་མེད་ན་ནི། །
དོན་དུ་གཞན་ཉིད་ག་ལ་འགྱུར། །

༦༧ ཕྱོགས་གཅིག་གམ་ཅི་ཐམས་ཅད་དུ། །
ཟད་པས་སྐད་ཅིག་འགྱུར་གྲང་ན། །
མི་འདྲ་བ་ཉིད་མི་དམིགས་ཕྱིར། །
དེ་རྣམ་གཉིས་འདང་རིགས་ལྡན་མིན།།

༦༨ སྐད་ཅིག་ཡིན་ན་རེ་ལ་མེད་ཕྱིར།།
རྙིང་པ་འགའ་ལྟ་ག་ལ་ཞིག །
བརྟན་ཕྱིར་སྐད་ཅིག་མ་ཡིན་ན། །
རྙིང་པ་འགའ་ལྟ་ག་ལ་ཞིག །

༦༩ ཇི་ལྟར་སྐད་ཅིག་མཐའ་ཡོད་པ། །
དེ་བཞིན་ཐོག་དང་དབུས་བརྟག་དགོས།།
དེ་ལྟར་སྐད་ཅིག་གསུམ་བདག་ཕྱིར། །
འཇིག་རྟེན་སྐད་ཅིག་གནས་པ་མིན། །

༧༠ ཐོག་མ་དབུས་དང་ཐ་མ་ཡང་། །
སྐད་ཅིག་བཞིན་དུ་བསམ་བྱས་ན། །
ཐོག་མ་དབུས་དང་ཐ་མ་ཉིད། །
རང་གཞན་ལས་ཀྱང་མ་ཡིན་ནོ། །

༥༡ ཐ་དད་ཕྱོགས་ཕྱིར་གཅིག་པུ་མིན།།
ཕྱོགས་མེད་པ་ནི་འགའ་ཡང་མེད།།
གཅིག་མེད་པར་ནི་དུ་མ་འང་མེད། །
ཡོད་པ་མེད་པར་མེད་པ་འང་མེད། །

༥༢ ཞིག་པ་འམ་ནི་གཉེན་པོ་ཡིས། །
ཡོད་ཉིད་མེད་པར་འགྱུར་གྲང་ན། །
ཡོད་པ་སྲིད་པ་མ་ཡིན་ཕྱིར། །
འཇིག་པའམ་གཉེན་པོར་ཇི་ལྟར་འགྱུར།།

༥༣ དེ་ཕྱིར་མྱ་ངན་འདས་པ་ཡིས།།
འཇིག་རྟེན་དོན་དུ་འགྲོ་བ་མི་འགྱུར།།
འཇིག་རྟེན་མཐའ་དང་ལྡན་ནམ་ཞེས།།
ཞུས་ནས་རྒྱལ་བ་མི་གསུང་བཞུགས།།

༥༤ གང་ཕྱིར་དེ་ལྟར་ཟབ་པའི་ཆོས། །
སྣོད་མིན་འགྲོ་ལ་མི་གསུང་བ། །
དེ་ཉིད་ཕྱིར་ན་མཁས་རྣམས་ཀྱིས།།
ཀུན་མཁྱེན་ཐམས་ཅད་མཁྱེན་པར་ཤེས།།

༥༥ དེ་ལྟར་ངེས་པར་ལེགས་པའི་ཆོས། །
ཟབ་མོ་ཡོངས་སུ་འཛིན་མེད་ཅིང༌། །
གནས་མེད་པ་ནི་རྫོགས་སངས་རྒྱས།།
ཐམས་ཅད་གཟིགས་པ་རྣམས་ཀྱིས་གསུངས།།

༥༦ གནས་མེད་ཆོས་འདིས་སྐྲག་པ་ཡི། །
སྐྱེ་བོ་གནས་ལ་མངོན་དགའ་ཞིང༌། །
ཡོད་དང་མེད་ལས་མ་འདས་པ། །
མི་མཁས་རྣམས་ནི་ཕུང་བར་འགྱུར། །

༥༧ འཇིགས་མེད་གནས་འཇིགས་དེ་དག་ནི། །
ཕུང་ལ་གཞན་ཡང་ཕུང་བར་བྱེད། །
རྒྱལ་པོ་ཕུང་བ་དེ་དག་གིས། །
ཅི་ནས་མི་ཕུང་དེ་ལྟར་གྱིས། །

༥༨ རྒྱལ་པོ་ཁྱོད་ནི་མི་ཕུང་བར། །
བགྱི་སླད་འཇིག་རྟེན་འདས་ཀྱི་ཚུལ། །
གཉིས་ལ་མི་བརྟེན་ཡང་དག་པ། །
ཇི་བཞིན་ལུང་གི་དབང་གིས་བཤད། །

༧༩ སྨིག་དང་བསྙད་ནམས་བྱ་བ་འདས།།
ཟབ་མོ་བཀྲོལ་བའི་དོན་དང་ལྡན། །
མུ་སྟེགས་གཞན་དང་རང་གི་ཡང་། །
གནས་མེད་འཇིགས་པས་མཇུངས་པའོ།།

༨༠ སྐྱེས་བུ་ས་མིན་ཆུ་མ་ཡིན། །
མེ་མིན་རླུང་མིན་ནམ་མཁའ་མིན།།
རྣམ་ཤེས་མ་ཡིན་ཀུན་མིན་ན། །
དེ་ལས་གཞན་ན་སྐྱེས་བུ་གང་།།

༨༡ སྐྱེས་བུ་ཁམས་དྲུག་འདུས་པའི་ཕྱིར།།
ཡང་དག་མ་ཡིན་ཇི་ལྟ་བར།།
དེ་བཞིན་ཁམས་ནི་རེ་རེ་ཡང་།
འདུས་ཕྱིར་ཡང་དག་ཉིད་དུ་མིན།།

༨༢ ཕུང་པོ་བདག་མིན་དེར་དེ་མིན། །
དེ་ལ་དེ་མིན་དེ་མེད་མིན། །
ཕུང་པོ་མེ་ཤིང་ལྟར་འདྲེས་མིན།།
དེ་ཕྱིར་བདག་ནི་ཇི་ལྟར་ཡོད། །

༨༣ འབྱུང་གསུམ་ས་མིན་འདི་ལ་མིན།།
དེ་ལ་འདི་མིན་དེ་མེད་མིན། །
རེ་རེ་རང་དེ་བཞིན་ཡིན་དེའི་ཕྱིར། །
འབྱུང་བ་རྣམས་ཀྱང་བདག་བཞིན་བརྫུན།།

༨༤ ས་ཆུ་མེ་དང་རླུང་རྣམས་ནི། །
རེ་རེའང་ངོ་བོ་ཉིད་དུ་མེད། །
གང་གསུམ་མེད་པར་རེ་རེ་མེད།།
གཅིག་མེད་པར་ཡང་གསུམ་མེད་དོ།།

༨༥ ག་ལ་ཏེ་གསུམ་མེད་རེ་རེ་མེད། །
གཅིག་མེད་པར་ཡང་གསུམ་མེད་ན།།
སོ་སོ་རང་ཡོད་མ་ཡིན་ཏེ། །
ཇི་ལྟར་འདུས་པ་སྐྱེ་བར་འགྱུར། །

༨༦ འོན་ཏེ་སོ་སོ་རང་ཡོད་ན། །
བུད་ཤིང་མེད་པར་མེ་ཅིས་མེད། །
གཡོ་དང་སྡོམས་དང་སྡུད་པ་དག །
ཆུ་དང་རླུང་དང་ས་དེ་བཞིན། །

༥༧ ངོན་ཏེ་མི་འདི་གྲགས་ཡིན་ན། །
ཇི་ལྟར་ཕྱོད་ཀྱི་གསུམ་གཞན་རང་། །
གསུམ་པོ་རྟེན་ཅིང་འབྱུང་བ་དང་། །
ཆོས་མི་མཐུན་པར་འགྱུར་བ་འང་མིན།།

༥༨ སོ་སོ་རང་རང་ཡོད་དེ་དག་ནི། །
ཇི་ལྟ་བུན་བཙན་ཆུན་ཡོད། །
སོ་སོ་རང་རང་ཡོད་མ་ཡིན་པ། །
དེ་དག་ཇི་ལྟར་བཙན་ཆུན་ཡོད། །

༥༩ གལ་ཏེ་སོ་སོར་རང་མེད་ཀྱི། །
གདན་གཅིག་དེར་ལྷག་མ་རྣམས། །
མ་འདྲེས་པ་རྣམས་གཅིག་གནས་མེད།།
འདྲེས་པ་སོ་སོར་རང་ཡོད་མིན། །

༦༠ སོ་སོར་རང་མེད་འབྱུང་བ་རྣམས། །
སོ་སོ་ནི་རང་མཚན་ག་ལ་ཡོད། །
སོ་སོར་རང་མེད་ཤས་ཆེ་འང་མེད།།
མཚན་ཉིད་དག་ནི་ཀུན་རྫོབ་བ་བཤད།།

༦༡ ཁ་དོག་དྲི་རོ་རེག་པ་གང་། །
དེ་དག་ལ་ཡང་རྒྱུ་ལ་འདི་ཡིན། །
མིག་དང་རྣམ་ཤེས་གཟུགས་རྣམས་དང་། །
མ་རིག་ལས་དང་སྐྱེ་བ་དང་། །

༦༢ བྱེད་པོ་ལས་དང་བྱ་བ་གྲངས། །
ལྡན་དང་རྒྱུ་འབྲས་དུས་དང་ནི། །
ཐུང་དང་རིང་སོགས་ཤེས་བྱ་དང་། །
མིང་དང་མིང་ཅན་དེ་བཞིན་ནོ། །

༦༣ ས་དང་ཆུ་དང་མེ་དང་རླུང་། །
རིང་ཐུང་ཕྲ་དང་སྦོམ་ཉིད་དང་། །
དགེ་སོགས་ཉིད་ནི་རྣམ་ཤེས་སུ།།
འགག་པར་འགྱུར་ཞེས་ཐུབ་པས་གསུངས།།

༦༤ རྣམ་ཤེས་བསྟན་མེད་མཐའ་ཡས་པ། །
ཀུན་ཏུ་བདག་པོ་དེ་ལ་ནི། །
ས་དང་ཆུ་དང་མེ་དང་ནི། །
རླུང་གི་གནས་མཐོང་འགྱུར་མ་ཡིན། །

༩༥ འདིར་ནི་རིང་དང་ཐུང་བ་དང་། །
ཕྲ་རགས་དགེ་དང་མི་དགེ་དང་། །
འདིར་ནི་མིང་དང་གཟུགས་དག་ཀྱང་། །
མ་ལུས་པར་ནི་འགག་པར་འགྱུར། །

༩༦ སྔར་མ་ཤེས་ཕྱིར་རྣམ་ཤེས་ལ། །
སྔོན་ཆད་སྣང་བ་དེ་ཀུན་ནི། །
དེ་ཤེས་ཕྱིར་ན་རྣམ་ཤེས་སུ། །
ཕྱིས་ནི་དེ་ལྟར་འགག་པར་འགྱུར།།

༩༧ རྣམ་ཤེས་མེ་ཡི་བུད་ཤིང་ནི། །
འགྲོ་ཆོས་འདི་ཀུན་ཡིན་པར་འདོད། །
དེ་དག་ཇི་བཞིན་རབ་འབྱེད་པའི། །
འོད་དང་ལྡན་པས་བསྲེགས་ནས་ནི། །

༩༨ མི་ཤེས་པས་ནི་སྔོན་བརྟགས་པ། །
ཕྱིས་ནི་དེ་ཉིད་ངེས་པ་དང་། །
གང་ཚེ་དངོས་པོ་མི་རྙེད་པ། །
དེ་ཚེ་དངོས་མེད་ག་ལ་འགྱུར།།

༩༩ གཟུགས་ཀྱི་དངོས་པོ་མིང་ཙམ་ཕྱིར། །
ནམ་མཁའ་ཡང་ནི་མིང་ཙམ་མོ། །
འབྱུང་མེད་གཟུགས་ལྟ་ག་ལ་ཡོད། །
དེ་ཕྱིར་མིང་ཙམ་ཉིད་ཀྱང་མེད། །

༡༠༠ ཚོར་དང་འདུ་ཤེས་འདུ་བྱེད་དང་། །
རྣམ་ཤེས་འབྱུང་བ་ལྔ་པོ་དང་། །
བདག་བཞིན་དུ་ནི་ཁམས་ལྔ་སྟེ།།
དེ་ཕྱིར་ཁམས་དྲུག་བདག་མེད་དོ།།

རིན་པོ་ཆེའི་ཕྲེང་བ་ལས་མངོན་པར་མཐོ་བ་དང་
ངེས་པར་ལེགས་པ་བསྟན་པ་སྟེ་ལེའུ་དང་པོའོ།། ༎

༡༠༡ ཇི་ལྟར་ཆུ་ཤིང་ཡན་ལག་དག །
མ་ལུས་བཅས་ཏེ་བཤིག་བྱས་ན། །
ཅི་ཡང་མེད་ལྟར་སྐྱེས་བུ་ཡང་། །
ཁམས་བཅས་བཤིག་ན་དེ་དང་འདྲ།།

༡༠༢ ཆོས་རྣམས་ཐམས་ཅད་བདག་མེད་ཅེས། །
དེ་ཕྱིར་རྒྱལ་བ་རྣམས་ཀྱིས་གསུངས། །
ཁམས་དྲུག་དེ་ཀུན་བདག་མེད་པར། །
ཁྱོད་ལ་གཏན་ལ་ཕབ་པ་ཡིན། །

༡༠༣ དེ་ལྟར་བདག་དང་བདག་མེད་པ། །
ཡང་དག་ཇི་བཞིན་དམིགས་སུ་མེད།།
བདག་དང་བདག་མེད་ལྟ་བ་དག། །
དེ་ཕྱིར་ཐུབ་པ་ཆེན་པོས་བཟློག། །

༡༠༤ མཐོང་དང་ཐོས་སོགས་ཐུབ་པ་ཡིས།།
བདེན་མིན་བརྫུན་པ་མིན་པར་གསུངས།།
ཕྱོགས་ལས་མི་མཐུན་ཕྱོགས་འགྱུར་ན།།
དེ་ནི་གཉི་ག་དོན་དུ་མིན། །

༡༠༥ དེ་ལྟར་དམ་པའི་དོན་དུ་ན། །
འཇིག་རྟེན་འདི་ནི་བདེན་བརྫུན་འདས།།
དེ་ཉིད་ཕྱིར་ན་ཡང་དག་ཏུ།
ཡོད་ཅེས་མེད་ཅེས་ཁས་མི་བཞེས།།

༡༠༦ གང་ཞིག་དེ་ལྟར་རྣམ་ཀུན་ཏུ།།
ཡོད་མིན་དེ་ནི་ཀུན་མཁྱེན་གྱིས།།
མཐའ་ཡོད་མཐའ་མེད་གཉི་ག་དང་།།
གཉིས་མ་ཡིན་ཞེས་ཇི་ལྟར་བསྟན།།

༡༠༧ སངས་རྒྱས་གྲངས་མེད་གཤེགས་དེ་བཞིན། །
འབྱོན་འགྱུར་བ་དང་ད་ལྟར་བཞུགས། །
སེམས་ཅན་རྣམས་ནི་བྱེ་བར་འགྱུར། །
དེ་ལས་དུས་གསུམ་གནས་པ་དགོངས།།

༡༠༨ ཟད་པ་དུས་གསུམ་གནས་པ་ནི། །
འཇིག་རྟེན་འཕེལ་བའི་རྒྱུ་མ་ཡིན།།
ཐམས་ཅད་མཁྱེན་པས་ཇི་ལྟར་དེའི།།
སྔོན་མཐའ་ལུང་མ་བསྟན་པར་མཛད།།

༡༠༩ སོ་སོའི་སྐྱེ་བོ་ལ་གསང་བ། །
གང་ཡིན་དེ་ནི་ཟབ་མོའི་ཆོས།།
འཇིག་རྟེན་སྒྱུ་མ་ལྟ་བུ་ཉིད། །
སངས་རྒྱས་བསྟན་པ་བདུད་རྩི་ཡིན།།

༡༡༠ ཇི་ལྟར་སྒྱུ་མའི་གླང་པོ་ལ། །
སྐྱེ་དང་འཇིག་པ་ཉིད་སྣང་ཡང་། །
དེ་ལ་དོན་གྱི་ཡང་དག་ཏུ། །
སྐྱེ་དང་འཇིག་པ་ཉིད་མེད་ལྟར། །

༡༡༡ དེ་བཞིན་སྒྱུ་འདྲའི་འཇིག་རྟེན་ལ། །
སྐྱེ་དང་འཇིག་པ་ཉིད་སྣང་ཡང་། །
དམ་པའི་དོན་དུ་སྐྱེ་བ་དང་། །
འཇིག་པ་ཉིད་ནི་ཡོད་མ་ཡིན། །

༡༡༢ ཇི་ལྟར་སྒྱུ་མའི་གླང་པོ་ནི། །
གང་ནས་མ་འོངས་གར་མི་འགྲོ། །
སེམས་རྨོངས་ཙམ་དུ་ཟད་པས་ན། །
ཡང་དག་ཉིད་དུ་གནས་པ་མེད། །

༡༡༣ དེ་བཞིན་འཇིག་རྟེན་སྒྱུ་འདྲ་བ། །
གང་ནས་མ་འོངས་གར་མི་འགྲོ། །
སེམས་རྨོངས་ཙམ་དུ་ཟད་པས་ན། །
ཡང་དག་ཉིད་དུ་གནས་པ་མེད། །

༡༡༤ དེ་ལྟར་དུས་གསུམ་འདས་བདག་ཉིད། །
ཐ་སྙད་གདགས་པ་མ་གཏོགས་པར། །
གང་ཞིག་ཡོད་དམ་མེད་འགྱུར་བའི། །
འཇིག་རྟེན་དོན་དུ་ཅི་ཞིག་ཡོད། །

༡༡༥ སངས་རྒྱས་ཀྱིས་ནི་རྒྱུ་འདི་ལས། །
མཐའ་ཡོད་པ་དང་མཐའ་མེད་དང་། །
གཉིས་དང་གཉིས་མིན་རྣམ་པ་བཞི། །
ལུང་མ་བསྟན་མཛད་ལས་གཞན་མིན། །

༡༡༦ རེ་ཞིག་ལུས་འདི་མི་གཙང་ཉིད། །
རགས་ཤིང་མངོན་སུམ་སྤྱོད་ཡུལ་བ། །
རྟག་ཏུ་སྣང་བའང་གང་གི་ཚེ། །
སེམས་ལ་གནས་པམ་ཡིན་པ། །

༡༡༧ དེ་ཚེ་དམ་ཆོས་གནས་མེད་པ། །
ཕྲ་རབ་མངོན་སུམ་མ་ཡིན་པ། །
ཟབ་མོ་དེ་ཀོ་ཇི་ལྟ་བུར། །
སེམས་ལ་བདེ་བླག་འཇུག་པར་འགྱུར། །

༢༢༨ ཆོས་འདི་ཟབ་ཕྱིར་སྐྱེ་བོ་ཡིས། །
ཤེས་པར་དཀའ་བར་ཐུགས་ཆུད་དེ། །
དེས་ན་ཐུབ་པ་སངས་རྒྱས་ནས། །
ཆོས་བསྟན་པ་ལས་ལོག་པར་འགྱུར། །

༢༢༩ ཆོས་འདི་ལོག་པར་ཤེས་གྱུར་ན། །
མི་མཁས་རྣམས་ནི་ཆུད་ཀྱང་ཟ། །
འདི་ལྟར་མེད་པར་ལྟ་བ་ཡི། །
མི་གཙང་དེར་ནི་བྱིང་བར་འགྱུར། །

༢༣༠ གཞན་ཡང་འདི་ནི་ལོག་བཟུང་ན། །
བླུན་པོ་མཁས་པའི་ང་རྒྱལ་ཅན། །
སྤོང་བས་མ་རུང་བདག་ཉིད་ཅན། །
མནར་མེད་པར་ནི་སྤྱི་འཚུགས་འགྲོ། །

༢༣༡ ཇི་ལྟར་ཁ་ཟས་བཟའ་ཉེས་པས། །
ཕུང་བ་དག་ཏུ་འགྱུར་བ་དང་། །
བཟའ་ལེགས་ཚེ་དང་ནད་མེད་དང་། །
སྟོབས་དང་བདེ་བར་འགྱུར་བ་ལྟར། །

༢༣༢ དེ་བཞིན་ལོག་པར་བཟུང་བ་དེས། །
ཕུང་བ་དག་ནི་ཐོབ་འགྱུར་ཞིང་། །
ལེགས་པར་ཤེས་པས་བདེ་བ་དང་། །
བྱང་ཆུབ་བླ་ན་མེད་པ་འཐོབ། །

༢༣༣ དེ་ཕྱིར་འདི་ལ་སྐྱོན་བ་དང་། །
མེད་པའི་ལྟ་བ་སྤངས་ནས་ནི། །
དོན་ཀུན་བསྒྲུབ་ཕྱིར་ཡང་དག་པའི། །
ཤེས་ལ་ནན་ཏན་མཆོག་མཛོད་ཅིག །

༢༣༤ ཆོས་འདི་ཡོངས་སུ་མ་ཤེས་ན། །
ངར་འཛིན་པ་ནི་རྗེས་སུ་འཇུག །
དེ་ལས་དགེ་དང་མི་དགེའི་ལས། །
དེ་ལས་སྐྱེ་བ་བཟང་དང་ངན། །

༢༣༥ དེ་ཕྱིར་ཇི་སྲིད་ངར་འཛིན་པ། །
སེལ་བའི་ཆོས་འདི་མ་ཤེས་པ། །
དེ་སྲིད་སྦྱིན་དང་ཚུལ་ཁྲིམས་དང་། །
བཟོད་པའི་ཆོས་ལ་གུས་པར་མཛོད། །

༡༢༦ ལས་རྣམས་སྔོན་དུ་ཆོས་བཏང་ཞིང་། །
བར་དུ་ཆོས་ལྡན་ཐ་མར་ཡང་། །
ཆོས་ལྡན་བསྒྲུབ་པའི་རིས་བདག་ནི། །
འདི་དང་གཞན་དུ་གནོད་མི་འགྱུར། །

༡༢༧ ཆོས་ཀྱིས་འདིར་གྲགས་བདེ་བ་དང་། །
འདི་དང་འཆི་ཀ་ར་འཇིགས་པ་མེད། །
འཇིག་རྟེན་གཞན་དུ་བདེ་བརྒྱས། །
དེ་བས་རྟག་ཏུ་ཆོས་བསྟེན་མཛོད། །

༡༢༨ ཆོས་ནི་ལུགས་ཀྱི་དམ་པ་སྟེ། །
ཆོས་ཀྱིས་འཇིག་རྟེན་མདོན་དགར་འགྱུར། །
འཇིག་རྟེན་དགའ་བར་གྱུར་པས་ཀྱང་། །
འདི་དང་གཞན་དུ་བསླུས་མི་འགྱུར། །

༡༢༩ ཆོས་མིན་པས་ནི་ལུགས་འདོད་གང་། །
དེ་ཡིས་འཇིག་རྟེན་མི་དགའ་འགྱུར། །
འཇིག་རྟེན་མི་དགའ་ཉིད་ཀྱི་ཕྱིར། །
འདི་དང་གཞན་དུ་དགར་མི་འགྱུར། །

༡༣༠ དོན་མེད་རིག་པ་ངན་འགྲོའི་ལམ། །
གཞན་བསླུ་ལྷུར་ལེན་མི་བཟད་པ། །
ཤེས་རབ་འཆལ་བ་རྣམས་ཀྱིས་ནི། །
ཇི་ལྟར་དོན་འགྱུར་རིག་པར་བྱས། །

༡༣༡ པ་རོལ་བསླུ་བ་ལྷུར་ལེན་པ། །
དོན་དུ་ཇི་ལྟར་ལུགས་ལྡན་ཡིན། །
དེས་ནི་ཚོར་བས་སྟོང་ཕྲག་ནི། །
མང་པོར་བདག་ཉིད་བསླུས་པར་འགྱུར། །

༡༣༢ དགྲ་ལ་གནོད་པ་བྱིན་ཡང་། །
སྐྱོན་རྣམས་བཏང་སྟེ་ཡོན་ཏན་བསྟེན། །
དེས་ནི་ཕྱོད་ཀྱིས་རང་ཕན་ཐོབ། །
དགྲ་བོ་ཡང་ནི་མི་དགར་འགྱུར། །

༡༣༣ སྦྱིན་དང་སྙན་པར་སྨྲ་བ་དང་། །
མཐུན་དང་དོན་གཅིག་སྤྱོད་པ་སྟེ། །
དེ་དག་རྣམས་ཀྱིས་འཇིག་རྟེན་དང་། །
ཆོས་ཀྱང་བསྡུ་བ་ཉིད་དུ་མཛོད། །

༡༨༤ རྒྱལ་པོ་དག་ལ་ཇི་ལྟར་བྱུར། །
བདེན་ཚིག་ཡིད་ཆེས་བརྟན་བསྐྱེད་པ། །
དེ་བཞིན་དེ་ལ་བརྫུན་པ་ནི། །
ཡིད་མི་ཆེས་པར་བྱེད་པའི་མཆོག །

༡༨༥ བསླུ་བ་མེད་ལྡན་བདེན་སྨྲ་སྟེ། །
བསམ་པས་བསྒྱུར་བ་དོན་དུ་མིན། །
གཞན་ལ་གཅིག་ཏུ་ཕན་པ་བདེན། །
མི་ཕན་ཕྱིར་ན་ཅིག་ཤོས་བརྫུན། །

༡༨༦ ཇི་ལྟར་རྒྱལ་པོའི་ཉེས་པ་དག །
སྤྲིན་གསལ་ལ་གཅིག་གིས་སྒྲིབ་པ་ལྟར། །
དེ་བཞིན་འཛུངས་པའང་དེ་དག་གི །
ཡོན་ཏན་བརྡོག་པ་ཐམས་ཅད་འཇོམས། །

༡༨༧ ཉེ་བར་ཞི་བ་ཟབ་པའི་ཕྱིར། །
མཆོག་ཏུ་གུས་པ་བྱེད་པར་འགྱུར། །
གུས་པས་བརྗོད་ལ་བཀའ་ཡང་བཙན། །
དེ་བས་ཉེ་བར་ཞི་བ་བསྟེན། །

༡༨༨ ཤེས་རབ་ལྡན་པས་བློ་མི་འཁྲུགས། །
གཞན་གྱི་དྲིང་མི་འཇོག་ཅིང་བརྟན། །
བསླུ་བས་མི་རྒྱུགས་རྒྱལ་པོ་སྟེ། །
དེ་བས་ཤེས་རབ་ལྷུར་བླང་མཛོད། །

༡༨༩ བདེན་གཏོང་ཞི་དང་ཤེས་རབ་སྟེ། །
བཞི་པོ་བཟང་བའི་མི་དབང་ནི། །
ཆོས་བཟང་རྣམ་པ་བཞི་ལྟ་བུར། །
ལྷ་མི་རྣམས་ཀྱིས་བསྟོད་པར་འགྱུར། །

༡༩༠ ཕེབས་པར་སྨྲ་ཞིང་དག་སྤྱུར་པ། །
ཤེས་རབ་སྙིང་རྗེ་དྲི་མེད་དང་། །
ལྷན་ཅིག་འགྲོགས་ན་རྟག་ཏུ་ཡང་། །
ཤེས་རབ་དང་ནི་ཆོས་ཀྱང་འཕེལ། །

༡༩༡ ཕན་པར་སྨྲ་བ་དཀོན་པ་སྟེ། །
ཉན་པར་བྱེད་པ་ཤིན་ཏུ་དཀོན། །
དེ་དག་བས་ཀྱང་མི་སྙན་ཡང་། །
ཕན་པ་མྱུར་དུ་བྱེད་པ་དཀོན། །

༡༩༢ དེ་ལྟ་བས་ན་མི་སྨན་ཡང་། །
ཕན་པར་མཁྱེན་ནས་སྒྱུར་དུ་སྤྱོད།།
ནད་གསོའི་དོན་དུ་བདག་བྱམས་པ།།
མི་བཟད་པ་ཡི་སྨན་ཡང་འཐུང་།།

༡༩༣ སྲོག་དང་ནད་མེད་རྒྱལ་སྲིད་དག །
མི་རྟག་ཉིད་དུ་རྟག་དགོངས་ཏེ།།
དེ་ནས་ཡང་དག་བརྩོན་ལྡན་པར།།
ཆོས་ལ་གཅིག་ཏུ་ནན་ཏན་མཛོད།།

༡༩༤ གདོན་མི་ཟ་བར་འཆི་འགྱུར་ཞིང་།།
ཤི་ནས་སྡིག་པས་སྡུག་བསྔལ་བ།།
གཟིགས་ཏེ་འཕྲལ་དུ་བདེན་ཡང་།།
སྡིག་པ་བགྱི་བར་མི་རིགས་སོ། །

༡༩༥ ལ་ལར་འཇིགས་པ་མེད་མཐོང་ཞིང་།།
དུས་འགར་འཇིགས་པ་མཐོང་འགྱུར་བ།།
གལ་ཏེ་གཅིག་ལ་ཡིད་རྟོན་ན། །
གཅིག་ལ་ཕྱེད་ནི་ཅིས་མི་འཇིགས།།

༡༩༦ ཆང་གིས་འཇིག་རྟེན་བརྙས་འགྱུར་ཞིང་། །
དོན་ཡལ་འཐོར་ཡང་ཟད་པར་འགྱུར། །
མྱོས་པས་བྱ་བ་མིན་བྱེད་ད། །
དེ་བས་རྟག་ཏུ་ཆང་ནི་སྤོངས། །

༡༩༧ རྒྱན་པོ་ཆགས་དང་མི་དགའ་འདང་།།
ཞེ་སྡང་གཡོ་སྒྱུ་རྫོད་པའི་གནས། །
བརྫུན་དང་ཀྱལ་པ་ཚིག་རྩུབ་རྒྱུ། །
དེ་བས་རྟག་ཏུ་སྤང་བར་མཛོད། །

༡༩༨ བུད་མེད་ཆགས་པ་ཕལ་ཆེར་ནི། །
བུད་མེད་གཟུགས་ས་གཙང་སེམས་ལས་བྱུང་།།
བུད་མེད་ལུས་ལ་དོན་དུ་ནི། །
གཙང་བ་ཕྲན་ཟད་ཡོད་མ་ཡིན།།

༡༩༩ ཁ་ནི་བཀྲུ་རུལ་བ་དང་། །
སོ་སྐྱག་མི་གཙང་སྣོད་ཡིན་ནོ། །
སྣ་ནི་སྣ་གསྣབས་སྣ་ཆུའི་སྣོད།།
མིག་ནི་མིག་རྫུལ་མཆི་མའི་སྣོད།།

༡༥༠ ཕྱོ་བ་འི་ཕོ་ང་ཉེ་ས་ཤང་གཅི་དང་།།
སྒྲོ་བ་མཆིན་པ་འི་སྦྱོད་ཡིན་པར།།
སྨོངས་པས་བུད་མེད་མ་མཐོང་བས།།
དེ་ཡི་ལུས་ལ་ཆགས་པར་བྱེད།།

༡༥༡ མི་ཤེས་འགའ་ཞིག་མི་གཙང་བའི།།
བུམ་པ་རྒྱན་ལ་ཆགས་པ་ལྟར། །
འཇིག་རྟེན་མི་ཤེས་རྨོངས་པ་ཡིས།།
བུད་མེད་རྣམས་ལ་དེ་བཞིན་ནོ། །

༡༥༢ ལུས་ཡུལ་ཤིན་ཏུ་དྲི་ང་བ། །
ཆགས་བྲལ་རྒྱུ་ནི་གང་ཡིན་པ།།
དེ་ལའང་འཇིག་རྟེན་ཆེར་ཆགས་ན།།
གང་གིས་འདོད་ཆགས་བྲལ་བར་བགྱི།།

༡༥༣ ཇི་ལྟར་བཤང་དང་གཅི་གཞི་ལ།།
ངན་སྐྱུགས་ཕག་རབ་ཆགས་པ་ལྟར།།
དེ་བཞིན་བཤང་དང་གཅི་གཞི་ལ།།
འདོད་ལྡན་ངན་སྐྱུགས་ཕག་རྣམས་ཆགས།།

༡༥༤ ལུས་ཀྱི་གྲོང་ཁྱེར་མི་གཙང་བ། །
འབྱུང་བའི་བུག་དོད་པ་གང་། །
དེ་ནི་སྐྱེ་བོ་བླུན་པོ་ཡིས། །
དགའ་བའི་དོན་དུ་ཉེ་བར་བརྟགས།།

༡༥༥ ཁྱོད་བདག་ཉིད་ཀྱིས་བཤང་གཅི་སོགས།།
སོ་སོར་མི་གཙང་མཐོང་ནས་ནི།།
དེ་འདྲས་ལུས་ལ་ཇི་ལྟ་བུར། །
ཡིད་དུ་འོང་བ་ཉིད་དུ་འགྱུར། །

༡༥༦ ཁྲག་དང་ཁུ་བ་འདྲེས་པ་ཡི། །
ས་བོན་མི་གཙང་སྙིང་པོས་བསྐྱེད།།
མི་གཙང་གཟུགས་སུ་ཤེས་བཞིན་དུ།།
འདི་ལ་འདོད་པ་གང་གིས་ཆགས།།

༡༥༧ མི་གཙང་ཕུང་པོ་དེ་རླན་གྱིས། །
བརླན་པའི་པགས་པས་གཡོགས་པ་གང་།།
ཉལ་བ་དེ་ནི་བུད་མེད་ཀྱི། །
ཀུ་སོ་ལི་བོ་ངས་ན་···ཉལ་བར་ཟད། །

༡༥༨ གཟུགས་བཟང་བ་དང་གཟུགས་ངན་ནམ།།
རྒན་ནམ་ཡང་ན་གཞོན་པ་དར་རུང་། །
བུད་མེད་གཟུགས་ཀུན་མི་གཙང་ན། །
ཁྱེད་ཆགས་ཁྱད་པར་གང་ལས་སྐྱེ། །

༡༥༩ གལ་ཏེ་མི་གཙང་ཁ་དོག་བཟང་། །
ཤིན་ཏུ་གསར་ལ་དབྱིབས་ལེགས་ཀྱང་། །
དེ་ལ་ཆགས་པར་མི་འོས་ལྟར། །
བུད་མེད་གཟུགས་ལའང་དེ་བཞིན།།

༡༦༠ ཁོང་རུལ་ལ་ཕྱི་རོལ་པགས་པས་གཡོགས། །
རོ་རྨུགས་འདི་ཡི་རང་བཞིན་ནི། །
ཤིན་ཏུ་མི་བཟད་སྣང་བཞིན་དུ།།
ཇི་ལྟ་བུར་ན་མཐོང་མི་འགྱུར། །

༡༦༡ པགས་པ་འདི་ཡང་མི་གཙང་མིན།།
ར་ལ་ག་བཞིན་དུ་འདུག་ཅེ་ན། །
མི་གཙང་ཕུང་པོའི་པགས་པ་ལྟར།།
ཇི་ལྟ་བུར་ན་གཙང་བར་འགྱུར། །

༡༦༢ མི་གཙང་གང་བའི་བུམ་པ་ནི།།
ཕྱི་རོལ་བཀྲ་ཡང་སྨད་པ་ཡིན། །
མི་གཙང་བ་ཡི་རང་བཞིན་ལུས།།
མི་གཙང་གང་བ་ཅིས་མི་སྨད། །

༡༦༣ གལ་ཏེ་ཁྱོད་ནི་མི་གཙང་སྨོད།།
དྲི་དང་ཕྲེང་བ་བཟའ་བཏུང་ནི།།
གཙང་མའང་མི་གཙང་བྱེད་པ་གང་།།
ལུས་འདི་ཅི་ཡི་ཕྱིར་མི་སྨད།།

༡༦༤ ཇི་ལྟར་རང་རྣམ་གཞན་དག་གི །
མི་གཙང་སྨད་པར་བྱ་བ་ལྟར། །
དེ་བཞིན་རང་དང་གཞན་དག་གི།
མི་གཙང་གཟུགས་ནི་ཅིས་མི་སྨད།།

༡༦༥ ཇི་ལྟར་བུད་མེད་གཟུགས་མི་གཙང་།།
ཁྱོད་ཀྱི་རང་ལུས་དེ་དང་འདྲ། །
དེ་བས་ཕྱི་དང་ནང་ཉིད་ལ། །
འདོད་ཆགས་བྲལ་བར་རིགས་མིན་ནམ།།

༡༦༦ རྨ་དགུ་དག་ནས་འཛག་པ་ཅན། །
བདག་ཉིད་དམ་ངོན་སུམ་འབྲུ་ཕྱེད་ཀྱང་།།
ལུས་མི་གཙང་བར་མི་རྟོགས་ན། །
ཁྱོད་ལ་བཤད་པས་ཅི་ཞིག་ཕན། །

༡༦༧ གང་དག་མི་གཙང་ལུས་འདི་ལ། །
སྙེག་ཚོགས་སྐྱན་ངག་བྱེད་པ་ནི། །
ཨེ་མ་ཧོ་གཟུ་ལུམས་ཨེ་མ་ཧོ་བླུན།།
ཨེ་མ་ཧོ་སྐྱེ་བོས་ཁྲེལ་ལ་ད་རུང་། །

༡༦༨ མི་ཤེས་མུན་པས་བསྒྲིབས་པ་ཡི། །
སེམས་ཅན་འདི་ནི་ཕལ་ཆེར་ཡང་། །
འདོད་པའི་དོན་དུ་རྩོད་འབྱུང་བ། །
མི་གཙང་དོན་དུ་ཁྱི་རྣམས་བཞིན། །

༡༦༩ གཡན་པ···ཕྲུགས་ན་བདེར་འགྱུར་བ།།
དེ་བས་གཡན་པ་མེད་པ་བདེ། །
དེ་བཞིན་འཇིག་རྟེན་འདོད་ལྡན་བདེ།།
འདོད་པ་མེད་པ་དེ་བས་བདེ། །

༡༧༠ གལ་ཏེ་དེ་ལྟར་བརྟགས་ན་ཁྱོད། །
འདོད་ཆགས་བྲལ་བར་མ་གྲུབ་ཀྱང་། །
འོན་ཀྱང་འདོད་ཆགས་བསྲབ་བས་ན་ཡིས།།
བུད་མེད་ཆགས་པར་མི་འགྱུར་རོ། །

༡༧༡ ཚོ་སྦྱང་འཛིགས་དང་སྡུག་བསྔལ་དང་།
དམྱལ་བའི་རྒྱུ་ནི་མི་ཟད་པ། །
རིངས་ལ་ཡེངས་ཏེ་དེ་ལྟ་བས། །
རྟག་ཏུ་གསོད་མེད་བརྟན་པར་མཛོད།།

༡༧༢ ཡན་ལག་ཐམས་ཅད་མི་གཙང་བས། །
བསྐུས་པའི་སྦྲུལ་གདུག་འཛག་པ་ལྟར།།
གང་ལ་བརྟེན་ནས་ལུས་ཅན་རྣམས། །
སྡུག་པར་འགྱུར་བ་དེ་རེ་དན། །

༡༧༣ ཆར་སྤྲིན་ཆེན་པོ་ལངས་པ་ན། །
ཞིང་པ་རྣམས་ནི་ཇི་ལྟ་བར། །
གང་ལ་བརྟེན་ནས་ལུས་ཅན་རྣམས།།
དགའ་བར་འགྱུར་བ་དེ་རེ་བཟང་། །

༡༧༤ དེ་བས་ཆོས་མིན་སྤང་བྱས་ཏེ། །
གཡེལ་བ་མེད་པར་ཆོས་ལ་བརྟེན། །
བདག་ཉིད་དང་ནི་འཇིག་རྟེན་འདིས། །
བླ་མེད་བྱང་ཆུབ་ཐོབ་འདོད་ན། །

༡༧༥ དེ་ཡི་རྩ་བ་བྱང་ཆུབ་སེམས། །
རི་དབང་རྒྱལ་པོ་ལྟར་བརྟན་དང་། །
ཕྱོགས་མཐས་གཏུགས་པའི་སྙིང་རྗེ་དང་། །
གཉིས་ལ་མི་བརྟེན་ཡེ་ཤེས་ལགས། །

༡༧༦ རྒྱལ་པོ་ཆེན་པོ་སྐྱེས་ཆེན་གྱི། །
མཚན་ནི་སུམ་ཅུ་རྩ་གཉིས་ཀྱིས། །
ཇི་ལྟར་ཁྱོད་སྐུ་བརྒྱན་འགྱུར་པ། །
དེ་ལྟ་བུ་དག་གསན་པར་མཛོད། །

༡༧༧ མཆོད་རྟེན་མཆོད་འོས་འཕགས་པ་དང་། །
རྒན་རབས་དག་ནི་ལེགས་བཀུར་བས། །
དཔལ་ལྡན་ཕྱག་ཞབས་འཁོར་ལོ་ཡིས། །
མཚན་པའི་འཁོར་ལོས་སྒྱུར་བར་འགྱུར། །

༡༧༨ རྒྱལ་པོ་ཆོས་ལ་རྟག་པར་ནི། །
ཡང་དག་བླངས་པ་བརྟན་པོར་མཛོད། །
དེས་ནི་ཤིན་ཏུ་ཞབས་གནས་པའི། །
བྱང་ཆུབ་སེམས་དཔར་འགྱུར་བ་ལགས། །

༡༧༩ སྦྱིན་དང་སྙན་པའི་ཚིག་དང་ནི། །
ཕན་དང་དོན་གཅིག་སྤྱོད་པ་ཡིས། །
དཔལ་ལྡན་ཕྱག་སོར་དྲ་བ་ཡིས། །
འབྲེལ་བའི་ཕྱག་རིས་ཅན་དུ་འགྱུར། །

༡༨༠ བཟའ་བ་དང་ནི་བཏུང་བའི་མཆོག །
རབ་ཏུ་མང་པོ་སྦྱིན་པ་ཡིས། །
དཔལ་ལྡན་ཕྱག་དང་ཞབས་མཉེན་ཞིང་། །
ཕྱག་དང་ཞབས་དང་ཐལ་གོང་དང་། །
ལྟག་པའི་ཕྱོགས་རྣམས་མཐོ་བའི་ཕྱིར། །
སྐུ་ཆེ་བདུན་དག་མཐོ་བར་འགྱུར། །

༡༨༡ འཆི་མེད་གསོད་པ་ཕར་བྲལ་བས། །
སྐུ་མཛེས་དྲང་ཞིང་ཆེ་བ་དང་། །
ཆེ་རིང་སོར་མོ་རིང་བ་དང་། །
རྟིང་པ་ཡངས་པ་དག་ཏུ་འགྱུར། །

༡༨༢ ཡང་དག་བླངས་པའི་ཆོས་རྣམས་ནི། །
སྤེལ་བས་དཔལ་ལྡན་མདོག་བཟང་ཞིང་། །
ཞབས་ཀྱི་ལོང་བུ་མི་མངོན་དང་། །
བསྤུ་གྱེན་དུ་ཕྱོགས་མཚན་འགྱུར། །

༡༨༣ རིག་དང་བཟོ་ལ་སོགས་པའི་ལས། །
གུས་པས་ལེན་དང་སྦྱིན་པས་ཕྱོད། །
ཨེ་ན་ཡ་ཡི་བྱིན་པ་དང་། །
ཡིད་ཉེ་ཤེས་རབ་ཆེན་པོར་འགྱུར། །

༡༨༤ རང་གི་ནོར་བདོག་བསླངས་གྱུར་ན། །
མྱུར་དུ་གཏོང་བའི་བརྟུལ་ཞུགས་ཀྱིས། །
ཕྱག་རྒྱས་བདེ་དང་འཇིག་རྟེན་གྱི། །
རྣམ་པར་འདྲེན་པ་ཉིད་དུ་འགྱུར། །

༡༨༥ གཉེན་པ་ཤེས་པ་ཉན་རྒྱུན་བརྗེ་བ་དག །
ཡང་དག་བསྒྲུམ་པ་བྲལ་བ་ཡིས། །
དཔལ་ལྡན་འདོམས་ཀྱི་སྦ་བ་ནི། །
སྦུབས་སུ་ནུབ་པའི་དམ་པར་འགྱུར། །

༡༨༦ ཁང་བཟང་དང་ནི་གདིང་བ་དག །
བདེ་ཞིང་བཟང་བར་སྦྱིན་པས། །
གསེར་ནི་གཙོ་མ་དྲི་མེད་པ། །
ཤིན་ཏུ་འཇམ་པོའི་མདོག་འདྲར་འགྱུར། །

༡༨༧ བླ་ན་མེད་པའི་དབང་བྱིན་ཞིང་། །
རིགས་པར་བླ་མའི་རྗེས་འཇུག་པས། །
དཔལ་ལྡན་བསྤུ་ཉག་རེ་དང་། །
ཞལ་ནི་མཛོད་སྤུས་བརྒྱན་པར་འགྱུར། །

༡༨༨ སྨན་ཅིང་དགའ་བར་སྨྲ་བ་དང་། །
ལེགས་པར་སྨྲས་དང་མཐུན་བྱས་པས། །
ཕྱེད་ནི་དཔུང་མགོ་ཟླུམ་བ་དང་། །
རོ་…སྟོད་སེང་གེ་འདྲ་བར་འགྱུར། །

༡༥༩ ནད་པ་རྣམས་ལ་རིམ་གྲོ་དང་། །
གསོས་པས་ཐལ་གོང་རྒྱས་པ་དང་།།
བདག་ཉིད་རྣལ་དུ་གནས་པ་དང་། །
རོ་བྲོ་བ་ཡི་མཆོག་ཏུ་འགྱུར། །

༡༦༠ ཆོས་དང་མཐུན་པའི་བྱ་བ་ལ།།
ཐོག་དྲངས་ཚོད་ཀྱི་དབུ་གཙུག་ཏོར། །
ལེགས་གནས་ཉ་གྲོ་དྷ་ལྟ་བུར། །
རྒྱུ་ཞིང་གབ་པ་དག་ཏུ་འགྱུར། །

༡༦༡ ཚིག་ནི་བདེན་ལ་འཇམ་པོ་དག །
ཡུན་རིང་དུས་སུ་བརྗོད་པ་ཡིས།།
མི་བདག་ལྗགས་ནི་རིང་བ་དང་།།
ཚངས་པའི་དབྱངས་སུ་འགྱུར་བ་ལགས།།

༡༦༢ རྟག་པར་རྒྱུན་མི་འཆད་པར་སྨྲ། །
བདེན་པའི་ཚིག་ནི་སྨྲས་པ་ཡིས།།
འགྲམ་པ་སེང་གེའི་ལྟ་བུ་དང་། །
དཔལ་ལྡན་ཐུབ་པར་དཀའ་བར་འགྱུར།།

༡༦༣ ལྷག་པར་གུས་དང་བཀུར་སྟི་དང་། །
ཇི་ལྟར་རིགས་པར་རྗེས་འཇུག་པས།།
ཚེམས་ནི་ཤིན་ཏུ་དཀར་བ་དང་། །
མདོག་ལྡན་མཉམ་པའི་ཚེམས་སུ་འགྱུར།།

༡༦༤ བདེན་དང་ཕྲ་མ་མེད་པ་ཡི། །
ཚིག་ནི་ཡུན་རིང་གོམས་པ་ཡིས། །
དཔལ་ལྡན་ཚེམས་ནི་བཞི་བཅུ་ཚང་། །
མཉམ་པར་ཐགས་ཀྱང་བཟང་བར་འགྱུར།།

༡༦༥ ཆགས་དང་སྡང་དང་རྨོངས་མེད་ཅིང་། །
བྱམས་པས་སེམས་ཅན་བལྟས་པ་ཡིས།།
སྤྱན་ནི་བཀྲག་ཅན་མཐོན་མཐིང་ལ། །
རྫི་མ་བ་ཡི་ལྟ་བུར་འགྱུར། །

༡༦༦ དེ་ལྟར་མདོར་ན་རྒྱུར་བཅས་པའི། །
སུམ་ཅུ་རྩ་གཉིས་དེ་དག་ནི། །
སྐྱེས་བུ་སེང་གེ་ཆེན་པོ་ཡི། །
མཚན་རྣམས་ལེགས་པར་མཁྱེན་པར་མཛོད།།

༡༩༧ དཔེ་བྱད་བཟང་པོ་བརྒྱད་བཅུ་ནི། །
བྱམས་པའི་རྒྱུ་མཐུན་ལས་བྱུང་བ། །
གཞུང་ཆེ་མང་དུ་དོགས་པ་ཡིས། །
རྒྱལ་པོ་ཁྱོད་ལ་མ་བཤད་དོ། །

༡༩༨ འཁོར་ལོས་བསྒྱུར་བ་ཐམས་ཅད་ལ། །
འདི་དག་ཡོད་པར་འདོད་མོད་ཀྱི། །
དག་དང་མཛེས་དང་གསལ་བ་ནི། །
སངས་རྒྱས་རྣམས་ཀྱི་ཆར་མི་ཕོད། །

༡༩༩ འཁོར་ལོས་བསྒྱུར་བའི་མཚན་དང་ནི། །
དཔེ་བྱད་བཟང་པོ་གང་དག་གཅིག །
ཐུབ་དབང་པོ་ལ་སེམས་དད་པའི། །
ཡན་ལག་གཅིག་ལས་བྱུང་བཤད་པ། །

༢༠༠ བསྐལ་པ་བྱེ་བ་བརྒྱ་ཕྲག་ནི། །
གཅིག་ཏུ་བསགས་པའི་དགེ་བས་ཀྱང་། །
སངས་རྒྱས་བ་སྤུ་ཁུང་གཅིག་ཀྱང་། །
བསྐྱེད་པར་ནུས་པ་མ་ཡིན་ནོ། །
ཉི་མ་རྣམས་ཀྱི་འོད་བྱེད་པ། །
མེ་ཁྱེར་རྣམས་དང་བག་འདྲ་ལྟར། །
སངས་རྒྱས་རྣམས་ཀྱི་མཚན་ཀྱང་ནི། །
འཁོར་ལོས་བསྒྱུར་བ་རྣམས་དང་འདྲ། །

རིན་པོ་ཆེའི་ཕྲེང་བ་ལས་སྤེལ་མ་
ཞེས་བྱ་བསྟེ་ལེའུ་གཉིས་པའོ། ། ། །

༢༠༡ ༄ བསོད་ནམས་བསམ་གྱིས་མི་ཁྱབ་ལས། །
ཇི་ལྟར་སངས་རྒྱས་མཚན་འབྱུང་བ། །
ཐེག་པ་ཆེན་པོའི་ལུང་ཆེན་ལས། །
རྒྱལ་པོ་ཆེན་པོ་དེ་བཞིན་གསོན། །

༢༠༢ རང་སངས་རྒྱས་ཀུན་ལས་བྱུང་དང་། །
སློབ་དང་མི་སློབ་ལས་བྱུང་དང་། །
འཇིག་རྟེན་མ་ལུས་ཀུན་བསོད་ནམས། །
འཇིག་རྟེན་བཞིན་དུ་དཔག་མེད་གང་། །

༣༠༣ དེ་ཙམ་བཅུར་ནི་བསྒྲེས་པ་ཡིས། །
བསྐྱུའི་བུ་ག་གཅིག་འགྲུབ་སྟེ།།
སངས་རྒྱས་བསྐྱུའི་བུ་ག་ནི། །
ཐམས་ཅད་དེ་དང་འདྲ་བར་འགྱུར།།

༣༠༤ བསྐྱུའི་བུ་ག་ཐམས་ཅད་ནི།
སྐྱེད་པར་བྱེད་པའི་བསོད་ནམས་གང་།།
དེ་དག་བརྒྱར་ནི་བསྒྱུར་བ་ཡིས། །
དཔེ་བྱད་བཟང་པོ་གཅིག་ཏུ་བཞེད།།

༣༠༥ བསོད་ནམས་དེ་སྟེད་དེ་སྟེད་ཀྱིས། །
རྒྱལ་པོ་དཔེ་བྱད་བཟང་པོ་ནི། །
གཅིག་མཐར་ཕྱིན་ཏེ་དེ་ལྟ་བུར།།
བརྒྱད་ཅུའི་བར་དུ་འབྱུང་བར་འགྱུར།།

༣༠༦ དཔེ་བྱད་བཟང་པོ་བརྒྱད་ཅུ་དག །
འགྲུབ་པའི་བསོད་ནམས་ཚོགས་གང་ཡིན།།
དེ་དག་བརྒྱར་ནི་བསྒྱུར་བ་ཡིས། །
སྐྱེས་བུ་ཆེན་པོའི་མཚན་གཅིག་གོ།

༣༠༧ མཚན་ནི་སུམ་ཅུ་འགྲུབ་པའི་རྒྱུ། །
བསོད་ནམས་རྒྱ་ཆེན་གང་ཡིན་པ།།
དེ་དག་སྟོང་དུ་བསྒྱུར་བ་ཡིས། །
ཟླ་བ་ཉ་འདྲའི་མཛོད་སྤུ་འོ། །

༣༠༨ མཛོད་སྤུ་ཡི་ནི་བསོད་ནམས་དག །
སྟོང་ཕྲག་བརྒྱ་ནི་བསྒོམས་པ་ཡིས།།
སྤྱི་གཙུག་ལྷུར་ནི་མི་སྣང་བ། །
སྐྱོབ་པའི་གཙུག་ཏོར་བསྐྱེད་པར་བྱེད།།

(གཙུག་ཏོར་བསོད་ནམས་བྱེ་བ་དག །འབུམ་ཕྲག་བརྒྱ་ནི་བསྒྲེས་པ་ཡིས།།
གྲངས་མེད་རྒྱ་ཆེན་བཅུ་པོ་དག །སངས་རྒྱས་གསུང་གི་སྒྲ་དབྱངས་ནི། །
ཡན་ལག་དྲུག་ཅུ་བསྐྱེད་པའི་མཆོག །).

༣༠༩ དེ་ལྟར་བསོད་ནམས་ཚད་མེད་ཀྱང་། །
ཇི་ལྟར་འཇིག་རྟེན་ཕྱོགས་ཀུན་ཏུ། །
བཅུས་བསྒྲེས་མ་ལུས་བརྗོད་པ་ལྟར།།
ཚད་དང་ལྡན་པ་བག་ཙམ་བརྗོད།།

༣༧༠ གང་ཚེ་སངས་རྒྱས་གཟུགས་སྐུ་ཡི། །
རྒྱུ་ཡང་དེ་ལྟར་འཛིག་རྟེན་བཞིན། །
གཞལ་མེད་དེ་ཚེ་ཆོས་ཀྱི་སྐུའི། །
རྒྱུ་ལ་ཇི་ལྟར་གཞལ་དུ་ཡོད། །

༣༧༡ ཐམས་ཅད་ཀྱི་ནི་རྒྱུ་ཆུང་ཡང་། །
འབྲས་བུ་རྒྱ་ཆེན་སྐྱེ་འགྱུར་ན། །
སངས་རྒྱས་རྒྱུ་ནི་དཔག་མེད་ལ། །
འབྲས་བུ་དཔག་ཡོད་བསམ་ཐག་ཆད། །

༣༧༢ སངས་རྒྱས་རྣམས་ཀྱི་གཟུགས་སྐུ་ནི། །
བསོད་ནམས་ཚོགས་ལས་བྱུང་བ་སྟེ། །
ཆོས་ཀྱི་སྐུ་ནི་མདོར་བསྡུ་ན། །
རྒྱལ་པོ་ཡེ་ཤེས་ཚོགས་ལས་བྱུང་། །

༣༧༣ དེ་ལྟ་བས་ན་ཚོགས་འདི་གཉིས། །
སངས་རྒྱས་ཉིད་ནི་འཐོབ་པའི་རྒྱུ། །
དེ་ལྟར་མདོར་ན་བསོད་ནམས་དང་། །
ཡེ་ཤེས་འདི་ནི་རྟག་བསྟེན་མཛོད། །

༣༧༤ རིགས་པ་དང་ནི་ལུང་བསྟན་པའི། །
དབུགས་འབྱིན་བྱེད་པའི་རྒྱུ་འདི་ཡིས། །
བྱང་ཆུབ་བསྒྲུབ་···པའི་བསོད་ནམས་ནི། །
འདི་ལ་སྒྱིད་ལུགས་མི་བྱའོ། །

༣༧༥ ཕྱོགས་རྣམས་ཀུན་ཏུ་ནམ་མཁའ་དང་། །
ས་དང་ཆུ་དང་མེ་དང་རླུང་། །
ཇི་ལྟར་མཐའ་ཡས་དེ་བཞིན་དུ། །
སྡུག་བསྔལ་སེམས་ཅན་མཐའ་ཡས་འདོད། །

༣༧༦ སེམས་ཅན་མཐའ་ཡས་དེ་དག་ནི། །
བྱང་ཆུབ་སེམས་དཔའ་སྙིང་བརྩེ་བས། །
སྡུག་བསྔལ་དག་ལས་དྲངས་བྱས་ཏེ། །
སངས་རྒྱས་ཉིད་ལ་དགོད་པར་ངེས། །

༣༧༧ དེ་ལྟར་བརྟན་པར་གནས་དེ་ནི། །
མ་ཉལ་བའམ་ཉལ་ཡང་རུང་། །
ཡང་དག་བླངས་པ་ནས་བཟུང་སྟེ། །
བག་མེད་གྱུར་ཀྱང་སེམས་ཅན་རྣམས། །

༣༢༨ མཐའ་ཡས་ཕྱོར་ན་སེམས་ཅན་བཞིན།།
བསོད་ནམས་མཐའ་ཡས་རྟག་སོག ····འཕྱུར།།
མཐའ་ཡས་དེས་ན་སངས་རྒྱས་ཉིད། །
མཐའ་ཡས་ཐོབ་མི་དཀའ་ཞེས་བྱ། །

༣༢༩ གང་ཞིག་དཔག་མེད་དུས་གནས་ཏེ། །
ལུས་ཅན་དཔག་ཏུ་མེད་དོན་དུ། །
བྱང་ཆུབ་དཔག་ཏུ་མེད་འདོད་ཅིང་། །
དགེ་བ་དཔག་ཏུ་མེད་བྱེད་པ། །

༣༣༠ དེས་ཀོ་བྱང་ཆུབ་དཔག་མེད་ཀྱང་། །
དཔག་ཏུ་མེད་པ་རྣམ་བཞི་ཡི། །
ཚོགས་ཀྱིས་རིང་པོར་མི་ཐོགས་པར།།
ཇི་ལྟ་བུར་ན་ཐོབ་མི་འགྱུར། །

༣༣༡ བསོད་ནམས་མཐའ་ཡས་ཞེས་པ་དང་།།
ཡེ་ཤེས་མཐའ་ཡས་ཞེས་པ་དེས། །
ལུས་དང་སེམས་ཀྱི་སྡུག་བསྔལ་དག།
མྱུར་བ་ཉིད་དུ་སེལ་བར་བྱེད། །

༣༣༢ སྡིག་པས་ངན་འགྲོར་ལུས་ཀྱི་ནི། །
སྡུག་བསྔལ་བཀྲེས་སྐོམ་ལ་སོགས་འབྱུང་། །
དེས་སྡིག་མི་བྱས་བསོད་ནམས་ཀྱིས། །
སྐྱིད་པ་གཞན་ན་དེ་མེད་དོ། །

༣༣༣ རྨོངས་པས་ཡིད་ཀྱི་སྡུག་བསྔལ་ནི། །
ཆགས་སྡང་འཇིགས་དང་འདོད་ལ་སོགས། །
དེས་རྟེན་མེད་པའི་ཤེས་པ་ཡིས། །
དེ་ནི་མྱུར་བ་ཉིད་དུ་སྤོང་། །

༣༣༤ ལུས་དང་ཡིད་ཀྱི་སྡུག་བསྔལ་གྱིས། །
དེ་ལྟར་ཤིན་ཏུ་མ་སྨས་ན། །
གལ་ཏེ་འཇིག་རྟེན་མཐས་གཏུགས་པར། །
འཇིག་རྟེན་འདྲེན་ཀྱང་ཅི་སྟེ་སྐྱོ། །

༣༣༥ སྡུག་བསྔལ་བ་ལ་དུས་ཐུང་ཡང་། །
བཟོད་དཀའ་ཡུན་རིང་སྨོས་ཅི་དགོས།།
སྡུག་བསྔལ་མེད་ཅིང་བདེ་བ་ལ། །
མཐའ་ཡས་དུས་ཀྱང་ཅི་ཞིག་གནོད། །

༣༢༦ དེ་ལ་ལུས་ཀྱི་སྡུག་བསྔལ་མེད། །
ཡིད་ཀྱི་སྡུག་བསྔལ་ག་ལ་ཡོད། །
དེ་ནི་སྙིང་རྗེས་འཇིག་རྟེན་སྡུག །
དེ་ཉིད་ཀྱིས་ནི་ཡུན་རིང་གནས། །

༣༢༧ དེ་བས་སངས་རྒྱས་རིང་ཐོགས་ཞེས། །
བློ་དང་ལྡན་པ་སྐྱིད་མི་ལུག །
ཉེས་ཟད་ཡོན་ཏན་དོན་དུ་ནི། །
འདི་ལ་རྟག་ཏུ་འབད་པར་བྱ། །

༣༢༨ ཆགས་དང་ཞེ་སྡང་གཏི་མུག་དག །
ཉེས་པ་མཁྱེན་ནས་ཡོངས་སུ་སྤོངས། །
མ་ཆགས་མི་སྡང་གཏི་མུག་མེད། །
ཡོན་ཏན་མཁྱེན་ནས་གུས་པར་བསྟེན། །

༣༢༩ ཆགས་པས་ཡི་དྭགས་འགྲོ་བར་འགྲོ། །
ཞེ་སྡང་གིས་ནི་དམྱལ་བར་འཕེན། །
རྨོངས་པས་ཕལ་ཆེར་དུད་འགྲོར་འགྲོ། །
བཟློག་པས་ལྷ་དང་མི་ཉིད་དོ། །

༣༣༠ སྐྱོན་སྤངས་ཡོན་ཏན་འཛིན་པ་ནི། །
མངོན་པར་མཐོ་བ་པ་ཡི་ཆོས། །
ཤེས་པས་འཛིན་པ་ཡོངས་ཟད་པ། །
ངེས་པར་ལེགས་པ་པ་ཡི་ཆོས། །

༣༣༡ སངས་རྒྱས་སྐུ་གཟུགས་མཆོད་རྟེན་དང་། །
གཙུག་ལག་ཁང་དག་གུས་ཚུལ་དུ། །
ཤིན་ཏུ་རྒྱ་ཆེན་གནས་ལ་སོགས། །
རྒྱ་ཆེན་ཕྱུག་པོ་བསྒྲུབ་པར་མཛོད། །

༣༣༢ རིན་ཆེན་ཀུན་ལས་བགྱིས་པ་ཡིས། །
སངས་རྒྱས་སྐུ་གཟུགས་དབྱིབས་ལེགས་ཤིང་། །
ལེགས་པར་བྲིས་པ་བདྨ་ལ། །
བཞུགས་པ་དག་དང་རིན་པོ་ཆེ། །
ཀུན་གྱིས་བརྒྱན་པ་བགྱིད་དུ་གསོལ། །

༣༣༣ དམ་ཆོས་དགེ་སློང་དགེ་འདུན་དག །
ནན་ཏན་ཀུན་གྱིས་བསྐྱང་བར་མཛོད། །
གསེར་དང་རིན་ཆེན་དྲ་བ་དག །
ཉིད་ཀྱིས་མཆོད་རྟེན་རྣམས་ལ་ཐོགས། །

༣༣༤ གསེར་དང་དངུལ་གྱི་མེ་ཏོག་དང་། །
རྡོ་རྗེ་བྱུ་རུ་མུ་ཏིག་དག །
ཨན་དྲ་ནི་ལ་དང་བཻ་ཌཱུརྱ། །
མཐོན་ཀ་ཆེན་པོས་མཆོད་རྟེན་མཆོད། །

༣༣༥ དམ་ཆོས་སྐུ་ལ་མཆོད་པ་ནི། །
རྟེན་དང་བཀུར་སྟི་དང་ལྡན་པ། །
དགའ་བར་འགྱུར་བ་རྣམས་བགྱི་ཞིང་། །
ཆོས་ནི་ངེས་པར་བསྟེན་པར་མཛོད། །

༣༣༦ བླ་མར་རིམ་གྲོ་གུས་ཅན་དང་། །
ཞབས་འབྲིང་དང་ནི་མདངས་གསོལ་དང་། །
བྱང་ཆུབ་སེམས་དཔའ་རྣམས་ལ་ཡང་། །
རྟག་ཏུ་གུས་པས་མཆོད་པར་མཛོད། །

༣༣༧ ཁྱོད་ཀྱིས་མུ་སྟེགས་ཅན་གཞན་ལ། །
གུས་དང་མཆོད་ཕྱག་མི་བགྱི་སྟེ། །
མི་ཤེས་པ་རྣམས་དེའི་རྐྱེན་གྱིས། །
སྐྱོན་དང་བཅས་ལ་ཆགས་འགྱུར་གདའ། །

༣༣༨ ཐུབ་དབང་གསུང་དང་དེས་བྱུང་བའི། །
གཞུང་རྣམས་བྲི་དང་གླེགས་བམ་ནི། །
སྣག་ཚ་དག་དང་སྨྱུ་གུ་དག །
སྔོན་དུ་འགྲོ་བ་སྦྱིན་པར་མཛོད། །

༣༣༩ ཡུལ་དུ་ཡི་གེའི་གྲྭ་ཁང་དུ། །
སློབ་དཔོན་འཚོ་བའི་བྱ་བ་དང་། །
ཞིང་བསྐྱ་ལ་བ་ཡི་ངེས་པ་ནི། །
ཡེ་ཤེས་སྤེལ་བའི་ཐབས་སུ་མཛོད། །

༣༤༠ རྒན་དང་བྱིས་པ་ནད་པ་ཡི། །
སེམས་ཅན་སྡུག་བསྔལ་བསལ་བས་ལ་སླད་དུ། །
ཡུལ་དུ་སྨན་པ་འཚོ་མ་ཞིང་དག །
ཞིང་གིས་བརྟན་པ་འཛོག་ཏུ་གསོལ། །

༣༤༡ འགྲོན་གནས་ཀུན་དགའ་ཆུ་ལོན་དང་། །
རྫིང་དང་མདུན་ཁང་རྒྱུར་དག །
མལ་ཟས་རྩྭ་དང་ཤིང་ལྡན་པ། །
ཤེས་རབ་བཟང་པོ་བཀྱིད་དུ་སྩོལ། །

༣༩༢ གྲོང་དང་གཙུག་ལག་ཁང་དག་དང་། །
གྲོང་ཁྱེར་ཀུན་ཏུ་མདུན་ཁང་དང་། །
རྒྱུ་དཀོན་ལ་མཉམས་ཐམས་ཅད་དུ། །
རྒྱུར་དང་གཞི་བགྱིད་དུ་སྩོལ། །

༣༩༣ ནད་པ་མགོན་མེད་སྡུག་བསྔལ་གྱིས། །
ཉམས་ཐག་དམན་པ་ངན་པ་དག །
སྙིང་རྗེས་རྟག་ཏུ་ཡོངས་གཟུང་ཞིང་། །
དེ་དག་གསོ་ཕྱིར་གུས་བསྙེན་མཛོད། །

༣༩༤ དུས་སུ་ཐུང་བའི་ཟས་སྐོམ་དང་། །
བཅའ་བ་འབྲུ་དང་ཤིང་ཏོག་དག །
དགེ་སློང་དགེ་སློང་བའི་སྐྱོ་བོ་ལ། །
མ་སྨྲ་ལ་བར་དུ་གསོལ་མི་རིགས། །

༣༩༥ ལྷམ་དང་གདུགས་དང་ཆུ་ཚགས་དང་། །
ཚེར་མ་འབྱུང་བའི་ཆ་སྐྱ་དང་། །
ཁབ་སྐུད་དང་ནི་བསིལ་ཡབ་དག །
རྒྱུར་ཡི་ནི་གནས་སུ་བཞག །

༣༩༦ འབྲས་བུ་གསུམ་དང་ཚ་བ་གསུམ། །
མར་དང་སྦྲང་རྩི་མིག་སྨན་དང་། །
དུག་སེལ་རྒྱུ་རར་གཞག་བགྱི་ཞིང་། །
གྲུབ་པའི་སྔགས་དང་སྨན་སྦྱར་བྲི། །

༣༩༧ ལུས་དང་རྐང་པ་མགོ་བསྐུ་དང་། །
བལ་དང་ཁྲི་འུ་སྒྲོམ་དང་། །
བུམ་པ་ཟངས་དང་དགྲ་སྣ་སོགས། །
རྒྱུར་དག་ཏུ་འཛེག་ཏུ་གསོལ། །

༣༩༨ ཏིལ་དང་འབྲས་དང་འབྲུ་དང་ཟས། །
བུ་རམ་སྦྲུམ་དང་ལྷན་པ་ཡི། །
རྒྱུར་རྒྱུད་དུ་བསིལ་གྱི་བ་ཏུ། །
ཐུང་བའི་རྒྱུས་པ་ཀང་བགྱིད་དུ་སྩོལ། །

༣༩༩ གྲོག་སྦྲུར་ཚང་གི་སྒོ་དག་ཏུ། །
ཟས་དང་ཆུ་དང་བུ་རམ་དང་། །
འབྲུ་ཡི་སྤུང་པོ་རྟ་ག་པ་ར་ཞི། །
བྱུགས་པ་བརྟན་མི་རྣམས་བགྱིད་དུ་གསོལ། །

༣༥༠ བཙོས་གསོལ་སྔོན་དང་འོག་དག་ཏུ། །
ཡི་དྭགས་ཁྱི་དང་གྲོག་སྦྲུར་དང་། །
བྱ་ལ་སོགས་པ་ཚི་བདེ་བར། །
རྟག་ཏུ་ཟས་དག་སྩལ་བར་མཛོད། །

༣༥༡ གཙེས་པ་དང་ནི་ལོ་ཉེས་དང་། །
གནོད་པ་དང་ནི་ཡམས་ནད་དང་། །
ཕམ་གྱུར་ཡུལ་དུ་འཇིག་རྟེན་ལ། །
རྗེས་སུ་གཟུང་བ་རྒྱ་ཆེན་མཛོད། །

༣༥༢ ཞིང་པ་ཉམ་ཐག་གྱུར་རྣམས་ལ། །
ས་བོན་ཟས་ཀྱིས་རྗེས་སུ་གཟུང་། །
ནད་ཀྱི་དཔྱ་ཁྲལ་བཏང་བ་དང་། །
ཤགས་རྣམས་ཀྱང་ནི་བསྐྱུང་བ་དང་། །

༣༥༣ ཆགས་ཉེན་པ་ལས་ཡོངས་བསྐྱབ་དང་། །
ཤོ་གམ་གཏད་དང་ཤོ་གམ་དབྲི། །
དེ་དག་སྐྱོན་སྤྱོད་པ་ཡི། །
ཉོན་མོངས་ལས་ཀྱང་བཟློག་པར་མཛོད། །

༣༥༤ རང་གི་ཡུལ་དང་ཡུལ་གཞན་གྱི། །
ཆོམ་རྐུན་རྣམས་ཀྱང་ཞི་བར་མཛོད། །
དབྱིག་གི་སློགས་ནི་མཉམ་པ་དང་། །
རིན་ཐང་རིགས་པར་མཛད་དུ་གསོལ། །

༣༥༥ སྔོན་པོས་ཚི་དང་ཚི་གསོལ་བ། །
ཉིད་ཀྱིས་ཀུན་ཏུ་མཁྱེན་མཛད་ནས། །
འཇིག་རྟེན་སྨན་པ་གང་དང་གང་། །
དེ་དང་དེ་ཀུན་རྟག་ཏུ་མཛོད། །

༣༥༦ བདག་ཕན་ཚི་དང་ཚི་བྱ་ཞེས། །
ཇི་ལྟར་ཁྱོད་ལ་གུས་ཡོད་པ། །
གཞན་ཕན་ཚི་དང་ཚི་བྱ་ཞེས། །
དེ་བཞིན་ཁྱོད་ན་གུས་པར་མཛོད། །

༣༥༧ ས་དང་ཆུ་དང་མེ་དང་རླུང་། །
སྨན་དང་ནགས་ཀྱི་ཤིང་བཞིན་དུ། །
བདག་ཉིད་ཡུད་ཙམ་གཅིག་ཏུ་ཡང་། །
འདོད་དགུར་སྤྱད་པ་ཉིད་དུ་མཛོད། །

༣༥༨ གོམ་པ་བརྟུན་པའི་དུས་སུ་ཡང་། །
བདོག་པ་ཀུན་གཏོང་སེམས་འཆང་བའི།།
བྱང་ཆུབ་སེམས་དཔའ་རྣམས་ལ་ནི། །
བསོད་ནམས་མཁའ་འདྲ་དཔག་མེད་སྐྱེ།།

༣༥༩ བུ་མོ་གཟུགས་མཛེས་ལེགས་བརྒྱན་པ། །
དེ་དོན་གཉེར་བ་རྣམས་སྩལ་ན། །
དེས་ནི་དམ་ཆོས་ཡོངས་འཛིན་པའི། །
གཟུངས་ནི་སོ་སོར་འཐོབ་པར་འགྱུར།།

༣༦༠ རྒྱན་རྣམས་ཀུན་དང་ལྡན་པ་ཡི། །
བུ་མོ་སྟོང་ཕྲག་བརྒྱད་ཅུ་དག །
ཡོ་བྱད་ཀུན་དང་ལྷན་ཅིག་ཏུ། །
ཐུབ་པ་ཡིས་ནི་སྔོན་སྩལ་ཏོ། །

༣༦༡ སྣ་ཚོགས་པ་དང་འོད་གསལ་བའི། །
བགོ་བ་དག་དང་རྒྱན་རྣམས་དང་། །
དྲི་དང་ཕྲེང་བ་ལོངས་སྤྱོད་དག །
སློང་བ་རྣམས་ལ་བརྩེ་བས་སྩོལ། །

༣༦༢ གང་ལ་ཆོས་དོན་གང་མེད་ན། །
ཤིན་ཏུ་ཉམས་ཐག་གྱུར་པ་དེ།།
དེ་ཡི་མོད་ལ་དེ་སྩལ་ན། །
དེ་ལས་སྦྱིན་མཆོག་མ་མཆིས་སོ།།

༣༦༣ གང་ལ་དུག་ནི་ཕན་འགྱུར་ན།།
དེ་ལ་དུག་ཀྱང་སྦྱིན་པར་བགྱི།།
ཁ་ཟས་མཆོག་ཀྱང་མི་ཕན་ན།།
དེ་ལ་དེ་ནི་སྦྱིན་མི་བགྱི། །

༣༦༤ སྦྲུལ་གྱིས་ཟིན་ལ་ཇི་ལྟ་བུར། །
སོར་མོ་བཅད་ན་ཕན་པ་ལྟར། །
དེ་བཞིན་ཐུབ་པས་གཞན་ཕན་པ།།
མི་བདེ་བ་ཡང་བྱ་བར་གསུངས། །

༣༦༥ དམ་པའི་ཆོས་དང་ཆོས་སྨྲ་ལ། །
ཉིད་ཀྱིས་བཀུར་སྟི་མཆོག་དང་ནི།།
གུས་པར་བྱས་ཏེ་ཆོས་ཉན་ཅིང་།།
ཆོས་ཀྱི་སྦྱིན་པ་དག་ཀྱང་མཛོད།།

༢༦༦ འཇིག་རྟེན་གཏམ་ལ་དགའ་མ་མཛོད།།
འཇིག་རྟེན་འདས་ལ་དགྱེས་པར་མཛོད།།
བདག་ལ་ཇི་ལྟ་དེ་བཞིན་དུ། །
གཞན་ལ་ཡོན་ཏན་བསྐྱེད་པར་མཛོད། །

༢༦༧ གསན་པའི་ཆོས་ཀྱིས་མི་ངོམས་ཤིང་། །
དོན་གཟུང་རྣམ་པར་དཔྱད་པ་དང་། །
བླ་མ་དག་ལ་ཡོན་འབུལ་བ། །
རྟག་ཏུ་གུས་པས་མཛད་དུ་གསོལ།།

༢༦༨ འཇིག་རྟེན་རྒྱང་ཕན་སོགས་མི་གདོན།།
ང་རྒྱལ་དོན་དུ་རྩོད་པ་སྤང་། །
རང་གི་ཡོན་ཏན་མི་བསྔགས་ཤིང་། །
དགྲ་ལའང་ཡོན་ཏན་བརྗོད་པར་མཛོད། །

༢༦༩ གནད་ལ་དབབ་པར་མི་བགྱི་ཞིང་། །
གཞན་རྣམས་ལ་ནི་ངན་སེམས་ཀྱིས། །
གླེང་བར་མི་བགྱི་བདག་ཉིད་ཀྱི། །
འཁྲུལ་པ་སོ་སོར་བརྟག་པར་བྱ། །

༢༧༠ ཉེས་པ་གང་གིས་གཞན་དག་ལ། །
མཁས་པས་རྟག་ཏུ་ཁ་བྱ་བ། །
དེ་ཉིད་རང་གིས་ཡོངས་སྤང་ཞིང་། །
ནུས་པས་གཞན་ཡང་བཟློག་པར་མཛོད།།

༢༧༡ གཞན་གྱིས་གནོད་པ་བགྱིས་པ་ལ།།
སྔོན་གྱི་ལས་དགོངས་ཁྲོ་མི་བགྱི། །
སྡུག་བསྔལ་ཡང་འབྱུང་མི་འགྱུར་བས།།
རང་གི་ཉེས་པ་མེད་པར་བགྱི། །

༢༧༢ ཕན་ལ་རེ་བ་མ་མཆིས་པར། །
གཞན་དག་ལ་ནི་ཕན་པར་མཛོད། །
སྡུག་བསྔལ་གཅིག་པུས་གནག་བགྱི་ཞིང་།།
བདེ་བ་སློང་དང་ལྷན་ཅིག་སྤྱད། །

༢༧༣ ལྷ་ཡི་ཕུན་སུམ་ཚོགས་པས་ཀྱང་། །
ཁེངས་པ་ཉིད་དུ་མི་བྱ་ཞིང་། །
ཡི་དྭགས་བཞིན་དུ་དབུལ་བ་ཡི། །
རྒུད་པས་ཀྱང་ནི་ཞུམ་མི་བགྱི། །

༢༧༤ བདེན་པ་གང་གིས་རང་དོན་ལ། །
འཆི་འམ་ཡང་ན་རྒྱལ་པོའི་སྲིད། །
ཉམས་འགྱུར་དེ་ནི་རྟག་བརྗོད་ཅིང༌། །
དེ་ལས་གཞན་དུ་བརྗོད་མི་བགྱི། །

༢༧༥ ཇི་སྐད་གསུངས་པ་དེ་བཞིན་དུ། །
མཛད་པའི་བརྟུལ་ཞུགས་རྟག་བསྟེན་མཛོད། །
དེས་ན་དཔལ་ལ་ལྷུན་ས་སྐྱེང་དུ། །
ཚད་མ་ཡི་ནི་དམ་པར་འགྱུར། །

༢༧༦ ཁྱོད་ནི་རྟག་ཏུ་ཐམས་ཅད་ལ། །
ལེགས་པར་བརྟགས་ཏེ་མཛད་པ་དང༌། །
ཡང་དག་ཇི་བཞིན་དོན་གཟིགས་པས། །
གཞན་གྱི་དྲིང་མི་འཇོག་པར་མཛོད། །

༢༧༧ ཆོས་ལས་རྒྱལ་སྲིད་བདེ་བ་དང༌། །
ཕྱོགས་རྣམས་ཀུན་ཏུ་གྲགས་པ་ཡི། །
བླ་རེ་རྒྱ་ཆེན་འབྱུང་འགྱུར་ཞིང༌། །
བློན་པོ་རྣམས་ཀྱང་ཀུན་ཏུ་འདུད། །

༢༧༨ འཆི་བའི་རྐྱེན་ནི་མང་བ་སྟེ། །
གསོན་པའི་རྒྱུ་ནི་ཉུང་ཟད་ཅིག །
དེ་དག་ཉིད་ནི་འཆི་བའི་ཡང༌། །
དེ་བས་རྟག་ཏུ་ཆོས་མཛོད་ཅིག །

༢༧༩ འདི་ལྟར་རྟག་ཏུ་ཆོས་མཛད་ན། །
འཇིག་རྟེན་ཀུན་དང་བདག་ཉིད་ལ། །
ཉམས་བདེར་འགྱུར་བ་གང་ཡིན་པ། །
དེ་ཉིད་རེ་ཞིག་ལྡོག་མོ་ལགས། །

༢༨༠ ཆོས་ཀྱིས་བདེ་བར་གཉིད་ལོག་ཅིང༌། །
བདེ་བར་སད་པ་དག་ཏུ་འགྱུར། །
ནང་གི་བདག་ཉིད་སྐྱོན་མེད་པས། །
མི་ལམ་དག་ཀྱང་བདེ་བ་མཐོང༌། །

༢༨༡ ཕ་མ་སྲི་ཞུ་ལྷུར་ལེན་དང༌། །
རིགས་ཀྱི་གཙོ་ལ་རིམ་གྲོ་དང༌། །
ལོངས་སྤྱོད་ལེགས་སྤྱོད་བཟོད་གཏོང་དང༌། །
ཚིག་འཇམ་ཕྲ་མ་མེད་བདེན་པའི། །

༣༤༢ བརྟུལ་ཞུགས་ཆེ་གཅིག་བྱས་པ་དེས། །
ཀླུ་ཡི་དབང་པོ་ཉིད་ཐོབ་ནས། །
ད་དུང་དུ་ཡང་ཀླུ་དབང་བགྱིད། །
དེ་བས་དེ་འདྲའི་ཚེས་བསྙེན་མཛོད།།

༣༤༣ རྫི་ཙུ་བཙོས་སུམ་བརྒྱའི་ཁ་ཟས་དག །
ཉིན་རེ་དུས་གསུམ་བྱིན་པས་ཀྱང་།།
བྱམས་པ་ཡུད་ཙམ་ཐང་ཅིག་གི །
བསོད་ནམས་དག་ལ་ཆར་མི་ཕོད།།

༣༤༨ ལྷ་མི་བྱམས་པར་འགྱུར་བ་དང་། །
དེ་དག་ཀྱང་ནི་བསྲུང་བ་དང་། །
ཡིད་བདེ་བ་དང་བདེ་མང་དང་།།
དུག་དང་མཚོན་གྱིས་གནོད་མེད་དང་།།

༣༤༥ འབད་པ་མེད་པར་དོན་ཐོབ་དང་།།
ཚངས་པའི་འཇིག་རྟེན་སྐྱེ་འགྱུར་ཏེ།།
གལ་ཏེ་གྲོལ་བར་མ་གྱུར་ཀྱང་།།
བྱམས་ཆོས་ཡོན་ཏན་བརྒྱད་འཐོབ་བོ།།

༣༤༦ སེམས་ཅན་རྣམས་ནི་བྱང་ཆུབ་ཏུ། །
སེམས་བསྐྱེད་བཙུག་ཅིང་བརྟན་བྱས་ན།།
རི་དབང་རྒྱལ་པོ་ལྟར་བརྟན་པའི། །
བྱང་ཆུབ་སེམས་ནི་རྟག་ཏུ་འཐོབ། །

༣༤༧ དད་པས་མི་ཁོམ་འགྲོ་མི་འགྱུར། །
ཁྲིམས་ཀྱིས་འགྲོ་བ་བཟང་པོར་འགྲོ།།
སྟོང་པ་ཉིད་ལ་གོམས་པ་ཡིས། །
ཆོས་རྣམས་ཀུན་ལ་ཆགས་མེད་འཐོབ།།

༣༤༤ གཡོ་མེད་པས་ནི་དྲན་ལྡན་འཐོབ། །
སེམས་པར་བྱེད་པས་བློ་གྲོས་འཐོབ།།
བཀུར་སྟི་བྱས་པས་དོན་རྟོགས་ལྡན།།
ཆོས་བསྲུངས་ཤེས་རབ་ཅན་དུ་འགྱུར།།

༣༤༩ ཆོས་ཉན་པ་དང་སྦྱིན་པ་དག །
སྒྲིབ་པ་མེད་པར་བྱས་པ་ཡིས། །
སངས་རྒྱས་རྣམས་དང་འགྲོགས་པ་ཉིད།།
འདོད་པ་མྱུར་དུ་འཐོབ་པར་འགྱུར། །

༣/༨༠ མཆགས་པས་ནི་དོན་འགྲུབ་སྟེ། །
སེར་སྣ་མེད་པས་ལོངས་སྤྱོད་འཕེལ། །
ང་རྒྱལ་མེད་པས་གཙོ་བོར་འགྱུར། །
ཆོས་ལ་བཟོད་པས་གཟུངས་འཐོབ་བོ། །

༣/༨༡ སྙིང་པོ་ལྔ་རྣམས་སྦྱིན་པ་དང༌། །
འཇིགས་ལ་མི་འཇིགས་སྦྱིན་པ་ཡིས། །
བདུད་རྣམས་ཀུན་གྱིས་མི་ཚུགས་ཤིང༌། །
སྟོབས་པོ་ཆེ་ཡི་མཆོག་ཏུ་འགྱུར། །

༣/༨༢ མཆོད་རྟེན་མར་མེ་ཕྲེང་བ་དང༌། །
མུན་ཁུང་དག་ཏུ་སྒྲོན་མ་དང༌། །
མར་མེ་འབྲུ་མར་སྦྱིན་པ་ཡིས། །
ལྷ་ཡི་མིག་ནི་འཐོབ་པར་འགྱུར། །

༣/༨༣ མཆོད་རྟེན་མཆོད་པར་རོལ་མོ་དང༌། །
དྲིལ་བུ་དག་ནི་ཕུལ་བ་དང༌། །
དུང་དང་རྔ་ནི་རབ་ཕུལ་བས། །
ལྷ་ཡི་རྣ་བ་འཐོབ་པར་འགྱུར། །

༣/༨༤ གཞན་གྱི་འཁྲུལ་པ་མི་སྒྲོགས་ཤིང༌། །
ཡན་ལག་ཉམས་པ་རྣམས་མི་བརྗོད། །
སེམས་ནི་རྗེས་སུ་བསྲུངས་པས་ན། །
གཞན་གྱི་སེམས་ནི་ཤེས་པ་ཐོབ། །

༣/༨༥ ལྷམ་དང་བཞོན་པ་སྦྱིན་པ་དང༌། །
ཉམ་ཆུང་བཀུར་བ་བྱས་པ་དང༌། །
གཞོན་པས་བླ་མ་བཀུར་བ་ཡིས། །
མཁས་པས་རྫུ་འཕྲུལ་འཐོབ་པར་འགྱུར། །

༣/༨༦ ཆོས་ཀྱི་ཆེད་དང་དེ་བཞིན་དུ། །
ཆོས་གཞུང་དོན་དག་དྲན་པ་དང༌། །
ཆོས་ཀྱི་སྦྱིན་པ་དྲི་མེད་པས། །
ཚེ་རབས་དྲན་པ་འཐོབ་པར་འགྱུར། །

༣/༨༧ དངོས་རྣམས་ངོ་བོ་ཉིད་མེད་པར། །
ཡང་དག་ཇི་བཞིན་ཡོངས་ཤེས་པས། །
མངོན་ཤེས་དྲུག་པ་ཟག་པ་ཀུན། །
ཟད་པ་མཆོག་ནི་འཐོབ་པར་འགྱུར། །

༢༩༨ སེམས་ཅན་ཐམས་ཅད་སྒྲོལ་བའི་ཕྱིར།།
དེ་བཞིན་ཉིད་ཤེས་མཉམ་ལྡན་པ། །
སྙིང་རྗེས་བརླན་པ་བསྒོམས་པ་ཡིས། །
རྣམ་པའི་མཆོག་ལྡན་རྒྱལ་བར་འགྱུར།།

༢༩༩ སྨོན་ལམ་སྣ་ཚོགས་དག་པ་ཡིས། །
སངས་རྒྱས་ཞིང་ནི་དག་པར་འགྱུར། །
ཐུབ་དབང་རིན་ཆེན་ཕུལ་བ་ཡིས། །
མཐའ་ཡས་འོད་ནི་རྣམ་པར་འགྲོ། །

༣༠༠ དེ་བས་དེ་ལྟར་ལས་འབྲས་དག །
མཐུན་པར་མཁྱེན་མཛད་དོན་དུ་ནི།།
འགྲོ་ལ་ཕན་པ་རྟག་ཏུ་མཛོད།།
དེ་ཉིད་ཁྱོད་ལ་ཕན་པ་ལགས།།

རིན་པོ་ཆེའི་ཕྲེང་བ་ལས། བྱང་ཆུབ་ཀྱི་ཚོགས་
བསྡུས་པ་ཞེས་བྱ་བ་སྟེ་ལེའུ་གསུམ་པའོ།། །།

༣༠༡ ༄ གང་ཕྱིར་བཟོད་པ་མི་བཟོད་པ། །
ཤེས་པར་དཀའ་བས་རྒྱལ་པོ་ནི། །
ཆོས་མིན་རིགས་པ་མིན་སྤྱོད་ཀྱང་། །
རྗེས་སུ་འཚོ་བས་རྒྱལ་པོ་ལ། །
ཕལ་ཆེར་བསྟོད་པ་དེ་ཡི་ཕྱིར། །
སྨན་དང་མི་སྨན་མཁྱེན་པར་དཀའ།།

༣༠༢ རེ་ཞིག་གཞན་སུའང་རུང་བ་ལ།།
མི་སྙན་སྨན་པ་བརྗོད་དཀའ་ན།།
ས་ཆེན་མངའ་བའི་རྒྱལ་ཁྱོད་ལ།།
དགེ་སློང་བདག་ལྟ་ཅི་ཞིག་སྨོས།།

༣༠༣ ཁྱོད་ཀྱིས་དགྱེས་པ་མཛད་སླད་དང་།།
འགྲོ་བ་ལ་ཡང་བརྩེ་སླད་དུ། །
ཁྱོད་ལ་མི་སྙན་ཡང་སྨན་པ། །
བདག་ལྟ་གཅིག་པུ་ཏེ་བོར་གསོལ།།

༣༠༤ བདེན་འཛམ་དོན་ལྡན་འཁྲོད་པ་ནི། །
བརྩེ་བས་དུས་སུ་སློབ་མ་ལ། །
བརྗོད་པར་བྱ་ཞེས་བཅོམ་ལྡན་གསུང་། །
དེ་ལྟ་བསན་འདི་སྐད་བརྗོད། །

༣༠༥ བརྟན་པ་···ཁྲོ་བ་མེད་པ་ཡི། །
བདེན་པའི་ཚིག་ནི་བསྒྲགས་པ་ན། །
ཁྲུས་བྱེད་བཟང་པོའི་ཆུ་བཞིན་དུ། །
མཉན་འོས་ཡོངས་སུ་ལེན་པར་བགྱིད། །

༣༠༦ ཁྱོད་ལ་བདག་གིས་འདི་དང་ནི། །
གཞན་དུ་བརྟད་པ་བརྗོད་བགྱིད་པ། །
མཁྱེན་པར་མཛོད་དེ་བདག་ཉིད་དང་། །
གཞན་ལ་སྨན་པར་འགྱུར་དེ་མཛོད། །

༣༠༧ སློང་ལ་སྔོན་ཆད་སྦྱིན་བགྱིས་པས། །
དོན་བརྙེས་···གྱུར་ནས་མ་སྦྱིན་ན། །
བྱས་མི་བཟོ···དང་ཆགས་པ་ཡིས། །
སྦྱིནས་དོན་རྣམས་ཐོབ་མི་འགྱུར། །

༣༠༨ འཇིག་རྟེན་འདིན་ལས་བྱེད་པ། །
གླ་མེད་ལམ་རྒྱགས་ཁྱེར་མི་གཅུབ། །
སློང་བ་དམན་པ་མཇན་པར། །
ཁྱིམ་འཚེ་ལ་བརྒྱ་འགྱུར་ཁྱེར། །

༣༠༩ རྟག་ཏུ་ཐུགས་རྒྱ་ཆེན་པོ་དང་། །
མཛད་པ་རྒྱ་ཆེན་ལ་དགྱེས་མཛོད། །
རྒྱ་ཆེན་ལས་ལས་འབྲས་བུ་ནི། །
ཐམས་ཅད་རྒྱ་ཆེན་འབྱུང་བར་འགྱུར། །

༣༡༠ རྒྱལ་པོ་དམན་པ་རྣམས་ཀྱིས་ནི། །
ཡིད་ལ་འང་བསམ་པ་མ་གྱུར་པའི། །
ཆོས་གཞི་དཀོན་མཆོག་གསུམ་གྱི་རྟེན། །
གྲགས་པ་དཔལ་དང་ལྡན་པར་མཛོད། །

༣༡༡ ཆོས་གཞི་གང་ཞིག་ཀུན་འབྱོར་པའི། །
རྒྱལ་པོ་བསྒྱུ་མི་ལྡང་བ། །
ཤིན་འང་སྐྱེན་པར་མི་འགྱུར་བས། །
རྒྱལ་པོ་དེ་ནིམ་བྱས་བླ། །

༣༧༢ རྒྱུར་བ་ཆེ་ཕྱིར་རྒྱུ་ཆེན་རྣམས།།
བསྐྱེམས་བྲལ་སྤྲོ་བ་བསྐྱེད་བྱེད་ཅིང་།།
དམན་རྣམས་སྤྲོ་བ་འཛེམས་བྱེད་པ།།
བདག་···པ་ཐམས་ཅད་གཏུགས་ཏེ་མཛོད།།

༣༧༣ ཁྱོད་ནི་བདག་པ་ཀུན་བོར་ནས། །
དབང་མེད་ག་ཤེད་ག་ཤེགས་འཚོལ་ལ་ན།།
ཆོས་ཀྱི་སྣང་དུ་སྣང་པ་ཀུན།།
ཁྱོད་ཀྱི་མདུན་དུ་འོང་བ་ཉིད།།

༣༧༤ མི་དབང་སྤྲུ་མའི་བདག་པ་ཀུན།།
གསར་པ་ཡིན་ནི་དབང་འགྱུར་ན།།
སྤྲུ་མའི་ཆོས་ལམ་བདེ་བ་རམ།།
གྲགས་པ་དག་ཏུ་འགྱུར་རམ་ཅི།།

༣༧༥ ཉོར་སྐྱུད་པ་ཡིས་འདི་ལ་བདེ། །
བྱིན་པས་གཞན་དུ་བདེ་བར་འགྱུར།།
མ་སྐྱུད་མ་བྱིན་ཆུང་ཟློས་པས། །
སྡུག་བསྔལ་འབབ་ཞིག་ག་ལ་བདེ།།

༣༧༦ འཆི་ཀར་སློན་པོ་རྗེས་དན་ཅན། །
གཅེས་པར་མི་རྗེ་རྒྱལ་པོ་གསར།།
བྱམས་པར་འདོད་པ་རྣམས་ཀྱིས་ནི།།
དབང་མེད་བྱས་པས་སྐྱིན་མི་སྤྱོད།།

༣༧༧ དེ་བས་རྣལ་གནས་མྱུར་དུ་ནི། །
བདག་པ་ཀུན་གྱིས་ཆོས་གཞི་མཛོད།།
འཆི་བདག་རྐྱེན་གྱི་ནང་གནས་པ།།
ལྷུང་དམར་ནང་འདུག་མར་མེ་བཞིན།།

༣༧༨ སྔོན་གྱི་རྒྱལ་པོས་ཆོས་ཀྱི་གཞི། །
ལྷ་ཁང་ལ་སོགས་གཞན་བཀྱིས་པ།།
གང་དག་ལགས་པ་དེ་དག་ཀྱང་། །
སྤྱིར་ལུགས་བཞིན་དུ་བསྐྱང་བར་མཛོད།།

༣༧༩ དེ་དག་འཚོ་མེད་དགེ་སྐྱོད་ཅིང་།།
བརྟུལ་ཞུགས་ལ་གནས་བློ་བུར་བྱམས།།
བདེན་བརྗོད་འཐབ་ཀྲོལ་མ་མཆིས་པ།།
རྟག་ཏུ་བརྩོན་གནས་སྤྱོད་དུ་གསོལ།།

༣༣༠ ལོང་བ་ནད་པ་དམན་པ་དང་།།
མགོན་མེད་སྡུག་ཕོངས་ཡན་ལག་ཉམས།།
དེ་དག་ཀྱང་ནི་ཟས་དང་སྐོམ།།
དགག་པ་མེད་པར་སྙོམས་ཐོབ་མཛོད།།

༣༣༡ ཆོས་ལྡན་དོན་དུ་མི་གཉེར་བ།།
རྒྱལ་པོ་གཞན་ཡུལ་གནས་རྣམས་ལའང་།།
རྗེས་སུ་གཟུང་བ་བྱ་བ་དག །
ཅི་རིགས་དམ་ཞི་རབ་ཏུ་མཛོད།།

༣༣༢ ཆོས་ཀྱི་གཞི་ནི་ཐམས་ཅད་དུ།།
ཆོས་འཁོར་སྨྲ་བོ་མི་གཡེལ་བར།།
མི་གཟན་མཁས་ཤིང་ཆོས་མཐུན་པ།།
དེ་དག་རྣམས་ལ་མི་གནོད་བསྐོས།།

༣༣༣ ལུགས་ཤེས་ཆོས་དང་ལྡན་ལ་འཛར།།
གཙང་ཞིང་སྙིང་ཉེ་མི་སྡར་བ།།
རིགས་བཟང་ངང་དང་ཚུལ་ཕུན་སུམ་ལྡན།།
བྱས་པས་བཟོ་བའི་བློན་པོ་བསྐོས།།

༣༣༤ གཏོང་ཕོད་མཆགས་དཔའ་བ་དང་།།
འཛམ་ཞིང་ངན་སྤྱོད་བརྟན་པ་དང་།།
རྟག་ཏུ་བག་ནི་ཡོད་པ་དང་།།
ཆོས་དང་ལྡན་པའི་དམག་དཔོན་བསྐོས།།

༣༣༥ ཆོས་ཀྱི་ངང་ཚུལ་གཙང་ལ་བཟོ།།
དོན་ཤེས་གཙུག་ལག་ལ་མཁས་པ།།
ཚུལ་ལྡན་སྙོམས་ཤིང་དང་འཛམ་པ།།
རྒན་རབས་རྣམས་ནི་སྣ་བོར་བསྐོས།།

༣༣༦ ཟླ་རེ་ཞིང་ནི་དེ་དག་ལ།།
ཉིད་ཀྱིས་འདུ་འགོད་ཀུན་གསོན་ཏེ།།
གསན་ནས་ཆོས་ཀྱི་གཞི་སོགས་ཀྱི།།
དོན་ཀུན་ཉིད་ཀྱིས་བཀའ་སྩོལ་ཅིག།

༣༣༧ ཁྱོད་ཀྱི་རྒྱལ་སྲིད་ཆོས་དོན་དུ།།
གྲགས་དོན་འདོད་སྣང་མ་ལགས་ན།།
དེས་ནི་ཤིན་ཏུ་འབྲས་བུར་བཅས།།
དེ་ལས་གཞན་འགྱུར་དོན་མེད་འབྲས།།

༣༢༨ མི་དབང་དེ་ལྟར་འཇིག་རྟེན་ན། །
ཕལ་ཆེར་ཕན་ཚུན་སྨོར་འཇུག་པས། །
ཇི་ལྟར་ཁྱོད་ཀྱི་རྒྱལ་སྲིད་དང་། །
ཆོས་སུ་འགྱུར་བ་དེ་བཞིན་གསོན། །

༣༢༩ ཤེས་པས་རྒན་ཞིང་རིགས་པ་བཟང་བ། །
རིགས་པ་ཤེས་པ་སྡིག་ལ་འཛེམ། །
ནང་མ་ཤིན་དགོས་པ་མཐོང་འགྱུར་བ། །
མང་པོ་རྟག་ཏུ་ཁྱོད་ཀྱིས་སོགས། །

༣༣༠ དེ་དག་ཆད་པ་གཞུང་བཏེག་སོགས། །
ག་ལ་དེ་རིགས་པས་བྱེད་ནའང་། །
ཁྱོད་ནི་སྙིང་རྗེས་བརླན་གྱུར་ནས། །
རྟག་ཏུ་རྗེས་སུ་གཟུང་བར་མཛོད། །

༣༣༡ མི་བཟད་སྡིག་པ་བྱེད་པ་ཡི། །
ལུས་ཅན་དག་ནི་ཐམས་ཅད་ལའང་། །
རྒྱལ་པོ་ཁྱོད་ཀྱིས་རྟག་པར་ཡང་། །
སྙིང་རྗེས་ཕན་སེམས་ཁོ་ན་བསྐྱེད། །

༣༣༢ མི་བཟད་སྡིག་ཅན་གསོད་བྱེད་ལ། །
ཁྱད་པར་དུ་ཡང་སྙིང་རྗེ་བསྐྱེད། །
བདག་ཉིད་ཉམས་པ་དེ་དག་ཉིད། །
བདག་ཉིད་ཆེན་པོའི་སྙིང་རྗེའི་གནས། །

༣༣༣ ཉིན་གཅིག་བཞིན་ནམ་ཞག་ལྔ་ཞིང་། །
ཉམས་ཆུང་བཙོན་རྣམས་གཏང་བར་མཛོད། །
ལྷག་མ་རྣམས་ཀྱང་ཅི་རིགས་པར། །
འགའ་ཡང་མི་དགྲོལ་བ་མེད་པར་མཛོད། །

༣༣༤ ཁྱོད་ནི་གང་ལ་གཏང་སེམས་མེད། །
དེ་ལས་སྡོམ་པ་མིན་པ་སྐྱེ། །
སྡོམ་པ་མ་ཡིན་དེ་ལས་ནི། །
རྒྱུན་མི་འཆད་པར་སྡིག་པ་སོག །

༣༣༥ བཙོན་ནི་ཇི་སྲིད་མ་བཏང་བ། །
དེ་སྲིད་བར་དུ་འདྲེག་མཁན་དང་། །
ཁྲུས་དང་བཟའ་དང་བཏུང་བ་དང་། །
སྨན་དང་ལྷན་པས་བདེ་བར་བགྱི། །

༣༣༦ སྣོད་མིན་པ་ཡི་བུ་དག་ལ། །
སྣོད་དུ་རུང་བར་བྱ་འདོད་ཕྱིར། །
སྙིང་རྗེ་ཡིས་ནི་ཚར་གཅད་བྱའི། །
སྡང་བས་མ་ཡིན་ནོར་ཕྱིར་མིན། །

༣༣༧ རབ་སྡང་གསོད་པར་བགྱིས་པའི་མི། །
བརྟགས་ཏེ་ལེགས་པར་ཤེས་བགྱིས་ནས། །
མི་བསད་གནོད་པར་མི་བགྱི་བར། །
ཡུལ་ལས་བསྐྲད་པ་དག་ཏུ་མཛོད། །

༣༣༨ རང་དབང་ཡོད་པར་ཡུལ་ཀུན་ཡང་། །
བྲ་མ་ཧྲ་ཡི་སྤྱན་གྱིས་གཟིགས། །
རྟག་ཏུ་བག་ཡོད་དྲན་ལྡན་པར། །
ཆོས་དང་མཐུན་པའི་དོན་མཛོད་ཅིག །

༣༣༩ ཡོན་ཏན་གནས་ལ་བདག་ཉིད་ཀྱིས། །
རབ་སྦྱིན་བཀུར་སྟི་རིམ་གྲོ་དག །
རྒྱ་ཆེན་རྗེས་སུ་མཐུན་སྦྱོར་ཞིང་། །
ལྷག་མ་རྣམས་ལའང་ཅི་རིགས་བགྱི། །

༣༤༠ རྒྱལ་པོའི་ལྗོན་ཤིང་བཟོད་གྲིབ་ཅན། །
བཀུར་སྟིའི་མེ་ཏོག་རྒྱས་ཕྱུར་ཅིང་། །
རབ་སྦྱིན་འབྲས་བུ་ཆེ་ལྡན་ལ། །
དམངས་ཀྱི་བྱ་རྣམས་བརྟེན་པར་འགྱུར། །

༣༤༡ རྒྱལ་པོ་གཏོང་བའི་ངང་ཚུལ་ཅན། །
བརྗིད་དང་ལྡན་ན་དགའ་འགྱུར་ཏེ། །
སུག་སྨེལ་ལན་ལེ་ཤམ་རྩུ་བ་པའི། །
ཤ་ཁ་ར་ཡི་ལ་དུ་བཞིན། །

༣༤༢ དེ་ལྟར་རིགས་པས་དཔྱད་ན་ནི། །
ཁྱོད་ཀྱི་རྒྱལ་སྲིད་འགྲོངས་མི་འགྱུར། །
རིགས་པ་⋯མ་ཡིན་མི་འགྱུར་ཞིང་། །
ཆོས་མིན་མ་ཡིན་ཆོས་སུ་འགྱུར། །

༣༤༣ རྒྱལ་སྲིད་འཇིག་རྟེན་པ་རོལ་ནས། །
བསྣམས་ཏེ་མཚོན་བསྣམ་མི་འགྱུར། །
ཆོས་ཀྱིས་བརྙེས་པས་དེ་སླད་དུ། །
ཆོས་མིན་ཚེད་ཀྱིས་བསྐྱེ་མི་རིགས། །

༣༤༤ འཚོག་ཆས་ཟོང་ཞི་རྒྱལ་སྲིད་ཀྱིས།།
སྡུག་བསྔལ་འཚོག་ཆས་བརྒྱུད་པ་དག །
ཅིནས་འགྲུབ་པར་མི་འགྱུར་བར། །
རྒྱལ་པོ་དེ་ལྟར་ཞན་ཏན་མཛོད། །

༣༤༥ འཚོག་ཆས་ཟོང་ཞི་རྒྱལ་སྲིད་ཀྱིས། །
རྒྱལ་སྲིད་འཚོག་ཆས་བརྒྱུད་པ་དག །
རྒྱལ་པོ་ཅིནས་བརྟེས་འགྱུར་བ། །
དེ་ལྟ་བུ་ཞིག་ཞན་ཏན་མཛོད། །

༣༤༦ གླིང་བཞི་པ་ཡིས་ཐོབ་ཀྱང་། །
འཁོར་ལོས་སྒྱུར་བའི་བདེ་བ་ནི།།
ལུས་ཀྱི་དག་དང་སེམས་ཀྱི་སྡེ།།
འདི་གཉིས་ཕོན་ནར་ཟད་པར་འདོད།།

༣༤༧ ལུས་ཀྱི་རྫོར་བ་བདེ་བ་ནི། །
སྡུག་བསྔལ་ཕྱིར་ནི་བཅོས་པ་ཙམ།།
སེམས་ཀྱི་འདུ་ཤེས་རང་བཞིན་ཏེ།།
རྟོག་པས་བྱས་པ་ཕོན་ནར་ཟད། །

༣༤༨ འཇིག་རྟེན་བདེ་བའི་བཙོག་པ་ཀུན། །
སྡུག་བསྔལ་ཕྱིར་ཞི་བཅོས་ཙམ་དང་། །
རྟོག་ཙམ་ཉིད་ཡིན་དེ་ཡི་ཕྱིར། །
དེ་ཞི་དོན་དུ་དོན་མེད་དོ། །

༣༤༩ གླིང་དང་ཡུལ་དང་གནས་དང་ཁྱིམ། །
ཁྱོགས་དང་སྟན་དང་གོས་རྣམས་དང་།།
མལ་ཆ་བཟའ་བཏུང་གླང་པོ་རྟ། །
བུད་མེད་སྤྱད་བྱ་རེ་རེར་ཟད། །

༣༥༠ གང་ཚེ་གང་ལ་སེམས་འགྱུར་བ། །
དེ་ཚེ་དེ་ཡིས་བདེ་ཞེས་གྲགས། །
ལྷག་མ་ཡིད་ལ་མི་བྱེད་པས། །
དེ་ཚེ་དོན་དུ་དོན་མེད་ཉིད། །

༣༥༡ མིག་ལ་སོགས་པའི་དབང་པོ་ལྔས། །
ཡུལ་ལྔ་འཛིན་ཚེ་གང་གི་ཕྱིར། །
རྟོག་པར་མི་བྱེད་དེ་ཡི་ཕྱིར། །
དེ་ཚེ་དེ་ལ་བདེ་བ་མེད། །

༣༥༢ གང་ཚེ་ཡུལ་ནི་གང་དང་གང་། །
དབང་པོ་གང་གིས་ཤེས་གྱུར་པ། །
དེ་ཚེ་ལྷག་མས་ལྷག་མ་མིན། །
གང་ཕྱིར་དེ་ཚེ་དོན་མེད་ཉིད། །

༣༥༣ དབང་པོ་ཡིས་ནི་དམིགས་གྱུར་པ། །
འདས་པའི་ཡུལ་གྱི་རྣམ་པ་ལ། །
ཡིད་ཀྱིས་དམིགས་ནས་རྟོག་པ་ན། །
བདེའོ་སྙམ་དུ་རློམ་པར་བྱེད། །

༣༥༤ འདིན་དབང་པོ་གཅིག་གིས་ནི། །
དོན་གཅིག་ཤེས་པ་གང་ཡིན་པ། །
དེ་ཡང་དོན་མེད་པར་དོན་མེད། །
དོན་ཡང་དེ་མེད་པར་དོན་མེད། །

༣༥༥ ཇི་ལྟར་ཕ་དང་མ་དག་ལ། །
བརྟེན་ནས་བུ་ནི་འབྱུང་བཤད་པ། །
དེ་བཞིན་མིག་དང་གཟུགས་བརྟེན་ནས། །
རྣམ་པར་ཤེས་པ་འབྱུང་བར་བཤད། །

༣༥༦ ཡུལ་ནི་འདས་དང་མ་འོངས་རྣམས། །
དབང་པོ་དང་བཅས་དོན་མེད་ལ། །
དེ་གཉིས་ལས་ཐ་དད་མེད་ཕྱིར། །
གང་དག་ད་ལྟར་ཡང་དོན་མེད། །

༣༥༧ ཇི་ལྟར་མིག་ནི་འཁྲུལ་པ་ཡིས། །
མགལ་མེའི་འཁོར་ལོ་འཛིན་བྱེད་པ། །
དེ་བཞིན་དབང་པོ་རྣམས་ཀྱིས་ནི། །
ད་ལྟའི་ཡུལ་དག་འཛིན་པར་བྱེད། །

༣༥༨ དབང་པོ་རྣམས་དང་དབང་དོན་རྣམས། །
འབྱུང་བ་རྣམས་ཀྱི་རང་བཞིན་འདོད། །
འབྱུང་བ་སོ་སོར་དོན་མེད་པས། །
འདི་དག་དོན་དུ་དོན་མེད་དོ། །

༣༥༩ འབྱུང་རྣམས་སོ་སོར་ཐ་དད་ན། །
བུད་ཤིང་མེད་པའི་མེ་ཐལ་འགྱུར། །
འདུས་ན་མཚན་ཉིད་མེད་འགྱུར་ཏེ། །
ལྷག་མ་ལ་ཡང་དེ་ལྟར་ངེས། །

༣༥༠ དེ་ལྟར་འབྱུང་རྣམས་རྣམ་གཉིས་སུ་འང་། །
དོན་མེད་པས་ན་འདུས་དོན་མེད། །
འདུས་པ་དོན་མེད་ཉིད་ཀྱི་ཕྱིར། །
གཟུགས་ཀྱང་དོན་དུ་དོན་མེད་དོ། །

༣༥༡ རྣམ་ཤེས་ཚོར་དང་འདུ་ཤེས་དང་། །
འདུ་བྱེད་རྣམས་ཀྱང་ཐམས་ཅད་དུ། །
སོ་སོར་བདག་ཉིད་དོན་མེད་ཕྱིར། །
དམ་པའི་དོན་དུ་དོན་མེད་དོ། །

༣༥༢ ཇི་ལྟར་སྡུག་བསྔལ་ཕྱིར་བཅོས་ལ། །
དོན་དུ་བདེ་བར་ང་རྒྱལ་བྱེད། །
དེ་བཞིན་བདེ་འཇོམས་འགྱུར་བ་ལ། །
སྡུག་བསྔལ་དུ་ཡང་ང་རྒྱལ་བྱེད། །

༣༥༣ དེ་ལྟར་ངོ་བོ་ཉིད་མེད་ཕྱིར། །
བདེ་དང་ཕྲད་པའི་སྲེད་པ་དང་། །
སྡུག་བསྔལ་འབྲལ་བའི་སྲེད་པ་སྤོང་། །
དེ་ཕྱིར་དེ་ལྟར་མཐོང་བ་གྲོལ། །

༣༥༤ གང་གིས་མཐོང་བར་འགྱུར་ཞེན། །
ཐ་སྙད་དུ་ནི་སེམས་བརྗོད་དེ། །
སེམས་འབྱུང་མེད་པར་སེམས་མི་འབྱུང་། །
དོན་མེད་ལྷན་ཅིག་མི་འདོད་དོ། །

༣༥༥ དེ་ལྟར་ཡང་དག་ཇི་བཞིན་དུ། །
འགྲོ་བ་དོན་མེད་ཤེས་ནས་ནི། །
རྒྱུ་མེད་པ་ཡི་མེ་བཞིན་དུ། །
གནས་མེད་ལེན་མེད་མྱ་ངན་འདའ། །

༣༥༦ དེ་ལྟར་བྱང་ཆུབ་སེམས་དཔས་ཀྱང་། །
མཐོང་ནས་བྱང་ཆུབ་ངེས་པར་འདོད། །
དེ་ནི་སྙིང་རྗེ་འབའ་ཞིག་གིས། །
བྱང་ཆུབ་བར་དུ་སྲིད་མཚམས་སྦྱོར། །

༣༥༧ དེ་བཞིན་གཤེགས་པས་ཐེག་ཆེན་ལས། །
བྱང་ཆུབ་སེམས་དཔའ་ཚོགས་བསྟན་ན། །
དེ་ལ་ཀུན་ཏུ་རྨོངས་པ་རྣམས། །
རབ་ཏུ་སྡང་བས་སྨོད་པར་བྱེད། །

༣༦༨ ཡོན་ཏན་སྐྱོན་དག་མི་ཤེས་པ་འམ།།
ཡོན་ཏན་སྐྱོན་དུ་འདུ་ཤེས་པ་འམ།
ཡང་ན་ཡོན་ཏན་སྨད་པ་ཞིག །
ཐེག་པ་ཆེ་ལ་སྨོད་བྱེད་གྲང་།།

༣༦༩ གཞན་ལ་གནོད་པ་སྐྱོན་དང་ནི། །
གཞན་ལ་ཕན་པ་ཡོན་ཏན་ཏུ།།
ཤེས་ནས་ཐེག་པ་ཆེན་པོ་ལ།།
སྨོད་བྱེད་ཡོན་ཏན་སྨད་ཞེས་བརྗོད།།

༣༧༠ རང་གི་དོན་ལ་མི་ལྟ་ཕྱིར།།
གཞན་དོན་རོ་གཅིག་དགའ་བ་གང་།།
ཡོན་ཏན་འབྱུང་གནས་ཐེག་ཆེན་ཏེ།།
དེ་ལ་སྡང་བ་དེ་བསྲེག་འགྱུར། །

༣༧༡ དད་པ་ཅན་ནི་གཟུང་ཉེས་པས།
ཅིག་ཤོས་སྡང་ཕྱིར་ཁྲོས་པ་ཡིས།།
དད་པ་ཅན་ཡང་བསྲེག་བཤད་ན།།
སྡང་བས་ཕྱིར་ཕྱོགས་སྨོས་ཅི་དགོས།།

༣༧༢ དུག་གིས་དུག་ནི་བསལ་བྱ་བར།།
ཇི་ལྟར་སྨན་དཔྱད་ལས་བཤད་བཞིན།།
སྡུག་བསྔལ་གྱིས་ཀྱང་མི་ཕན་པ།།
བསལ་བར་བྱ་བ་ཅི་ཞིག་འགལ།།

༣༧༣ ཆོས་རྣམས་སྔོན་དུ་ཡིད་འགྲོ་ཞིང་།།
ཡིད་ནི་གཙོ་བོ་ཞེས་གྲགས་པས།།
སྡུག་བསྔལ་གྱིས་ཀྱང་ཕན་ཡིད་ཅན།།
ཕན་པར་བྱེད་པ་ཅིས་མི་ཕན། །

༣༧༤ མི་བདེ་འང་ཕྱིས་རྗེས་ཕན་འགྱུར་བ།།
བྱ་ན་བདག་དང་གཞན་དག་ལ། །
བདེ་ཕན་ལྟ་ཞིག་ཅི་སྨོས་ཏེ། །
ཆོས་འདི་གནའ་ཡི་ལུགས་ཡིན་ནོ།།

༣༧༥ གལ་ཏེ་བདེ་ཆུང་ཡོངས་བཏང་བས། །
བདེ་བ་རྒྱ་ཆེན་མཐོང་འགྱུར་ན། །
བརྟན་པས་བདེ་བ་ཡོངས་གཟིགས་ལ།།
བདེ་བ་ཆུང་དུ་བཏང་བར་མཛོད། །

३७६ གལ་ཏེ་དེ་ཡང་མི་བཟོད་ན། །
དེས་ན་སྨན་པ་དག་གིས་ནི། །
མི་ཞིམ་སྨན་ནི་སྦྱིན་བྱེད་པ། །
གཏུགས་འགྱུར་དེ་ནི་བཏང་མ་ཡིན། །

३७७ གནོད་པར་མཐོང་བ་གང་ཡིན་དེ། །
ལ་ལར་མ་ཁབས་པས་ཕན་པར་མཐོང་། །
སྦྱོར་བཏང་དམིགས་ཀྱིས་བས་ལ་བ་ནི། །
བསྟན་བཅོས་ཀུན་ལ་རབ་ཏུ་བསྔགས། །

३७८ ཐེག་པ་ཆེན་པོ་གང་ཞིག་ལས། །
སྙིང་རྗེ་སྔོན་བཏང་སྤྱོད་པ་དང་། །
ཡེ་ཤེས་དྲི་མ་མེད་བཤད་པ། །
སེམས་ཡོད་སུ་ཞིག་དེ་ལ་སྨོད། །

३७९ ཤིན་ཏུ་རྒྱ་ཆེ་རབ་ཟབ་ལ། །
སྐྱིད་ལུག་བདག་ཉིད་མ་སྦྱངས་པ། །
བདག་གཞན་དགྲ་རྣམས་རྨོངས་པ་ཡིས། །
འདི་ན་ཐེག་པ་ཆེ་ལ་སྨོད། །

३८० སྦྱིན་དང་ཚུལ་ཁྲིམས་བཟོད་བརྩོན་འགྲུས། །
བསམ་གཏན་ཤེས་རབ་སྙིང་རྗེ་འི་བདག །
ཐེག་ཆེན་ཡིན་ན་དེ་ཡི་ཕྱིར། །
འདི་ལ་ཉེས་པར་བཤད་ཅི་ཞིག་ཡོད། །

३८१ ཚུལ་ཁྲིམས་སྦྱིན་པས་གཞན་གྱི་དོན། །
བརྩོན་འགྲུས་བཟོད་པས་བདག་ཉིད་ཀྱི། །
བསམ་གཏན་ཤེས་རབ་ཐར་པའི་རྒྱུ། །
ཐེག་ཆེན་དོན་ནི་བསྡུས་པ་ཡིན། །

३८२ བདག་དང་གཞན་ཕན་ཐར་པའི་དོན། །
མདོར་ན་སངས་རྒྱས་བསྟན་དེ་དག །
ཕ་རོལ་ཕྱིན་དྲུག་ཁོང་ན་ཡོད། །
དེ་བས་འདི་ནི་སངས་རྒྱས་བཀའ། །

३८३ བྱང་ཆུབ་ལམ་ཆེན་བསོད་ནམས་དང་། །
ཡེ་ཤེས་རང་བཞིན་སངས་རྒྱས་ཀྱིས། །
གང་ལས་བསྟན་པའི་ཐེག་ཆེན་འདི། །
མི་ཤེས་ལྡོངས་རྣམས་མི་བཟོད་དོ། །

༣༥༤ ཡོན་ཏན་མཁའ་ལྟར་བསམ་ཡས་པས། །
རྒྱལ་བའི་ཡོན་ཏན་བསམ་ཡས་གསུངས། །
གང་ཕྱིར་སངས་རྒྱས་བདག་ཉིད་ཆེ། །
ཐེག་ཆེན་ལས་བཤད་འདིར་བཟོད་ཀྱིས། །

༣༥༥ འཕགས་པ་ཤཱ་རདྭ་ཏིའི་བུས། །
ཚུལ་ཁྲིམས་ཙམ་ཡང་མ་ཤེས་པས། །
དེས་ན་སངས་རྒྱས་བདག་ཉིད་ཆེ། །
དེ་བསམ་ཡས་པར་ཅིས་མི་བཟོད། །

༣༥༦ ཐེག་པ་ཆེ་ལས་སྐྱེ་མེད་བསྟན། །
གཞན་གྱི་ཟད་པ་སྟོང་པ་ཉིད། །
ཟད་དང་མི་སྐྱེ་དོན་དུ་ནི། །
གཅིག་པས་དེ་ཕྱིར་བཟོད་པར་གྱིས། །

༣༥༧ སྟོང་ཉིད་སངས་རྒྱས་ཆེ་བདག་ཉིད། །
དེ་ལྟར་རིགས་པས་རྗེས་ལྟས་ན། །
ཐེག་ཆེན་གཅིག་ཤོས་ལས་གསུངས་པ། །
མཁས་པ་རྣམས་ལ་ཅིས་མི་མཉམ། །

༣༥༨ དེ་བཞིན་གཤེགས་དགོངས་གསུངས་པ་རྣམས། །
ཤེས་པར་སླ་མིན་དེ་ཡི་ཕྱིར། །
ཐེག་གཅིག་ཐེག་པ་གསུམ་གསུངས་པས། །
བཏང་སྙོམས་ཀྱིས་ནི་བདག་བསྲུང་བྱ། །

༣༥༩ བཏང་སྙོམས་ཀྱིས་ནི་སྡིག་མི་འགྱུར། །
སྡང་བས་སྡིག་འགྱུར་དགེར་མི་འགྱུར། །
དེ་བས་ཐེག་ཆེན་ཞེ་སྡང་བ། །
བདག་ལེགས་འདོད་པས་བྱ་མི་རིགས། །

༣༦༠ ཉན་ཐོས་ཐེག་པ་དེ་ལས་ནི། །
བྱང་ཆུབ་སེམས་དཔའི་སྨོན་ལམ་དང་། །
སྤྱོད་པ་ཡོངས་བསྔོ་མ་བཤད་དེས། །
བྱང་ཆུབ་སེམས་དཔར་ག་ལ་འགྱུར། །

༣༦༡ བྱང་ཆུབ་སེམས་དཔའི་བྱང་ཆུབ་ཕྱིར། །
རྟེན་རྣམས་སངས་རྒྱས་ཀྱིས་མ་བཤད། །
དོན་འདི་ལ་ནི་རྒྱལ་བ་ལས། །
ལྷག་པའི་ཚད་མ་གཞན་སུ་ཡོད། །

༣༨༢ ཆོས་དང་འཕགས་པའི་བདེན་དོན་དང་། །
བྱང་ཆུབ་ཕྱོགས་མཐུན་ལྡན་པ་ཡི། །
ལམ་ནི་ཉན་ཐོས་ཐུན་མོང་ལས། །
སངས་རྒྱས་འབྲས་བུ་གང་གིས་ལྷག །

༣༨༣ བྱང་ཆུབ་སྤྱོད་ལ་གནས་པའི་དོན། །
མདོ་སྡེ་ལས་ནི་བཀའ་མ་སྩལ། །
ཐེག་པ་ཆེ་ལས་བཀའ་སྩལ་པ། །
དེ་ཕྱིར་མཁས་པ་རྣམས་ཀྱིས་བཟུང་། །

༣༨༤ བརྡ་སྤྲོད་པ་དག་ཇི་ལྟ་བུར། །
ཡི་གེ་ཕྱི་མོ་ཀློག་འཇུག་ལྟར། །
དེ་བཞིན་སངས་རྒྱས་གདུལ་བྱ་ལ། །
ཇི་ཙམ་བཟོད་པའི་ཆོས་སྟོན་ཏོ། །

༣༨༥ ཁ་ཅིག་ལ་ནི་སྡིག་པ་ལས། །
རྣམ་པར་བཟློག་ཕྱིར་ཆོས་སྟོན་ཏེ། །
ཁ་ཅིག་བསོད་ནམས་འགྲུབ་བྱའི་ཕྱིར། །
ཁ་ཅིག་ལ་ནི་གཉིས་བརྟེན་པ། །

༣༨༦ ཁ་ཅིག་ལ་ནི་གཉིས་མི་བརྟེན། །
ཟབ་མོ་ཁྲེ་འཕྲིག་ཅན་འཇིགས་པ། །
སྟོང་ཉིད་སྙིང་རྗེའི་སྙིང་པོ་ཅན། །
བྱང་ཆུབ་བསྒྲུབ་པ་ཁ་ཅིག་ལའོ། །

༣༨༧ དེ་ལྟས་མཁས་པས་ཐེག་ཆེན་ལ། །
ཁོང་ཁྲོ་བ་ནི་ཟད་བྱ་ཞིང་། །
རྫོགས་པའི་བྱང་ཆུབ་བསྒྲུབ་བྱའི་ཕྱིར། །
ལྷག་པར་རབ་ཏུ་དད་པར་བྱ། །

༣༨༨ ཐེག་པ་ཆེ་ལ་རབ་དད་ཞིང་། །
དེ་ལས་བཤད་པ་སྤྱད་པ་ཡིས། །
བླ་མེད་བྱང་ཆུབ་ཐོབ་འགྱུར་ཞིང་། །
བདེ་བ་ཀུན་ཀྱང་ཞར་ལ་འགྲུབ། །

༣༨༩ དེར་ནི་སྦྱིན་དང་ཚུལ་ཁྲིམས་དང་། །
བཟོད་པའི་ཆོས་ནི་ཁྱད་པར་དུ། །
ཁྱིམ་པ་ལ་བཤད་སྙིང་རྗེ་ཡི། །
སྙིང་པོ་ཅན་དེ་བརྟན་གོམས་མཛོད། །

༩༠༠ འོན་ཏེ་འཇིག་རྟེན་མི་བསྲུན་ཕྱིར། །
ཆོས་ཀྱིས་རྒྱལ་སྲིད་བསྐྱོད་དཀའ་ན།།
དེས་ན་མཆོད་དང་གྲགས་དོན་དུ། །
ཁྱོད་ཀྱིས་རབ་བྱུང་འཐོབ་མཛད་རིགས།།

རིན་པོ་ཆེའི་ཕྲེང་བ་ལས་རྒྱལ་པོའི་ཚུལ་
བསྟན་པ་སྟེ་ལེའུ་བཞི་པའོ།། ༎

༩༠༡ ༄ དེ་ནས་རབ་ཏུ་བྱུང་བ་ཡིས། །
དང་པོར་བསླབ་ལ་རབ་གུས་བྱ།།
སོ་སོར་ཐར་པ་འདུལ་བཅས་དང་།།
མང་ཐོས་དོན་གཏན་དབབ་ལ་བསྒྲིམ།།

༩༠༢ དེ་ནས་ཉེས་པ་ཕྲན་ཚེགས་ཞེས།།
བྱ་བའི་གཞི་རྣམས་སྤང་བར་བྱ།།
ལྔ་བཅུ་རྩ་བདུན་བསྒྲགས་པ་རྣམས།།
འབད་དེ་ངེས་པར་རྟོགས་པར་བྱ།།

༩༠༣ ཁྲོ་བ་སེམས་ཀྱི་འཁྲུག་པ་སྟེ། །
དེ་དང་རྗེས་འབྲེལ་ཁོན་དུ་འཛིན།།
འཆབ་པ་སྡིག་པ་འཆབ་པ་སྟེ།།
ཚིག་པ་སྡིག་ལ་ཞེན་པའོ། །

༩༠༤ གཡོ་ནི་ཟོལ་ཏུ་བསླུ་བ་སྟེ། །
སྒྱུ་ནི་སེམས་རྒྱུད་གྱ་གྱུ་བ།།
ཕྲག་དོག་གཞན་གྱི་ཡོན་ཏན་གདུང་།
སེར་སྣ་གཏོང་བས་འཇིགས་པ་ཉིད།།

༩༠༥ ངོ་ཚ་མེད་དང་ཁྲེལ་མེད་པ། །
རང་དང་གཞན་ལ་མི་འཛེམ་པའོ།།
ཁེངས་པ་འདུད་པར་མི་བྱེད་པའོ།།
ཉེས་རྩོམ་ཁྲོ་བས་བསླད་པའོ། །

༩༠༦ རྒྱགས་པ་དྲེགས་པ་བག་མེད་པ། །
དགེ་བ་རྣམས་ལ་མི་སྦྱོར་བའོ། །
ང་རྒྱལ་རྣམ་པ་བདུན་ཡིན་ཏེ། །
དེ་ཉིད་རབ་ཏུ་ཕྱེ་སྟེ་བཤད། །

༤༠༧ དེ་ལ་མངོན་པར་སྙོམ་བྱེད་བདག །
དམན་པས་དམན་ཞིང་མཉམ་དང་མཉམ། །
དམན་པ་བས་ནི་ལྷག་པའམ་མཉམ། །
བདག་ཉིད་ང་རྒྱལ་ཞེས་བྱའོ། །

༤༠༨ ཚོས་གང་བདག་ཉིད་ཁྱད་འཕགས་དང་། །
མཉམ་པར་སྙོམས་པ་གང་ཡིན་ཏེ། །
ལྷག་པའི་ང་རྒྱལ་ཁྱད་འཕགས་པས། །
ཁྱད་པར་འཕགས་པར་སྙོམས་པ་གང་། །

༤༠༩ ཤིན་ཏུ་མཐོ་བས་མཐོ་སྙམ་པ། །
ང་རྒྱལ་ལས་ཀྱང་ང་རྒྱལ་ཏེ། །
འབྲས་ཀྱི་སྟེང་དུ་ཐོལ་མིག་དག །
སྐྲང་བ་བཞིན་དུ་བྲུ་བ་ཡིན། །

༤༡༠ ཉེ་བར་ལེན་པ་ཞེས་བྱ་བ། །
ལྔ་པོ་སྟོང་པ་དེ་དག་ལ། །
སྨོངས་པས་ང་སྙམ་འཛིན་པ་གང་། །
དེ་ནི་ངར་སྙམ་པར་བཤད། །

༤༡༡ འབྲས་མ་ཐོབ་པར་ཐོབ་སྙམ་པ། །
གང་ཡིན་མངོན་པའི་ང་རྒྱལ་ཏེ། །
སྡིག་ལས་བྱེད་ལ་བསྟོད་པ་ནི། །
མཁས་པས་ལོག་པའི་ང་རྒྱལ་རྟོགས། །

༤༡༢ བདག་དགོས་མེད་པ་ཉིད་དོ་ཞེས། །
བདག་ཉིད་སྨོད་པ་གང་ཡིན་ཏེ། །
དམན་པའི་ང་རྒྱལ་ཞེས་བྱ་སྟེ། །
དེ་དག་མདོར་བསྡུས་བཤད་པ་ཡིན། །

༤༡༣ ཚུལ་འཆོས་རྙེད་དང་བཀུར་སྟིའི་ཕྱིར། །
དབང་པོ་སྡོམ་པར་བྱེད་པ་སྟེ། །
ཁ་གསག་རྙེད་དང་བཀུར་སྟིའི་ཕྱིར། །
ཚིག་འཇམ་སྨྲ་ནི་སྨྲ་བའོ། །

༤༡༤ གཞོགས་སློང་དེ་ནི་ཐོབ་བྱའི་ཕྱིར། །
གཞན་གྱི་རྫས་ལ་བསྔགས་བྱེད་པའོ། །
ཐོབ་ཀྱིས་འཇལ་བ་བརྙེད་པའི་ཕྱིར། །
མངོན་སུམ་གཞན་ལ་སྨོད་བྱེད་པ། །

༤༡༥ ཉེད་པས་ཉེད་བ་རྣམས་འདོད་པ། །
སླར་ཐོབ་པ་ལ་བསླུ་གས་བྱེད་པའོ།།
སྨིན་གྲོལ་གཞན་གྱི་འཁྲུལ་སྐྱུར་པ།།
དེ་དང་དེ་ནི་གང་གྲོལ་པའོ།།

༤༡༦ སྐྱུངས་མེད་སོ་སོར་མ་བརྟགས་པར། །
ནད་ལས་གྱུར་པའི་སློང་བའོ།།
ཀུན་ཆགས་བདག་གི་ཡོ་བྱད་དང་། །
ཆགས་པ་ལེ་ལོ་ཅན་གྱི་ཡིན། །

༤༡༧ ཐ་དད་འདུ་ཤེས་འདུ་ཤེས་གང་།
ཆགས་སྡང་ལྡན་གྱིས་བསྒྲིབས་པའོ།།
ཡིད་ལ་མི་བྱེད་གང་ཡིན་དེ། །
སེམས་ལ་ལྟ་བ་མེད་པར་བཤད།།

༤༡༨ མཐུན་པར་བྱ་བ་རྣམས་ལ་ནི། །
ལོ་ལོས་བཀུར་སྟི་ཉམས་པ་གང་།།
བླ་མར་བཙོམ་ལྡན་རྒྱལ་མེན་ཏེ།།
སྐྱོ་བོ་ངན་པ་ཡིན་པར་འདོད། །

༤༡༩ ཞེན་པ་ཀུན་ནས་དཀྲིས་པ་རྒྱུད། །
འདོད་པའི་འདོད་ཆགས་ལས་བྱུང་བའོ།།
ཡོངས་ཞེན་འདོད་པ་ལས་བྱུང་བའི། །
ཀུན་ནས་དཀྲིས་པ་ཆེར་བ་ཡིན། །

༤༢༠ ཆགས་པ་རང་གི་རྫས་ལ་ནི། །
ཆགས་པའི་འདོད་ཆགས་ལྡན་པའི་ཡིད།།
གཞན་གྱི་རྫས་ལ་ཞེན་པ་ནི། །
མི་རིགས་ཆགས་པ་ཞེས་བྱའོ།།

༤༢༡ སྙང་བྱ་བུད་མེད་ཆགས་བསྐྱོད་པ།།
ཆོས་མ་ཡིན་པའི་འདོད་ཆགས་སོ།།
སྡིག་འདོད་ཡོན་ཏན་མེད་བཞིན་དུ། །
ཡོན་ཏན་ལྡན་པར་ཀྱལ་འཚོས་པའོ།།

༤༢༢ འདོད་ཆེན་ཤིན་ཏུ་བཀམ་པ་སྟེ། །
ཆོག་ཤེས་དཔལ་ལས་འདའ་བའོ།།
ཐོབ་འདོད་བདག་ཉིད་ཅི་ནས་ཀྱང་།།
ཡོན་ཏན་ཡང་དག་ལྡན་ཤེས་འདོད།།

༤༣༣ མི་བཟོད་དགོད་པ་བྱེད་པ་དང་། །
སྡུག་བསྔལ་དག་ཀྱང་མི་བཟོད་པའོ། །
ཚུལ་མེད་སློབ་དཔོན་བླ་མ་ཡི། །
བྱ་བ་རྣམས་ལ་མ་གུས་པའོ། །

༤༣༤ བཀའ་འགྲོ་བདེ་བམ་ཡིན་གང་། །
ཆོས་མཐུན་ཚིག་སྨྲ་མ་གུས་པའོ། །
ཉེ་དུ་དང་འབྲེལ་རྣམ་རྟོག་ནི། །
ཉེ་དུ་ལ་བྱམས་ཆགས་པའོ། །

༤༣༥ དེ་བཞིན་ཡུལ་སྲིད་དེ་དོན་དུ། །
དེ་ཡི་ཡོན་ཏན་བརྗོད་པའོ། །
དེ་བཞིན་མི་འཆིར་རྟོག་པ་གང་། །
འཆི་བའི་འཇིགས་པས་མི་དོགས་པའོ། །

༤༣༦ རྗེས་རྣམ་རིག་དང་ལྡན་རྟོག་ནི། །
བདག་ཉིད་ཅི་ནས་གཞན་དག་གིས། །
ཡོན་ཏན་བརྗོད་པའི་རྣམ་པ་ཡིས། །
བླ་མར་བྱེད་པར་འགྱུར་རློམ་པའོ། །

༤༣༧ གཞན་རྗེས་ཆགས་དང་ལྡན་པ་ཡི། །
རྣམ་རྟོག་གང་ཡིན་གཞན་དག་ལ། །
ཆགས་དང་གནོད་སེམས་རིག་པ་ཡིས། །
ཕན་དང་མི་ཕན་སེམས་པའོ། །

༤༣༨ མི་དགའ་བརྟན་པ་མེད་པའོ། །
ཕྲད་འདོད་བརྙོགས་པའི་ཡིད་ཡིན་ནོ། །
སྙོམས་པ་བརྩོན་པ་མེད་པའི་ལུས། །
སྒྲིད་ལུག་དོན་གྱི་ལེ་ལོ་ཡིན། །

༤༣༩ འགྱུར་བ་ཉོན་མོངས་དབང་གིས་ནི། །
ལུས་དང་ཁ་དོག་འགྱུར་བའོ། །
ཟས་མི་འདོད་པ་བཟའ་དྲགས་པས། །
ལུས་མི་བདེ་བ་ཡིན་པར་བཤད། །

༤༤༠ སེམས་ནི་ཤིན་ཏུ་དམའ་བ་ཉིད། །
སེམས་ཞུམ་འཇིགས་པ་ཡིན་པར་བསྟན། །
འདོད་འདུན་ཡོན་ཏན་ལྔ་དག་ལ། །
འདོད་པ་དོན་དུ་གཉེར་བ་ཉིད། །

༩༣༡ གནོད་སེམས་བདག་དང་གྲོགས་དང་དགྲའི། །
ཕྱོགས་ལ་དུས་གསུམ་དོན་མིན་པའི། །
དོགས་པ་གཞན་ལ་གནོད་པའི་སེམས། །
རྒྱུ་དགུ་ལས་ནི་བྱུང་བ་ཡིན། །

༩༣༢ ལུས་སེམས་ལྷི་ཕྱིར་ལས་བྲལ་བ། །
གང་ཡིན་པ་ནི་རྨུགས་པའོ། །
གཉིད་ནི་གཉིད་དོ་ཆོད་པ་ནི། །
ལུས་སེམས་རབ་ཏུམ་ཞི་བའོ། །

༩༣༣ འགྱོད་པ་ངན་པར་བྱས་ལ་འགྱོད། །
ཕྱིས་གདུང་བ་ལས་བྱུང་བའོ། །
བདེན་དང་དཀོན་མཆོག་གསུམ་སོགས་ལ། །
བློ་རྣམ་གཉིས་ནི་ཐེ་ཚོམ་མོ། །

༩༣༤ དེ་དག་བྱང་ཆུབ་སེམས་དཔས་སྤང་། །
སྒོམ་བརྩོན་ཅན་གྱིས་ལྷག་པར་སྤང་། །
ཉེས་པ་དེ་རྣམས་དང་བྲལ་ན། །
ཡོན་ཏན་རྣམས་ལ་བདེ་བླག་བརྟེན། །

༩༣༥ དེ་ལ་བྱང་ཆུབ་སེམས་དཔའ་ཡིས། །
ཡོན་ཏན་མཛོར་བསྙེན་བྱ་བ་ནི། །
སྦྱིན་དང་ཚུལ་ཁྲིམས་བཟོད་བརྩོན་འགྲུས། །
བསམ་གཏན་ཤེས་རབ་སྙིང་རྗེ་སོགས། །

༩༣༦ སྨིན་པ་རང་འོར་ཡོངས་གཏོང་བ། །
ཚུལ་ཁྲིམས་གཞན་ལ་ཕན་བྱེད་པའོ། །
བཟོད་པ་ཁྲོ་བ་སྤངས་པ་སྟེ། །
བརྩོན་འགྲུས་དགེ་ལ་སྤྲོ་བ་ཉིད། །

༩༣༧ བསམ་གཏན་རྩེ་གཅིག་ཉོན་མོངས་མེད། །
ཤེས་རབ་བདེན་དོན་གཏན་ལ་འབེབས། །
སྙིང་བརྩེ་སེམས་ཅན་ཐམས་ཅད་ལ། །
སྙིང་རྗེར་གཅིག་བློ་གྲོས་སོ། །

༩༣༨ སྦྱིན་པས་ལོངས་སྤྱོད་ཁྲིམས་ཀྱིས་བདེ། །
བཟོད་པས་མདངས་ལྡན་དགེ་བས་བརྗིད། །
བསམ་གཏན་གྱིས་ཞི་བློ་ཡིས་གྲོལ། །
སྙིང་བརྩེ་བས་ནི་དོན་ཀུན་འགྲུབ། །

༩༣༩ བདུན་པོ་འདི་དག་མ་ལུས་པར། །
ཅིག་ཅར་ཕ་རོལ་ཕྱིན་པ་ཡིས། །
ཡེ་ཤེས་བསམ་གྱིས་མི་ཁྱབ་ཡུལ། །
འཇིག་རྟེན་མགོན་པོ་ཉིད་ཐོབ་འགྱུར།།

༩༤༠ ཀྱཻ་ལྷར་ཉན་ཐོས་ཐེག་པ་ལ། །
ཉན་ཐོས་ས་ནི་བརྒྱད་བཤད་པ།།
དེ་བཞིན་ཐེག་པ་ཆེན་པོ་ལ། །
བྱང་ཆུབ་སེམས་དཔའི་ས་བཅུའོ།།

༩༤༡ དེ་དག་དང་པོ་རབ་དགའ་བ། །
བྱང་ཆུབ་སེམས་དཔའ་དགའ་འབྱེད་ཕྱིར།།
ཀུན་ཏུ་སྦྱོར་བ་གསུམ་སྤངས་ཤིང་། །
དེ་བཞིན་གཤེགས་པའི་རིགས་སྐྱེས་ཕྱིར།།

༩༤༢ དེ་ཡི་རྣམ་པར་སྨིན་པས་ན། །
སྦྱིན་པའི་ཕ་རོལ་ཕྱིན་མཆོག་འགྱུར།།
འཇིག་རྟེན་ཁམས་ནི་བརྒྱ་གཡོ་ཞིང་།།
འཛམ་གླིང་དབང་ཕྱུག་ཆེན་པོར་འགྱུར།།

༩༤༣ གཉིས་པ་དྲི་མ་མེད་ཅེས་བྱ། །
ལུས་དང་ངག་དང་སེམས་ཀྱི་ལས། །
བཅུ་ཆར་དྲི་མ་མེད་པའི་ཕྱིར། །
དང་གིས་དེ་དག་ལ་གནས་ཕྱིར།།

༩༤༤ དེ་ཡི་རྣམ་པར་སྨིན་པས་ན། །
ཚུལ་ཁྲིམས་ཕ་རོལ་ཕྱིན་མཆོག་འགྱུར།།
དཔལ་ལྡན་རིན་ཆེན་བདུན་གྱི་བདག །
འགྲོ་ཕན་འཁོར་ལོས་སྒྱུར་བར་འགྱུར། །

༩༤༥ ས་གསུམ་པ་ནི་འོད་བྱེད་པ། །
ཡེ་ཤེས་ཞི་བའི་འོད་འབྱུང་ཕྱིར།།
བསམ་གཏན་མངོན་ཤེས་བསྐྱེད་པ་དང་།།
འདོད་ཆགས་ཞེ་སྡང་ཡོངས་ཟད་ཕྱིར།།

༩༤༦ དེ་ཡི་རྣམ་པར་སྨིན་པས་ན། །
བཟོད་པའི་སྤྱོད་པ་ལྷག་པར་སྤྱོད། །
ལྷ་ཡི་དབང་ཆེན་མཁས་པ་སྟེ། །
འདོད་པའི་འདོད་ཆགས་བཟློག་པ་ཡིན།།

༤༤༧ བཞི་པ་འོད་འཕྲོ་ཅན་ཞེས་བྱ། །
ཡང་དག་ཡེ་ཤེས་འོད་འབྱུང་ཕྱིར།།
བྱང་ཆུབ་ཕྱོགས་མཐུན་ལྷུར་ལེན་པ།།
ཁྱད་པར་དུ་ནི་བསྒོམ་པའི་ཕྱིར། །

༤༤༨ དེ་ཡི་རྣམ་པར་སྨིན་པས་ན། །
རབ་འཐབ་བྲལ་གནས་ལྷ་རྒྱལ་འགྱུར།།
འཇིག་ཚོགས་ལྟ་བ་རབ་འབྱུང་བ། །
ཀུན་ནས་འཇོམས་བྱེད་མཁས་པ་ཡིན།།

༤༤༩ ལྔ་པ་ཤིན་ཏུ་སྦྱང་དཀའ་བདུད། །
ཀུན་གྱིས་ཤིན་ཏུ་ཐུབ་དཀའ་ཕྱིར།།
འཕགས་པའི་བདེན་སོགས་ཕྲ་མོའི་དོན།། །
ཤེས་ལ་མཁས་པ་འབྱུང་བའི་ཕྱིར། །

༤༥༠ དེ་ཡི་རྣམ་པར་སྨིན་པས་ན། །
དགའ་ལྡན་གནས་ཀྱི་ལྷ་རྒྱལ་འགྱུར།།
མུ་སྟེགས་བྱེད་པ་ཐམས་ཅད་ཀྱི། །
ཉོན་མོངས་ལྟ་གནས་བཟློག་བྱེད་པ།།

༤༥༡ དྲུག་པ་མངོན་ཕྱོགས་ཞེས་བྱ་སྟེ། །
སངས་རྒྱས་ཆོས་ལ་མངོན་ཕྱོགས་ཕྱིར།།
ཞི་གནས་ལྷག་མཐོང་གོམས་པ་ཡིས།།
འགོག་པ་ཐོབ་པས་རྒྱས་པའི་ཕྱིར།།

༤༥༢ དེ་ཡི་རྣམ་པར་སྨིན་པས་ན། །
ལྷ་ཡི་རྒྱལ་པོ་རབ་འཕྲུལ་འགྱུར། །
ཉན་ཐོས་རྣམས་ཀྱིས་མི་འཕྲོག་པ། །
ལྷག་པའི་ང་རྒྱལ་ཅན་ཞི་བྱེད། །

༤༥༣ བདུན་པ་རིང་དུ་སོང་བ་སྟེ། །
གྲངས་ནི་རིང་དུ་སོང་ལྡན་ཕྱིར། །
གང་ཕྱིར་སྐད་ཅིག་སྐད་ཅིག་ལ།།
དེར་ནི་འགོག་ལ་སྙོམས་པར་འཇུག །

༤༥༤ དེ་ཡི་རྣམ་པར་སྨིན་པས་ན། །
དབང་བསྒྱུར་ལྷ་ཡི་བདག་པོར་འགྱུར།།
འཕགས་པའི་བདེན་མངོན་རྟོགས་ཤེས་པའི།།
སློབ་དཔོན་ཇུ་མཆོག་ཆེན་པོར་འགྱུར།།

༥༥༥ དེ་བཞིན་བརྒྱད་པ་གཞོན་ནུ་རིས། །
མི་གཡོ་བ་སྟེ་མི་རྟོག་ཕྱིར། །
མི་གཡོ་དེ་བཞིན་ལུས་དང་ནི། །
ངག་སེམས་སྤྱོད་ཡུལ་བསམ་མི་ཁྱབ། །

༥༥༦ དེ་ཡི་རྣམ་པར་སྨིན་པས་ན། །
སྟོང་གི་བདག་པོའི་ཚངས་པར་འགྱུར། །
དགྲ་བཅོམ་རང་སངས་རྒྱས་སོགས་ཀྱིས། །
དོན་གཏན་འབེབས་ལ་འགྲོགས་པ་མེད། །

༥༥༧ ས་དགུ་པ་ནི་ལེགས་པ་ཡི། །
བློ་གྲོས་ཞེས་བྱ་རྒྱལ་ཚབ་བཞིན། །
གང་ཕྱིར་སོ་སོར་ཡང་དག་རིག །
ཐོབ་པས་འདི་ལ་བློ་གྲོས་བཟང་། །

༥༥༨ དེ་ཡི་རྣམ་པར་སྨིན་པས་ན། །
སྟོང་གཉིས་བདག་པོའི་ཚངས་པར་འགྱུར། །
སེམས་ཅན་བསམ་པ་དྲིས་པ་ལ། །
དགྲ་བཅོམ་སོགས་ཀྱིས་འགྲོགས་པ་མེད། །

༥༥༩ བཅུ་པ་ཆོས་ཀྱི་སྤྲིན་ཡིན་ཏེ། །
དམ་པའི་ཆོས་ཀྱི་ཆར་འབེབས་ཕྱིར། །
བྱང་ཆུབ་སེམས་དཔའ་སངས་རྒྱས་ཀྱིས། །
འོད་ཟེར་དབང་གིས་དབང་བསྐུར་ཕྱིར། །

༥༦༠ དེ་ཡི་རྣམ་པར་སྨིན་པས་ན། །
གནས་གཙང་ལྷ་ཡི་བདག་པོར་འགྱུར། །
བསམ་ཡས་ཡེ་ཤེས་ཡུལ་གྱི་བདག །
དབང་ཕྱུག་ཆེན་པོ་མཆོག་ཡིན་ནོ། །

༥༦༡ དེ་ལྟ་བཅུ་པོ་དེ་དག་ནི། །
བྱང་ཆུབ་སེམས་དཔའི་ས་བཅུར་བསྒྲགས། །
སངས་རྒྱས་རྣམས་ཀྱིས་གཞན་ཏེ། །
རྣམ་པ་ཀུན་ཏུ་གཞལ་ཡས་པར། །

༥༦༢ རྒྱ་ཆེན་དེ་ནི་སྟོབས་བཅུ་དང་། །
ལྡན་པ་ཡིན་པ་ཙམ་ཞིག་བརྗོད། །
དེ་ཡི་སྟོབས་ནི་རེ་རེ་ཡང་། །
འགྲོ་བ་ཀུན་བཞིན་དཔག་ཏུ་མེད། །

༩༥༣ སངས་རྒྱས་རྣམས་ཀྱི་ཚད་མེད་ཉིད། །
ཕྱོགས་མཚམས་ཀུན་གྱི་ནམ་མཁའ་དང་། །
ས་ཆུ་མེ་རླུང་ཇི་ལྟ་བ། །
དེ་ཙམ་ཞིག་ཏུ་བརྗོད་པར་བས། །

༩༥༤ ག་ལ་ཏེ་རྒྱུ་ནི་དེ་ཙམ་དུ། །
ཚད་མེད་ཉིད་དུ་མ་མཐོང་ན། །
སངས་རྒྱས་རྣམས་ཀྱི་ཚད་མེད་པ། །
དེ་ལ་ཡིད་ཆེས་མི་འགྱུར་བས། །

༩༥༥ དེ་ཕྱིར་སྐུ་གཟུགས་མཆོད་རྟེན་གྱི། །
སྤྱན་སྔ་འམ་ཡང་ན་གཞན་དུའང་རུང་། །
ཚིགས་སུ་བཅད་པ་ཉི་ཤུ་འདི། །
ཉིན་གཅིག་ཅིང་ཡང་དུས་གསུམ་བརྗོད། །

༩༥༦ སངས་རྒྱས་དམ་ཆོས་དགེ་འདུན་དང་། །
བྱང་ཆུབ་སེམས་དཔའ་རྣམས་ལ་ཡང་། །
རྣམ་ཀུན་བཏུད་དེ་སྐྱབས་མཆིས་ནས། །
མཆོད་འོས་རྣམས་ལ་ཕྱག་འཚལ་ལོ། །

༩༥༧ སྡིག་པ་རྣམས་ལས་ལྡོག་པ་བགྱི་ཞིང་། །
བསོད་ནམས་ཐམས་ཅད་ཡོངས་སུ་གཟུང་། །
ལུས་ཅན་ཀུན་གྱི་བསོད་ནམས་དག །
ཀུན་ལ་རྗེས་སུ་ཡི་རང་ངོ་། །

༩༥༨ བདག་ནི་སྤྱིས་བཏུད་ཐལ་སྦྱར་ཏེ། །
ཆོས་ཀྱི་འཁོར་ལོ་བསྐོར་སླད་དང་། །
འགྲོ་གནས་བར་དུ་བཞུགས་སླད་དུ། །
རྫོགས་པའི་སངས་རྒྱས་རྣམས་ལ་གསོལ། །

༩༥༩ དེ་ལྟར་བགྱིས་པའི་བསོད་ནམས་དང་། །
བདག་གིས་བགྱིས་དང་མ་བགྱིས་གང་། །
དེས་ནི་སེམས་ཅན་ཐམས་ཅད་ཀྱང་། །
བླ་མེད་བྱང་ཆུབ་སེམས་ལྡན་ཤོག །

༩༦༠ སེམས་ཅན་ཐམས་ཅད་དྲི་མེད་དབང་། །
ཡོངས་རྫོགས་མི་ཁོམ་····ཀུན་འདས་ཤིང་། །
སྤྱོད་པ་རང་དབང་ཡོད་པ་དང་། །
འཚོ་བ་བཟང་དང་ལྡན་པར་ཤོག །

༤༧༡ ལུས་ཅན་དག་ནི་ཐམས་ཅད་ཀྱང་། །
ལག་ན་རིན་ཆེན་ཉིད་ལྡན་ཞིང་། །
ཡོ་བྱད་ཐམས་ཅད་མཐའ་ཡས་པ། །
འཁོར་བ་སྲིད་དུ་མི་ཟད་ཤོག །

༤༧༢ བུད་མེད་ཐམས་ཅད་དུས་ཀུན་ཏུ། །
སྐྱེས་མཆོག་ཉིད་དུ་འགྱུར་བར་ཤོག །
ལུས་ཅན་ཐམས་ཅད་རིག་པ་དང་། །
རྐང་པར་ལྡན་པ་ཉིད་དུ་ཤོག །

༤༧༣ ལུས་ཅན་ཁ་དོག་ལྡན་པ་དང་། །
གཟུགས་བཟང་གཟི་བརྗིད་ཆེ་བ་དང་། །
བལྟ་ན་སྡུག་ཅིང་ནད་མེད་དང་། །
སྟོབས་ཆེན་ཚེ་དང་ལྡན་པར་ཤོག །

༤༧༤ ཐམས་ཅད་ཐབས་ལ་མཁས་གྱུར་ཏེ། །
སྡུག་བསྔལ་ཀུན་ལས་ཐར་བ་དང་། །
དཀོན་མཆོག་གསུམ་ལ་གཞོལ་བ་དང་། །
སངས་རྒྱས་ཆོས་ནོར་ཆེར་ལྡན་ཤོག །

༤༧༥ བྱམས་དང་སྙིང་རྗེ་དགའ་བ་དང་། །
ཉོན་མོངས་བཏང་སྙོམས་གནས་པ་དང་། །
སྦྱིན་དང་ཚུལ་ཁྲིམས་བཟོད་བརྩོན་འགྲུས། །
བསམ་གཏན་ཤེས་རབ་ཀྱིས་བརྒྱན་ཅིང་། །

༤༧༦ ཚོགས་རྣམས་ཐམས་ཅད་ཡོངས་རྫོགས་ཏེ། །
མཚན་དང་དཔེ་བྱད་གསལ་བ་དང་། །
བསམ་གྱིས་མི་ཁྱབ་ས་བཅུ་དག །
རྒྱུན་མི་འཆད་པར་བགྲོད་པར་ཤོག །

༤༧༧ བདག་ཀྱང་ཡོན་ཏན་དེ་དག་དང་། །
གཞན་ཀུན་གྱིས་ཀྱང་རྣམ་བརྒྱན་ཏེ། །
ཉེས་པ་ཀུན་ལས་གྲོལ་བ་དང་། །
སེམས་ཅན་ཀུན་མཆོག་བྱམས་པ་དང་། །

༤༧༨ སེམས་ཅན་ཀུན་ཡིད་རེ་བ་ཡི། །
དགེ་བ་ཐམས་ཅད་རྫོགས་བགྱིད་ཅིང་། །
རྟག་ཏུ་ལུས་ཅན་ཐམས་ཅད་ཀྱི། །
སྡུག་བསྔལ་སེལ་བར་བགྱིད་པར་ཤོག །

༩༠༩ འཇིག་རྟེན་ཀུན་ལ་སྐྱོ་བོ་གང་། །
སྡུ་དག་འཇིགས་པས་སྐྱོ་བ་དེ། །
བདག་གི་མིང་ཙམ་ཐོས་པས་ཀྱང་། །
ཤིན་ཏུ་འཇིགས་པ་མེད་པར་ཤོག །

༩༡༠ བདག་ནི་མཐོང་དང་དྲན་པ་དང་། །
མིང་ཙམ་ཐོས་པས་སྐྱེ་བོ་རྣམས། །
རབ་དགའ་འཁྲུལ་མེད་རྣལ་མ་དང་། །
རྫོགས་པའི་བྱང་ཆུབ་ངེས་པ་དང་། །

༩༡༡ ཚེ་རབས་······ཀུན་ཏུ་རྗེས་འབྲང་བའི། །
མངོན་ཤེས་ལྔ་པོ་ཐོབ་པར་ཤོག །
སེམས་ཅན་ཀུན་ལ་རྣམ་ཀུན་ཏུ། །
རྟག་ཏུ་ཕན་བདེ་བསྒྲུབ་པར་ཤོག །

༩༡༢ འཇིག་རྟེན་ཀུན་ན་སྐྱེ་བོ་གང་། །
སྡིག་པ་བྱེད་པར་འདོད་གྱུར་པ། །
དེ་དག་ཐམས་ཅད་གནོད་མེད་པར། །
རྟག་ཏུ་ཅིག་ཅར་བཟློག་གྱུར་ཅིག །

༩༡༣ ས་དང་ཆུ་དང་མེ་དང་རླུང་། །
སྨན་དང་དགོན་ནགས་ཤིང་བཞིན་དུ། །
རྟག་ཏུ་སེམས་ཅན་ཐམས་ཅད་ཀྱིས། །
རང་དགར་དགག་མེད་སྤྱོད་བྱར་ཤོག །

༩༡༤ སེམས་ཅན་རྣམས་ལ་སྲོག་བཞིན་ཕངས། །
བདག་ལ་དེ་དག་ཆེས་ཕངས་ཤོག །
བདག་ལ་དེ་དག་སྡིག་སྨིན་ཅིང་། །
བདག་དགེ་མ་ལུས་དེར་སྨིན་ཤོག །

༩༡༥ ཇི་སྲིད་སེམས་ཅན་འགའ་ཞིག་ཀྱང་། །
གང་དུ་མ་གྲོལ་དེ་སྲིད་དུ། །
དེ་ཕྱིར་བླ་ན་མེད་པ་ཡི། །
བྱང་ཆུབ་ཐོབ་ཀྱང་གནས་གྱུར་ཅིག །

༩༡༦ དེ་སྐད་བརྗོད་པའི་བསོད་ནམས་གང་། །
ག་ལ་ཏེ་དེ་ནི་གཟུགས་ཅན་གྱུར། །
གནྨའི་ཁྱོམ་སྐྱེད་ཀྱི་ནི། །
འཇིག་རྟེན་ཁམས་ཀྱང་ཤོང་མི་འགྱུར། །

༩༥༧ དེ་ནི་བཅོམ་ལྡན་འདས་ཀྱིས་གསུངས། །
གཏན་ཚིགས་ཀྱང་ནི་འདི་ལ་སྣང་། །
སེམས་ཅན་ཁམས་ནི་ཚད་མེད་ལ། །
ཕན་འདོད་དེ་ནི་དེ་འདྲ་ནོ། །

༩༥༨ དེ་ལྟར་བདག་གིས་ཁྱོད་ལ་ནི། །
མདོར་བསྡུས་ཆོས་བཤད་གང་ཡིན་དེ། །
ཁྱོད་ལ་ཇི་ལྟར་རྟག་ཏུ་སྐུ། །
ཕངས་པ་བཞིན་དུ་ཕངས་པར་མཛོད། །

༩༥༩ གང་ལ་ཆོས་དེ་ཕངས་གྱུར་པ། །
དེ་ལ་དོན་དུ་བདག་ལུས་ཕངས། །
ཕངས་ལ་ཕན་པ་བྱ་དགོས་ན། །
དེ་ནི་ཆོས་ཀྱིས་བྱེད་པར་འགྱུར། །

༩༦༠ དེ་བས་ཆོས་ནི་བདག་བཞིན་བསྟེན། །
ཆོས་བཞིན་དུ་ནི་བསྒྲུབ་པ་དང་། །
བསྒྲུབ་པ་བཞིན་དུ་ཤེས་རབ་དང་། །
ཤེས་རབ་བཞིན་དུ་མཁས་པ་བསྟེན། །

༩༦༡ གཙང་ཞིང་བྱམས་ལ་བློ་ལྡན་པ། །
ཕེབས་པས་ཕན་པར་སྨྲ་བ་ལ། །
གང་ཞིག་བདག་ངན་དོགས་བྱེད་པ། །
དེ་ནི་རང་དོན་རྒྱུད་ཀྱང་གནོན། །

༩༦༢ དགེ་བའི་བཤེས་གཉེན་དེ་དག་གི། །
མཚན་ཉིད་མདོར་བསྡུས་མཁྱེན་པར་མཛོད། །
ཆོག་ཤེས་སྙིང་རྗེ་ཚུལ་ཁྲིམས་ལྡན། །
ཉོན་མོངས་སེལ་བའི་ཤེས་རབ་ཅན། །

༩༦༣ དེ་དག་གིས་ནི་ཁྱོད་བསྟན་ན། །
ཁྱོད་ཀྱིས་མཁྱེན་གྱིས་གུས་པར་མཛོད། །
ལུགས་ནི་ཕུན་སུམ་ཚོགས་པ་འདིས། །
གྲུབ་པ་ཡི་ནི་མཆོག་ཐོབ་འགྱུར། །

༩༦༤ བདེན་དང་སེམས་ཅན་འཇམ་སྨྲ་ཞིང་། །
བདེ་བའི་ངང་རྒྱལ་བསྙེན་དཀའ་བ། །
རྒྱལ་ལྡན་ཁྲེད་དུ་གསོད་མི་འདོད། །
རང་དབང་ལེགས་པར་སྨྲ་བར་མཛོད། །

༤༩༥ ལེགས་དུལ་བག་ལ་ཉལ་གཏོང་དང་། །
བརྗིད་བག་ལྡན་ཞིང་སེམས་ཞི་བ། །
རྩོད་པ་མེད་ཅིང་མཐའ་མི་རིང་། །
གཡོ་མེད་པ་དང་ངེས་པར་སྨྲ། །

༤༩༦ ཟླ་བ་ཉ་བ་ངེས་པ་དང་། །
སྟོན་གྱི་ཉི་བཞིན་གཟི་ལྡན་དང་། །
རྒྱ་མཚོ་བཞིན་དུ་ཟབ་པ་དང་། །
རི་རབ་བཞིན་དུ་བརྟན་པར་མཛོད། །

༤༩༧ ཉེས་པ་ཀུན་ལས་རྣམ་གྲོལ་ཞིང་། །
ཡོན་ཏན་ཀུན་གྱིས་བརྒྱན་གྱུར་ཏེ། །
སེམས་ཅན་ཀུན་གྱི་ཉེར་འཚོ་དང་། །
ཐམས་ཅད་མཁྱེན་པ་ཉིད་དུ་མཛོད། །

༤༩༨ ཆོས་འདི་རྒྱལ་པོ་འབའ་ཞིག་ལ། །
བསྟན་པ་ཁོ་ནར་མ་པས་ཏེ། །
སེམས་ཅན་གཞན་ལའང་ཅི་རིགས་པར། །
ཕན་པར་འདོད་པས་བསྟན་པ་ལགས། །

༤༩༩ བདག་དང་གཞན་རྣམས་ཡང་དག་པར། །
རྫོགས་པའི་བྱང་ཆུབ་འགྲུབ་བགྱི་སླད། །
རྒྱལ་པོ་གཏམ་དུ་བྱ་བ་འདི། །
གདུགས་རེ་ཞིང་ཡང་བསམ་པའི་རིགས། །

༥༠༠ ཚུལ་ཁྲིམས་སྐྱེ་བོ་བླ་མ་མཆོག་བཀུར་བཟོད་དང་དེ་བཞིན་
ཕྲག་དོག་མེད། །
སེར་སྣ་དང་བྲལ་རེ་བ་མེད་པར་བྱས་ནས་གཞན་དོན་
ནོར་ཅན་དང་། །
ཕོངས་པ་ཕྱུར་ལ་ཕན་བྱེད་མཆོག་དང་མཆོག་མིན་ཡོངས་
གཟུངས་དོར་བ་དང་། །
དམ་ཆོས་ཡོངས་གཟུང་བྱང་ཆུབ་ཕྱིར་དོན་གཉེར་བ་རྣམས་
ཀྱིས་རྟག་ཏུ་བྱ། །

རིན་པོ་ཆེའི་ཕྲེང་བ་ལས། བྱང་ཆུབ་སེམས་དཔའི་
སྤྱོད་པའི་ལེའུ་བསྟན་པ་སྟེ་ལྔ་པའོ།། ། །

རྒྱལ་པོ་ལ་གཏམ་བྱ་བ་རིན་པོ་ཆེའི་ཕྲེང་བ་ཞེས་བྱ་བ།
སློབ་དཔོན་ཆེན་པོ་འཕགས་པ་ཀླུ་སྒྲུབ་ཀྱིས་མཛད་
པ་རྫོགས་སོ།། ||

རྒྱ་གར་གྱི་མཁན་པོ་བིདྱཱ་ཀཱ་ར་པྲ་བྷཱ་དང་། བོད་ཀྱི་ལོ་ཙཱ་བ་བནྡེ་དཔལ་ལ
བརྩེགས་ཀྱིས་བསྒྱུར་ཅིང་ཞུས་ཏེ་གཏན་ལ་ཕབ་པའོ།། ||སླད་ཀྱིས་
རྒྱ་གར་གྱི་མཁན་པོ་ཀྀ་ཀ་ན་ཀ་ཝརྨ་དང་། བོད་ཀྱི་བནྡེ་པ་ཚབ་ཉི་མ་
གྲགས་ཀྱིས་རྒྱ་དཔེ་གསུམ་ལ་གཏུགས་ནས། འཕགས་པ་ཡབ་སྲས
ཀྱི་དགོངས་པ་ཐུན་མོང་···མ་ཡིན་པ་དང་མི་མཐུན་པར་བསྒྱུར་བ་ལ་
སོགས་པ་བཅོས་ཤིང་གཏན་ལ་ཕབ་པའོ།། ||འདི་ཞོལ་པར་ཁང་དུ་
བཞུགས་པ་ནས་ཞལ་བ་ཕུས་པ་དགེའོ།། ||

GUIDE TO THE TOPICS: TIBETAN

In his *Illumination of the Essential Meanings of (Nāgārjuna's) "Precious Garland of Madhyamaka"* Gyel-tsap Dar-ma-rin-chen breaks Nāgārjuna's text into a complicated series of sections and sub-sections in order to clarify shifts of topic and inter-relations of points. I have extracted this guide and placed it here as a table of contents. The edition used is from his Collected Works, *ka* (New Delhi: Guru Deva, 1982), which is a reproduction from the 1897 old *zhol* (*dga' ldan phun tshogs gling*) blocks. (The pagination of the 1897 *zhol* edition used in the notes differs slightly from this one even though they are both 78 folios.)

GYEL-TSAP	TOPIC AND NUMBER OF DIVISIONS	VERSE
6b.4	(1) རྒྱས་པར་བཤད་པ།༣	8-24ab
6b.4	(a) མངོན་མཐོའི་ཆོས་བཤད་པ།༤	8-21
6b.4	1' མངོན་མཐོའི་ཆོས་བཅུ་དྲུག་བཤད་པ།༣	8-10
6b.5	a' གང་ལས་ལྡོག་པའི་ཆོས་བཅུ་གསུམ།༢	8-10ab
6b.6	1" མི་དགེ་བཅུ་ལས་ལྡོག་པ།	8-9
7a.5	2" ཁ་ན་མ་ཐོ་བ་གཞན་ལས་ལྡོག་པ།	10ab
7b.6	b' འཇུག་པའི་ཆོས་གསུམ།	10bc
8a.1	c' དོན་བསྡུ་བ།	10d
8a.2	2' ཆོས་འདི་པ་ལས་གཞན་ལ་དེ་དག་མེད་པར་བསྟན་པ།༣	11-13
8a.2	a' ལམ་གོལ་བར་ཞུགས་པས་རང་གཞན་ལ་གནོད་པ།	11
8a.4	b' གོལ་བར་འགྲོ་བའི་གང་ཟག	12
8a.6	c' གོལ་བར་ཞུགས་པའི་ཉེས་པ།	13
8b.3	3' ཆོས་དེ་དག་ལ་ལོག་པར་ཞུགས་པའི་འབྲས་བུ།༣	14-19
8b.3	a' མི་དགེ་བའི་རྒྱུ་མཐུན་གྱི་འབྲས་བུ་ཚེ་ཐུང་བ་སོགས་སུ་འགྱུར་བ།	14-18b
9a.b	b' རྣམ་སྨིན་གྱི་འབྲས་བུ་ངན་འགྲོ་འགྲོ་བ།	18cd
9b.2	c' དགེ་བའི་ལས་ཀྱི་འབྲས་བུ་དེ་ལས་ལྡོག་སྟེ་འབྱུང་བ།	19
9b.4	4' དགེ་མི་དགེའི་རྒྱུ་འབྲས་སོ་སོར་བཤད་པ།	20-21
10a.1	(b) ཇི་ལྟར་ཉམས་སུ་བླང་བའི་ཚུལ།	22
10a.3	(c) ཉམས་སུ་བླངས་པའི་འབྲས་བུ།	23-24b
10a.5	(2) དོན་བསྡུ་བ།	24cd

GYEL-TSAP	TOPIC AND NUMBER OF DIVISIONS	VERSE
10a.6	b. ངེས་ལེགས་ཀྱི་འབྲས་བཤད་པ།༣	25-100
10a.6	(1) མདོ་ལས་ཇི་ལྟར་གསུངས་པའི་ཚུལ།༣	25-77
10a.6	(a) རྒྱལ་བས་གསུངས་པའི་ཚུལ་མདོར་བསྟན་པ།༣	25-27
10b.1	1' ཇི་ལྟ་བུ་གསུངས་པ།	25
10b.3	2' མཁས་རྨོངས་ཟབ་མོའི་དོན་ལ་སྐྲག་པ་སྐྱེ་མི་སྐྱེད་ཀྱི་ཁྱད་པར།	26
10b.6	3' སྐྲག་པ་དེ་ཡང་བདག་འཛིན་ལས་བྱུང་བར་སྟོན་པས་གསུངས་པ།	27
11a.2	(b) དེའི་དོན་རྒྱས་པར་བཤད་པ།༣	28-74
11a.2	1' ང་དང་ང་ཡིར་འཛིན་པ་རྫུན་པར་བསྒྲུབ་པ་དངོས།༢	28-34
11a.2	a' དངོས།	28-29
11a.6	b' དེ་སྤངས་པས་ཐར་པ་འཐོབ་པར་བསྟན་པ།	30
11b.2	c' དེ་ཉིད་གཟུགས་བརྙན་གྱི་དཔེས་བཤད་པ།༣	31-33
11b.2	1" གང་ཟག་དང་ཕུང་པོ་བདེན་མེད་དུ་རྟོགས་པས་སྡུག་ཀུན་ལྡོག་པའི་ རྗེས་འགྲོའི་དཔེ་དོན།	31-32
11b.6	2" ལྡོག་པའི་དོན།	33
12a.3	d' སྟོང་ཉིད་རྟོགས་པ་ཐར་པའི་རྒྱུར་བསྟན་པ།	34
12a.5	2' བཅིངས་ཐར་རང་བཞིན་གྱིས་དགག་པ།༢	35-45
12a.6	a' འཁོར་བར་འཇུག་པའི་རིམ་པ།༣	35-36
12b.6	1" འཁོར་བའི་རྩ་བ་ངོས་བཟུང་བ།	35
12b.6	2" དེ་ལ་བརྟེན་ནས་འཁོར་བའི་དཔེ།	36
13a.3	b' འཁོར་བ་ལས་ལྡོག་པའི་རིམ་པ།	37-38

GYEL-TSAP	TOPIC AND NUMBER OF DIVISIONS	VERSE
13a.5	c' སྟོང་ཉིད་རྟོགས་པའི་ཕན་ཡོན།	39
13b.1	d' ཐར་པའི་རང་བཞིན་བཤད་པ།༤	40-45
13b.2	1" ཕུང་པོ་ལྷག་མེད་ཀྱི་གནས་སྐབས་ན་བདེན་འཛིན་ཟད་པ་ལ་འཇིགས་པར་མི་རིགས་པ།	40
13b.4	2" བདེན་འཛིན་མཐའ་དག་ཟད་པ་ཐར་པར་བསྟན་པ།༣	41-42
13b.4	a" དངོས་མེད་རང་བཞིན་གྱིས་གྲུབ་པ་ཐར་པར་མི་འཐད།	41
13b.6	b" ཐར་པ་དངོས་པོར་མི་འཐད།	42ab
14a.2	c" དངོས་ཀྱི་དོན།	42cd
14a.3	3" ལོག་ལྟ་དང་ཡང་དག་པའི་ལྟ་བའི་ཁྱད་པར་ལྷག་བཅས་ཀྱི་དུས་ན་ཡང་བདེན་འཛིན།	43-44
14a.6	4" ཟད་པ་ཐར་པར་བསྟན་པ།	45
14b.3	3' ཆོས་ཀུན་རྟག་ཆད་ཀྱི་མཐའ་དང་བྲལ་བར་བསྟན་པ།༤	46-74
14b.3	a' རྒྱས་པར་བཤད་པ།༤	46-56
14b.4	1" རྒྱུ་འབྲས་རང་བཞིན་གྱིས་གྲུབ་པ་དགག་པ།༣	46-47
14b.4	a" རྒྱུ་འབྲས་ཡོད་མེད་ཀྱི་མཐའ་དང་བྲལ་བ།	46
14b.6	b" རྒྱུ་འབྲས་རང་བཞིན་གྱིས་གྲུབ་པ་དགག་པ།	47
15a.1	2" གྲགས་པ་དང་འགལ་བ་སྤང་བ།	48-49
15a.5	3" གཉིས་མེད་ཀྱི་དོན་རྟོགས་པས་གྲོལ་བ།	50-51
15b.2	4" ཤེས་བྱེད་ཀྱི་དཔེ་བཤད་པ།༣	52-56
15b.2	a" དངོས་པོའི་དེ་ཁོ་ན་ཉིད་རྟོགས་པ་དང་མ་རྟོགས་པའི་དཔེ།	52-53

GYEL-TSAP	TOPIC AND NUMBER OF DIVISIONS	VERSE
15b.5	b" ཕུང་པོ་རང་བཞིན་གྱིས་གྲུབ་པ་དགག་པ།	54
15b.6	c" ཡོད་མེད་དུ་ལྟ་བ་མ་སྤངས་ན་འཁོར་བ་ལས་མི་གྲོལ་བ།	55-56
16a.2	b' དེ་ལ་ཆད་པར་ཐལ་བའི་ཉེས་པ་མེད་པ།༣	57-60
16a.2	1" ཐར་པ་ཐོབ་པ་ལ་གཉིས་མེད་རྟོགས་དགོས་པར་བསྟན་པ།	57
16a.5	2" མཐའ་བྲལ་རྟོགས་པ་ཡོད་མེད་ཀྱི་ལྟ་བ་ཅན་དུ་ཐལ་བ་འཕང་པ།	58-59
16b.1	3" སྤྲོལ་བྲལ་ཁོང་དུ་ཆུད་པ་ལ་ཆད་པ་ལ་ཆད་པའི་ཉེས་པ་མེད་པ།	60
166.4	c' མཐའ་བྲལ་སངས་རྒྱས་ཀྱི་ཐུན་མོང་མ་ཡིན་པའི་ཁྱད་ཆོས་སུ་བསྟན་པ།	61-62
17a.6	d' དངོས་པོ་རང་བཞིན་གྱིས་གྲུབ་པ་དགག་པ།༤	63-74
17a.6	1" འགྲོ་འོང་རང་བཞིན་གྱིས་གྲུབ་པ་དགག་པ།	64
17b.3	2" འདུས་བྱས་ཀྱི་མཚན་ཉིད་སྐྱེ་འཇིག་གནས་གསུམ་རང་བཞིན་གྱིས་གྲུབ་པ་དགག་པ།	65
17b.4	3" ཞར་ལ་གཞན་སྡེའི་འདོད་པ་དགག་པ།༢	66-68
17b.4	a" བྱེ་བྲག་པས་རྡུལ་ཕྲན་རྟག་པར་འདོད་པ་དགག་པ།	66-67
18a.4	b" ཁྱབ་འཇུག་པ་སྐྱེས་བུ་རྟག་པར་འདོད་པ་དགག་པ།	68
18a.6	4" སྐད་ཅིག་མ་རང་བཞིན་གྱིས་གྲུབ་པ་དགག་པ།༤	69-74
18a.6	a" སྐད་ཅིག་ལ་ཆ་བཅས་ཀྱིས་ཁྱབ་པ་བསྟན་པ།	69
18b.4	b" ཆ་བཅས་རང་བཞིན་གྱིས་གྲུབ་པ་དགག་པ།	70
18b.6	c" གཅིག་དང་དུ་བྲལ་གྱི་གཏན་ཚིགས་ཀྱིས་དངོས་པོ་རང་བཞིན་གྱིས་གྲུབ་པ།	71-73b

GYEL-TSAP	TOPIC AND NUMBER OF DIVISIONS	VERSE
19a.5	d" འཇིག་རྟེན་མཐའ་ལྡན་དུ་མི་བཟུང་བའི་རྒྱ་མཚན།	73cd-74
19b.2	(c) དོན་བསྡུ་བ།༣	75-77
19b.2	1' ཟབ་མོ་རྒྱལ་བས་གསུངས་པ།	75
19b.4	2' དེ་ལ་སྐྲག་པའི་ཉེས་དམིགས།	76-77b
20a.4	3' རྒྱལ་པོས་ཀྱང་ཟབ་མོའི་དོན་རྟོགས་པར་གདམས་པ།	77cd
20a.b	(2) རྒྱལ་པོས་ཀྱང་ཟབ་མོའི་དོན་ལ་བསླབ་པར་གདམས་པ།༣	78-100
20a.6	(a) སྐབས་དགོད་པ།	78-79
20b.2	(b) བདག་མེད་གཉིས་བཤད་པ།༣	80-100
20b.2	1' གང་ཟག་གི་བདག་མེད་བཤད་པ།༣	80-82
21a.6	a' ཁམས་དྲུག་གང་ཟག་ཏུ་མི་རུང་བ།	80-81
21b.4	b' དཔྱད་པ་ལྔའི་སྒོ་ནས་གང་ཟག་རང་བཞིན་གྱིས་གྲུབ་པ་དགག་པ།	82
22a.1	2' ཆོས་ཀྱི་བདག་མེད་བཤད་པ།༣	83-100
22a.1	a' གཟུགས་ཕུང་རང་བཞིན་གྱིས་གྲུབ་པ་དགག་པ།༢	83-99
22a.1	1" རྟེན་འབྱུང་རང་བཞིན་གྱིས་གྲུབ་པ་དགག་པ།༢	83-90
22a.1	a" གཅིག་དང་དུ་མའི་རང་བཞིན་དུ་མ་གྲུབ་པ།	83
22a.5	b" དེས་ན་འབྱུང་བ་རང་བཞིན་གྱིས་མེད་པ།	84
22a.5	c" འདུས་པ་རང་བཞིན་གྱིས་མ་གྲུབ་པ།༣	85-87
22a.6	1: ལྡོས་ན་འདུས་པ་རང་བཞིན་གྱིས་གྲུབ་པ་འགལ་བ།	85
22b.1	2: དེའི་ལན་དགག་པ།	86
22b.3	3: རྩོད་པ་སྤོང་བ།	87

GYEL-TSAP	TOPIC AND NUMBER OF DIVISIONS	VERSE
22b.	d" སྒྲུབ་བྱེད་དགག་པ།	88-90
23a.4	2" བརྟེན་པ་འབྱུང་འགྱུར་རང་བཞིན་གྱིས་གྲུབ་པ་དགག་པ།	91ab
23a.5	3" ཆོས་གཞན་ལ་སྦྱར་བ།༣	91c-98
23a.5	a" དངོས།	91cd-92
23b.2	b" རང་བཞིན་གྱིས་སྟོང་པའི་ཤེས་བྱེད།༤	93-98
23b.2	1: ཆོས་ཀུན་རང་བཞིན་གྱིས་སྟོང་པའི་དོན་བསྟན་པ།	93
23b.3	2: བཤད་པ།	94-95
23b.6	3: སྒྲུབ་བྱེད་དགོད་པ།	96-97
24a.5	4: ཚད་ལྟར་ཐལ་བའི་སྐྱོན་མེད་པ།	98
24b.2	4" ནམ་མཁའ་རང་བཞིན་གྱིས་གྲུབ་པ་དགག་པ།	99
24b.4	b' ཕུང་པོ་ལྷག་མ་རྣམས་ལ་སྦྱར་བ།	100
24b.6	B. མངོན་མཐོ་ངེས་ལེགས་རྒྱུ་འབྲས་སྤེལ་མར་བཤད་པ།༣	101-200
24b.6	1. ངེས་ལེགས་རྒྱུ་འབྲས།༣	101-123
25a.1	a. མཐར་འཛིན་གྱི་ལྟ་བ་དགག་པ།༣	101-115
25a.1	(1) དཔེ་གཞན་གྱིས་བཤད་ཟིན་དྲན་པར་བྱེད་པ།	101
25a.4	(2) དགག་པ་དངོས།༣	102-114
25a.4	(a) བདག་དང་བདག་མེད་རང་བཞིན་གྱིས་མ་གྲུབ་པ།	102-103
25b.1	(b) དངོས་པོར་ཡོད་མེད་རང་བཞིན་གྱིས་མ་གྲུབ་པ།༣	104-106
25b.2	1' དངོས།	104-105
25b.5	2' མཐའ་བཞིར་ལུང་མ་བསྟན་པའི་རྒྱུ་མཚན།	106

GYEL-TSAP	TOPIC AND NUMBER OF DIVISIONS	VERSE
25b.6	(c) འཁོར་བའི་ཕྱི་མཐའ་ལུང་མ་བསྟན་པ་མི་འཐད་པའི་རྩོད་པ་སྤང་བ།༈	107-114
25b.6	1' རྩོད་པ།	107-108
26a.4	2' ལན།༈	109-114
26a.4	a' འཁོར་བ་ལ་སྐྱེ་འགག་རང་བཞིན་གྱིས་མ་གྲུབ་པའི་དཔེ།༈	109-114
26a.4	1" སྣོད་མིན་ལ་གསང་བ་གང་ཟབ་མོར་བསྟན་པ།	109
26b.1	2" དངོས།	110-112
26b.5	b' འགྲོ་འོང་རང་བཞིན་གྱིས་མ་གྲུབ་པའི་དཔེ།	112-113
27a.1	c' མིང་དུ་བཏགས་པ་ཙམ་དུ་ཟད་པ།	114
27a.2	(3) དེས་ན་མཐའ་བཞིར་ལུང་མ་བསྟན་པ།	115
27a.5	b. ཟམ་མོ་རྟོགས་པར་དཀའ་བའི་ཚུལ།༈	116-123
27a.5	(1) ཟམ་མོ་རྟོགས་པར་དཀའ་བའི་རྒྱུ་མཚན།	116-117
27b.4	(2) ཐུབ་པས་སྣོད་མིན་ལ་ཟབ་མོ་མི་གསུང་བའི་རྒྱུ་མཚན།	118
27b.5	(3) རྒྱུ་མཚན་དེ་ཉིད་བཤད་པ།༈	119-123
27b.5	(a) ཟམ་མོ་ལོག་པར་བཟུང་བའི་ཉེས་དམིགས།	120
28a.5	(b) བཟུང་ལེགས་ཉེས་ཀྱི་ཕན་ཡོན་དང་ཉེས་དམིགས་ཀྱི་དཔེ་བཤད་པ།	121-122
28b.1	(c) ཟབ་མོ་རྟོགས་པ་ལ་བག་དང་ལྡན་པར་གདམས་པ།	123
28b.2	2. མངོན་མཐོ་རྒྱུ་འབྲས།༈	124-174b
28b.3	a. སྐབས་དགོད།༈	124-125
28b.4	(1) སྟོང་ཉིད་མ་རྟོགས་པས་འཁོར་བར་འཁོར་བ།	124
28b.4	(2) དེ་མ་རྟོགས་པ་དེ་སྲིད་མངོན་མཐོ་ལ་འབད་པར་གདམས་པ།	125

GYEL-TSAP	TOPIC AND NUMBER OF DIVISIONS	VERSE
28b.5	b. དངོས་ཀྱི་དོན།༣	126-174b
28b.5	(1) མངོན་མཐོའི་རྒྱུ་སྒྲུབ་པ།༣	126-143
28b.6	(a) མངོན་མཐོའི་རྒྱུ་ལ་བསླབ་པ་སྤྱིར་བསྟན་པ།༣	126-132
28b.6	1' ཕན་ཡོན་ལྡོ་ལྡན་གྱི་རྒྱུ་ལ་བསླབ་པ།	126-127
29a.3	2' སྤྱིར་དམ་པའི་ལུགས་ལ་བསླབ་བ།	128
29a.4	3' དམ་པ་མ་ཡིན་པའི་ལུགས་སྤང་བ།༣	129-132
29a.4	a' ལུགས་ཀྱི་བསྟན་བཅོས་ངན་པ་ལ་བརྟེན་པར་མི་རིགས་པ་	129
29a.6	b' དེ་ལ་སྨད་པ།	130-131
29b.3	c' ཆོས་ཀྱི་ལུགས་ཁྱད་པར་དུ་འཕགས་པ།	132
29b.4	(b) མངོན་མཐའི་རྒྱུ་ཁྱད་པར་ཅན་ལ་བསླབ་པ།༣	133-143
29b.4	1' བསྡུ་བ་བཞི་ལ་བསླབ་པ།	133
30a.1	2' བདེན་པ་སྨྲ་བ་སོགས་བཞི་ལ་བསླབ་པ།༣	134-139
30a1	a' སོ་སོར་བསྟན་པ།༤	134-138
30a.1	1" བདེན་པ་ལ་བསླབ་པ།	134-135
30a.5	2" གཏོང་བ་ལ་བསླབ་པ།	136
30a.6	3" ཉེ་བར་ཞི་བ་ལ་བསླབ་པ།	137
30b.1	4" ཤེས་རབ་བཟང་པོ་ལ་བསླབ་པ།	138
30b.2	b' བསྡུས་ཏེ་བསྟན་པ།	139
30b.3	3' དགེ་བ་འཕེལ་བའི་རྒྱུ་གྲོགས་ཁྱད་པར་ཅན་ལ་བསྟེན་པ།༣	140-143
30b.4	a' གྲོགས་ཁྱད་པར་ཅན་གྱི་མཚན་ཉིད།	140

GYEL-TSAP	TOPIC AND NUMBER OF DIVISIONS	VERSE
30b.6	b' དེའི་རྗེས་སུ་འཇུག་པར་རིགས་པ།	141-142
31a.2	c' འཆི་བ་མི་རྟག་པ་རྒྱུན་དུ་སྒོམ་པ།	143
31a.3	(2) ངན་འགྲོའི་རྒྱུ་སྤང་བ།༢	143-173
31a.4	(a) མདོར་བསྟན་པ།	144-145
31b.1	(b) རྒྱས་པར་བཤད་པ།༣	146-173
31b.1	1' ཆང་ལ་ཆགས་པ་དགག	146
31b.3	2' རྒྱན་པོ་ལ་ཆགས་པ་དགག་པ།	147
31b.4	3' བུད་མེད་ལ་ཆགས་པ་དགག་པ།༢	148-170
31b.4	a' བུད་མེད་ཀྱི་ལུས་གཙང་བ་སྤྱིར་དགག	148
31b.6	b' སོ་སོར་དགག་པ།༢	149-169
31b.6	1" བུད་མེད་ཀྱི་ཡན་ལག་མཛེས་པ་དགག་པ།༤	149-154
31b.6	a" མི་གཙང་བའི་རང་བཞིན་འབའ་ཞིག་ཡིན་པས་ཆགས་པར་མི་རིགས་པ།	149-150
32a.3	b" དེའི་དཔེ།	151
32a.4	c" བུད་མེད་ལ་ཆགས་ན་ཆགས་བྲལ་གྱི་གནས་མེད་པར་འགྱུར་བ།	152
32a.5	d" མི་གཙང་ཡང་བླུན་པོས་དགའ་བའི་རྒྱུར་བཏགས་པ།	153-154
32b.1	2" ལུས་ཡག་ལག་ཅན་མཛེས་པ་དགག་པ།༤	155-168
32b.1	a" བུད་མེད་ཀྱི་ལུས་ལ་ཆགས་པ་སྤྱིར་དགག་པ།	155-157
32b.4	b" ཁ་དོག་དང་དབྱིབས་ལ་ཆགས་པ་དགག་པ།༢	158-165b
32b.4	1: བུད་མེད་ཀྱི་ཁ་དོག་དང་དབྱིབས་ལ་ཆགས་པ་སྤྱིར་དགག་པ།	158

GYEL-TSAP	TOPIC AND NUMBER OF DIVISIONS	VERSE
32b.6	2: གཟུགས་མཛེས་པ་ལ་ཆགས་པ་དགག་པ།༣	159-163
32b.6	a: ཆགས་པར་མི་རིགས་པ།	159-161
33a.2	b: སྨད་པར་རིགས་པ།	162-163
33a.4	3: བུད་མེད་ཀྱི་ལུས་དང་འདྲ་བར་རང་གི་ལུས་ཀྱང་མི་གཙང་བར་བསམ་པ།	164-165ab
33a.5	c" དེས་ན་བུད་མེད་ཀྱི་ལུས་ལ་ཆགས་པར་མི་རིགས་པ།	165c-166
33b.1	d" བུད་མེད་ལ་བསྟོད་པའི་གང་ཟག་སྨད་པ།	167-168
33b.3	3" བུད་མེད་ལ་ཆགས་པ་བདེ་བའི་རྒྱུ་ཡིན་པ་དགག་པ།	169
33b.4	c' མི་གཙང་བ་བསྒོམས་པའི་འབྲས་བུ།	170
33b.5	4' ལིངས་དགག་པ།༣	171-173
33b.5	a' སྲོག་གཅོད་སྤང་བ།	171
34a.1	b' གཞན་ལ་སྐྲག་པ་སྐྱེད་པ་སྤང་བ།	172
34a.2	c' དགའ་བ་སྐྱེད་པ་བསྟན་པ།	173
34a.3	(3) ཆོས་མིན་སྤངས་ནས་ཆོས་སྒྲུབ་པའི་དོན་བསྡུ་བ།	174ab
34a.4	3. ངེས་ལེགས་རྒྱུ་འབྲས་བཤད་པ།༤	174c-200
34a.4	a. བླ་ན་མེད་པའི་བྱང་ཆུབ་ཀྱི་རྒྱུའི་གཙོ་བོ་གསུམ་དུ་བསྡུས་ནས་དེ་ལ་བསླབ་པ།	174c-175
34b.6	b. སངས་རྒྱས་ཀྱི་མཚན་སོ་གཉིས་འགྲུབ་པའི་རྒྱུ་ལ་བསླབ་པ།༣	176-196
34b.6	(1) ཉན་པར་སྐུལ་བ།	176
35a.1	(2) བཤད་པ་དངོས།	177-196
36b.4	c. དཔེ་བྱད་ཀྱི་རྒྱུ་འབྲས་འདིར་རྒྱས་པར་མ་སྨོས་པའི་རྒྱུ་མཚན།	197

GYEL-TSAP	TOPIC AND NUMBER OF DIVISIONS	VERSE
36b.5	d. སངས་རྒྱས་དང་འཁོར་ལོས་བསྒྱུར་བའི་རྒྱལ་པོའི་མཚན་དཔེའི་ཁྱད་པར།༣	198-200
36b.6	(1) འབྲས་བུའི་ཁྱད་པར།	198
37a.2	(2) རྒྱུའི་ཁྱད་པར།	199-200d
37a.3	(3) དཔེ་བཤད་པ།	200efgh
37a.5	C. བླ་ན་མེད་པའི་བྱང་ཆུབ་ཀྱི་རྒྱུ་ཚོགས་གཉིས་ལ་བསླབ་པར་གདམས་པ།༦	201-300
37a.b	1. ཚོགས་སུ་འགྱུར་བའི་ཚུལ།༢	201-11
37a.1	a. རྒྱལ་པོ་ལ་ཉན་པར་སྐུལ་བ།	201
37b.4	b. བསོད་ནམས་ཀྱི་ཚོགས་མཐའ་ཡས་པའི་ཚུལ།༣	202-209
37b.4	(1) དངོས།༥	202-208
37b.4	(a) རང་རྒྱལ་སོགས་ཀྱི་བསོད་ནམས་བཅུར་བསྒྱུར་བའི་ཚད་ཀྱིས་ཐུབ་པའི་བ་སྤུའི་བུ་ག་གཅིག་འགྲུབ་པ།	202-203
38a.2	(b) བ་སྤུའི་བུ་ག་ཐམས་ཅད་འགྲུབ་པའི་བསོད་ནམས་བརྒྱ་འགྱུར་གྱིས་དཔེ་བྱད་གཅིག་འགྲུབ་པ།	204-205
38a.4	(c) དཔེ་བྱད་ཐམས་ཅད་སྐྱེད་པའི་བསོད་ནམས་བརྒྱ་འགྱུར་གྱིས་མཚན་གཅིག་འགྲུབ་པ།	206
38a.4	(d) མཚན་ཐམས་ཅད་སྐྱེད་པའི་བསོད་ནམས་སྟོང་འགྱུར་གྱིས་མཛེད་སྤུ་འགྲུབ་པ།	207
38a.5	(e) དེ་སྐྱེད་པའི་བསོད་ནམས་སྟོང་ཕྲག་བརྒྱར་བསྒྱུར་བས་གཙུག་ཏོར་འགྲུབ་པ།	208
38a.5	(2) ཚད་མེད་ཀྱང་གདུལ་བྱའི་སེམས་ངོར་ཚད་དང་ལྡན་པར་བསྟན་པ།	209

GYEL-TSAP	TOPIC AND NUMBER OF DIVISIONS	VERSE
38b.1	c. ཡེ་ཤེས་ཀྱི་ཚོགས་མཐའ་ཡས་པའི་ཚུལ།	210
38b.1	d. དེ་གཉིས་ཀྱི་འབྲས་བུ་མཐའ་ཡས་པའི་ཚུལ།	211
38b.3	2. འབྲས་བུ་གང་གི་ཚོགས་ཡིན་པ།	212-213
39a.6	3. ཚོགས་གཉིས་གསོག་པ་ལ་སྒྱིད་ལུགས་མི་བྱ་བར་གདམས་པ།༣	214-227
39a.6	a. མདོར་བསྟན་པ།	214
39b.2	b. རྒྱས་པར་བཤད་པ།༢	215-226
39b.2	(1) བསོད་ནམས་ཀྱི་ཚོགས་ལ་སྒྱིད་ལུག་མི་བྱ་བར་གདམས་པ།༣	215-220
39b.3	(a) བྱང་ཆུབ་ཏུ་སེམས་བསྐྱེད་པའི་བསོད་ནམས་མཐའ་ཡས་པ།	215-216
39b.5	(b) རྒྱུ་ངེས་སངས་རྒྱས་ཐོབ་སླ་བ།	217-218
40a.3	(c) དཔག་མེད་བཞི་ལྡན་གྱི་རྒྱུ་མཚན་གྱིས་སངས་རྒྱས་ཐོབ་སླ་བ།	219-220
40a.5	(2) ཚོགས་གཉིས་གསོག་པ་ལ་སྒྱིད་ལུག་མི་བྱ་བར་གདམས་པ།༥	221-226
40a.5	(a) ཚོགས་གཉིས་ཀྱིས་ལུས་སེམས་ཀྱི་སྡུག་བསྔལ་སེལ་བ་སྤྱིར་བསྟན་པ།	221
40b.1	(b) བསོད་ནམས་ཀྱིས་ལུས་ཀྱི་སྡུག་བསྔལ་སེལ་བ།	222
40b.3	(c) ཡེ་ཤེས་ཀྱིས་ཡིད་ཀྱི་སྡུག་བསྔལ་སེལ་བ།	223
40b.6	(d) ཚོགས་གསོག་པ་ལ་སྐྱོ་བའི་རྒྱུ་མེད་པ།	224-225
41a.2	(e) སྙིང་རྗེ་ཆེན་པོའི་ནུས་མཐུ་བསྟན་པ།	226
41a.4	c. དོན་བསྡུ་བ།	227
41a.5	4. ཚོགས་གཉིས་ཀྱི་ངོ་བོ།༣	228-230
41a.5	a. བསོད་ནམས་ཀྱི་འགལ་ཟླ་སྤང་ཞིང་ངོ་བོ་བསྙེན་པར་གདམས་པ།	228
41b.1	b. དུག་གསུམ་དང་དེ་ལས་ལོག་པའི་འབྲས་བུ།	229

GYEL-TSAP	TOPIC AND NUMBER OF DIVISIONS	VERSE
41b.2	c. ཚོགས་གཉིས་དངོས།	230
41b.3	5. ཚོགས་གཉིས་ཀྱི་ཡན་ལག༣	231-276
41b.4	a. མདོར་བསྟན་པ།༣	231-239
41b.4	(1) བསོད་ནམས་ཀྱི་ཚོགས་ཀྱི་ཡན་ལག༣	231-237
41b.4	(a) མཆོད་ཡུལ་སྒྲུབ་པ།༢	231-233
41b.5	1' གསར་དུ་སྒྲུབ་པ།	231-232
42a.1	2' གྲུབ་ཟིན་མཆོད་པ།	233
42a.2	(b) དེ་ལ་མཆོད་པ།	234-236
42a.6	(c) མཆོད་ཡུལ་མིན་པ་མཆོད་པ་དགག་པ།	237
42b.1	(2) ཡེ་ཤེས་ཀྱི་ཚོགས་ཀྱི་ཡན་ལག	238-239
42b.3	b. རྒྱས་བཤད།༢	240-276
42b.3	(1) བསོད་ནམས་ཀྱི་ཚོགས་ཀྱི་ཡན་ལག༤	240-264
42b.4	(a) རང་གི་རྫས་དངོས་སུ་བྱིན་པའི་ཚོགས།	240-251
43b.4	(b) དེ་ལས་གཞན་པའི་སྦྱིན་པ།	252-256
44a.3	(c) བདོག་པ་ཀུན་བཏང་བ།	257-258
44a.5	(d) དོན་དུ་གཉེར་བའི་ཁྱད་པར་ལ་ལྟོས་པའི་སྦྱིན་པ།༣	259-264
44a.5	1' མོའི་བྱེ་བྲག་དོན་དུ་གཉེར་བ་ལ་བྱིན་པ།	259-260
44b.2	2' བདོག་པ་ཀུན་དོན་དུ་གཉེར་བ་ལ་སྦྱིན་པ།	261
44b.3	3' ཆོས་དང་མཐུན་པའི་སྦྱིན་པ།	262-264
44b.5	(2) ཡེ་ཤེས་ཀྱི་ཚོགས་ཀྱི་ཡན་ལག	265-276

GYEL-TSAP	TOPIC AND NUMBER OF DIVISIONS	VERSE
45b.6	6. ཚོགས་གསོག་པ་པོ་ཕན་ཡོན་འབྱུང་བའི་ཚུལ།༣	277-300
46a.1	a. ཐུན་མོང་གི་ཡོན་ཏན་ལྔ་འབྱུང་བ།	277-280
46a.6	b. ཁྱད་པར་གྱི་ཡོན་ཏན་ཉེར་ལྔ་འབྱུང་བ།	281-300
48a.5	D. རྒྱལ་པོའི་སྤྱོད་ཚུལ་ཁ་ན་མ་ཐོ་བ་མེད་པ་ལ་བསླབ་པར་གདམས་པ།༢	301-400
48a.6	1. འབྲེལ་དགོད་པ།༣	301-306
48a.6	a. རྒྱལ་པོའི་ངོར་སྨྲ་མི་ནུས་ཤིང་ཕལ་ཆེར་བསྔོད་པས་ཞིགས་བཤད་གསན་ b. རིགས་པ།	301-303
48b.4	c. ཕན་པའི་ཚིག་ཉན་པར་སྟོན་པས་གསུངས་པ་བཞིན་བསླབ་པར་བསྟན་པ།	304
48b.6	2. རང་གཞན་ལ་ཕན་པའི་ཚིག་ཉན་པར་སྐུལ་བ་དངོས།	305-306
49a.2	2. རྒྱས་པར་བཤད་པ།༣	307-398
49a.2	a. རྒྱལ་པོའི་ཚུལ་ལུགས།༥	307-327
49a.3	(1) སྦྱིན་གཏོང་སྤེལ་བ།	307-308
49b.1	(2) གཙུག་ལག་ཁང་བཟུང་བ།༣	309-317
49b.1	(a) བསམ་སྦྱོར་རྒྱ་ཆེ་བ་ལ་བསླབ་པ།	309
49b.2	(b) ཚོས་བཞི་པོ་རབ་སྒྲུབ་པ།	310
49b.3	(c) ཁྱད་པར་སྒྲུབ་པ།	311-317
50a.5	(3) སྔར་ཡོད་ཀྱི་ནར་མའི་ཟས་ལ་སོགས་པ་བསྐྱང་བ།༣	318-320
50a.6	(a) སྤྱིར་བསྟན་པ།	318
50a.1	(b) གཉེར་པ་བསྐོ་བ།	319
50b.2	(c) སྔོམས་པར་བསྐྱང་བ།	320

GYEL-TSAP	TOPIC AND NUMBER OF DIVISIONS	VERSE
50b.3	(4) དོན་དུ་མི་གཉེར་བ་ཡང་རྗེས་སུ་བཟུང་བ།	321
50b.4	(5) དཔོན་སྣ་བསྒོ་བའི་ཚུལ།༤	322-327
50b.4	(a) ཆོས་དཔོན་བསྒོ་བ།	322
50b.6	(b) བཀའ་ལ་གཏོགས་པ།	323
51a.2	(c) དམག་དཔོན་བསྒོ་བ།	324
51a.3	(d) ནོར་གྱི་གཉེར་ལ་སོགས་པ་སྒོ་བ།	325-327
51b.1	b. མི་ཉམས་ཤིང་འགྲུབ་པར་བསླབ་པ།༢	328-345
51b.2	(1) ཆོས་སྤྱོར་ཡོད་མི་ཉམས་པ་ལ་བསླབ་པ།༢	328-337
51b.2	(a) འབྲེལ་དགོད་པ།	328
51b.4	(b) དངོས་ཀྱི་དོན།༤	329-337
51b.4	1' དབང་བྱེད་ཁྱད་པར་ཅན་བསྟུ་བ།	329
52a.1	2' རང་ཉིད་བརྩེ་བ་དང་ལྡན་པ་བྱ་བ།༣	330-332
52a.2	a' བརྩེ་བས་བཟུང་བར་བྱ་བ།	330
52a.3	b' སྡིག་བྱེད་པ་ལ་ཁྱད་པར་དུ་སྙིང་རྗེ་བྱ་བ།	331
52a.4	c' དེའི་འཐད་པ།	332
52a.6	3' བཙོན་བཏང་ཞིང་བཙོན་གྱི་ཚེ་ཡང་བདེ་བར་བྱ་བ།༣	333-336
52b.4	4' ལས་རུང་དུ་བྱ་མི་རུང་ན་ཡུལ་ནས་བསྐྲད་པ།	337
52b.6	(2) ཆོས་སྤྱོར་མེད་འགྲུབ་པ་ལ་བསླབ་པ།༢	338-345
52b.6	(a) ཆོས་སྒྲུབ་པ།༢	338-342
52b.6	1' བྱ་མ་རྟ་ཁྱད་པར་ཅན་བྱ་བ།	338-339

GYEL-TSAP	TOPIC AND NUMBER OF DIVISIONS	VERSE
53a.3	2' དེའི་དཔེ།	340-342
53a.6	(b) ཆོས་མིན་དགག་པ།	343-345
53b.4	c. ཐར་པ་ཐོབ་ཅིང་ཐེག་པ་ཆེན་པོའི་སྤྱི་སྟོད་མི་སྤྱོང་བ།༣	346-398
53b.4	(1) ཐར་པའི་ལམ་ལ་བསླབ་པ།༣	346-66
53b.4	(a) སྲིད་པའི་ཡུལ་ཚོར་བ་བདེ་སྡུག་རང་བཞིན་གྱིས་གྲུབ་པ་དགག་པ།༣	346-364
53b.6	1' ཚོར་བ་བདེ་བ་རང་མཚན་པ་དགག་པ།༣	346-361
53b.6	a' འབྲེལ་དགོད།	346-347
54a.6	b' མདོར་བསྟན་པ།	348
54b.1	c' རྒྱས་པར་བཤད་པ།༣	349-361
54b.1	1" བདེ་བ་རང་མཚན་པའི་སྒྲུབ་བྱེད་དགག་པ།༣	349-361
54b.1	a" ཡིད་ཀྱི་བདེ་བ་རང་མཚན་པའི་སྒྲུབ་བྱེད་དགག་པ།	349-350
54b.5	b" ལུས་ཀྱི་བདེ་བ་རང་མཚན་པའི་སྒྲུབ་བྱེད་དགག་པ།༣	351-360
54b.5	1: ཡུལ་ལྔ་བསྡུས་པ་དེའི་སྒྲུབ་བྱེད་ཡིན་པ་དགག་པ།	351-353
55a.4	2: རེ་རེ་བ་སྒྲུབ་བྱེད་ཡིན་པ་དགག་པ།༣	354-360
55a.4	a: དངོས།	354
55a.6	b: སྒྲུབ་བྱེད་དགག་པ།༣	355-360
55a.6	1* རྣམ་ཤེས་རང་བཞིན་གྱིས་གྲུབ་པ་དགག་པ།	355
55b.3	2* ཡུལ་རང་བཞིན་གྱིས་གྲུབ་དགག་པ།	356-357
56a.1	3* དབང་པོ་རང་བཞིན་གྱིས་གྲུབ་དགག་པ།༣	358-360

GYEL-TSAP	TOPIC AND NUMBER OF DIVISIONS	VERSE
56a.1	a* འབྱུང་བ་རང་བཞིན་གྱིས་གྲུབ་པ་བཀག་པས་དབང་དོན་རང་བཞིན་གྱིས་གྲུབ་པ་དགག་པ།	358
56a.3	b* འབྱུང་བ་རང་བཞིན་གྱིས་གྲུབ་དགག་པ།	359
56a.3	c* དེས་ན་གཟུགས་རང་བཞིན་གྱིས་མ་གྲུབ་པ།	360
56a.5	2" བདེ་བ་རང་མཚན་པའི་ངོ་བོ་དགག་པ།	361
56b.1	2' སྡུག་བསྔལ་རང་བཞིན་གྱིས་གྲུབ་པ་དགག་པ།	362
56b.4	3' བཀག་པའི་འབྲས་བུ།༢	363-364
56b.4	a' སྟོང་ཉིད་རྟོགས་པས་གྲོལ་བར་བསྟན་པ།	363
56b.6	b' སྟོང་ཉིད་རྟོགས་པའི་ཡུལ་ཅན་གྱི་བློ་ངོས་བཟུང་བ།	364
57a.5	(b) ཐེག་པ་ཆེ་ཆུང་གཉིས་ཀས་སྟོང་ཉིད་ཕྲ་མོ་རྟོགས་པ་མཚུངས་པར་བསྟན་པ།༢	365-366
57a.5	1' ཐར་པ་ཙམ་ཐོབ་པ་ལ་སྟོང་ཉིད་ཕྲ་མོ་རྟོགས་དགོས་པ།	365
57b.2	2' ཐེག་པ་ཆེ་ཆུང་གི་ཁྱད་པར།	366
57b.4	(2) ཐེག་ཆེན་གྱི་སྡེ་སྣོད་སྤོང་བ་དགག་པ།༢	367-398
57b.5	(a) རྒྱས་པར་བཤད་པ།༣	367-396
57b.5	1' ཐེག་ཆེན་གྱི་སྡེ་སྣོད་སྤོང་བ་མི་རིགས་པའི་རྒྱུ་མཚན།༢	367-379
57b.6	a' ཐེག་ཆེན་ལ་སྨོད་པའི་ཉེས་དམིགས།༢	367-371
57b.6	1" ཐེག་ཆེན་ལ་སྨོད་པའི་ཚུལ།	367
58a.2	2" སྨོད་པའི་རྒྱུ།	368-369
58a.5	3" སྨོད་པའི་ཉེས་དམིགས།	370-371

GYEL-TSAP	TOPIC AND NUMBER OF DIVISIONS	VERSE
58b.2	b' ངེས་ན་སྤང་བར་མི་རིགས་པ།༥	372-379
58b.2	1" སྡུག་བསྔལ་ཆུང་ངུས་ཀྱང་ཆེན་པོ་བསལ་རིགས་པ།	372
58b.3	2" ཐེག་ཆེན་གྱི་སྤྱོད་པ་ལ་སྡུག་བསྔལ་བ་ཙུང་ཟད་ཡོད་ཀྱང་གཏན་གྱི་སྡུག་བསྔལ་སེལ་བྱེད་དེ་ལ་སྤང་མི་རིགས་པ།	373-374
59a.3	3" བདེ་བ་ཆེན་པོའི་དོན་དུ་འབད་རིགས་ཀྱི་ཆུང་ངུ་ལ་ཆགས་པ་མི་རིགས་པ།	375-377
59b.2	4" ཐེག་པ་ཆེན་པོ་ལ་དགའ་བར་རིགས་པ།	378
59b.4	5" དོན་བསྡུ་བ།	379
59b.6	2' ཐེག་ཆེན་གྱི་སྡེ་སྣོད་བཀར་སྒྲུབ་པ།༣	380-389
59b.6	a' ཕར་ཕྱིན་གྱི་སྤྱོད་པ་བསྟན་པ།༣	380-382
60a.1	1" ཐེག་ཆེན་གྱི་སྡེ་སྣོད་ལ་ཉེས་བཤད་ཙུང་ཟད་ཀྱང་མེད་པ།	380
60a.3	2" ཐེག་པ་ཆེན་པོའི་དོན་དེ་ལས་བསྟན་པ།	381
60a.6	3" དེས་ན་སྡེ་སྣོད་དེ་ཉིད་བཀར་གྲུབ་པ།	382
60b.2	b' བྱང་ཆུབ་ཆེན་པོའི་ལམ་རྟོགས་པ་དེ་ལས་ཤེས་དགོད་པ།	383
60b.3	c' སངས་རྒྱས་ཀྱི་ཆེ་བའི་བདག་ཉིད་དེ་ལས་རྟོགས་པར་ཤེས་དགོས་པས་བཀར་སྒྲུབ་པ།༣	384-389
60b.3	1" གཟུགས་སྐུའི་རྒྱུ་མཐའ་ཡས་པ་ཐེག་ཆེན་ལས་གསུངས་པ།	384-385
61a.3	2" ཐེག་དམན་གྱི་སྡེ་སྣོད་ནས་བཤད་པའི་ཟད་པའི་ཤེས་པ་དང་། ཐེག་ཆེན་གྱི་སྡེ་སྣོད་ནས་བཤད་པའི་ཟད་སྐྱེ་མི་ཤེས་པ་སྟོང་ཉིད་རྟོགས་པའི་དོན་དུ་གཅིག་པ།	386-387

GYEL-TSAP	TOPIC AND NUMBER OF DIVISIONS	VERSE
61b.6	3" ཐེག་པ་ཆེན་པོའི་དོན་མ་རྟོགས་ན་བཏང་སྙོམས་སུ་བཞག་པར་རིགས་ཀྱི་སྨད་པར་མི་རིགས་པ།	388-389
62a.2	3' ཐེག་དམན་གྱི་སྡེ་སྣོད་ནས་བཤད་པ་ཐེག་པ་ཆེན་པོའི་ལམ་འབྲས་རྫོགས་པ་མིན་པ།༣	390-393
62a.3	a' ཉན་ཐོས་ཀྱི་སྡེ་སྣོད་ལས་བྱང་ཆུབ་སེམས་དཔའི་སྤྱོད་པ་རྫོགས་པར་མ་གསུངས་པ།	390-391
62b.3	b' བདེན་བཞི་དང་ཕྱོགས་མཐུན་ཙམ་ཉམས་སུ་བླངས་པས་སངས་རྒྱས་མི་འགྲུབ་པ།	392
62b.5	c' མཁས་པས་ཐེག་ཆེན་གྱི་སྡེ་སྣོད་བཀར་བཟུང་རིགས་པ།	393
62b.6	4' ཐེག་པ་གསུམ་བསྟན་པའི་དགོས་པ།	394-396
63b.5	(b) དོན་བསྡུ་བ།	397-398
63b.1	3. དོན་བསྡུ་བ།	399
63b.2	4. རྒྱལ་པོའི་ཀུན་སྤྱོད་ཁྱད་པར་ཅན་ལ་སློབ་མི་ནུས་ན་རབ་འབྱུང་བྱ་བ་གདམས་པ།	400
63b.4	E. ཐར་པ་མྱུར་དུ་ཐོབ་པར་འདོད་པའི་བྱང་ཆུབ་སེམས་དཔས་ཀྱང་རབ་ཏུ་འབྱུང་བར་གདམས་པ།༣	401-487
63b.4	1. ཁྱིམ་པ་དང་རབ་ཏུ་བྱུང་བའི་བྱང་ཆུབ་སེམས་དཔའི་བླང་དོར་གྱི་གནས་མདོར་བསྟན་པ།༣	401-402
64a.1	2. རྒྱས་པར་བཤད་པ།༣	403-487
64a.1	a. སྐྱོན་སྤང་བ།༣	403-434b
64a.1	(1) རྒྱས་པར་བཤད་པ།༣	403-434b

GYEL-TSAP	TOPIC AND NUMBER OF DIVISIONS	VERSE
64a.2	(a) ཁྲོ་བ་སོགས་དང་པོ་བཅོ་ལྔར་བཤད་པ།༣	403-413
64a.2	1' ཁྲོ་བ་སོགས་བཅུ་བཞི་བཤད་པ།	403-406b
64b.1	2' ང་རྒྱལ་བཤད་པ།	406c-412
65a.2	(b) ཚུལ་ཆོས་ནས་ཞི་གཅིག་པ་མི་འཆི་བའི་ཏོག་པའི་བར་བཤད་པ།	413-425
66a.2	(c) ཞི་གཉིས་པ་རང་གི་ཡོན་ཏན་སྒྲོག་པ་སོགས་བཤད་པ།	426-433
66b.5	(2) དོན་བསྡུ་བ།	434ab
66b.6	b. ཡོན་ཏན་བླང་བ།༣	434c-487
66b.6	(1) གནས་སྐབས་ཀྱི་ཡོན་ཏན།༣	434c-461b
66b.6	(a) སྤྱིར་བསྟན་པ།༢	434c-439
67a.1	1' ཡོན་གྱི་ངོ་བོ་བསྡུས་ཏེ་བསྟན་པ།	434c-435
67a.3	2' སོ་སོའི་ངོ་བོ་ངོས་བཟུང་བ།	436-437
67a.6	3' སོ་སོའི་འབྲས་བུ།	438
67b.1	4' ཐུན་མོང་གི་འབྲས་བུ།	439
67b.2	(b) ས་བཅུའི་ཡོན་ཏན།༣	440-461b
68a.6	1' ཉན་ཐོས་ཀྱི་ས་བརྒྱད་ཡོད་པ་ལྟར་བྱང་ཆུབ་སེམས་དཔའི་ས་བཅུ་དབྱེ་ བ།	440
68b.2	2' ས་བཅུའི་སོ་སོའི་ངོ་བོ་ཡོན་ཏན་དང་བཅས་པ།	441-460
71a.4	3' དོན་བསྡུ་བ།	461ab
71a.5	(2) མཐར་ཐུག་གི་ཡོན་ཏན།༣	461c-487
71a.6	(a) སངས་རྒྱས་ཀྱི་ཡོན་ཏན་རེ་རེའང་ཚད་མེད་པར་བསྟན་པ།༣	461c-463

GYEL-TSAP	TOPIC AND NUMBER OF DIVISIONS	VERSE
71a.6	1' སངས་རྒྱས་ཀྱི་ཡོན་ཏན་མཐའ་ཡས་པ་སྟོབས་བཅུ་ལ་བརྟེན་པ།	461c-462b
71b.1	2' ཡོན་ཏན་ཚད་མེད་པའི་དཔེ།	462c-463
71b.2	(b) དེ་ལ་ཡིད་ཆེས་ཤིང་མོས་པ་སྐྱེད་པའི་རྒྱུ།༢	464-487
71b.3	1' སངས་རྒྱས་ཀྱི་ཡོན་ཏན་ཚད་མེད་པ་དེའི་རྒྱུ་མཚན་དེ་ཡི་རྒྱུ་ཕྱུག་ལ་སོགས་པ་བསོད་ནམས་ཚད་མེད་པ།༣	464-468
71b.4	a' སངས་རྒྱས་ཡོན་ཏན་ཚད་མེད་པའི་ཤེས་བྱེད།	464
71b.6	b' བསོད་ནམས་ཚད་མེད་གསོག་པའི་ཚུལ།	465
72a.2	c' ཡན་ལག་བདུན་པར་བསྡུས་ཏེ་བསྟན་པ།	465-468
72a.6	2' ཕན་བྱ་ཚད་མེད་པ་ལ་ཕན་པར་སྨོན་པས་རྒྱུ་ཚད་མེད།	469-485
73b.6	3' ཡོན་ཏན་གྱི་བསོད་ནམས་ཚད་བཟུང་མི་ནུས་པ།	486
74a.2	4' ཤེས་བྱེད་དགོད་པ།	487
74a.5	III. བཤད་པ་མཐར་ཕྱིན་པའི་བྱ་བ།༥	488-500
74a.5	A. ཆོས་ལ་སྤྲོ་བ་སྐྱེད་ཅིང་ཆོས་བཞི་བསྟེན་པར་གདམས་པ།༣	488-490
74b.6	B. དགེ་བའི་བཤེས་གཉེན་ལ་སྐྲག་པའི་ཉེས་དམིགས་དགེ་བཤེས་ཀྱི་མཚན་ཉིད་དང་བཅས་པ།༣	491-493b
75a.4	C. སྤྱོད་ཚུལ་ཕུན་སུམ་ཚོགས་པས་འབྲས་བུ་མཆོག་འགྲུབ་པ།༣	493c-497
75a.4	1. འབྲས་བུ་མཆོག་འགྲུབ་པ།	493cd
75a.5	2. སྤྱོད་ཚུལ་ཁྱད་པར་ཅན་བྱ་བར་གདམས་པ།༣	494-497
75a.5	a. སྤྱོད་ཚུལ་རྒྱས་པ།	494-495
75b.3	b. བསྡུས་པ།	496

GYEL-TSAP	TOPIC AND NUMBER OF DIVISIONS	VERSE
75b.4	c. ཤིན་ཏུ་བསྟུས་པ།	497
75b.5	D. ཆོས་འདི་རྒྱལ་པོར་མ་ཟད་གཞན་དང་ཡང་ཐུན་མོང་བ་ཡིན་པ།	498
76a.1	E. རྒྱལ་པོ་དེ་ལ་ཉན་པར་བསྐུལ་བ།༢	499-500
76a.1	1. གཞན་དོན་རྒྱུན་དུ་བསམ་པར་རིགས་པ།	499
76a.3	2. ཡོན་ཏན་བླང་བར་རོགས་པ།	500

Emendations to the Tibetan Text

Key

G = Gyel-tsap, *dbu ma rin chen 'phreng ba'i snying po'i don gsal bar byed pa,* Collected Works (lha sa: zhol par khang, 15th rab 'byung in the fire rooster year, i.e., 1897), *ka* (78 folios).

P = *Tibetan Tripiṭaka* (Tokyo-Kyoto: Tibetan Tripiṭaka Research Foundation, 1956), translated by the Indian Jñānagarbha and the Tibetan L̄u-gyel-tsen (*klu'i rgyal mtshan*) and emended by the Indian Kanakavarman and the Tibetan B̄a-tsap Nyi-ma-drak (*pa tshab nyi ma grags*).

S = P. L. Vaidya, *Madhyamakaśāstra of Nāgārjuna,* Buddhist Sanskrit Texts: 10 (Darbhanga: Mithila Institute, 1960), 296-310; and Michael Hahn, *Nāgārjuna's Ratnāvalī,* vol. 1, The Basic Texts (Sanskrit, Tibetan, and Chinese), (Bonn: Indica et Tibetica Verlag, 1982).[a]

Z = *zhol* edition, Translated by the Indian Vidyākaraprabha (*rigs byed 'od zer*) and the Tibetan Translator from Shu-chen B̄el-d̄zek (*zhu chen kyi lo tstsha ba dpal brtsegs*) and emended by the Indian Kanakavarman and the Tibetan B̄a-tsap Nyi-ma-drak (*pa tshab nyi ma grags*).

verse	*zhol edition*	*emendation*	*source*
13b	shid	shing	GPS
27d	pu	tu	GP
29c	gis	gi	GS (P: gis)
31a	de	ji	GPS
31c	ni	na	GP
34b	thob	thos	PS (G: thob)
37a	bzhin	gzhan	GPS
38b	na	nas	GPS
39b	pas	pa	GPS
41d	khyo ko ces	khyod ko cis	GPS
45c	yi	yis	GS (P: yi)
47b	min don	med do	GP[b]
49a	med	yod	G (P: ring po lta na thung ba nyid)[c]

[a] The Sanskrit references are primarily to the former since the editorial work was mostly done in 1972 and thus do not take account of Hahn's emendations.

[b] The Sanskrit is *hetur āhetur 'rthataḥ* (Hahn, 20), which translated into Tibetan more likely would be *rgyu ni don du rgyu med do.*

[c] The Sanskrit could be either.

verse	*zhol edition*	*emendation*	*source*
between 49b & 49c	*extra line eliminated:* yod min rang bzhin las min phyir		GPS
50c	pa	pas	GP
51d	brtan	brten	GP
54d	mngon	don	GPS
61c	pa	la	GPS
62a	kyis	kyi	GPS
62d	kyis	gyis	GS
63a	na	nas	G
67d	rnams	rnam	GS (P: rnams)
71c	du ma dang	du ma'ang med	GPS
79a	'dis	'das	GP
81d	gang	yang	GP
87a	gzhan bdag med	grags yin na	GP
88c	yod pa yin pa	yod ma yin pa	GP
98a	sdun	sngon	GP
102c	pa	par	G
103a	par	pa	G
106b	med	min	GS
106d	*variant:* Z: ji ltar; GP: ji skad		
115a	gnyis	kyis	GS
122b	po	ba	GPS
123a	yod pa	spong ba	GPS
124b	par	pa	G
128b	kyi	kyis	GS
132c	de	des	G
135a	min te	smra ste	G (P: min)
135b	pa las byung	pas bsgyur ba	GP
135c	na	la	GPS
135c	pu	tu	GPS
137d	bstan	bsten	GPS
138a	pa	pas	GPS
140b	rjes	rje	P
143a	dang	dag	GPS
145a	mang	med	GPS
149d	mi rdu	mig rdul	Ajitamitra
153d	kha cig	phag rnams	GP
155a	kyi	kyis	G
156a	yis	yi	G
158d	las	la	GP
161a	bzhin du	'di yang	GP

verse	*zhol edition*	*emendation*	*source*
163a	snod	smod	GP
168a	bsgrubs	bsgribs	GP
171d	spong byed brten por	gsod med brtan por	P (G: gsod med brten par)
176c	gyur	'gyur	G
181c	tshe	che	G (P: tshe)
184a	blangs	bslangs	G
185a	dang	dag	GP
185c	lba	sba	GP
185d	pa dag tu	pa'i dam par	GP
187b	pas	par	GP
192c	ge	ge'i	GP
194a	yis	yi	GP
194d	thag	thags	G
201c	lung can	lung chen	GP
between 208 & 209	*extra five-line stanza eliminated:* gtsug tor bsod nams bye ba dag/ 'bum phrag brgya ni bsgres pa yis/ grangs med rgya chen bcu po dag/ sangs rgyas gsung gi sgra dbyangs ni/ yan lag drug cu bskyed pa'i mchog//		G
209a	de dag	de ltar	GP
211d	bag	dpag	GP
212a	'dir	ni	GP
213b	zhing	nyid	GP
218b	sogs	sog	G
218d	zhes	shes	G
223b	dang	sdang	GP
223c	de ni de brten med par shes	des rten med pa'i shes pa yis	GP
224b	smras	smas	GP
228b	spong	spongs	GP
229b	gi	gis	GP
231a	can	dang	GP
232a	la	las	G
233b	bskyed	bskyang	GP
235a	dang	ni	GP
235c	kyi	bgyi	GP
235d	chos drug gus pas	chos ni nges par	both given in G
238c	snyug	smyug	GP
239c	bstsal	brtsal	P
240d	brngan	brtan	G
241a	'dron	'gron	G (P: 'dron)
241b	bdun	mdun	GP
242b	bdun	mdun	GP

verse	*zhol edition*	*emendation*	*source*
243d	bstan	bsten	(P: brten; G: bstan)
246c	ras	rar	GP
247b	byis pa'i	bal dang	GP
247c	bzang	zangs	GP
248c	dang	tu	GP
249b	'bru mar	bu ram	GP
251c	'pham 'gyur	pham gyur	GP
253a	nyon	nyen	GP
255a	blun po	blon pos	GP
255b	mdzod	mdzad	G
257d	spyod	spyad	GP
265a	smras	smra	GP
266a	mdzad	mdzod	G (P: mdzad)
273a	tshegs	tshogs	GP
274c	nyam	nyams	GP
275c	ni	na	GP
280d	bde bar	bde ba	GP
281d	pas	pa'i	GP
286b	brten	brtan	GP
296b	dang	dag	GP
296d	thob	'thob	GP
299d	'gro	'phro	GP
301b	ba'i	bas	GP
301c	pas	pa	GPS
303a	kyi	kyis	GP
305c	pa'i	po'i	GPS
306b	bgyis	bgyid	PS
307b	brnyed	brnyes	GPS
308c	rngan	dman	GPS
309b	bgyis	dgyes	GPS
314b	sar	gsar	G
316d	stong	spyod	G
318c	legs	lags	GPS
322b	gna'	sna	GPS
325b	gna'	sna	GPS
329b	rig	rigs	GS
329c	bshin	gshin	GPS
330a	sbyo	sogs	combining GPS
333b	brtson	btson	GPS
337c	bgyis par	bgyi bar	GP

verse	*zhol edition*	*emendation*	*source*
339c	rjes mthun sbyar bya zhing	rjes su mthun sbyor zhing	G
between 341 & 342	*two lines eliminated:* des na de ltar rigs pa bsten/ rigs pa yis ni rgyal srid 'gyur		GP
343b	bsnams	bsnam	GS
343c	rnyed	brnyes	GS
346c	ngang	ste	P
350b	grag	grags	GP
between 353a & 353b	*one line eliminated:* rnam par shes pa 'byung bar bshad[a]		GS
356bcd	de gnyis las ni ma 'das phyir/ dbang por bcas don med la gang/ da lta'i yang ni don med do	dbang po dang bcas don med la/ de gnyis[b] las tha dad med phyir/ gang dag da ltar yang don med	PS (G incorporates both)
362a	de	ji	GPS
364a	sems mthong	mthong bar	G (P: sems mthong)
364b	brjod pa ste	sems brjod de	G
365d	'das	'da'	PS
366ab	byang chub sems dpa'ang de ltar na/ drzogs pa'i byang chub nges par 'dod	de ltar byang chub sems dpas kyang/ mthong nas byang chub nges par 'dod	GPS
367d	pos smad	bas smod	GPS
373b	pa	pas	GPS
374a	phyi	phyis	GPS
386b	khyed kyis	gzhan gyi	GPS
387b	bstan	ltas	GPS
391a	dpas	dpa'i	GPS
392a	*variant:* Z: rten rnams; GP, byin rlabs		
393d	zung	bzung	GPS
396b	'phrig	'khrig	GPS
398d	zhing las	zhar la	GPS
400b	kyi	kyis	GS
400b	bgyi bka'	bgyid dka'	GP
404b	rgyu	sgyu	GP
406d	bye	phye	GP
407d	mnyam pa'i	bdag nyid	GP
408a	dman	chos	GP
408bc	*(missing)*	mnyam par rlom pa gang yin te/ lhag pa'i nga rgyal khyad 'phags pas/	GP
414d	gsum	sum	GP

[a] This line is given later at 355d.

[b] P: nyid.

verse	*zhol edition*	*emendation*	*source*
417a	kyi	gang	GP
422a	bskam	brkam	GP
422b	mchog	chog	GP
424c	'bral	'brel	GP
425d	pas dogs	pas mi dogs	G (P: mi dgongs)
426c	dogs	bdog	GP
428c	snyom	snyoms	GP
429b	kha ni	kha dog	P
433c	par	dang	GP
434b	gyis ni	can gyis	GP
434c	nas	na	GP
435a	yi	yis	GP
435b	bstan	bsten	GP
436d	ba yongs 'dzin pa'o	la spro ba nyid	GP
439a	pas	par	GP
454 c	pa'i phyir	shes pa'i	GP
456d	'phrog	'phrogs	GP
458d	'phrog	'phrogs	GP
471b	cen	chen	G
472a	dri	bud	GP
479b	'jig	'jigs	GP
480c	mar	ma	GP
482b	'gyur	gyur	GP
491c	don	ngan	GP
493a	bsten	bstan	G (P: bsnyen)
493b	khyed kyis mkhyen gyi	khyod kyis mkhyen gyis	GP
495a	stong	gtong	GP
495d	nges par	des par	see n. a, 164
495d	nges pa	des pa	see n. b, 164
497b	'gyur	gyur	GP
499b	bsgrub	'grub	GP
500c	phangs	phongs	GP
chap. title	*(missing)*	rin po che'i phreng ba las/ byang chub sems dpa'i spyod pa'i le'u bstan pa ste lnga pa'o//	P

BIBLIOGRAPHY

Sūtras and tantras are listed alphabetically by English title in the first section. Indian and Tibetan treatises are listed alphabetically by author in the second section; other works are listed alphabetically by author in the third section.

"P," standing for "Peking edition," refers to the *Tibetan Tripiṭaka* (Tokyo-Kyoto: Tibetan Tripiṭaka Research Foundation, 1956). "Toh" refers to the *Complete Catalogue of the Tibetan Buddhist Canons*, ed. by Prof. Hukuji Ui, and *A Catalogue of the Tohuku University Collection of Tibetan Works on Buddhism*, ed. by Prof. Yensho Kanakura (Sendai, Japan: 1934 and 1953). "Dharma" refers to the *sde dge* edition of the Tibetan canon published by Dharma Publishing—the *Nying-ma Edition of the sDe-dge bKa'-'gyur and bsTan-'gyur* (Oakland, CA: Dharma Publishing, 1980). "Tokyo *sde dge*" refers to the *sDe dge Tibetan Tripitaka—bsTan hgyur preserved at the Faculty of Letters, University of Tokyo*, (Tokyo: 1977ff.). "Karmapa *sde dge*" refers to the *sde dge mtshal par bka' 'gyur: a facsimile edition of the 18th century redaction of Si tu chos kyi 'byung gnas prepared under the direction of H.H. the 16th rgyal dbang karma pa* (Delhi: Delhi Karmapae Chodhey Gyalwae Sungrab Partun Khang, 1977). "*Golden Reprint*" refers to the *gser bris bstan 'gyur* (Sichuan, China: krung go'i mtho rim nang bstan slob gling gi bod brgyud nang bstan zhib 'jug khang, 1989).

1 SŪTRAS AND TANTRAS

Descent Into Laṅkā Sūtra
laṅkāvatārasūtra
lang kar gshegs pa'i mdo
P775, vol. 29
Sanskrit: *Saddharmalaṅkāvatārasūtram*. P. L. Vaidya, ed. Buddhist Sanskrit Texts No. 3. Darbhanga: Mithila Institute, 1963. Also: Bunyiu Nanjio, ed. Bibl. Otaniensis, vol. I. Kyoto: Otani University Press, 1923.
English translation: D. T. Suzuki. *The Lankavatara Sutra*. London: Routledge and Kegon Paul, 1932.

Excellent Golden Light Sūtra
suvarṇaprabhāsottama
phags pa gser 'od dam pa mcho tu rnam par rgyal ba'i mdo sde'i rgyal po theg pa chen po'i mdo
P174, vol. 6-7
Sanskrit: Nobel, Johannes, ed. *Suvarnaprabhāsottamasūtra, Das Goldglanz-Sūtra*. Leiden: Brill, 1950.

Great Drum Sūtra
mahābherīhārakaparivartasūtra
rnga bo che chen po'i le'u'i mdo
P888, vol. 35

Mañjushrī Root Tantra
mañjuśrīmūlakalpa
'jam dpal tsa ba'i rtog pa
P162, vol. 6

Sūtra on the Ten Grounds
daśabhūmikasūtra
mdo sde sa bcu pa
P761.31, vol. 25
Sanskrit: *Daśabhūmikasūtram*. P. L. Vaidya, ed. Buddhist Sanskrit Texts No.7. Darbhanga: Mithila Institute, 1967
English translation: M. Honda. "An Annotated Translation of the 'Daśabhūmika'." in D. Sinor, ed, *Studies in Southeast and Central Asia*, Śatapitaka Series 74. New Delhi: 1968, 115-276

2 OTHER SANSKRIT AND TIBETAN WORKS

Ajitamitra (*mi pham bshes gnyen*)
Extensive Commentary on (Nāgārjuna's) "Precious Garland"
ratnāvaliṭīkā
rin po che'i phreng ba'i rgya cher bshad pa
P5659, vol. 129; Golden Reprint, vol. 183, *nge*

Āryadeva (*'phags pa lha*, second to third century, C.E.)
Compilation of the Essence of Wisdom
jñānasārasamuccaya

ye shes snying po kun las btus pa
P5251, vol. 95

Four Hundred/ Treatise of Four Hundred Stanzas
catuḥśatakaśāstrakārikā
bstan bcos bzhi brgya pa zhes bya ba'i tshig le'ur byas pa
P5246, vol. 95
Edited Tibetan and Sanskrit fragments along with English translation: Karen Lang. "Āryadeva on the Bodhisattva's Cultivation of Merit and Knowledge." Ann Arbor: University Microfilms, 1983.
English translation: *Yogic Deeds of Bodhisattvas: Gyel-tsap on Āryadeva's Four Hundred.* Commentary by Geshe Sonam Rinchen, translated and edited by Ruth Sonam. Ithaca: Snow Lion Publications: 1994.
Italian translation of the last half from the Chinese: Giuseppe Tucci, "La versione cinese del Catuḥśataka di Āryadeva, confronta col testo sanscrito et la traduzione tibetana." *Rivista degli Studi Orientalia* 10 (1925), 521-567.

Chandrakīrti (*zla ba grags pa,* seventh century)

[Auto]commentary on the "Supplement to (Nāgārjuna's) 'Treatise on the Middle Way'"
madhaymakāvatārabhāṣya
dbu ma la 'jug pa'i bshad pa/ dbu ma la 'jug pa'i rang 'grel
P5263, vol. 98. Also: Dharamsala: Council of Religious and Cultural Affairs, 1968.
Edited Tibetan: Louis de la Vallée Poussin. *Madhyamakāvatāra par Candrakīrti.* Bibliotheca Buddhica IX. Osnabrück: Biblio Verlag, 1970.
French translation (up to VI.165): Louis de la Vallée Poussin. *Muséon* 8 (1907), 249-317; *Muséon* 11 (1910), 271-358; and *Muséon* 12 (1911), 235-328.
German translation (VI.166-226): Helmut Tauscher. *Candrakīrti-Madhyamakāvatāraḥ und Madhyamakāvatārabhāṣyam.* Wien: Wiener Studien zur Tibetologie und Buddhismuskunde, 1981.

Clear Words, Commentary on (Nāgārjuna's) "Treatise on the Middle"
mūlamadhyamakavṛttiprasannapadā
dbu ma rtsa ba'i 'grel pa tshig gsal ba
P5260, vol. 98. Also: Dharamsala: Tibetan Publishing House, 1968.
Sanskrit: *Mūlamadhyamakakārikās de Nāgārjuna avec la Prasannapadā Commentaire de Candrakīrti.* Louis de la Vallée Poussin, ed. Bibliotheca Buddhica IV. Osnabrück: Biblio Verlag, 1970.
English translation (Ch. I, XXV): T. Stcherbatsky. *Conception of Buddhist Nirvāṇa.* Leningrad: Office of the Academy of Sciences of the USSR, 1927; revised rpt. Delhi: Motilal Banarsidass, 1978, 77-222.
English translation (Ch. II): Jeffrey Hopkins. "Analysis of Coming and Going." Dharamsala: Library of Tibetan Works and Archives, 1974.
Partial English translation: Mervyn Sprung. *Lucid Exposition of the Middle Way, the Essential Chapters from the Prasannapadā of Candrakīrti translated from the Sanskrit.* London: Routledge, 1979 and Boulder: Prajñā Press, 1979.
French translation (Ch. II-IV, VI-IX, XI, XXIII, XXIV, XXVI, XXVII): Jacques May. *Prasannapadā Madhyamaka-vṛtti, douze chapitres traduits du sanscrit et du tibétain.* Paris: Adrien-Maisonneuve, 1959.
French translation (Ch. XVIII-XXII): J. W. de Jong. *Cinq chapitres de la Prasannapadā.* Paris: Geuthner, 1949.
French translation (Ch. XVII): É. Lamotte. "Le Traité de l'acte de Vasubandhu, Karmasiddhiprakaraṇa," *MCB* 4 (1936), 265-288.
German translation (Ch. V and XII-XVI): St. Schayer. *Ausgewahlte Kapitel aus der Prasannapadā.* Krakow: Naktadem Polskiej Akademji Umiejetnosci, 1931.
German translation (Ch. X): St. Schayer. "Feuer und Brennstoff." *Rocznik Orjentalistyczny* 7 (1931), 26-52.

Commentary on (Āryadeva's) "Four Hundred Stanzas on the Yogic Deeds of Bodhisattvas"
bodhisattvayogacaryācatuḥśatakaṭīkā
byang chub sems dpa'i rnal 'byor spyod pa gzhi brgya pa'i rgya cher 'grel pa
P5266, vol. 98; Toh 3865, Tokyo *sde dge* vol. 8
Edited Sanskrit fragments: Haraprasād Shāstri, ed. "Catuḥśatika of Ārya Deva," Memoirs of the Asiatic Society of Bengal, III no. 8 (1914), 449-514. Also (Ch. 8-16): Vidhusekhara Bhattacarya, ed. *The Catuḥśataka of Āryadeva: Sanskrit and Tibetan texts with copious extracts from the commentary of Candrakīrti,* Part II. Calcutta: Visva-Bharati Bookshop, 1931.

Commentary on (Nāgārjuna's) "Seventy Stanzas on Emptiness"
śūnyatāsaptativṛtti
stong pa nyid bdun cu pa'i 'grel pa
P5268, vol. 99

Commentary on (Nāgārjuna's) "Sixty Stanzas of Reasoning"
yuktiṣaṣṭikāvṛtti
rigs pa drug cu pa'i 'grel pa
P5265, vol. 98
Supplement to (Nāgārjuna's) "Treatise on the Middle"
madhyamakāvatāra
dbu ma la 'jug pa
P5261, P5262, vol. 98
Edited Tibetan: Louis de la Vallée Poussin. *Madhyamakāvatāra par Candrakīrti.* Bibliotheca Buddhica IX. Osnabrück: Biblio Verlag, 1970.
English translation (Ch. I-V): Jeffrey Hopkins. In *Compassion in Tibetan Buddhism.* Valois, NY: Gabriel Snow Lion, 1980.
English translation (Ch. VI): Stephen Batchelor, trans. In Geshé Rabten's *Echoes of Voidness.* London: Wisdom, 1983, 47-92. *See also* references under Chandrakīrti's *[Auto]-Commentary on the "Supplement."*

Ḍzong-ka-ḇa Ḷo-sang-drak-ḇa (*tsong kha pa blo bzang grags pa,* 1357-1419)
Four Interwoven Annotations on (Ḍzong-ka-ḇa's) "Great Exposition of the Stages of the Path"
The Lam rim chen mo of the incomparable Tsong-kha-pa, with the interlineal notes of Ba-so Chos-kyi-rgyal-mtshan, Sde-drug Mkhan-chen Ngag-dbang-rab-rtan, 'Jam-dbyangs-bshad-pa'i-rdo-rje, and Bra-sti Dge-bshes Rin-chen-don-grub
New Delhi: Chos-'phel-legs-ldan, 1972
Illumination of the Thought, Extensive Explanation of (Chandrakīrti's) "Supplement to (Nāgārjuna's) 'Treatise on the Middle Way'"
dbu ma la 'jug pa'i rgya cher bshad pa dgongs pa rab gsal
P6143, vol. 154. Also: Sarnath, India: Pleasure of Elegant Sayings Press, 1973
English translation (first five chapters): Jeffrey Hopkins. In *Compassion in Tibetan Buddhism.* Valois, New York: Snow Lion, 1980.
English translation (commentary on stanzas 1-7 of sixth chapter): Jeffrey Hopkins and Anne C. Klein. In Anne C. Klein *Path to the Middle: Madhyamaka Philosophy in Tibet: The Oral Scholarship of Kensur Yeshay Tupden.* Albany: SUNY Press, 1994. 147-183 and 252-271.
Ocean of Reasoning, Explanation of (Nāgārjuna's) "Treatise on the Middle Way"/ Great Commentary on (Nāgārjuna's) "Treatise on the Middle Way"
dbu ma rtsa ba'i tshig le'ur byas pa shes rab ces bya ba'i rnam bshad rigs pa'i rgya mtsho
P6153, vol. 156. Also: Sarnath, India: Pleasure of Elegant Sayings Printing Press, no date. Also: in *rJe tsong kha pa'i gsung dbu ma'i lta ba'i skor,* vol. 1 and 2, Sarnath, India: Pleasure of Elegant Sayings Press, 1975.

Gyel-tsap-dar-ma-rin-chen (*rgyal tshab dar ma rin chen,* 1364-1432)
Illumination of the Essential Meanings of (Nāgārjuna's) "Precious Garland of Madhyamaka"
dbu ma rin chen 'phreng ba'i snying po'i don gsal bar byed pa
Collected Works, *ka.* lha sa: zhol par khang, 15th rab 'byung in the fire rooster year, i.e., 1897 (78 folios); also, Collected Works, *ka.* New Delhi: Guru Deva, 1982 (349-503, 78 folios), "reproduced from a set of prints from the 1897 lha-sa old zhol (*dga' ldan phun tshogs gling*) blocks." [These are two separate editions.]

Jam-ȳang-shay-ḇa Nga-w̄ang-ḏzön-drü (*'jam dbyangs bzhad pa ngag dbang brtson grus,* 1648-1721)
Great Exposition of Tenets/ Explanation of 'Tenets,' Sun of the Land of Samantabhadra Brilliantly Illuminating All of Our Own and Others' Tenets and the Meaning of the Profound [Emptiness], Ocean of Scripture and Reasoning Fulfilling All Hopes of All Beings
grub mtha' chen mo/ grub mtha'i rnam bshad rang gzhan grub mtha' kun dang zab don mchog tu gsal ba kun bzang zhing gi nyi ma lung rigs rgya mtsho skye dgu'i re ba kun skong
Musoorie: Dalama, 1962
English translation (beginning of the chapter on the Consequence School): Jeffrey Hopkins. In *Meditation on Emptiness.* London: Wisdom Publications, 1983.
Great Exposition of the Middle/ Analysis of (Chandrakīrti's) "Supplement to (Nāgārjuna's) 'Treatise on the Middle,'" Treasury of Scripture and Reasoning, Thoroughly Illuminating the Profound Meaning [of Emptiness], Entrance for the Fortunate
dbu ma chen mo/ dbu ma 'jug pa'i mtha' dpyod lung rigs gter mdzod zab don kun gsal skal bzang 'jug ngogs
Buxaduor: Gomang, 1967

Maitreya (*byams pa*)
Great Vehicle Treatise on the Sublime Continuum/ Treatise on the Later Scriptures of the Great Vehicle
mahāyānottaratantraśāstra
theg pa chen po rgyud bla ma'i bstan bcos
P5525, vol. 108

Sanskrit: E. H. Johnston (and T. Chowdhury) ed. *The Ratnagotravibhāga Mahāyānottaratantraśāstra.* Patna: Bihar Research Society, 1950.

English translation: E. Obermiller. "Sublime Science of the Great Vehicle to Salvation." *Acta Orientalia,* 9 (1931), 81-306. Also: J. Takasaki. *A Study on the Ratnagotravibhāga.* Rome: IS. M.E.O., 1966.

Nāgārjuna (*klu sgrub,* first to second century, C.E.)

Praise of the Element of Qualities
dharmadhātustotra
chos kyi dbyings su bstod pa
P2010, vol. 46

Six Collections of Reasoning

1 *Precious Garland of Advice for a King*
rājaparikathāratnāvalī
rgyal po la gtam bya ba rin po che'i phreng ba
P5658, vol. 129; Golden Reprint, vol. 183

Sanskrit, Tibetan, and Chinese in: Michael Hahn. *Nāgārjuna's Ratnāvalī, vol. 1, The Basic Texts (Sanskrit, Tibetan, and Chinese).* Bonn, Indica et Tibetica Verlag, 1982.

Tibetan (with photo off-set of Sanskrit): Ācārya Ngawang Samten. *Ratnāvalī of Ācārya Nāgārjuna with the Commentary by Ajitamitra.* Bibliotheca Indo-Tibetica Series-XXI. Sarnath: Central Institute of Higher Tibetan Studies, 1990.

English translation: John Dunne and Sara McClintock. *The Precious Garland: An Epistle to a King.* Boston: Wisdom Publications, 1997.

English translation of 223 stanzas (I. 1-77, II. 1-46, IV. 1-100): Giuseppe Tucci. "The *Ratnāvalī* of Nāgārjuna." *Journal of the Royal Asiatic Society,* 1934, 307-25; 1936, 237-52, 423-35.

Japanese translation: URYŪZU Ryushin. *Butten II, Sekai Koten Bungaku Zenshu.* Edited by NAKAMURA Hajime. vol. 7. Tokyo: Chikuma Shobō. July, 1965, 349-72; *Daijō Butten.* vol. 14. *Ryūju Ronshū.* Edited by KAJIYAMA Yuichi and URYŪZU Ryushin. Tokyo: Chūōkōronsha, 1974, 231-316.

Danish translation: Christian Lindtner. *Nagarjuna, Juvelkaeden og andre skrifter.* Copenhagen: 1980.

2 *Refutation of Objections*
vigrahavyāvartanīkārikā
rtsod pa bzlog pa'i tshig le'ur byas pa
P5228, vol. 95; Toh 3828, Tokyo *sde dge* vol. 1

Edited Sanskrit text: E. H. Johnston. *The Ratnagotravibhāga Mahāyānottaratantraśāstra.* Patna: Bihar Research Society, 1950.

English translation: K. Bhattacharya. *The Dialectical Method of Nāgārjuna.* New Delhi: Motilal Banarsidass, 1978.

Edited Tibetan and Sanskrit: Christian Lindtner, *Nagarjuniana.* Indiske Studier 4, 70-86. Copenhagen: Akademisk Forlag, 1982.

Translation from the Chinese: Giuseppe Tucci. *Pre-Diṅnāga Buddhist Texts on Logic from Chinese Sources.* Gaekwad's Oriental Series, 49. Baroda: Oriental Institute, 1929.

French translation: S. Yamaguchi. "Traité de Nāgārjuna pour écarter les vaines discussion (Vigrahavyāvartanī) traduit et annoté." *Journal Asiatique* 215 (1929), 1-86.

3 *Seventy Stanzas on Emptiness*
śūnyatāsaptatikārikā
stong pa nyid bdun cu pa'i tshig le'ur byas pa
P5227, vol. 95; Toh 3827, Tokyo *sde dge* vol. 1

Edited Tibetan and English translation: Christian Lindtner. *Nagarjuniana.* Indiske Studier 4, 34-69. Copenhagen: Akademisk Forlag, 1982.

English translation: David Ross Komito. *Nāgārjuna's "Seventy Stanzas": A Buddhist Psychology of Emptiness.* Ithaca: Snow Lion Publications, 1987.

4 *Sixty Stanzas of Reasoning*
yuktiṣaṣṭikākārikā
rigs pa drug cu pa'i tshig le'ur byas pa
P5225, vol. 95; Toh 3825, Tokyo *sde dge* vol. 1

Edited Tibetan with Sanskrit fragments and English translation: Christian Lindtner in *Nagarjuniana.* Indiske Studier 4, 100-119. Copenhagen: Akademisk Forlag, 1982.

5 *Treatise Called the Finely Woven*
vaidalyasūtranāma
zhib mo rnam par 'thag pa zhes bya ba'i mdo

P5226, vol. 95

6 *Treatise on the Middle/ Fundamental Treatise on the Middle, Called "Wisdom"*
madhyamakaśāstra/ prajñānāmamūlamadhyamakakārikā
dbu ma'i bstan bcos/ dbu ma rtsa ba'i tshig le'ur byas pa shes rab ces bya ba
P5224, vol. 95
Edited Sanskrit: *Nāgārjuna, Mūlamadhyamakakārikāḥ.* J. W. de Jong, ed. Adyar: Adyar Library and Research Centre, 1977. Also: Christian Lindtner in *Nāgārjuna's Filosofiske Vaerker.* Indiske Studier 2, 177-215. Copenhagen: Akademisk Forlag, 1982.
English translation: Frederick Streng. *Emptiness: A Study in Religious Meaning.* Nashville, New York: Abingdon Press, 1967. Also: Kenneth Inada. *Nāgārjuna: A Translation of his Mūlamadhyamakakārikā.* Tokyo, The Hokuseido Press, 1970. Also: David J. Kalupahana. *Nāgārjuna: The Philosophy of the Middle Way.* Albany: State University Press of New York, 1986. Also: Jay L. Garfield. *The Fundamental Wisdom of the Middle Way.* New York: Oxford University Press, 1995.
Italian translation: R. Gnoli. *Nāgārjuna: Madhyamaka Kārikā, Le stanze del cammino di mezzo.* Enciclopedia di autori classici 61. Turin: P. Boringhieri, 1961.
Danish translation: Christian Lindtner in *Nāgārjuna's Filosofiske Vaerker.* Indiske Studier 2, 67-135. Copenhagen: Akademisk Forlag, 1982.

Nga-w̄ang-b̄el-den (*ngag dbang dpal ldan*, b. 1797), also known as B̄el-den-chö-jay (*dpal ldan chos rje*)
Annotations for (Jam-ȳang-shay-b̄a's) "Great Exposition of Tenets," Freeing the Knots of the Difficult Points, Precious Jewel of Clear Thought
grub mtha' chen mo'i mchan 'grel dka' gnad mdud grol blo gsal gces nor
Sarnath: Pleasure of Elegant Sayings Press, 1964

3 OTHER WORKS

Apte, Vaman Shivaram. *Sanskrit-English Dictionary.* Poona: Prasad Prakashan, 1957.

Chandra, Lokesh, ed. *Materials for a History of Tibetan Literature.* Śata-piṭaka series, vol. 28-30. New Delhi: International Academy of Indian Culture, 1963.

Das, Sarat Chandra. *A Tibetan-English Dictionary.* Calcutta, 1902.

Dunne, John and McClintock, Sara. *The Precious Garland: An Epistle to a King.* Boston: Wisdom Publications, 1997.

Hahn, Michael. *Nāgārjuna's Ratnāvalī, vol.1, The Basic Texts (Sanskrit, Tibetan, and Chinese).* Bonn, Indica et Tibetica Verlag, 1982.

Hahn, Michael. "On a Numerical Problem in Nāgārjuna's Ratnāvalī." *Indological and Buddhist Studies: Volume in Honour of Professor J. W. de Jong on his Sixtieth Birthday.* Canberra: Faculty of Asian Studies, 1982, 161-185.

Hopkins, Jeffrey, trans. "Analysis of Going and Coming," by Chandrakīrti. Dharamsala: Library of Tibetan Works and Archives, 1976.

Hopkins, Jeffrey. *Emptiness Yoga.* Ithaca: Snow Lion, 1987, 1996.

Hopkins, Jeffrey. *Meditation on Emptiness.* London: Wisdom Publications, 1983; Boston: Wisdom Publications, 1996.

Hopkins, Jeffrey, trans. *Practice of Emptiness.* Dharamsala: Library of Tibetan Works and Archives, 1974.

Jong, Jan W. de. *Cinq chapitres de la Prasannapadā.* Paris: Libraire Orientaliste de Paul Geuthner, 1949.

Joshi, L. M. "Facets of Jaina Religiousness in Comparative Light," L. D. Series 85, [Ahmedabad: L. D. Institute of Indology, May 1981], 53-8.

Klein, Anne C. *Path to the Middle: Madhyamaka Philosophy in Tibet: The Oral Scholarship of Kensur Yeshay Tupden.* Albany: SUNY Press, 1994.

Kuijp, Leonard W. J. van der. "Notes on the Transmission of Nagarjuna's Ratnavali in Tibet." *The Tibet Journal,* Summer 1985, vol. X, no. 2, pp. 3-19.

Lang, Karen. "sPa tshab Nyi ma grags and the Introduction of Prāsaṅgika Madhyamaka into Tibet." *Reflections on Tibetan Culture: Essays in Memory of Turrell V. Wylie.* Ed. by Lawrence Epstein and Richard Sherburne. Lewiston, NY: Edwin Mellen Press, 1990.

Lhalungpa, L. P. *Dbuma Rigs Tshogs Drug: The Six Yuktishastra of Madhyamika.* Delhi: 1970.

Lindtner, Christian. *Nagarjuniana.* Indiske Studier 4. Copenhagen: Akademisk Forlag, 1982.

Monier-Williams, Sir Monier. *A Sanskṛit-English Dictionary.* London: Oxford, 1899; reprint, Delhi: Motilal, 1976.

Nobel, Johannes, ed. *Suvarnaprabhāsottamasūtra, Das Goldglanz-Sūtra.* Leiden: Brill, 1950.

Obermiller, E., trans. *History of Buddhism In India and Tibet by Bu-ston.* Heidelberg: Heft, 1932; rpt. Delhi: Sri Satguru Publications, 1986.

Poussin, Louis de la Vallée, trans. *Madhyamakāvatāra. Muséon* 8 (1907), 249-317; 11 (1910), 271-358; and 12 (1911), 235-328.

Poussin, Louis de la Vallée. *Madhyamakāvatāra par Candrakīrti*. Bibliotheca Buddhica IX. Osnabrück: Biblio Verlag, 1970.

Poussin, Louis de la Vallée, ed. *Mūlamadhyamakakārikās de Nāgārjuna avec la Prasannapadā Commentaire de Candrakīrti*. Bibliotheca Buddhica IV. Osnabrück: Biblio Verlag, 1970.

Rinchen, Geshe Sonam. *Yogic Deeds of Bodhisattvas: Gyel-tsap on Āryadeva's Four Hundred*. Translated and edited by Ruth Sonam. Ithaca: Snow Lion Publications: 1994.

Roerich, George N. *The Blue Annals*. Delhi: Motilal Banarsidass, rpt. 1979.

Ruegg, David Seyfort. *The Literature of the Madhyamaka School of Philosophy in India*. Wiesbaden: Otto Harrassowitz, 1981.

Sakaki, Ryōzaburō, ed. *Bon-zō-kan-wa yon'yaku taiko Mahabuyuttopatti*. 2 vols. Tokyo: Kokusho kankokai, 1981. Also: *Quadralingual Mahāvyutpatti*. Reproduced by Lokesh Chandra. New Delhi: International Academy of Indian Culture, 1981.

Samten, Ācārya Ngawang. *Ratnāvali of Ācārya Nāgārjuna with the Commentary by Ajitamitra*. Bibliotheca Indo-Tibetica Series-XXI. Sarnath: Central Institute of Higher Tibetan Studies, 1990.

Sastri, Heramba Chatterjee. *The Philosophy of Nāgārjuna as contained in the Ratnāvālī*. Calcutta: Saraswat Library, 1977.

Thurman, Robert A. F. "Nagarjuna's Guidelines for Buddhist Social Action." *Engaged Buddhist Reader*. Ed. by Arnold Kotler. Berkeley: Parallax, 1996, 79-90.

Tsong-ka-pa, Kensur Lekden, and Hopkins, Jeffrey. *Compassion in Tibetan Buddhism*. London: Rider and Company, 1980; repr. Ithaca: Snow Lion, 1980.

Vaidya, P. L., ed. *Saddharmalaṅkāvatārasūtram*. Buddhist Sanskrit Texts No. 3. Darbhanga: Mithila Institute, 1963.

Walleser, Max. "The Life of Nāgārjuna from Tibetan and Chinese Sources." *Asia Major*, Introductory Volume. Hirth Anniversary Volume. Leipzig: 1923; rpt. Delhi: Nag Publishers, 1979, 421-55.

Wogihara, Unrai, ed. *Abhisamayālaṃkārālokā Prajñā-pāramitā-vyākhyā. The Work of Haribhadra*. Tokyo: The Toyo Bunko, 1932-5; reprint ed., Tokyo: Sankibo Buddhist Book Store, 1973.

GUIDE TO THE TOPICS: ENGLISH

In his *Illumination of the Essential Meanings of (Nāgārjuna's) "Precious Garland of Madhyamaka"* Gyel-tsap Dar-ma-rin-chen breaks Nāgārjuna's text into a complicated series of sections and sub-sections in order to clarify shifts of topic and inter-relations of points. I have extracted this guide and placed it both beside the stanzas themselves and separately here as a table of contents. The numbers immediately after the entry are the respective stanzas; those in parentheses are the number of subdivisions for that item; those at the right hand margin are the page numbers.

ENDNOTES

[1] *lang kar gshegs pa'i mdo, laṅkāvatārasūtra;* Peking 775, vol. 29.

[2] *'phags pa sprin chen po zhes bya ba theg pa chen po'i mdo, āryamahāmeghanāmamahāyānasūtra;* Peking 898, vol. 35. As given in Louis de la Vallée Poussin's translation (*Muséon* 11, 275) the title is *āryadvādaśasahasramahāmegha* (*'phags pa sprin chen po stong phrag bcu gnyis pa*), this being how Chandrakīrti cites it.

[3] Jam-ȳang-shay-b̄a makes this point in the *Four Interwoven Annotations to (Ḏzong-ka-b̄a's) "Great Exposition of the Stages of the Path" / Clear Lamp of the Mahāyāna Path, Good Explanation by Way of the Four Annotations on the Difficult Points of the "Great Exposition of the Stages of the Path to Enlightenment" Composed by the Unequalled Foremost Venerable Ḏzong-ka-b̄a* (*lam rim mchan bzhi sbrags ma / mnyam med rje btsun tsong kha pa chen pos mdzad pa'i byang chub lam rim chen mo'i dka' ba'i gnad rnams mchan bu bzhi'i sgo nas legs par bshad pa theg chen lam gyi gsal sgron*) (New Delhi: Chophel Lekden, 1972), 153.3.

[4] *dbu ma rtsa ba'i tshig le'ur byas pa shes rab ces bya ba'i rnam bshad rigs pa'i rgya mtsho,* Peking 6153, vol. 156.

[5] Sarnath: Pleasure of Elegant Sayings Press, n.d., 3.14-4.4. The sūtra is Chapter X.163-66; see D. T. Suzuki, trans., *The Lankavatara Sutra* (London: Routledge, Kegan and Paul, 1932), 239-40. For the Sanskrit, see *Saddharmalaṅkāvatārasūtram,* ed. by Dr. P. L. Vaidya, Buddhist Sanskrit Texts No. 3 (Darbhanga: Mithila Institute, 1963), 118. The bracketed addition at the end of the second stanza is from Nga-w̄ang-b̄el-den's (*ngag dbang dpal ldan,* born 1797) *Annotations for (Jam-ȳang-shay-b̄a's) "Great Exposition of Tenets," Freeing the Knots of the Difficult Points, Precious Jewel of Clear Thought* (*grub mtha' chen mo'i mchan 'grel dka' gnad mdud grol blo gsal gces nor*) (Sarnath: Pleasure of Elegant Sayings Press, 1964), *dngos* 58a.1, as is the identification of Mahāmati as Mañjushrī.

[6] *dbu ma la 'jug pa'i rgya cher bshad pa dgongs pa rab gsal,* Peking 6143, vol. 154. See Anne C. Klein, *Path to the Middle: Madhyamaka Philosophy in Tibet: The Oral Scholarship of Kensur Yeshay Tupden* (Albany: SUNY Press, 1994), 154.

[7] *gser 'od dam pa, suvarṇaprabhāsottama;* Peking 174, vol. 6-7. See *Suvarṇaprabhāsottamasūtra, Das Goldglanz-Sūtra,* ed. Johannes Nobel (Leiden: Brill, 1944), Text, chapter II, 12.13-17.6. Liked-When-Seen-by-All-the-World is mentioned three times in the sūtra: 13.2, 14.1, and 16.2. (Thanks to Professor Shotaro Iida of the University of British Columbia for providing this edition.)

[8] *'jam dpal tsa ba'i rtog pa, mañjuśrīmūlakalpa;* Peking 162, vol. 6.

[9] *'phags pa rnga bo che chen po'i le'u zhes bya ba theg pa chen po'i mdo, āryamahābherīharakaparivartanāmamahāyānasūtra;* Peking 888, vol. 35.

[10] *dngos* 57b.4.

[11] Peking 888, vol. 35, 88.2.4. As indicated, the quotations from the *Great Drum Sūtra* and the *Great Cloud Sūtra* are taken from Jam-ȳang-shay-b̄a's *Great Exposition of the Middle* and *Great Exposition of Tenets.*

[12] *Four Interwoven Annotations to (Ḏzong-ka-b̄a's) "Great Exposition of the Stages of the Path,"* 153.6.

[13] Peking 888, vol. 35, 99.4.6.

[14] Peking 888, vol. 35, 97.5.4.

[15] Peking 888, vol. 35, 98.5.7.

[16] Peking 898, vol. 35, 251.4.3.

[17] Peking 898, vol. 35, 253.3.3-253.3.5.

[18] Peking 898, vol. 35, 253.4.8.

[19] Peking 898, vol. 35, 254.5.1.

[20] Peking 898, vol. 35, 255.2.6.

[21] Peking 898, vol. 35, 255.3.2.

[22] Peking 898, vol. 35, 266.1.2.

[23] *chos dbyings bstod pa, dharmadhātustotra;* Peking 2010, vol. 46.

[24] *Great Exposition of Tenets, ca* 4b.

[25] Peking 898, vol. 35, 254.4.6.

[26] Poona: Prasad Prakashan, 1957, 196.

[27] Tsong-ka-pa, Kensur Lekden, and Jeffrey Hopkins, *Compassion in Tibetan Buddhism*, 198-99.

[28] 1578.

[29] Gyel-tsap, 58b.3.

[30] Golden Reprint, vol. 183, 402.6-403.6.

[31] Golden Reprint, vol. 183, 403.1: *don du zhes bya ba ni don dam par ro.*

[32] XX.21-22.

[33] Peking 5227, vol. 95, 13.1.7.

[34] Peking 5231, vol. 95, 52.5.6ff.

[35] Peking 5262, vol. 98, 103.3.6, VI.99; Poussin's translation is *Muséon*, n.s. v. 11, 296.

[36] From Jeffrey Hopkins, "Analysis of Going and Coming," (Dharamsala: Library of Tibetan Works & Archives, 1976).

[37] 25cd.

[38] Golden Reprint, vol. 183, 411.4.

[39] Gyel-tsap, 19b.4.

[40] Golden Reprint, vol. 183, 422.3.

[41] Peking 5260, vol. 98, 53.1.8, commenting on XVIII.1; Poussin, 341.8.

[42] XXVII.12.

[43] XXVII.6.

[44] Peking 5262, vol. 98, 104.2.1ff, VI.127-28; Poussin's translation is *Muséon*, n.s. v.12, 292-4. Brackets are from Chandrakīrti's own commentary, Peking 5263, vol. 98, 142.5.5ff, and Ḏzong-ka-ɓa's *Illumination*, Peking 6143, vol. 154 84.5.4ff.

[45] XXVII.27.

[46] VI.127ab.

[47] XVIII.1.

[48] Peking 5224, vol. 95, 7.2.8, XVIII.1cd.

[49] Peking 5260, vol. 98, 53.3.1ff, commenting on XVIII.1cd; Poussin, 343.8; Buddhist Sanskrit Texts No. 10 146.20ff.

[50] Peking 5242, vol. 95, 120.4.4ff, commenting on XXII.1.

[51] Peking 5263, vol. 98, 145.4.6ff, commenting on VI.142; Poussin's translation is *Muséon*, n.s. v. 12, 310.

[52] Peking 5242, vol. 95, 120.4.5, commenting on XXII.1.

[53] Peking 5263, vol. 98, 145.5.2ff, commenting on VI.143; Poussin's translation is *Muséon*, n.s. v. 12, 311.

[54] 59b.5.

[55] Gyel-tsap, 58b.3.

[56] Ḏzong-ka-ɓa, *Illumination of the Thought* (*dgongs pa rab gsal*), (Dharamsala: Shes rig par khang edition, n.d.), 34.12.

[57] Gyel-tsap, 62a.4.

[58] Golden Reprint, vol. 113, 25.4.

[59] 64a.2.

[60] Gyel-tsap, 8b.6; see also Ajitamitra, Golden Reprint, vol. 183, 383.1.

[61] Ajitamitra, Golden Reprint, vol. 183, 416.2.

[62] The reading follows the Tibetan and Gyel-tsap (31b.6).

[63] Gyel-tsap, 34b.1.

[64] Gyel-tsap, 38a.3.

[65] Gyel-tsap, 39a.6.

[66] Gyel-tsap, 43b.6.

[67] Gyel-tsap, 44b.2.

[68] The bracketed additions in this section on "Other giving" are from Gyel-tsap, 45a.1-45a.6.
[69] Gyel-tsap, 45a.1.
[70] Gyel-tsap, 46a.1.
[71] Gyel-tsap, 46b.2.
[72] Gyel-tsap, 48a.2.
[73] Gyel-tsap, 51a.1.
[74] Gyel-tsap, 52a.6.
[75] Gyel-tsap, 58b.3.
[76] Gyel-tsap, 59a.4.
[77] Brackets in this stanza Gyel-tsap, 59a.5.
[78] Gyel-tsap, 59b.3.
[79] Brackets in this stanza from Gyel-tsap, 59b.3-59b.4.
[80] Gyel-tsap, 60a.2.
[81] Gyel-tsap, 60a.2.
[82] Gyel-tsap, 60a.5.
[83] Gyel-tsap, 61a.6.
[84] Gyel-tsap, 61b.3.
[85] Gyel-tsap, 61b.6.
[86] Gyel-tsap, 64a.6.
[87] Gyel-tsap, 64b.1.
[88] Gyel-tsap, 64b.2.
[89] Gyel-tsap, 65a.1.
[90] Gyel-tsap, 65a.5.
[91] Gyel-tsap, 65a.5.
[92] Gyel-tsap, 55b.2.
[93] Gyel-tsap, 70a.2.
[94] Gyel-tsap, 71a.4.
[95] Gyel-tsap, 71a.6.
[96] Brackets in this line from Gyel-tsap, 72b.2.
[97] Gyel-tsap, 72b.2.
[98] Brackets in this line from Gyel-tsap, 73b.1.
[99] Gyel-tsap, 73b.2.
[100] Gyel-tsap, 73b.4.
[101] Gyel-tsap, 73b.4.
[102] Gyel-tsap, 74b.1.
[103] Brackets in this line and the next from Gyel-tsap, 74b.4.
[104] Gyel-tsap, 75a.3.